ALSO BY DAVID HALBERSTAM

The Noblest Roman
The Making of a Quagmire
One Very Hot Day
The Unfinished Odyssey of Robert Kennedy
Ho
The Best and the Brightest
The Powers That Be
The Breaks of the Game
The Amateurs
The Reckoning
Summer of '49
The Next Century
The Fifties
War in a Time of Peace
Firehouse

OCTOBER
1964

OCTOBER 1964

David Halberstam

FAWCETT BOOKS • NEW YORK

For Bill Euler and Andy Oates

"There is nothing more vulnerable than entrenched success."

—GEORGE ROMNEY,
speaking to the author about the fate of
General Motors in the 1980s

Prologue

In the spring of 1964, the young Chicago Cub outfielder, rejoining his team in Arizona, was determined that this season he would finally make his breakthrough. It was his third full year in the major leagues, and he was approaching a critical point in his career. His employers were no longer confident of his abilities—and with good reason, for he had played well below his potential so far. The men who ran baseball, he believed, gave you three years to prove yourself, and in his first two years he had ended up right on the margin: he had not fielded well and had proved to be only a .250–.260 singles hitter. To their eyes that made him at best a journeyman, in an age when baseball teams did not keep black journeymen around on their benches.

Still, Lou Brock, child of rural Southern sharecroppers, was confident that he had the talent to play in the big leagues. The Cubs, intrigued by his promise as a college player (and particularly by his great speed), had paid a handsome bonus to sign him, a great deal more than most young black players were getting at the time. But so far he had given only the slightest hint of the skills that they and the representatives of competing organizations had seen. One Chicago sportswriter, Bob Smith of the *Daily News*, had written brutally about his playing—not always unfairly, Lou Brock later thought. After one play in which Brock had been thrown out trying to take an extra base, Smith wrote that he had pulled a Rock, as in Brock.

Then, in the 1963 season, Smith announced, "If you have watched all the Cub home games thus far you probably had come to the conclusion that Lou Brock is the worst outfielder in baseball history. He really isn't, but he hasn't done much to prove it."

Brock was about to turn twenty-five. He was aware that the other young Cub players his own age were just hitting their strides and beginning to move ahead of him: his friend Billy Williams, a year older than Brock, had hit 25 home runs and knocked in 95 runs in the 1963 season; Ron Santo, a year younger than Brock, had hit 25 home runs as well, knocking in 99 runs. Perhaps, Brock thought, 1964 would be his turn. Some of his teammates thought him withdrawn, and they found it hard to gauge his emotional state. Some in the press and in the stands considered him too casual about his job, but that was a misperception. In fact, he was driven, not merely by a desire, but by a rage to succeed. He was determined to show the people who owned the Cubs, the sportswriters on the Chicago papers, and, most of all, his fellow players in the National League that he would not be merely a good major-league player but a great one. Those disappointed by his performance during those first two years would have been surprised to learn that in his need to leave behind the memories of a sharecropper's life and seize on this rare chance to be a major-league ballplayer, he had wound himself so tight that he was unable to utilize his great natural abilities.

If some people in Chicago thought Brock not motivated enough, his Cub roommate, Ernie Banks, thought him *too* motivated, to the point that he had lost that most critical of athletic abilities: to relax and just play. In fact, Brock was so tense that he had trouble sleeping and eating. Banks, who recognized Brock's fierce ambition, told his friend again and again to relax, that he was blocking his baseball abilities. Unlike most young ballplayers, Brock kept records of every game he played in—which pitchers he had faced, what pitches they had thrown him, and how well he had done against them. Banks had never seen a player so determined or goal-oriented. Before a road trip, Brock would write down how many hits he should get and how many runs he should drive in. He talked all the time about how he *had* to make it as a major-league star, about how it would mean a life of success and affluence; whereas failing would send him back to the extreme poverty from which he had come. "I've got to make it here," Brock would say again and again. "I just can't go back to Louisiana and Arkansas. I've been there, and I know what's there." I am here to play baseball, Banks would think, but Lou is here to fight a war. Banks worried that Brock was getting no pleasure from the game; he was sure that the more pleasure you got, the more naturally and the better you played.

Brock faced an additional early handicap. The Cubs played him in right field, which in Wrigley Field was the sun field, a truly murderous place for young outfielders. Because Brock's minor-league career had been so brief—one season in Class C ball in Minnesota—he had never learned how to play a sun field. He had arrived in major-league baseball as a promising rookie, and yet no one had ever taught him how to flip down his sunglasses when a ball went into sun. As such, he not only kept losing balls in the sun, but worse, even when he did catch one, it appeared to be something of a life-and-death struggle. Playing on the road did not bother him, nor did playing on cloudy days in Chicago, but the mere thought of playing sunny day games at Wrigley would make him break into a sweat. If he misplayed a ball, the Cubs manager and coaches would have someone hit balls to him early the next morning, but somehow no one had yet figured out that the missing piece for him was how to handle the sun.

Brock had yet another worry as he arrived at spring training that season. The coaches saw him as a leadoff hitter, but, like most hitters, he believed himself a power hitter when he first reached the major leagues—for he had hit in the middle of the order in college and in the minor leagues. Suddenly he was supposed to hit at the top of the order, and the whole purpose of each at bat changed: he was to get on base, rather than to drive the ball. Some of the Cubs coaches were trying to mold him into becoming like Richie Ashburn, a classic leadoff hitter who knew how to hit to the opposite field and how to take a lot of pitches and draw walks from pitchers—on four occasions Ashburn had led the league in walks. But that was not Brock's style. He did things that Ashburn could not do, he had more power and speed than Ashburn, and he did not want to be made into a black Ashburn. He hoped the coaches would not try to mess with him anymore, that they would just let him hit. He feared that the Cub management might send him back to the minor leagues for more seasoning. That thought terrified him.

OCTOBER
1964

The Yankees arrived at spring training as confident as ever. Their marquee names—Maris, Mantle, Ford—still inspired awe and fear among opponents. Most Yankee players as well as their fans remained confident about the coming season, which promised to mark the fifteenth year of a Yankee dynasty that had started with the arrival of Casey Stengel: since 1949 the team had won the pennant thirteen times and the World Series nine times. Yankee fans expected now that their team would always manage to win the pennant. In those years the Yankees were a spectacular, finely honed machine. They depended on a deep farm system so skillfully run that when critical parts of the team wore down, new and perhaps even better parts were always found. If by some chance the farm system failed to deliver, it was so rich in other parts that a three-for-one trade could be worked out with some hapless have-not franchise. This was the case with Roger Maris, the right fielder who, with his short, compact swing, appeared to have been born to play in Yankee Stadium, and who only three years earlier had not only beaten out Mickey Mantle for the annual home-run title but also broken Babe Ruth's record for home runs in a single season as well.

The Yankee players themselves had come to believe in their invincibility. They were not merely the best, they were the toughest players as well: they almost always won the big games, and because they had played in so many big games, they were therefore better

prepared for the terrible pressures of a pennant race or a World Series. It was simply part of being a Yankee. All the best young players,
it was presumed, wanted to play for this, the most celebrated sports
franchise in America, not only because of the pride of playing with
the best but also because of the lure of so many World Series bonus
checks. In 1963, after Steve Hamilton joined the Yankees as a relief
pitcher, Clete Boyer, the third baseman, showed him his World Series ring. As Hamilton admired it, Boyer said, "Listen, Steve, the
good thing about the Yankees is that you don't just get a ring for
yourself. You get yours the first year, then you get one the next year
for your wife, and the year after that for your oldest kid, and after
that for your other kids." Boyer himself already had four World Series rings. Just as Boyer predicted, Steve Hamilton got his first ring
that year. The rings, along with the World Series checks, were built
into the expectations of being a Yankee in those years. It was part of
the lore of the team that Charlie Silvera, the Yankee backup catcher
for much of that period, cashed seven World Series checks for some
$50,000 (the actual total was $46,337.45)—a huge amount of money
in that era, particularly for someone who had played in only one
World Series game. Silvera would come to refer to the lovely house
he bought in suburban San Francisco as "the house that Yogi built,"
after the Yankee catcher whom he had played behind all those years.

Even in the matter of signing baseballs, the Yankees were set
apart by their fame and success. Players on other teams might sign,
at best, six boxes of a dozen balls a week, but the Yankees, because of
their promotional commitments, had to sign ten or twelve boxes of a
dozen balls a day. That was a daily chore few players liked, and there
was a competition among the players to see who could sign the balls
in the shortest amount of time. Whitey Ford was good at it, having
shortened his autograph name to Ed Ford in order to expedite the
process, saving four letters a ball, or forty-eight letters a box. As in
all things, Tony Kubek was efficient and businesslike at signing,
helped by the advantage of so short a name. Steve Hamilton thought
Kubek could do twenty balls in a minute, which was something of a
Yankee record. Hamilton himself was always slower, due to his long
last name, but he could usually do fifteen in a minute. The most

conscientious, in terms of ball signing, appeared to be Mickey Mantle, the team's great star. Hamilton liked to come to the park early to get such routine chores as baseball signing out of the way. But no matter how early he came in, Mantle had somehow already signed the requisite number of balls. For a long time Hamilton was impressed by Mantle's diligence, and then it struck him that in fact Mantle was *never* the first to arrive, that Hamilton was always there before Mantle. Since Mantle most assuredly did not do his signing at night after a long game, Hamilton even suspected that Pete Previte, the clubhouse boy, came in every morning and signed Mantle's baseballs for him—although he could find no proof of this.

Still, by this time there was considerable evidence that the team was wearing down physically, and that the other American League teams were now being run by richer, smarter people who were less willing to have their best players culled by the Yankees. At the end of the coming season, for the first time, major-league baseball would move to a draft for new players signing their first contracts, a change specifically designed by other owners to limit the huge bonuses being paid to untried, green players—but also weakening the power of both the Yankees and the Dodgers. In addition, by 1964 the Yankee farm system was not the majestic organization that had existed at the beginning of the dynasty, for it had been severely cut back because of economic constraints. There was one great new talent pool, that of young black players, but it was well known that the Yankees had moved slowly in this direction. Sure of their success, sure of their past, and sure of their own racial attitudes, they had essentially sat on the sidelines in the fifties as a number of National League teams had signed the best of these young, supremely gifted and determined athletes. In fact, most astute baseball observers believed now that the entire American League was inferior to the National League because it had lagged behind in signing black players. The owners even began to suspect that this difference in the talent was showing up in the attendance figures, and that the American League was in trouble, in part because the Yankees had dominated it for a generation, and in part because the National League players were far more exciting to watch.

There were already tangible signs that the Yankees were in the early stages of their decline. They had beaten the Giants by the narrowest of margins in a great seven-game World Series in 1962, a series decided only on the last out. Then, in 1963, the Los Angeles Dodgers (powered primarily by two great pitchers) had swept the Yankees in four games. Though the Yankees appeared to have a number of talented young pitchers just beginning to come into their own, they had not yet come up with a single sure big-game winner to replace Whitey Ford, who was, by the spring of 1964, already thirty-five years old and increasingly dependent upon his shrewdness and courage. In his first thirteen World Series decisions Ford had been 9-4; in his last four he was 1-3. Some of the Yankee players were aware that time was catching up with their once virtually unbeatable team.

The previous October, the Yankees had lost their first two World Series games to the Dodgers in New York, and on the day off, as the Series shifted to Los Angeles, Ralph Terry, one of the best Yankee pitchers, had gone to the racetrack with Hal Reniff, a Yankee relief pitcher. Reniff was a true aficionado of the horse races, a man who loved to figure the odds at the track and other sporting events, and in honor of his talents his teammates had obligingly nicknamed him "Clocker Dan." On this day, as he was going over the odds with Terry, Reniff asked Terry what he thought the odds were that the Dodgers would sweep the Yankees in four games. It was a long shot, answered Terry. A sweep of an ordinary team in a World Series was one thing, but a sweep of the *Yankees* was another. But Reniff continued to muse. It wasn't really *that* long a shot, if you thought about it, Reniff said. In fact it was a real possibility. Look at the quality of the Dodger pitching, with Koufax and Drysdale both set to pitch in Los Angeles. As for the Yankees themselves, they *seemed* to be dominating on paper, but a lot of the top Yankee players were either hurt or coming off subpar seasons. Maris had been hurt and missed much of the season (he would come up only five times in the Series) and Mantle was clearly wearing down—he had come to bat only 172 times in the 1963 season and was not swinging well. The Yankees, Reniff said with the cool eye of a racetrack tout, were not really in very good shape. Terry listened carefully, hearing something he had not yet been willing to admit to himself. The odds on a sweep of the mighty Yankees had to be at least 50–1 and maybe 100–1, Reniff said. If Terry and Reniff were really smart and unscrupulous, they would each very quietly put down five hundred dollars on it. "You know," Reniff finally said, "the Dodgers could really sweep our asses." That, of course, was exactly what happened: Drysdale and Koufax, who were having astonishing years, with 557 strikeouts between them, both won in Los Angeles. Still, most of the Yankee players went home feeling that they had had the better team, but the edge had gone to the Dodgers because of their magnificent pitching.

In the spring of 1964 there were other signs that the team was wearing down. Jerry Coleman, the former Yankee second baseman, by then a broadcaster, was struck as he watched spring training that this was somehow not as tough and as disciplined a team as he had witnessed in the past. It was hard to tell about the talent level because some of the players were young, but Coleman was sure something was missing, perhaps some depth. Just after his retirement five years earlier, Coleman had worked in the farm system, and as the economics of baseball had changed, he had been charged with the melancholy task of getting rid of both a Double A and a Triple A farm team. That was a sign that the Yankee high command was cutting back in a major way, and it meant that the Yankees would employ half the number of players that they once did in the de facto staging area for the major-league club. There was a ripple effect in this: if there were fewer clubs at the top level in the farm system, there would soon be fewer signings as well. In the brief time that Coleman was working in the player personnel department, he had been sent out to Kearney, Nebraska, to check out how much talent the Yankees had on their rookie team there. Roy Hamey, briefly the team's general manager, called Coleman in upon his return and asked what he had seen. "We have one pitcher who might make Triple A," Coleman said. That irritated Hamey, who immediately sent Coleman's superior, Bill Skiff, out to Kearney. Soon Skiff returned. "Well, Bill, how much have we got out there?" Hamey asked. "Jerry's right," he answered. "Almost nothing." Now, some five years later, the Yankees still had young talent, but not as much as in the past.

As Coleman watched spring practice in 1964, he thought a different kind of player was beginning to come up. In the past, the Yankees had always signed the toughest kids, often for less money than they were offered elsewhere. For many of them, and Coleman had felt this way himself, being a Yankee was almost a religion. Now, Coleman thought, the younger players were not so singularly focused on baseball as those of his generation had been. Going out for dinner with his broadcasting partner, Red Barber, Coleman said, "You know, Red, I don't think the Yankees are going to win it this year." And Barber answered, "I think you're right."

The center of attention at the Yankee camp was the new manager, who was in fact the old catcher, Yogi Berra. The Yankee front office was in a state of flux. In 1960, general manager George Weiss, the efficient if not entirely lovable architect of much of the previous decade's Yankee success, had been told by his employers that his services were no longer needed. Roy Hamey had come over from Milwaukee and briefly replaced Weiss (a fleeting moment when there was a good deal more interest in signing black players), but Hamey soon wanted out, and Ralph Houk was promoted to general manager after the 1963 season. Houk had managed the Yankees for the previous three seasons and had won the pennant all three times. Houk was known as a player's manager, which meant that he could not have been more different in his approach than Casey Stengel, whom he had replaced. Not only did Stengel show little personal interest in his players, except insofar as what they might do for him on the field, he seemed loath even to learn their names. Born in 1890, Stengel came from an era in American life when very little emphasis was placed on being nice or kind to employees, and he was, in fact, rarely kind or nice to his players. He was often caustic, frequently making fun of them and putting them down to his beloved sportswriters. Stengel might be standing near the batting cage when a young player such as Jerry Lumpe was taking his swings and hitting the ball sharply to all fields. If a writer mentioned the lovely quality of Lumpe's swing to Stengel, the old man would say, "Yes, he looks like the greatest hitter in the world until you play him."

Stengel had his eye not merely on winning pennants, which he certainly wanted to do, but on history as well, and as far as his players were concerned, he seemed to be interested chiefly in courting writers. As far as Stengel was concerned, the writers were the critical link to history, and in return, they glorified his professional skills. The writers had always been important to him, and he always basked in their attention; many seemed as interested in him as they were in the game itself, and their interest was seductive. On one of the rare occasions that his Yankees did not win the pennant—in 1954 when Cleveland beat them—Stengel was stunned to find the New York writers abandoning him and his team to follow the Indians as they moved on to the World Series. "Jesus," he told one reporter, "I'm losing my writers."

Many of the writers remembered him from his leaner years of bad teams and second-division finishes, nine seasons of managing, and only one team that finished above .500; when he became the greatest manager in the game of baseball, the legitimate heir to the great John McGraw, it was all the sweeter. After all, he represented not just the present in baseball but the past as well, and the writers were interested in the past, as the players were not. Once when Mantle was young and the Yankees were going to play the Dodgers in the World Series, Stengel took Mantle out on the field in Ebbetts Field and tried to explain to him how he had played this particularly treacherous right-field wall. "You mean you actually played here?" asked the astonished Mantle. Later, Stengel gathered his writers around him, told the story, and shook his head. "He thinks when I was born I was already sixty years old and had a wooden leg and came here to manage," Stengel said.

Later in his career with the Yankees, Stengel became even more drawn to the writers and, if anything, more protective of them. Aware that some of his players were less than hospitable to certain of the more irreverent journalists, Stengel often went out of his way to make sure that the shunned writers were taken care of. After more than a decade of Casey Stengel, the writers worshiped him, but the players had come to look upon him as a rather cold-blooded albeit wealthy grandfather who still controlled the family will and who turned on his very considerable charm only for outsiders. Ralph Houk changed that overnight. His loyalty was to the players. They were not just his players, they were his pals, or, in the vernacular he used, his "pardners." He was an extremely political man, and he had a shrewd sense of the mood in the clubhouse and the resentments that had festered under Stengel despite all those years of winning. Houk was very much aware that Mantle had come to resent Stengel's treatment of him and Stengel's thinly veiled criticism (which tended to show up in the stories of various New York writers). Stengel always seemed to imply that no matter how much Mantle did and how well he played, he might somehow achieve even more and play at an even higher level, that he somehow never quite lived up to his potential, and, worse, that he was not a particularly smart baseball player. There was even a standing joke in the Yankee locker room among the players: Mickey, a player would ask Mantle, when are you going to live up to your potential?

The relationship between Mantle and Stengel had evolved over the years. Stengel had been a mediocre ballplayer himself, and for much of his career he had managed ballplayers even more mediocre than himself; when he finally got the Yankee job late in his career, he had been uneasy with Joe DiMaggio, who was at the end of his career, and who was an icon beyond the reach of a rookie manager. But Mantle had come to him as a boy, the greatest player Stengel had ever seen—all that power, all that speed; "My God," said Stengel the first time he saw Mantle play, "the boy runs faster than Cobb!" Stengel had eagerly anticipated the chance to mold Mantle, to add to that magnificent body a mind filled with all the baseball knowledge and lore he had accumulated over four decades. "Mantle," as the sportswriter Milton Gross wrote at the time, "was to be the monument the old gent wanted to leave behind. Casey wanted his own name written in the record books as manager, but he also wanted a creation that was completely his own on the field every day, doing things that no other ballplayer ever did, rewriting all the records." But Mantle frustrated him; he remained pure Mantle, not a hybrid of Mantle/Stengel. It was then that Stengel tried to reach him by criticism, often meted out through the sportswriters. Again and again the player rejected Stengel's advice. He would play hard, drive himself relentlessly in his own way and on his own terms, but he would not be Stengel's creation.

There was already enough pressure on Mantle as it was—the pressure of playing in New York, the pressure of replacing the great DiMaggio, and, above all, the pressure of living up to his father's, Mutt Mantle's, high expectations for him. He needed no additional pressure, no more lessons; what he needed was a means of escaping the pressure. It took everything he had to get through each day, and the last thing he wanted was a father figure as boss. If his and Stengel's was to be a father-son relationship, it was, as the writer Robert Creamer noted, "that of an angry father and a stubborn son." Over the years the relationship continued to deteriorate. "Telling Mantle something is like telling him nothing," Stengel once told reporters, summing up his attitude toward his greatest player. To Stengel, Mantle was someone who had fallen short of his own true greatness, and to Mantle, his manager was more and more just a querulous old man who was never satisfied. It seemed even to the other players that Stengel saw not so much what Mantle did as what he did not do. To some degree Stengel's attitude colored the attitude not only of the New York writers but of the New York fans as well. The glory that should so readily have been Mantle's, the acclamation by the New York fans of his greatness and of his ability to carry the team year after year, came only after a decade of play and only when Roger Maris challenged him in the 1961 home-run derby. Then the fans somehow decided that it was Mantle's prerogative to challenge Ruth, not Maris's. Only then did they begin to cheer Mantle, as they jeered *Maris*. Hearing them boo Maris, Mantle noted with some degree of amusement, "Roger has stolen my fans."

Ralph Houk knew that this was Mantle's team, and the first thing he did as manager was to go to the center fielder and tell him what he knew: that Mantle was the leader of the team and therefore now the captain of it. That moment symbolized a significant change: Houk would cater almost exclusively to the players, often at the expense of the writers, whom he did not so much shun as treat as a necessary evil. In place of the brilliant press-conference soliloquies by Stengel, which some reporters thought worthy of Mark Twain, Houk gave the press a measure of bromides, reflecting both his eternal optimism and a shrewd awareness that his players would read his praise of them in the next day's newspapers. With Houk the writers sensed a bunker mentality, a them-against-us attitude. If Stengel had his eye always fixed on history as recorded by the sportswriters, Houk was content merely to win pennants and world championships.

No one appreciated that more than Mantle. The Houk years were largely happy ones for the players, and frequently less happy for the writers. The younger players, who often played with considerable anxiety and insecurity, found Houk reassuring, a sort of surrogate father. He had been an average ballplayer himself, a backup catcher during the Berra years. During World War II he distinguished himself in the Battle of the Bulge, and ended the war as a major. Some of the older writers still called him "Major" (which irritated the younger, more iconoclastic writers to no small degree). He possessed an intuitive sense of how to get the most out of his players, whether they were stars or journeymen, and he was very good at walking the delicate line between being their pal and knowing exactly when to draw the line. He gave the players a perfect example of that in the 1963 season when the Yankees went into Boston for a two-admission day-night doubleheader. As the Yankees arrived, one of the Boston papers printed an interview with Mantle in which the star discussed how much he loved to play for Houk and how if Houk asked him to go through a brick wall, he would ask only where the wall was. On the day of the doubleheader, the two teams were barely able to finish the first game, for it began to rain heavily during the late innings. As they waited for the rain to stop and the second game to start, the players became restless and bored, anxious to get on with it one way or another—either to go back to the hotel or to play. In the dugout, Mantle was passing the time by telling country-boy stories, including one about carnal relations with farm animals. When Houk walked by, Mantle asked, "Hey, Ralph, you ever done it with a sheep?" The atmosphere suddenly became tense and the other players realized that Mantle had crossed a line; Houk, good guy, abiding friend and pardner of the players, was not to be asked ribald questions, not by anyone, not even a star. His authority as manager was suddenly at stake. Houk called Mantle over, and then, as if he were speaking privately to him, but at the same time in a voice that everyone could hear, he thanked Mantle for the generous things he had said about him in the Boston paper. "Those are really kind words, Mickey, and I want to tell you they mean a lot to a manager." "That's okay, Ralph, I meant every word," Mantle answered. Then Houk continued, "Mickey, can you play in the second game if I need you?" Mantle shrugged and asked Houk to look at the field, where the rain was still pouring down. "Yeah, I know, Mickey, but with the field in that crappy condition I figure I may need you, because I'm thinking I don't want to take a chance on getting any of my regulars hurt." It was a masterful response, thought the players: Houk had held on to his authority and defused the situation, had even turned it to his advantage by using Mantle as his straight man, and yet in no way had he wounded the ego of the team's best and most beloved player.

Houk constantly told each player how good he was, how critical he was to the team's success, no matter how small his role. Every player talked to Ralph Houk and managed to hear what he had wanted to hear. If he did not seem to be entirely on their side in their negotiations with management for larger salaries, then at least he did not seem to be against them in such negotiations either—that is, until Houk was made general manager in time for the 1964 season. Suddenly the nature of his job changed dramatically. In an organization famed for its reluctance to pay top salaries and in which World Series checks were traditionally counted by management as part of a player's salary instead of as a bonus, Houk went overnight from player's man to company man. Some of the players suspected that he did it too readily and too completely, and that, like his predecessor George Weiss, he received a bonus based on how much he held down the team payroll. The previous fall, after the Dodgers swept the Yankees in the World Series, Steve Hamilton, a young relief pitcher who had had a good year, asked Houk for a raise. He found a very different Houk than the one who had just managed the team and who had always told Hamilton how important he was to the team's success. "You know, Hammy, I'd love to give you a better contract, but I can't. The Series, you know, only went four games and we didn't make any money," Houk said. The former manager had gone overnight, Hamilton, who still admired Houk, said later, from blowing smoke to blowing acid rain.

Houk's replacement as manager was a surprise to the team and to the media: Yogi Berra, the longtime star catcher. Berra was chosen, it was believed by those who knew the front office well, partly to compete with the upstart team in the New York area, the Mets, who were now managed by none other than the indefatigable Charles Dillon Stengel, soon to be seventy-four. Brilliant and verbal, live and in color, a nonstop one-man media show, Stengel could be safely called many things, but no one ever called him boring. The combination of the Mets' virtually pristine incompetence and Stengel's singular charm made the Mets a major draw, to the surprise of the Yankee ownership, which valued winning over fun. The more talented of the young New York sportswriters preferred covering the lowly Mets rather than the dynastic Yankees. The Yankees under George Weiss did not think in modern terms about the entertainment dollar, and the general manager had not wanted to broadcast the games on television, thinking that it was giving his product away for free. He had even been reluctant to sell the paraphernalia of modern baseball, including Yankee shirts, Yankee caps, and Yankee jackets. He did not want every kid in New York going around wearing a Yankee cap, he said, for it demeaned the Yankee uniform. The Mets were the reverse of this, and indeed part of their success in the earlier years happened because they successfully blurred the line between player and fan. The Mets were perceived as inept but lovable by a new generation of fans, while the Yankees were coming to be seen as the athletic equivalent of General Motors or U.S. Steel. Something profound was taking place in the larger culture and it was extremely troubling to the Yankee high command. In 1963 Yankee attendance slipped again, the second year in a row in which that had happened; it had surged to more than 1.7 million in 1961, the year Maris and Mantle had chased Ruth's record, but fell by more than 200,000 a year in the two years after. In 1963 the Yankees drew only about 220,000 more fans than the Mets, and it seemed likely that in 1964, when the Mets moved into their handsome new home at Shea Stadium, they might well outdraw the Yankees (which, in fact, they did, with 1.7 million customers, or nearly half a million more than the first-place Yankees). "My park," said Stengel, surveying Shea for the first time, "is lovelier than my team."

In a somewhat misguided effort to become more popular, the Yankees decided to make Yogi Berra their manager. Over the years the New York media had viewed Berra as something of a cartoon figure: funny, awkward, but lovable, much given to inelegant but ultimately wise aphorisms. Some of the famous Yogiisms were genuine, but a good many were manufactured by the writers, and the real Yogi Berra was quite different from the one that had been invented by the press. He was shy and wary with strangers, particularly the media, because of their jokes about his looks (his wife, Carmen, smart and extremely capable, *hated* those jokes) and about his lack of education. In the beginning the jokes were more than a little cruel, but Yogi was shrewd enough to go along with them; had he resisted, the jokes would have taken on a longer life. But it still did not mean he liked them. Nor was he the easiest of interviews. "Why do I have to talk to all these guys who make six thousand dollars a year when I make forty thousand dollars a year?" he once asked in what was to become a rallying cry for thousands of ballplayers yet unborn.

The truth was that the Yankees had made a serious miscalculation if they hired Berra because he was good with the media. Rather, the media was good with him—inventing a cuddly, wise, witty figure who did not, in fact, exist. It was no surprise that as the Yankee players arrived for their first workout that spring, there was a cartoon on the New York *Daily News* sports page entitled, "A Few Words Before the Season," which showed a grinning Berra in baseball uniform with a tiny cartoonist armed with pen and sketchbook standing on his arm and saying, "A cartoonist's dream! With that mug of yours I hope y' stick aroun' forever." As a player, Yogi had been surprisingly quick and nimble in a body that did not look particularly athletic, and he was a very dangerous late-inning hitter. "A rather strange fellow of very remarkable abilities," Stengel once said of him. His new assignment was going to be difficult: he was replacing a popular manager who was still close to the players and who was now his boss. Moreover, he was going to be managing his former teammates, who respected him as a player but who had frequently joked about him, and who thought him, among other things, uncommonly close with a dollar. Yogi was not a man who by his very presence inspired the respect of his teammates, as Mantle, Ford, and even Elston Howard, the catcher, did (though it was too early for anyone in baseball to think of a black man like Howard as a manager). When his friend and teammate Mickey Mantle was asked how the team would do now that Berra had replaced Houk, Mantle answered, "I think we can win in spite of it."

Berra was aware of the reservations of his teammates, and he was determined to get off to a good start with them. Before his first team meeting he stopped by to see Bobby Richardson, the veteran second baseman, in order to give a dry run of his first speech to the team as its new manager. "Okay," he was going to say, "this is a new season. We'll put 1963 behind us. We're going to have new rules: no swimming, no tennis, no golf, no fishing." Then he would pause and say, "I'm kidding. We'll play hard, we'll play together, we'll be relaxed, and we'll win." Richardson thought it a fine way to start the season, particularly for a manager addressing former teammates. But during the actual speech, when he got to the list of fake new rules, Mantle said very loudly, "I quit!" and the speech had been ruined. It was not a good start.

2

That spring Bing Devine knew his job was on the line. He had been general manager of the Cardinals since 1957, but he had not yet produced a pennant winner, and Cardinals owner Gussie Busch was hardly the most patient of men. Busch was the Budweiser tycoon, accustomed to having his every whim fulfilled. Since he was immensely successful in the beer business, he assumed that he would be equally successful in the world of baseball, about which he knew almost nothing. Busch was an extroverted, zestful man, "a booze-and-broads" kind of guy in the words of Harry Caray, the team's announcer, who by his own word was also a booze-and-broads guy and a close pal of Busch's until he got too close. Busch was a generous man, albeit generous on his own terms. He had to win at everything, most notably at card games. He did not like to be alone, and he tended to be followed by an entourage of cronies. Being truly claustrophobic, he did not like to fly on airplanes, so he traveled either in a massive custom-built and custom-outfitted bus or in his own luxuriously outfitted railroad car. On either of these vehicles there were likely to be a lot of drinking, cards, and attractive young women.

It was the rare Busch crony who did not believe in his heart that he was a baseball expert. Therefore, being a baseball manager or a general manager for Gussie Busch was a high-risk occupation. To make matters worse, the tycoon thought himself a man of the people and was prepared to listen to this endless parade of self-styled baseball experts he ran into every day. He was also readily accessible to local reporters, often, it turned out, after he already had a head start drinking either his own product or that of other alcohol manufacturers. If the team went on a losing streak, as it often did, and if a reporter reached Busch at home to ask if he was happy with the way the team was going, he was likely to say no, he goddamn well was not happy. That had happened when Eddie Stanky was managing and the team was on an eight-game losing streak. When the words were in print the next day, it was clear that time was running out for Stanky. Every day of August Busch's life, Bing Devine thought ruefully years later, there had to be any number of people telling him, "Hey, Gussie, you made a winner out of Bud, how come you can't make a winner out of the Cards?"

At the tail end of the 1963 season, the Cardinals had launched a furious if belated drive for the pennant, winning nineteen of twenty games, and that had whetted everyone's appetite for what was going to happen in 1964. Whether the 1964 team was as good as it had been in that miraculous, almost flawless three-week stretch was by no means a certainty. Devine had spent his entire life in the Cardinal organization, apprenticing from the bottom up, and there was no job so insignificant that he had not performed it. Back in the thirties, when Branch Rickey ran the organization, there were some thirty teams in the farm system, and Bing Devine made sixty-five dollars a month for the most menial of tasks. He began every day by collecting the telegrams from all the general managers of the different Cardinal farm clubs reporting what their team had done the previous day. Then Devine went to the various blackboards that listed each league and each Cardinal team, erased the old standings, and wrote in the new ones. He was therefore an expert on how a seemingly unbeatable team could unravel almost overnight based on an injury or two, he knew how two star players could have unexpectedly bad seasons at the same time and cripple a team, and he knew how the combination of these—an injury and an individual bad season—could end a team's chance as a pennant contender.

Devine was well aware that Busch was not a baseball man, but a *sportsman,* accustomed to winning. His explosive temper was fueled not merely by a fondness for his own product (which was never beer, but always a Bud; there was a fine at Gussie Busch's ongoing card game for anyone who asked for a beer, not a *Bud*), but even more so for what he called "silver bullets"—very, very dry martinis. In those days, a sportsman meant a rich man with a passion for hunting, fishing, and horse racing, a man who would shoot at the best lodges in the nation and fish distant waters for giant billfish, but who rarely knew about baseball, which was essentially a blue-collar sport. As a Budweiser executive, Busch was an unqualified success. His knowledge of the beer business was exceptional, and he had brought Budweiser to a position of dominance in the industry after World War II. But knowledge and expertise in one field did not travel lightly to another, as he had found after trying to purchase his first black player, Tom Alston, from the minor leagues.

Busch was irate when he found out that instead of being twenty-three years old, as he had been told, Alston was actually twenty-five. Busch was accustomed to buying machinery rather than human beings, and thereafter depreciating his machinery according to the wear on it. Since the average baseball player's career was ten years, as Busch had been told, and since Alston was two years older than had been claimed, then roughly 20 percent of his career was clearly gone, so Busch demanded twenty thousand dollars back on the price. That he did not get it was a sign of how difficult doing business was going to be with a rather worn-down baseball franchise. On another occasion he pushed for the signing of the son of a well-known former player named Dixie Walker. When his scouts and player-personnel people dissented, saying that they did not consider the younger Walker major-league potential, Busch became annoyed. He did not know baseball, he said, but he knew horses, and in the world of horses, you always went with the bloodlines and the gene pool—why not in baseball as well?

The Cardinals' previous owner, Sam Breadon, had come to baseball after owning an auto dealership in St. Louis, during the years when Branch Rickey was the general manager. Breadon was, if anything, cheaper than Rickey, a legendary skinflint: in 1942, when the young Musial had come in third in the National League batting race in his first big season, Breadon offered him the magnificent raise of $1,000 for his good work. With Rickey gone to Brooklyn as general manager, the Cardinals still managed to win regularly throughout the forties. But, getting older and fighting cancer, Breadon began in the mid-forties to sell or trade many of the team's better ballplayers. There was a ceiling on what a Cardinal ballplayer could make in those days, and it was $13,500. Only Marty Marion, as good a salesman as he was a shortstop, it was said, had been able to breach the 13.5 ceiling; he received $15,000 because he was a favorite of management and because, in 1944, he was also the Most Valuable Player in the National League. Generally, when a player reached $13,500, it was as good as buying a train ticket out of St. Louis. At one point, angered by the demands of the Cooper brothers for salaries as large as Marion's, Breadon essentially sold both of them off, getting $60,000 plus another ballplayer for Mort Cooper in 1945 from the Boston Braves, and, a few months later, selling Walker Cooper to the Giants for $175,000, then a record price. Breadon also allowed Branch Rickey's great farm system, which in the thirties and forties had fed so many great players into the team, to atrophy. The last hurrah for the old Cardinals came in 1949 when they dueled the Dodgers in a momentous pennant race. Up two games with only five games to play, they blew that lead at the end. On the train back to St. Louis late that season, Bob Broeg of the *Post-Dispatch* asked Eddie Dyer, the Cardinals' manager, when he thought the Cardinals might challenge for the pennant again. Dyer said, "Funny, Bob, I was just asking my wife the same thing." Then Dyer pondered the question for a moment. "Not for a long time," he said, for the farm system was gone and Branch Rickey, who had built it up, was gone, to archenemy Brooklyn, and there were not that many good young players coming up.

The era of the Cooper brothers, Whitey Kurowski, Terry Moore, and Howie Pollet was over. Soon only Musial and Red Schoendienst remained from the glory years. After the 1949 season Breadon sold the team to new owners, headed by a man named Fred Saigh. Saigh's role as a principal Cardinal owner was a cameo, as he was soon sentenced to a federal penitentiary for income-tax evasion. He was ordered to wind up his affairs before May 1953, which meant, among other things, getting rid of the Cardinals. Saigh wanted to sell the team locally, but, surprisingly, not a lot of buyers were interested. Saigh's main act of civic duty came when he sold it to The Brewery for $3.75 million, or an estimated half a million dollars less than he could have gotten from buyers in Milwaukee. That did not mean that Saigh came out of the deal badly, for as part of the transaction, according to Bob Broeg, he got an estimated $600,000 worth of Anheuser-Busch stock, which some forty years later, Broeg estimated, was worth about $60 million. But Gussie Busch, it turned out, had bought a name, a logo, and little else. The Cardinals did not even have their own ball park, playing in rickety old Sportsman's Park, which belonged to the lowly Browns.

The first lesson Gussie Busch learned was a painful one: he could not buy success overnight in baseball. What worked in the world of beer—hiring, if need be, the best men available—did not work in baseball. Great players were not for sale, no matter what the price. In his first season Busch asked Eddie Stanky, his manager, what it would take to create a championship team. Stanky answered that if he got a first baseman and a third baseman he would have a contending team. "Which would you rather have," Busch asked, "a first baseman or a third baseman?" Stanky thought about it for a bit. "A first baseman," he answered. Did Stanky have anyone in mind? Busch asked. "Sure," he answered, "and I think he'll play for me, Gil Hodges." Hodges, he explained, had just come off a bad World Series in Brooklyn and might want a change of venue. "No problem," said Busch. "Let's go and get Hodges." So, quite excited, Gussie Busch went the next day to visit with Walter O'Malley, in order to buy Gil Hodges. He came back in shock. What happened, Gussie? aides asked him. "O'Malley wanted six hundred thousand dollars for Hodges, and then he said even if I had the money he wouldn't sell him anyway because he was one of the most popular players on the Dodgers and he'd be run out of Brooklyn if he sold him. What kind of business is this anyway," he asked rather plaintively, "where they want six hundred thousand dollars for one player and even if you have the money they won't sell him?" A few years later he made another try at buying a player, this time Ernie Banks, the talented shortstop of the Cubs. Busch authorized Frank Lane, then his general manager, to go as high as $500,000 for him. But Lane returned empty-handed. "How high did you go?" Busch asked. "Five hundred thousand," answered Lane. "And you couldn't buy him?" asked an incredulous Busch. "Mr. Busch, I was politely reminded that Mr. Wrigley needs half a million just about as much as you do," Lane said. That was one trouble with being a sportsman: there were all those other sportsmen to deal with, and they were every bit as rich. Clearly, building a team was going to take time and cost a great deal of money. Neither spending nor waiting came easily for Busch, and one of his favorite retorts to the St. Louis writers when they told him what he ought to do, which trades he might make, or which deals he could pull off to strengthen the farm system was to say, "Pal, you're really good at spending other people's money."

A decade after Busch purchased the team, Bing Devine still had his job as general manager cut out for him: to rebuild the farm system on a smaller scale in a new and more expensive era while trying to jump-start the existing club. Busch was still looking for his first pennant. He had bought the franchise in part because he was a good citizen of St. Louis, and there was talk until the last minute when he entered the bidding that the team might leave St. Louis and relocate in Milwaukee, a rival midwestern city and, worse, a rival center of beer brewing. If Gussie Busch did not entirely understand baseball, he did understand that baseball could help sell beer. He presided over Budweiser at the precise moment of dramatic change in the industry brought about by modern communications, most notably televised advertising. Local breweries were on the way out, not because their beer was not as good as that of the giants but because they could not compete with them in terms of advertising dollars spent on national television. As with many aspects of American life during that postwar era, the big companies became bigger and richer, with new, handsome regional satellite plants, and the smaller ones withered away. Beer, more than most products, lent itself to national advertising, and it was part of Busch's genius that as his company expanded relentlessly in the fifties, he knew enough to increase the percentage of the corporate budget reserved for advertising—this was the means with which he could crush the competition. Busch realized that baseball was an effective and relatively inexpensive advertising vehicle for beer, and it was not entirely by accident that Bud's resurgence as the nation's best-selling beer coincided with The Brewery's purchase of the Cardinals in 1953. (From 1949 to 1955, Schlitz was the best-selling beer in the nation, but in 1955 Budweiser soared past Schlitz.)

Indeed, when Busch bought the Cardinals, he also bought Sportsman's Park, dilapidated though it was, and refurbished it. Ever the beer salesman, he tried to call his new ball park Budweiser Park, but was talked out of it by aides who said that you could not name a park after a beer. Phil Wrigley, they pointed out, had not named his stadium Spearmint Park after his chewing gum. Forced to choose between ego and advertising, Busch conceded: in Chicago it was Wrigley Field, and in St. Louis it would be Busch Stadium, not *Budweiser* Park.

Baseball turned out to have an added, unexpected advantage for Gussie Busch: owning a baseball team made him a celebrity. Before, as a beer magnate, his face might have been known to a fair number of people in St. Louis and to avid readers of *Fortune* magazine. When he called a press conference to announce the opening of a new regional multimillion-dollar brewery, though, there was little media interest. But now, as the owner of a major sports franchise, everything that Busch said was news. People coveted his friendship, and he loved it.

He seemed to have little patience for watching his own team play, and his interest quickly waned during the games. In fact, his closest friends doubted that he had followed baseball at all before he bought the Cardinals. To manage his team he tended to hire small, feisty overachievers, men who were considered strict disciplinarians. Two of his first three managers, Eddie Stanky, whom he liked, and Solly Hemus were cut from that cloth. Their very manner seemed to promise the owner that they would keep his young athletes in line;

after all, the players were being paid to *play a game*, and might therefore easily relax and exploit the essentially benign nature of the owner-sportsman.

Stanky, Hemus, and Fred Hutchinson, who served a tour as manager in the fifties, had either grown up in a tougher, harsher America or had apprenticed under men who had. They were not always supple in dealing with younger men who often had greater natural gifts than those once possessed by their managers. The Depression was a thing of the past, the country was dramatically more affluent than it had been, and such gifted athletes as Ray Sadecki, Tim McCarver, and Mel Stottlemyre often had other options in life, whether it was college or jobs in other fields. The nature of authority was slowly beginning to change. As for the black players, treating them with a harsh authoritarian hand had even more ominous implications and was likely to produce even less positive results, as Solly Hemus's handling of Bob Gibson and other players would soon show. Young baseball players, white or black, could no longer be treated as if they were recruits at a marine drill camp.

In the past, a manager intimidated his players. Stanky was the prototype of that breed, a tough little man whose nickname was "The Brat." As a player and a manager, he was always engaged in some kind of confrontation. Stanky knew a great deal about baseball and later turned out to be an exceptional scout and a valuable instructor within the Cardinal organization, but he was having trouble adjusting to a changing America. The time had come when he began to look at altogether too many young men and was unable to see a reflection of himself. During one game he told a young player named Tom Burgess who had hit .346 in the International League the year before, "Get out of here and go down to the bullpen. I'm sick of looking at you." Stanky's technique had worked with limited success when he first began to manage the club. But the more talented and sophisticated his ballplayers became the less effective the technique. Perhaps the moment that signaled the *end* of his effectiveness came one day at a team meeting when the manager was chewing out his players. There was nothing new in that, but while the tirade was going on, Stu Miller, one of the Cardinal pitchers, sat in the back reading *The Sporting News*. Stanky continued to lecture all the while, becoming angrier and angrier. Finally he yelled at his pitcher, "Miller, that'll cost you a hundred dollars!" Miller never looked up. He simply turned to Butch Yatkeman, the clubhouse attendant, and said, "Butch, can you go down to my locker and get a hundred dollars out of my wallet and give it to him?"

Hemus, the third of Busch's managers, saw himself as a Stanky disciple. Perhaps nothing reflected Hemus's attitude better than his way of rewarding a player who had had an unusually good day. He would reach into his pocket and give the player one hundred dollars in cash and tell him to take another player to dinner. That was what Hemus had seen managers do when he was coming up; it was the way big-timers operated. Hemus had got the job in part, the Cardinal players believed, by writing Busch a fawning letter when he himself had been traded from the Cardinals in 1956; the letter, many of the players felt, went far beyond the call of duty, particularly as it was addressed to an owner whose team had just sent him to another team. The contrast between his reverence for his superiors and the roughness with which he treated the players who worked for him did not increase his popularity with the players. Like Stanky, he was a prisoner of his own baseball experience, and he seemed to lack the capacity to treat different players in different ways. His blunt manner and words especially bothered some of the black players, who considered him racist.

In 1956, after some twenty years in the Cardinal organization and six years as general manager of its Triple A team in Rochester, Bing Devine was brought back to St. Louis, having been told that he was now going to be named general manager of the big-league club. But a man named Taylor Spink, editor of *The Sporting News*, a baseball weekly published in St. Louis, suggested to the owner that he hire Frank Lane, a professional baseball man known for his propensity to trade players. Egocentric, profane, and voluble, Lane was far better known than Devine at the time, and Busch hired him. Unfortunately, Lane was a man who traded not so much to build a better team, but almost out of psychological need, an irresistible impulse driving him to move players around. There was no particular grand scheme to Lane's trades, and it appeared likely that given the chance, he would continue to trade as an end in itself, thereby inevitably destabilizing his own team. The very act of trading seemed to feed his ego; a general manager who traded all the time became better known than all but the most famous of his players. Frank Lane's incessant trading in the end made Frank Lane the center of media attention rather than his players. In that sense he was not unlike George Steinbrenner, the owner of the Yankees who went about furiously hiring and firing managers some thirty years later—thereby guaranteeing himself endless coverage on the back pages of New York's tabloid press.

Lane became known as "Trader Lane." It was also true that the more important a ballplayer was to the team, the more seemingly inviolable his position within the Cardinals, the more irresistible was Frank Lane's urge to trade him. Thus Red Schoendienst, the great Cardinal second baseman, and a cherished link to the glory years of the forties, was dispatched for Alvin Dark, and the only reason that Lane did not trade Stan Musial, who was to most Cardinals fans the living embodiment of the team, was because Musial's restaurant partner learned of a proposed trade and managed to go public with it just in time, thereby stopping Lane. Had Musial not been a restaurateur as well as a great baseball player, he would have ended his career with the Philadelphia Phillies. From then on all major trades had to be cleared with Gussie Busch. In a way the attempt to trade Musial (for the great Robin Roberts) marked the high-water mark of the Lane era, and the beginning of his decline.

That became clear in the spring of 1957, when Gussie Busch went to a preseason sporting dinner in St. Louis under the impression that he did not have to make a speech. He was relaxed and in a good mood and he enjoyed several bottles of beer and several Scotches. Just as he was beginning to really enjoy the evening he was called to the rostrum to speak. He was not pleased by the request, and his mood quickly darkened. He got up and gave a brief speech saying that Frank Lane had better bring back a championship this coming year or he was going to be out on his ass. Lane happened to be in the audience, and instead of letting the remarks go—in the eyes of the

St. Louis sporting establishment this was simply Gussie being Gussie—he got up and jokingly explained to the audience that they had
just witnessed the perfect illustration of why baseball executives did
not dare send their laundry out—because they were not sure they
would be there when it came back. An expert on dealing with Busch
when he was in his cups would have let the matter go right then and
there. But Lane, perhaps knowing he was on his way out anyway,
drove out of town on his way to Florida the next day and sent Busch
a three-page telegram detailing a considerable list of demands—
principal among them, his insistence on a three-year contract.
Nothing that Lane had achieved so far in any way seemed to warrant
such a demand, and Busch's response was typical. He ordered a telegram sent to Lane saying, KISS MY ASS. It was not long after that that
Bing Devine became the general manager of the Cardinals. Lane
was soon gone to Cleveland, where, among other things, he was
noted for trading away the young talented Roger Maris to Kansas
City before Maris could reach his full potential.

It would have been hard to find a better human being in baseball
at that time, or a man more grounded in all its aspects, than Bing
Devine. He was a lifer in the best sense. He had played baseball in
college at Washington University of St. Louis, and had been good
but not good enough for the professional game, though many times
in his long career in the minor leagues, if on occasion a team was
short a player, he would dress and place himself on the roster. Devine had learned a lot about trading under Frank Lane, in particular
that you could not let one bad trade inhibit you, and that no matter
how shrewd and knowledgeable you were, certain trades were not
going to work out. At the same time, he understood that you could
not trade as an end in itself; you had to have purpose and method to
your moves. Devine envisioned a certain kind of baseball team and
traded systematically for it. He wanted speed, good defense, and,
above all, balance. Speed was important because if your players had
it, you not only improved your offense but your defense as well. He
differed from most general managers in one important way: he
would trade talented pitchers (not, he thought, supertalented ones,
but quality ones, fifteen-game winners) for everyday ballplayers. His

theory was that pitchers were the easiest players to scout, because a scout was likely to see far more of them on a given day than players at regular positions.

Within months of taking over from Lane, Devine began the process of building the team that would come together in the mid-sixties. His first important decision was *not* to trade a player—a young third baseman–outfielder named Ken Boyer, who had come up through the Cardinal organization. As far as Devine was concerned, Boyer would be the keystone of the next generation. He had played both infield and outfield in his first three seasons, and there were signs that he might be a budding star. He had both power and speed. Several teams coveted him, and Lane had been on the verge of trading him to Pittsburgh, but the trade was stopped. Then the Phillies made a strong offer for Boyer; they offered Richie Ashburn, a talented, speedy center fielder with more range and less power than Boyer, as well as Harvey Haddix, a former Cardinal coming to the end of his prime at thirty-two. Boyer was an adequate center fielder, but Devine suspected that he was out of position there. What distinguished him was not so much his speed as the quickness of his reflexes, a vital trait at third base. Having a third baseman who could field, and who also added power to the lineup, gave a team an edge. So Devine turned down the Phillies: "I'll bank what little reputation I have that Boyer will be a star, and at third base," he said at the time.

But that meant Devine went to the winter meetings at Colorado Springs in December 1957 without a center fielder. Day after day passed as the other baseball men made deals and seemed to be improving their teams, and yet Bing Devine, the newest member of this club, had yet to make a deal. He began to think this was something of a black mark against him, especially since his team was not that good. If he had learned anything from Frank Lane, he decided it was not only that you could trade too much but that you could also trade too little. It was part of the culture of baseball that you were supposed to leave those meetings with someone new, so that at the very least the fans would be optimistic about the coming season. On the last night of the meeting, when there was supposed to be a din-

ner, Gabe Paul of the Reds sought out Devine. "Look, you haven't
made a trade and we haven't made a trade. Let's skip the dinner and
sit down and make one." So they met in Gabe Paul's room, Paul
accompanied by Birdie Tebbetts, his manager, and Devine by Fred
Hutchinson, his manager at the time. They went back and forth for
more than three hours, and late in the session one of the Reds' officials, buoyed by the fact that they had a number of talented young
outfielders coming up in their farm system, including Vada Pinson,
suggested trading Curt Flood, a young black outfielder in their
minor-league system, to the Cardinals. Flood had the potential to be
a great player; he was not yet twenty, he had played two full seasons
in the minor leagues, and he had excelled both years. In his first
season in the Carolina League, playing under adverse conditions, he
had led the league in five categories, including hitting with a .340
batting average. The next year, he had again had a remarkable season, this time with Savannah in the Sally League. Mostly playing
third base, he had hit .299 with 14 home runs and 82 runs batted in.
Hutchinson had heard of Flood, checked around among his friends,
and liked what he had heard: that Flood was a good hitter, a good
fielder, better in the outfield than the infield, and a tough kid who
had withstood a lot of pressure in a hostile environment. Devine was
uneasy because it was his first deal, and because he had not only
never seen the player but he had no sense of him either. But Hutch
seemed confident of Flood's ability, and Devine had a good deal of
faith in Hutchinson's ability to judge talent. The Cardinals were offering one undistinguished big-league pitcher and two minor-
league pitchers for Flood, and while none of the three was
important in the Cardinal plans, if one of them blossomed later, it
could be embarrassing. After a lot of palavering, both sides decided
to recess. Devine, Hutchinson, and Dick Meyer, who was The
Brewery's man on baseball (because, it turned out, he had once
played baseball at a Lutheran seminary), caucused briefly in one
bedroom. "Well," said Meyer, "you're the baseball people, you
make the call." Devine still felt uneasy about the trade. What saved
the moment, Devine thought, was Fred Hutchinson's decisiveness:
"Make the deal. We'll fit him in somewhere. We think he can hit.

We know he can run. Maybe he can play center field for us," Hutch said.

Bolstered by his manager, Devine made his first deal. The Reds were willing to make the trade, virtually giving Flood away, because they already had Frank Robinson as a budding star in their outfield, where he had hit 67 home runs in his first two seasons, and because Pinson was a potential star in their farm system, having hit .367 with 20 home runs, 20 triples, and 40 doubles with their Visalia team in the California League. Pinson was bigger and stronger than Flood, and Flood himself always suspected they were not enamored of having an outfield of three black players. So Devine left Colorado Springs with two key pieces in place, one by taking a risk and listening to a manager he trusted, and one by *not* making a trade. For their part, the Reds lost the chance to have an outfield of Vada Pinson, Frank Robinson, and Curt Flood.

Slowly and steadily Devine continued to put together the right kind of team. The level of the team's speed and talent was going up constantly. There was the beginning of the right blend of veteran players and younger players. As the team began to emerge in the early sixties, almost everyone on the team could run, including the two power hitters, Bill White and Boyer. But then, in 1962, there was a dangerous move against Devine. A man named Bob Cobb, who ran the Brown Derby restaurant in Los Angeles, and who had in the days before expansion run Los Angeles's Triple A club, spent an evening with Busch, and sympathized with the plight of so wealthy a man who was so frustrated by the vagaries of baseball. Cobb suggested that Busch get the greatest baseball man of all time to help run his club, or at the very least to advise him. Who was that? Busch asked. Branch Rickey, of course, Cobb answered, the man who had created the Cardinals' farm system in their glory years, then had helped create the great Dodger teams of the fifties, and who was most notably revered in baseball history as the man who had signed Jackie Robinson to a Dodger contract and thereby broken the color line.

So it was that fifty-eight years after he first began as a player in St. Louis, fifty years after he first managed a big-league team, and thirty-eight years after he first became general manager of the Cardinals, Branch Rickey returned to St. Louis, principally, it seemed, at the expense of Bing Devine. Rickey joined the organization with the title of Special Consultant to Gussie Busch, and from the start, he set out to take over the team. Rickey was then in his eighties, and his health was beginning to fail. If the world of baseball had changed substantially by the mid-sixties from the one that he had helped create in the thirties and then dominated in the forties and fifties, nonetheless he was still an eminence, and no less ambitious than in the past. Rickey did not think of himself as old (as he had not thought of himself as young when he was young), and he was eager to remain a player in the front office, and to pull off one more miracle. He seemed to have little respect for Bing Devine, whom he remembered from Devine's days as a lowly clerk, even if most of Devine's peers saw him by then as one of the most subtle and skillful front-office men around. From the start Rickey made it clear to Devine that he did not intend to sit on the sidelines as a mere consultant. After their first day in the office together he asked Devine to drive him home. "Why do you think I'm here?" he asked the younger man. "Because Mr. Busch wants your counsel and advice," Devine said, hoping to put a positive spin on an untenable situation. "That's not why I'm here," Rickey said. "I'm here to make the final decisions on this ball club." Then Rickey asked, "Who do you think is going to run the ball club?" Devine answered that he intended to. "Then we have a problem," Rickey said. "Indeed I think we do," said Devine.

Branch Rickey was arguably the single most important front-office figure in modern baseball history. He had helped create the idea of the modern farm organization. By 1949, based on his amazing success in both the Cardinals and the Dodgers, as Jules Tygiel has pointed out in *Baseball's Great Experiment*, an estimated three out of eight major-leaguers had been developed in one of Rickey's two farm systems. His courage and foresight in challenging baseball's policy of segregation, and in sensing Jackie Robinson's greatness and selecting him as the instrument of his policy, guaranteed him a place in America's history books. But by reputation, he was, in the words of Leo Durocher, one of the men who managed for him, the worst operator in professional baseball—"the cheapest, the shrewdest, and the most hardhearted of men."

He was a Victorian man, born in and shaped by another century, much given to bloated rhetoric, at once shrewd and pious, honorable and duplicitous, quick to cover his base moves with high-minded speeches (and, on occasion, his more high-minded moves with primitive explanations). He had promised his mother that he would never play on Sunday and he kept that promise, never, even as an executive, going to the ball park on that day either. Some writers could not decide whether he was the most religious man of his era in baseball or simply the greatest con man. The room where he held press conferences was known by reporters as The Cave of the Winds. At one Rickey press conference John Drebinger of the *The New York Times* asked a question and Rickey took off on a twenty-minute soliloquy. "Does that answer your question, John?" he asked at the end. "I've forgotten the question," Drebinger answered. When he talked of his motivation in making a particular move, he often seemed to give the impression that the one person he had consulted was God. "The Mahatma," the sportswriter Tom Meany called him, a nickname that stuck; it came, of course, from Gandhi. It was the name given the Indian leader by his people, meaning "the great one." After all, John Gunther, the great journalist of the era, had described Gandhi as "a combination of God, your father, and Tammany Hall." To the sportswriters of the day that certainly sounded like Branch Rickey. Someone once laid down the basic rules for negotiating with Rickey: "Don't drink the night before, keep your mouth shut, and your hands in your pocket."

"El Cheapo," Jimmy Powers, the sports columnist called him, for his Calvinist view of society clearly forbade paying too much to a player: too much money might corrupt a player, and under no circumstances did Branch Rickey want to corrupt a young man. Better that the money should stay in his own coffers. In fact, the classic Rickey move with a gifted player was to wait until he had reached the apex of his career and his salary was beginning to reach its apex as well, and then trade him for a younger, less expensive but equally talented player on another team. That way he constantly kept the level of talent up, but kept his payroll down in the process. The ability to get something for as little as possible was a trademark of his technique, and even when he signed Robinson, he had not deigned to pay the Kansas City Monarchs anything for Robinson's contract. He knew that no black baseball official would dare block Robinson's chances for success in the white baseball world. Certainly, by the custom of the day, Rickey owed the Monarchs something, and had Robinson been a white player from a white team, Rickey would certainly have observed the amenities and paid the team something, even if Robinson had technically not been under contract. As criticism of the Robinson deal mounted within baseball circles, Rickey became quite self-righteous. Black baseball (which was in fact reasonably well organized) was nothing but a "booking agent's paradise," he said. "They are not leagues, and have no right to expect organized baseball to respect them," he added.

That Rickey did not recognize the changed world of baseball quickly became clear to Devine and other people in the Cardinal front office. His style of trading was premised on the luxury of an extremely deep farm system that allowed him maximum leverage in all deals, that is, both with other clubs and with his own players. By the late fifties and early sixties that kind of wealth was being swept away by the rising costs of baseball, the rising costs of minor-league teams, and the impact of television, which offered fans in small towns the chance to watch major-league games instead of their local Class B, C, and D games. Rickey's response to these changes did not seem very realistic to Devine. Aware that the price of players was going up because of the search for bonus babies, he devised an extremely curious new plan for major-league baseball, which he demanded that Devine sell to the other baseball owners. It was a detailed and oddly utopian plan, which called for the major leagues themselves to draft all the players, and then for the players to be divided up among the existing teams. Devine did not believe in it himself nor did he think it had the slightest chance to be picked up by the other owners and general managers.

There was clearly no room for the two of them. Getting around slowly on a cane or not, Rickey remained a powerful presence. He wore Devine down, making everything he did harder, making every day at the office more contentious, and making him argue harder for trades, which meant that if Devine finally got a trade, the expectations on the part of the owner were higher. Devine was working ever harder just to stay afloat; it was not an enviable situation.

In the fall of 1962 Devine decided that St. Louis badly needed a solid veteran shortstop. The Cardinals had played a rookie named Julio Gotay there in much of 1962, and they became dubious that Gotay would ever show the talent he had on occasion flashed in the minor leagues. Otherwise the infield was strong; Ken Boyer at third and Bill White at first were virtual all-stars, and Julian Javier at second was young but showing certain signs of greatness. Devine wanted a mature shortstop to play alongside Javier and help bring him along. Dick Groat, only two years earlier the Most Valuable Player in the National League, was available, the Pirates having become disenchanted with him. Groat was an unusual player. He was one of the smartest athletes in the game, a man who had to work exceptionally hard to maximize his abilities and overcome his physical limitations.

No one in any major professional sport was ever a better illustration of the difference between being fast and being quick. In terms of leg speed Dick Groat was slow, but in terms of his reflexes, he was exceptionally quick. He had been a college all-American as a basketball player and a professional basketball player as well. He had great hand-to-eye coordination and deft hands. But he also had minimal range. No one studied pitchers, his own as well as opposing ones, more closely than Dick Groat, because he had to know how to play each hitter since he lacked the natural speed to compensate for being even the slightest bit out of position. He loved playing behind veteran pitchers, for he felt that the more experienced a pitcher was, the better he could position himself to make the plays: if the pitcher threw where he was supposed to, then Groat had a very good chance of making the play. He was also an exceptional hitter, almost always around .300. He had great bat control, rarely struck out, and was very good on the hit-and-run. He had been a professional shortstop for eleven years, counting time spent in the service, and had never played in the minor leagues. At the time that Devine wanted to make the trade, Groat was thirty-two. The Cardinal scouts, headed by Eddie Stanky, believed that it was a good trade, that Groat was in great shape, was highly professional, still had several good seasons ahead of him, and was not likely to lose speed, since he had never had it. Rather, he would be a good influence on the younger players and could work alongside Javier, thus anchoring what was potentially a very good infield.

But Rickey hated the deal. It was anathema to everything he believed in, especially his most basic rule: never trade a young player for an older player. Devine tried to make the case for Groat for several weeks, but Rickey kept stonewalling it. Stanky, Harry Walker, a coach, and Johnny Keane, by then the manager, all wanted it. So, one day during the instructional meeting, they all descended on Rickey. "You seem to have this meeting loaded," Rickey said to Devine, and he was not pleased. Yes, Devine answered, he had loaded it up, but they all wanted Groat that badly. Then they made their pitch: Groat was the right player for a team that was ready to contend. It would have been nice to come up with a superb young shortstop in their farm system, but they did not have anyone ready in the minors. In the meantime, Groat was available, a good hitter, an absolute professional. Rickey listened, and the more he listened, the angrier he became. He knew that Devine had ambushed him brilliantly, and there was no alternative solution he could offer. "All right," he said, "I will tell Mr. Busch that I won't stand in the way of this deal, but I won't recommend it either." That meant that they could get Groat, but it also meant that Groat had better have a good year, and had better not slip.

Mercifully, they bet right; Groat was angered over his treatment by the hometown Pirates, and he was determined to show that his career was not over. He decided that he would throw from shortstop overhand, much like an outfielder, instead of sidearm like most infielders, and he spent the off-season building himself up with special weight drills to that end. He also ice-skated every day in order to strengthen his legs, and to diminish any chance of muscle pulls. He arrived in marvelous shape, and played very well for St. Louis. The Cardinal groundskeepers, so ordered by management, deliberately let the grass in the infield grow high, which slowed down the ball and gave him more range. The long grass pleased Groat the fielder, although Groat the hitter hated the very same grass and frequently complained to his teammates because it meant that he could not drive the ball through the infield so readily. In 1963 he made a solid challenge for the National League batting title at the end of the season, and that summer all four Cardinal infielders started in the All-Star Game. That in itself was a sign that Devine's master plan was coming along nicely.

But, if anything, Rickey became even more resentful when the Groat deal worked out, and in the spring of 1964, there was one more incident which showed that Devine was dealing from a base of limited power. Tim McCarver was set in spring training as the everyday catcher, but Johnny Keane badly wanted a new backup catcher. A young player named Bob Uecker, of limited experience, playing behind Del Crandall, Ed Bailey, and now Joe Torre at Milwaukee, was available, having told the Milwaukee management that if he was not traded, he would retire from baseball. Keane wanted to make the deal for him, giving up two minor players—Gary Kolb and Jimmie Coker, then the backup catchers. Rickey wanted no part of it; if anything, he seemed to like Kolb as a player. But as both Keane and Devine pushed hard for the trade, Rickey resisted, with a vehemence out of all proportion to the importance of the players at stake. It seemed to be more about territory than about personnel. Uecker was in fact a good defensive catcher with a good arm, and there was an additional advantage to getting him, because Uecker batted right-handed, while McCarver batted left-handed.

But every time Devine pressed for Uecker, Rickey used his leverage with Busch. Finally, just as the team was about to leave Florida, Keane went to Devine one last time to ask for Uecker. "Bing, we have to try one more time—we have to have a better backup catcher. If we don't, we're vulnerable there," Keane said. "I'm sorry, Johnny, but I can't go back there anymore," Devine said, "I've gone as far as I can go on that one." Keane could, if he wanted to, Devine suggested, go out that night and talk to Gussie Busch at his home about it himself. It was a sign of how seriously Keane took the matter that he did, in fact, go to Busch's house near the beach sometime after ten P.M. Around midnight a call came for Devine from Keane. He had talked to Busch and it was okay to make the Uecker trade. So Devine went ahead, and a few days later Bob Uecker became, in his own words, the first local Milwaukee boy to play for the Braves, the first to be sent down to the minor leagues by them, and then the first to be traded away by them. On his first day in the Cardinal locker room he was taken to meet the legendary Branch Rickey in the Cardinal clubhouse.

"Mr. Rickey," he said, extending his hand, "I'm Bob Uecker, and I've just joined your club." "Yes, I know," said Rickey, "and I didn't want you. I wouldn't trade a hundred Bob Ueckers for one Gary Kolb." And with that warm welcome, Rickey turned and walked away. (It should be noted that while Kolb came to bat 450 times in his big-league career, Uecker came to bat *731* in his.) Bing Devine knew that time was running out on him that year.

3

Just before the Cardinals broke camp, Johnny Keane sat talking with a group of sportswriters about how evenly balanced the National League was and how important a great player like Sandy Koufax of the Dodgers became in that situation. Koufax, he thought, had stood between the Cardinals and the pennant in 1963, and he was concerned that that one pitcher would once again make the difference. In 1963, Koufax, aided by an expanded strike zone, had a career year, winning 25, losing only 5, with an ERA of 1.88, and beating the Cardinals four times. Most critically, he had shut them out in the last matchup, when the Cards had been the hottest team in baseball, during their run at a pennant. The knowledge that any challenging team would eventually have to go against the Dodgers and beat Koufax head-to-head was an important advantage for the Dodgers, Keane said. Except for that one pitcher, the Cardinals might well have a better team than the Dodgers.

Keane continued to talk about his own team's prospects for the year. He thought his team was better than last year, but it was hardly without its weaknesses. No team had great hitting *and* great pitching, and no team since the Milwaukee Braves in 1957 and 1958 had won back-to-back pennants. Every year since 1958 a different team had won, and it was rarely the team that looked best on paper. Just a few days earlier 232 baseball writers around the country had been polled on who they thought would win the National League pennant. Eighty-four had picked the Giants with their great hitting, and 79 had picked the Dodgers with their great pitching. The Cardinals, with better balance, and off their late-season challenge last year, were third, chosen by 38 writers. San Francisco's pitching was suspect, Keane said. The Dodgers had great pitching and speed but little power, and had been looking for more than a year to make a deal for a consistent .300 hitter who could knock in 100 runs. Milwaukee might well have the toughest hitters in the league—Hank Aaron, Eddie Mathews, Joe Torre, Lee May, and Felipe Alou, recently traded from the Giants—but the great pitching staff that had carried the Braves to earlier pennants had aged, and the younger pitchers on whom the team had spent enormous bonus money had yet to come through. Pittsburgh had very good pitchers, with Bob Friend and Bob Veale, and a good batting order, with Bill Virdon, Roberto Clemente, and a rising star in Willie Stargell. Cincinnati had Frank Robinson, Vada Pinson, and a good pitching staff. Only 10 of the 232 writers favored Philadelphia, but Lee Petersen of UPI went out on a limb and picked the Phillies, because he thought they had the best pitching in the league, with Jim Bunning, just picked up in an off-season trade from Detroit; that gave them a formidable front-line pitcher to go with Art Mahaffey, Chris Short, and Dennis Bennett. The Phillies were a dark horse, but they worried other baseball men. Keane said he thought the Phillies would be tough.

The team that made it through was likely to be the one with the fewest injuries to key players, Keane said. In a league so evenly balanced, just one key player who was injured or performed significantly below expectations could cost a team the pennant. The Cardinals, Keane told his reporters, had to learn to beat the Dodgers this year. If you went head-to-head with your most important opponent and lost those big games, you did not deserve to win the pennant. The key to winning, Keane said, was for the Cardinals somehow to match Koufax; perhaps, he said, the Dodgers' luck might slip a little, Koufax might have an off season. An off year for Koufax was one in which he might win only twenty games instead of twenty-five. The odds favored it. It would be hard even for a pitcher that great to match what he had done the previous year, not to mention that Ron Perranoski, their top reliever, had gone 16-3, appearing in 69 games, with a 1.67 ERA, also a career year. Perhaps, Keane mused, if one or the other slipped just a bit, that might open the door a crack for the other teams.

The signing of Yankee players usually took place relatively painlessly, or at least relatively quickly. Management still held all the cards at contract time and retained all the negotiating leverage. In fact, there was no such thing as real negotiations, since it takes two sides to negotiate. Mantle had signed again for $100,000, and Maris for $65,000. But Jim (Bulldog) Bouton, who had pitched extremely well in 1963, winning 21 and losing only 7, with an earned run average of 2.53, the best on the staff, was asking for virtually a 100 percent raise for his third season; in 1963 he had made $10,500 and now he wanted $20,000. At first Ralph Houk had been optimistic about signing Bouton quickly. But the difference between them did not shrink. Houk was offering $18,000 and that was as high as he was going to go, he told the press. After all, he was offering Bouton 80 percent of what he wanted, which was fairly generous by contemporary standards. Bouton soon began to look like the one serious holdout on the team. Day by day Houk's irritation with the young pitcher increased, until by March 10, he announced that if Bouton did not sign, he would be fined $100 a day. ("The Yankees shortened the leash and tightened the collar on the 'Bulldog' today," the *Daily News* reported.) Houk said he was doing this for the good of the club. "I have no qualms about this," Houk told reporters. "If I gave him what he is asking it would not be fair to the others—my dealings with the rest of the club. I raised the figure and will not go any higher. Bouton had a good year and I hope he has many more . . . and that he gets more good raises. But he can't have it all at once. You have to earn your way to a star's salary." The next day Bouton conceded and signed for $18,000. BULLDOG STOPS BARKING, AGREES TO YANKS' $18,000, read the *News* headline.

As far as the Yankee management was concerned, Bouton's near holdout typified the danger of letting a young player, particularly a pitcher, have too good a season too early in his career. A twenty-game winner, management believed, had too much leverage with the club. In the Weiss-Stengel years, Yankee pitchers rarely won twenty games, and there was a reason for it. It was better to let them win fifteen or, at most, eighteen, which meant that the team could still win the pennant, but management would retain maximum leverage in negotiations the following year. That was as much a part of the Yankee tradition as winning the pennant and the World Series, and such great Yankee pitchers as Vic Raschi and Allie Reynolds had considered their contract struggles with Weiss to be virtual battles in which management belittled their achievements and did not like it if their previous seasons had been too good statistically. Those past Yankee teams had been so powerful and so dominating that not only could they win, they could do it while management kept one eye on statistics. Bouton, that spring, did not realize the degree to which he had violated Yankee tradition by winning too much too quickly. Years later he ran into Johnny Sain, who had been the pitching coach in 1963, and Sain filled him in on what had happened. Near the end of the season, with Bouton closing in on his twentieth victory, Houk had not been entirely pleased. "It's too soon for him to win twenty," Houk had told Johnny Sain at the time. "Look at how long it took Whitey to win twenty." This was a reference to the fact that it took Whitey Ford ten seasons to become a twenty-game winner. Besides, there was already some evidence that Bouton, who was later to emerge as a major iconoclast in the world of baseball, might turn into a difficult young man by Yankee terms—too outspoken, too quick to challenge management's decisions, too friendly with journalists, and in particular with journalists who were considered unfriendly to management. As Bouton neared his twentieth win, Houk had not kept him out of the rotation. But years later, after Bouton spoke with Sain, something clicked in his memory; he remembered the game that was his twentieth win. It had been in Minnesota, and he had been backed by a weird lineup, a goodly number of the Scrubeenies, as the bench players were known, with some of them out of position—Phil Linz, for example, in center field, and Johnny Blanchard in right. But Bouton had won his twentieth, and then, for good measure, he won his twenty-first.

After his twenty-first win his teammate Ralph Terry came over after the game, slapped him on the leg, and told him, "I'm glad you got the twenty-first—winning twenty games makes it look like you just barely made it. But twenty-one is really terrific."

There was a sense among the other players that although Bouton was entitled to more money, somehow he was different. He was part of the new breed who had joined the Yankee roster in recent years. Their style puzzled the old-time players. Bouton, Phil Linz, and Joe Pepitone—all of whom had played at Amarillo together in the Texas League—were considered distinctly un-Yankeelike by temperament. It was not that they were playboys, although Pepitone obviously liked being a major-league baseball player because it was not a disadvantage in meeting beautiful young women. If anything, both Bouton's and Linz's work ethic exceeded that of some more naturally gifted players from the past. Nor had they joined a team that scorned carousing, for the Yanks had more than their share of serious skirt chasers and drinkers, tough men who were throwbacks to the golden age of macho pursuits. Rather, their sin was in being lighter of heart than most Yankees, and of not taking defeat quite as hard as their predecessors did. (When Linz retired from the game and opened a restaurant-bar in New York, he did not, like most retired ballplayers cum restaurateurs, choose a name summoning up his past glory as a player; he called it Mister Laffs.) They were more exuberant than their teammates and their behavior on occasion puzzled them. Linz, for example, practiced self-hypnosis, and did it so successfully that after one early session of looking into a candle and repeating "I will time the ball perfectly . . . I will time the ball perfectly. I will hit the ball through the middle . . . I will hit the ball through the middle," he went 5-for-5. He reluctantly gave up the practice only because it was taking so much time, cutting into his sleep so that he arrived at the ball park tired.

Later some traditionalists claimed that the Yankee decline began with the arrival of the newcomers, that they had not understood the Yankee tradition of seriousness and commitment. However, while it was true that Pepitone squandered as much talent as any player who ever wore pinstripes, it is also true that no one played harder than Bouton or Linz. It was certainly true that Bouton was more political than most players, and more interested in arguing about the merits of politics than the merits of women; this was viewed as unnecessarily contentious and more than a little weird. Bouton was, among other things, quite possibly the only ballplayer in the major leagues who was for gun control. Nor was his friendship with such irreverent sportswriters of the day as Leonard Shecter, Stan Isaacs, and Maury Allen considered a plus by his teammates. Many of the complaints about Bouton, though, came only after his arm went bad, at which point his personality began to jar on his teammates. Linz was also a tough, aggressive player, and he loved being a Yankee. "Play me or keep me," he once told Houk.

Whether they represented the coming of a new and different generation, no one was sure. Frank Crosetti clearly disliked them. Crosetti was the third-base coach, who had broken in with the team in 1932, almost a decade before some of these players were born, and he had been playing or coaching ever since. He was the keeper of the flame, a man determined to force rookies to adhere to the Yankee rituals of the past. In particular, he did not think Linz took his job seriously enough. Their conflict was generational. Linz (and some of the other younger players) felt that much of what Crosetti stood for was not so much designed to make someone a better player as to inhibit personal freedom, to take the fun out of life. Linz also thought there was a double standard at work, that the stars on the team could take liberties without being criticized because they were the stars. The new breed, as some of the sportswriters (themselves the new breed as far as *their* colleagues were concerned) called them, flouted the code of conduct: those yet unproven were barely to be seen, let alone heard. Pepitone, a poor kid from a harsh environment in Brooklyn, managed to spend five thousand dollars the day he signed his first contract. He bought, among other things, a brand-new convertible, and showed up at his first spring training, barely out of D ball, driving the aforesaid convertible. Worse, it was hauling a giant boat, which he had no earthly idea how to use. Yankee rookies did not arrive in camp in flashy new convertibles, hauling brand-new boats, and he was given exactly twenty-four hours to sell the boat.

The new-breed players were not deferential to the veteran players. From the start they talked to the senior players—the great stars of the team—as if they were equals. The first time Pepitone was sent in to replace Moose Skowron for defensive purposes, the brash Pepitone told Skowron, "Moose, you must have the bad glove." Skowron, a veteran ballplayer and firm upholder of tradition, would walk through the locker room, looking at the younger players and shaking his head, saying that it had never been like this when he was a rookie. Pepitone answered by telling Skowron to watch out, because he was going to take his job, which in fact he eventually did. When in November 1962 Skowron was traded to the Dodgers, Pepitone sent him a cable after the trade: DEAR MOOSE: TOLD YOU SO. JOE PEP.

From the start, Pepitone, in particular, ignored the team hierarchy. If the normally unapproachable DiMaggio walked into the locker room, it was Pepitone who might yell out, "Hey, Clipper, how are you—do you want to have dinner tonight?" To everyone's amazement this seemed to please DiMaggio. It was Pepitone who, when asked by Mantle to bring him a beer, demanded that Mantle bring *him* a beer, which seemed to amuse Mantle as well. It quickly became clear that Pepitone loved Mantle, loved being Mantle's pal and basking in his reflected glory; in fact, Pepitone wanted nothing so much as to be Mantle's caddy. One or two of the older players thought there was a certain desperate quality to Pepitone's clowning, and his need for Mantle's approval. In the locker room, Pepi always had his eye on Mantle, watching to see if the great star approved of what he was doing. Some were reminded of school days when an insecure and not particularly popular kid wanted to win favor with the most popular boy in the class.

Generally Pepitone was successful in his attempts to charm Mantle. Pepitone, an amused Mantle said at the time, was "the freshest rookie I ever saw," but he also had a quick bat, a good swing, and could play both first and the outfield. Pepitone loved it when Mantle nicknamed him "Pepinose" (Stengel, in those days before ethnic slurs were taboo, called him "Pepperoni") and was thrilled when Mantle told a sportswriter that Pepitone was the key to the 1963 season. "I figure we'll win by a nose," Mantle said. Yet even the easygoing Mantle, a player always looking to be amused, thought there were times when Pepitone overstepped the bounds. Once, during batting practice, Pepitone jumped into the batting cage and got ready to take his swings when Mantle wanted to take extra swings because he wasn't hitting well. "Five swings, Slick," Pepitone said to an astonished and then enraged Mantle. The two exchanged sharp words, and even though Pepitone was embarrassed to have done the unthinkable, to have provoked his idol, he was in too deep and could not back down. Much to his regret, he heard himself telling Mantle to get to the ball park earlier and get himself wrapped earlier if he wanted extra swings, and not to hold up his teammates. It was not, as far as Mantle was concerned, a small matter, and he did not speak to Pepitone for several weeks, leaving Pep increasingly dispirited and desperate.

There were other sins. During spring training the Yankees had a dress code: the players were to come down to breakfast in the motel in their civilian clothes, which meant a sports jacket, and then go back to their rooms and change. On one occasion Pepitone and Linz came into the restaurant in their Yankee uniforms. Houk was furious, as if this were somehow demeaning the uniform, and he sent them right back to their rooms to change. Pepitone was the first Yankee to bring a hair dryer into the locker room, as much as anything else to fight his onrushing baldness. On occasion he seemed to enjoy going on the field without his cap, as if to unveil himself for the young women in the stands. He not only tended to wear his street clothes tighter than most of his teammates did (on the same day he bought his new convertible, he also bought several flashy suits, styled, in his words, like those of "the younger, sharper racket guys"), he also started to wear his uniform tighter than the prevailing style of the day for ballplayers.

Because they were young and ebullient and somewhat surprised to be playing for, of all teams, the Yankees, they showed their pleasure openly, especially to the younger sportswriters. Those writers were frustrated with the often unsympathetic older players, whose quotes seemed to come from some central clearinghouse of approved and sanitized athlete-speak, so, in turn, they were drawn to the extroverted new breed. But in the Yankee clubhouse the younger players were believed not only to talk too much, but to have talked before their turn. The ability to be quoted in a newspaper was not, in the Yankee tradition, a God-given right; rather, it was like being given a low rather than a high uniform number, something that was supposed to be earned, preferably over many years. They had not yet earned the right to be quoted.

This clubhouse code was set not by Mantle or Ford or Berra, who by and large could have cared less (and who were probably delighted to see the local sportswriters bothering someone other than themselves). Instead, it was the older players, more often than not the part-timers of marginal talents, who were bothered most. It was not surprising that the second-tier players were unusually zealous to protect their privileges as *Yankees*, for it was not individual play that secured their niche in baseball history, but their place on those dynastic teams. They viewed a younger player who talked too much and whose locker became something of a haven for the beat reporters as seeking too much publicity and promoting himself. He was a member, they said, of the Three-I League: I-I-I. In addition, there was a suspicion that a player who talked too much was somehow disloyal to the team, and might be giving away secrets. When Bouton or Linz or Pepitone were too available to reporters, the other players would pass their lockers and make a gesture with their fingers of a mouth moving, the implication being that the player was talking too much, and was too close to the press.

4

The Yankee roster was essentially set when spring training began. There was, the players believed, one additional place left—Yogi Berra was looking for a reliever, and in early spring it came down to a contest between a player named Tom Metcalf and one named Pete Mikkelsen. By all odds Metcalf, then twenty-three, was the favorite, for he had gone further and accomplished significantly more than Mikkelsen, twenty-four, whose career had been rocky. Metcalf had played for three years at Northwestern and pitched at a high level in the minor leagues: he had a wide variety of pitches, with a particularly good curve. Johnny Sain, the perceptive pitching coach, thought him just on the verge of becoming a good big-league pitcher. Metcalf had been brought up to New York from the Triple A farm club in Richmond in mid-1963 when Houk began to worry about his bullpen. Because he had spent time with the parent club, it did not occur to him until rather late in the spring of 1964 that he was competing with a pitcher who had never pitched above Class A. Even Pete Mikkelsen himself thought the fact that he had been invited to the major-league camp something of a fluke. He did not have a very good fastball ("at best it was mediocre") and he did not have a very good curve. He did have a wicked palm ball, a pitch that allowed him to rear back and throw with a violent arm motion, while the ball itself proceeded slowly toward the plate. In much of his career in the minors he had been on the edge of failure; in 1961 with

Binghamton he had been 4-10, and the next year, with Augusta, he had been 3-5 and he felt he had pitched badly. At that point he was sure he was on his way out of the world of professional baseball to one populated primarily by blue-collar workers, like most of his high school classmates from Staten Island. To make bad matters worse, in early 1963 he hurt his arm at the start of the season. Because of the pain, Mikkelsen had been forced to start throwing his fastball with a shoulder-high delivery instead of a straight overhand delivery as he had in the past. When he began to do that, the ball started to sink on the hitters, and they regularly beat the ball into the ground. He had become, quite involuntarily, a very good sinker-ball pitcher.

Rube Walker, Mikkelsen's manager in Class A, spotted the sinker and told him to stay with it. "Don't change a damn thing," he told Mikkelsen. Mikkelsen pitched well during 1963 with Augusta—his record there had been 11-6 in 49 games, and his ERA had dropped to 1.47—and much to his surprise he joined the big-league club in the spring of 1964, largely on Walker's recommendation, he was sure. He did not think he was pitching terribly well that spring, but he kept surviving the successive roster cuts. Finally, during the last two weeks in Florida, he realized that it had come down to himself and Metcalf. Mikkelsen later said, "Metcalf was a prospect, and I was a suspect." But Berra had liked sinker-ball pitchers in the past, and now that he was about to manage, he liked them even more, because they could come in during tense situations and get the batter to hit the ball on the ground. Walker kept telling Mikkelsen that he was doing well, that all he had to do was to keep throwing the sinker, which he did, even in batting practice, much to the annoyance of the veteran hitters. "All those hitters, they have this belief—thou shalt not pass," Walker said. "It's like a sin for them to get a walk. So they're going to swing and if you throw them the sinker, they'll beat it into the ground. And then you'll make the club."

Metcalf, in the meantime, thought he was throwing well, and not giving up very much in the way of hits or earned runs. He had not been pleased earlier in his career when the Yankees had turned him into a relief pitcher. He thought they had done it because he was tall (six feet two and a half inches) and slim (about 165 pounds), and they had decided that a player that skinny might lack the stamina necessary for a starter. His best pitch was a big roundhouse curve. Metcalf could throw it for a strike when he was behind in the count. "The Hammer," Ernie White, his manager in Augusta in the Sally League in 1962, liked to call it. There had been a clash of coaching wills that season when the Yankees sent the old Phillies reliever Jim Konstanty down for a few days as a pitching coach. Konstanty taught what the players called the Jim Konstanty Curve, which was a smaller curve that did not break as wide, but more sharply. Konstanty told Metcalf that his curve was too big, and that he needed to work on one that was smaller and sharper. "Your curve may break out of the strike zone," Konstanty said, "and maybe you won't get the call." So Metcalf had worked on the Konstanty Curve and started throwing it. As soon as he tried it in a game, Ernie White called time and ran out to the mound. "Where the hell is the Hammer, kid?" he asked. Metcalf said he was not throwing it anymore on Jim Konstanty's advice. "Listen, you dumb son of a bitch. You'll be riding the first train back to Whiskey Rapids or wherever the hell you're from if you don't go to the Hammer on the next pitch, and as for Konstanty, he'll be gone in two days, but I'll still be here managing this goddamn team, even if you're not on it." With that Metcalf went back to his big curve, winning 14 games and losing only 6. He reached Richmond in 1963, his third year in organized baseball, gaining a record of 9-5 there with an earned run average of 2.69 before being called up to New York. In New York he had one bad outing and appeared in seven other games. But with Hal Reniff, Marshall Bridges, and Steve Hamilton pitching well, the Yankees used Metcalf less and less. That bothered him, and late in the season he asked Ralph Houk to send him back to Richmond where he would be able to play regularly, but Houk said it was too risky, because the World Series rosters were set and if Metcalf were sent back, Houk might lose an eligible player. He said he was sorry the way things had turned out, but that Metcalf would get a good shot to make the roster and do some serious pitching next season.

Gradually that spring it dawned on Metcalf that he and Mikkelsen were competing for the last spot on the roster, that they were pitching on the same day against the same teams, to see how they did against the same hitters. That did not strike him as fair, since Mikkelsen had not yet pitched above Class A. *What do I have to prove?* Metcalf thought. *I've been in Triple A and I've done well, and he's never been above Class A.* There were stairs to climb, and in his mind he had climbed them and Mikkelsen had not. The other Yankee pitchers watched the competition with interest. They noticed one additional difference between the two players, and that was that Mikkelsen seemed to carry himself with more physical authority than most minor-leaguers. There was a sense that he would be grizzled one day, and there was an obvious physical toughness about him. By contrast, Metcalf had a cherubic face, innocent and unlined; he looked like someone who might be the most popular member of a college fraternity. This did not mean that Metcalf was, in fact, more innocent or gentler than Mikkelsen or that Metcalf cared any less about getting to the majors, but Metcalf *looked* innocent, and Mikkelsen *looked* tough. To some of the other players that was an important distinction, for they believed in the macho theory of baseball decision-making: you could put pictures of two equally talented players in front of several coaches and a manager, and they would, being pretty grizzled themselves, invariably choose the tougher-looking player.

As the competition continued, some players told Pete Mikkelsen that he was doing well, but he did not believe them. When there was a report in one of the New York papers about him and his improving prospects, the story referred to him as *Jim* Mikkelsen, which did not leave him optimistic. But he knew that Yogi liked sinker-ball pitchers, and the other players pointed out to him that if his name was in the papers, it was probably because Yogi had put it there—the sportswriters never pushed prospects without getting signals from the manager. But then the day came when he pitched against the Minnesota Twins, and he looked up at the plate to see the immense figure of Harmon Killebrew facing him. Here was the man believed by most players to be the only other hitter in the American League as strong as Mantle. *Harmon Killebrew at bat*, Mikkelsen thought. *I must be getting closer to the major leagues than I ever imagined if I'm pitching to him.* He gave Killebrew nothing but sinkers, and Killebrew drove four of them into the ground, foul. Although in the next inning Tony Oliva hit a ball off him that seemed to go past the flagpole in deepest center field, the fact that he had been able to handle Killebrew was something that the manager and the coaches had to have noticed.

Mikkelsen still believed that he was going to be sent back to a minor-league camp, although at a higher level than he had originally believed possible, when Rube Walker called him over. "Where do you think you're going next year?" Mikkelsen answered that he was hoping to go to Double A or, maybe with luck, Triple A. "You ain't going to no Double A, you're going to New York," Walker said. Mikkelsen said that they did not have a team in New York. "Yes, they do," Walker said. "You're going with the big club, the Yankees." Mikkelsen still did not believe Walker, but ten days later, when they were set to leave camp, Pete Sheehy, the clubhouse attendant, who knew every rumor ahead of everyone else on the team, asked him where he wanted his things shipped. "What do you mean where do I want them shipped?" he asked. "Where in New York?" Sheehy persisted. That was how Mikkelsen learned he had made the big-league roster. He later heard that there had been a split in the executive ranks—that Yogi and Rube Walker, a former catcher for Brooklyn and a close friend of Yogi's, had favored him, while Houk preferred Metcalf, but that Yogi had won out. What had made the difference, the other pitchers were sure, was the fact that Mikkelsen had one great pitch, the perfect go-to pitch for a reliever, because it produced ground balls. Metcalf, possibly more talented, had no comparable pitch that would serve a reliever so well.

Bruce Henry, the traveling secretary, asked Mikkelsen how many sports coats he owned. Mikkelsen answered that he owned one, because that was the way young men of limited means dressed in those days: one suit for weddings and funerals and one sports jacket. Henry told him that he had to buy some new clothes, that there was a dress code on the team and that one sports coat was not going to get him through the season.

Tom Metcalf was called in by Yogi Berra and told that he was being sent back to Richmond. Metcalf was sure he had outpitched Pete Mikkelsen, and he became extremely angry. He thought that their competition had been rigged, and that Mikkelsen had had the job from the start. He and Berra exchanged angry words. He asked to be traded, but it was clear that the Yankees had no interest in doing that, that they still saw him as a top prospect. Houk came over to him later that day and apologized, saying that it was Yogi's decision and Yogi's team. For a time Metcalf thought of not reporting to Richmond, but he realized that he would be challenging the entire structure of baseball, so he relented. That spring, having apparently learned a lesson in Florida, he began to work on a sinker ball. During one inning he tried to throw a sinker and felt a small, sharp pain in his elbow. When he left the mound, his arm did not hurt that much, but when he went back out to pitch, he bounced the first pitch halfway to home plate to Jake Gibbs, who was catching. Metcalf tried one more pitch and bounced that one too. The next day he had very little feeling in his fingers or in his arm from the elbow down. He had damaged the nerve in his right, or throwing, elbow, and he was done for that year. Though he made one major attempt to come back in 1965, his career was essentially finished, and he never made it back to the major leagues.

5

When a few years later, Marvin Miller, the labor negotiator, visited the various baseball camps during spring training for the first time to explain collective bargaining to the various players, he was quickly struck by the fact that the Cardinal camp was different from every other one he visited. The players were more relaxed, more mature, and better integrated, black with white. The friendships among the players seemed to transcend racial lines, and Miller was especially struck by the fact that not only were the players friendly with each other but their families were too. By the summer of 1964, the question of race hung heavily over the nation at large, as young blacks challenged existing segregation statutes in the South, and baseball too was going through its own period of dramatic racial change. It was now seventeen years since Jackie Robinson had broken in with the Dodgers, and had done it so brilliantly that he had not only helped lead Brooklyn to a pennant but had won the Rookie of the Year Award. That there was a great new talent pool of black athletes was hardly a secret among the white players themselves. The names of such great black players as Josh Gibson, Satchel Paige, and Judy Johnson had been well known to the many big-league players who had often barnstormed with them after the regular season was over (and who often made more money barnstorming on the all-white major league all-star teams than their colleagues had made playing in the World Series): they knew that the Negro leagues were filled with players who could hit and pitch, and, above all, who had speed. In the years since Robinson's historic arrival in the big leagues, certain teams had moved quickly to sign up the best black players. It was the equivalent of a bargain-basement sale at Tiffany's—great players available at discount prices, even as the price of young, untried white players was going up very quickly.

The talent search was not joined with equal enthusiasm by the two major leagues. In 1954 the Supreme Court of the United States had ruled that white Southern school districts should move with all deliberate speed to integrate; in baseball the National League moved with speed, but the American League moved with deliberation instead of speed. Because the Dodgers soon had Robinson, Roy Campanella, and Don Newcombe in their lineup, there was a ripple effect in the National League. The Dodgers' crosstown rivals, the Giants, had to move quickly in self-defense, and as both teams were adding speed and power, so other National League teams were forced to move as well. At first, they scouted the Negro league games, and then, as the younger players there were signed up, they began looking for ever younger players from the Deep South. Soon the Milwaukee Braves followed with Bill Bruton and Henry Aaron playing in the outfield, which led to the joke "What's black and catches flies?" The answer was the Braves' outfield. Hank Aaron did not think it very funny.

In the American League the tone was set by the New York Yankees. The Yankees were a dominating team, and their ownership in those critical years was, to be blunt, racist. They were winning and winning consistently without black players, about whom the ownership believed many of the existing stereotypes: that blacks were lazy and would not play well under pressure. George Weiss did not even want white rabble at his ball park, he told reporters. He wanted his fans to be from the white middle class, and he most emphatically did not want black fans who came to cheer black players. That, in his mind, would surely drive away his treasured white middle-class customers. In 1945, Weiss had stolen away one of Branch Rickey's best scouts, the famed Tom Greenwade, a man who worked the Ozarks and the Southwest. It was Greenwade who signed Mantle for the

Yankees, but it was less well known that he also had done the vital day-to-day scouting of Jackie Robinson when Rickey was making up his mind as to which black player would be the first to break the color line. Because of that, Greenwade knew as much or more about the available black talent as any white scout in the country, but Weiss was not interested. "Now, Tom," he told Greenwade in their first meeting working together, "I don't want you sneaking around down any back alleys and signing any niggers. We don't want them." That was that. Greenwade thought it bizarre. He was being tipped on such great young prospects as Ernie Banks, but was unable to move on them because of his marching orders. The Yankees, he later lamented to his son Bunch, lost an important decade by not going after black talent, and he told the story of Weiss setting limits on him with considerable bitterness and regarded it as the great regret of his career. Ironically, Mantle's greatness increased the arrogance of the front office, for his exceptional speed and power convinced the Yankees that they did not need to change. He helped bring them an additional decade of dominance, and in so doing, he helped create the attitude among their executives that would lead to their eventual decline. As most of the other American League teams followed suit, the National League gradually began to pull away as superior, with better teams and more exciting younger players.

By 1964 the National League had virtually all the best young black players, and it was therefore a league with more speed and power; its best young players flashed their speed on the base paths with increasing aggressiveness. The American League tended to rely on sluggers who were slow of foot (Mantle and Maris were exceptions), and tended toward a more cautious game, its managers by and large waiting for the big inning. The difference between the leagues was dramatic. After the 1963 season, Sandy Koufax, who had dominated the league as well as the Yankees during the World Series, was the National League's Most Valuable Player. The selection followed a decade in which nine of the previous ten winners were black, and in the one instance that a white player won—Dick Groat of the Pirates in 1960—it could as easily have been his teammate Roberto Clemente (who was enraged by Groat's selection and was convinced that he had lost because he was Puerto Rican and there-fore had encountered an additional layer of prejudice). The black winners were Roy Campanella of the Dodgers, winning the second of his three MVP awards, followed, in order, by Willie Mays, Cam-panella again, Don Newcombe, Hank Aaron, Ernie Banks, then Banks again, then Frank Robinson and Maury Wills. Wills was em-blematic of the change taking place. He was, first and foremost, a player who brought speed to the game, and he had languished in the Dodger organization for a long time. He came into his own when they moved from Ebbetts Field, a hitter's park, to the vast spaces of the Los Angeles Coliseum, which emphasized the importance of baserunning. Soon other National League teams were looking for their version of Maury Wills. By contrast, in the American League, Ellie Howard, the first black Yankee player, who was brought up in 1955, became the league's first black MVP in 1963. "Well, when they finally get me a nigger, I get the only one who can't run," joked Casey Stengel, his manager, whose attitudes on race were schizo-phrenic enough that he could at once use ethnic slurs and yet still appreciate Howard's obvious talents.

If, by 1964, the Cardinals had become something of a model in terms of their racial composition and attitudes, it had not always been that way. In fact the Cardinals had come to this more slowly than most National League teams. They were one of the teams that had, for a brief time, considered striking against Jackie Robinson in his first season. Before the Dodgers and Giants moved west in 1958, and before big-league baseball went to Kansas City and Atlanta, St. Louis was not only the farthest west team in professional baseball, it was the most southern as well. St. Louis was for a time the most segregated city in the big leagues, the city that visiting black players liked to visit least. The Chase Hotel, where the ball clubs stayed, was one of the last to admit black players. The regional pull of the surrounding territory affected the Cardinal decision-making, and the team drew some of its players and many of its fans from the South and Southwest, so it was loath to violate their racial preju-dices. KMOX, the radio station that beamed the Cardinal games, was a powerful signal throughout the South. It was the custom in the mid-fifties, in such places as Alabama, Mississippi, and Arkansas, for young, white working-class men, their work week finished, to load up a car with beer on Friday afternoons and take off for St. Louis. Driving and drinking, if necessary through the night, they would arrive in time to watch the Cardinals on Saturday and, if possible, in a Sunday doubleheader, before driving home all Sunday night. "In St. Louis they say that fans would never stand for Negroes on the Cardinals or Browns," wrcte the New York newspaperman Dan Daniel, after Larry Doby signed to become the first black player in the American League. "St. Louis, they insist, is too much a Southern city."

Among the players who agreed with that judgment was Minnie Minoso, the black Cuban player. In 1946, Minoso, one of the most gifted players in the history of the game, was playing in the Negro leagues. He was asked to a Cardinal tryout and arrived there with Jose Santiago, a Puerto Rican pitcher on the New York Cubans. In Minoso's eyes, he and Santiago were by far the best players at the tryout. Santiago struck out every batter he faced, while Minoso, playing in the infield, was told not to throw so hard to first, because the first baseman could not handle his throws. Nonetheless, Minoso could sense that the Cardinals were not interested in the two of them, that the tryout was a sham, and he left that day bitter and determined never again to attend a tryout for a white man's team. If white people wanted to scout him, he decided, they could come watch him play at Negro league games; he would pay no more house calls.

When the Cardinals finally did sign their first black player, they went about it ineptly. Gussie Busch was stunned to find that the team he had just purchased was all white. Since Budweiser, its executives believed, sold more beer to black people than any other beer company in the country, Busch was nervous for economic reasons about owning a lily-white team. He could easily visualize a black boycott of his beer, and, to his credit, he also thought it was simply morally wrong to exclude blacks. That first year he visited the team in spring training, he asked his manager and coaches, "Where are our black players?" There was a long silence and one of the coaches finally said, "We don't have any." Busch said, "How can it be the great American game if blacks can't play?" The silence hung heavily over everyone. "Hell," he added, in words that clearly represented the end of an era, "we sell beer to everyone."

Very quickly, as part of the new regime, two black players were signed, at the far-from-bargain-basement price of $100,000 each: Tom Alston, a minor-league first baseman who had played in San Diego and hit well there, and Memo Luna, a dark-skinned pitcher who was believed by the Cardinal ownership to be Cuban but was born in Mexico. Luna celebrated his good fortune at being signed by the Cardinals by pitching in both ends of a doubleheader and arrived in St. Louis with what was essentially a dead arm. He pitched less than one inning for the Cards in his career, gave up two walks and two hits, and retired from major-league baseball with an earned run average of 27.00. Busch did not regard this acquisition as a good start in improved race relations.

Tom Alston, by contrast, made a very good first impression on people in the Cardinal organization. At an early meeting, one of Busch's public-relations men, Al Fleishman, warned Alston of all the terrible things that were going to be said and done to him. Alston put his hand on Fleishman's knee and said, very gently, "I know I'm a Negro, and I know that there are going to be some people who hate me for nothing more than that. But that's not my problem, that's their problem." Then he visited a nearby teachers college, where he told young black students that times were changing and that people were going to be judged not by their color but by their ability. He said that a new day was coming, that doors once closed were going to open, and he ended movingly: "When it does, be ye ready." Alston, however, was not the answer to Busch's prayers. He was a first baseman with good feet and good hands but a weak bat. In 1954 he came up 244 times and hit .246, with only 4 home runs. Those were not good numbers for a first baseman, and the pressure on him, some teammates thought, exceeded what he could handle. Alston stayed around long enough to accumulate 27 more at bats over the next three years.

Later that same year the Cardinals brought up a young black

pitcher named Brooks Lawrence, who pitched exceptionally well; he had a record of 15-6 in 1954 and showed considerable promise for the future, but with Frank Lane as general manager, Lawrence was quickly traded away to Cincinnati. Clearly, putting talented young black players on the field was going to be harder than anyone expected, and was going to require far greater patience than the Cardinals had yet to display, as indeed putting together a first-rate team of any color was going to require greater patience than Busch had first expected. Yet, more than most teams, the Cardinal players came to deal with race with a degree of maturity and honesty rarely seen in baseball at that time. In 1961, a good fourteen years after Jackie Robinson's professional debut, Bill White, the Cardinal black first baseman, challenged the concept of an annual whites-only players breakfast in St. Petersburg. Local businessmen there traditionally honored the visiting Yankee and Cardinal players, but, according to local custom, invited only the white players. White leaked to a reporter the anger of the black players about the breakfast, and, even more important, their resentment over segregating white and black players in separate living facilities—the whites staying at the best local hotels, the blacks forced to stay as boarders with black families in the black section of town. The policy for the breakfast meeting was quickly reversed (when White found out how early he had to show up, he asked his white teammate Alex Grammas if Grammas would like to go in his place). The housing problem was stickier because of Florida law. Finally, a wealthy friend of Gussie Busch bought a motel, the Skyway, and the Cardinals leased it for six weeks and rented some rooms in an adjoining one, the Outrigger, so that the entire team and their families could stay together. A major highway ran right by the motel, and there, in an otherwise segregated Florida, locals and tourists alike could see the rarest of sights: white and black children swimming in the motel pool together, and white and black players, with their wives, at desegregated cookouts. That helped bring the team together. Even Stan Musial, who had both the right, as a senior star, and the money to rent a house for his family during spring training—something he had looked forward to in the past—stayed at the motel and was a part of the team. That made a great difference, for Musial was not only one of the two or three greatest players of his era, he was one of the most beloved as well: he seemed to live in a world without malice or meanness, where there was no prejudice, and where everyone was judged on talent alone. He had always been a generous teammate, and he was always willing to help teammates and opponents alike with batting tips—although he was so spectacular a hitter himself, with such great wrist and bat control and so great an eye, that his tips were not always helpful. Once the young Curt Flood asked him how to wait on the curveball. At the time Flood was having trouble learning how to adjust his own swing to wait that final millimeter of a second in order to time it properly. Musial duly considered Flood's request and then replied, "Well, you wait for a strike. Then you knock the shit out of it." (*I might as well*, Flood thought, *have asked a nightingale how to trill*.)

Another Cardinal player who set the tone was Ken Boyer, the third baseman and the captain of the team. By dint of his sheer professionalism and the nature of his personality, he was a role model to many of the younger white players. Boyer was from the Ozarks, which did not make him exactly a Southerner, but still a player from a region not necessarily known for its hospitality to blacks. But Boyer stayed at the motel too.

The Cardinals not only dealt with the white-black issue better than most teams, they did it, Tim McCarver noted years later, *before* the team had won a pennant, whereas most teams tended to come together on the question of race only after winning. The mutual respect Cardinal players had for each other cut across racial lines. The team bridge game was an important daily ritual, pitting Bill White and Ken Boyer against Bob Gibson and Dick Groat. While it was a game, it was more than a game, because if these men, the four leaders on the team, had to play together on the baseball field by law, what they did in the clubhouse was their own choice. That did not mean that they agreed on everything: White and Gibson liked and admired Boyer, and sensed that he had the capacity to grow on the issue of race, but they were aware that the changes in attitude that some younger men, such as Tim McCarver, were then undergoing might well be beyond Boyer's reach. Boyer was for integration in general, but he was made very uneasy by other aspects of more profound social change. Racial intermarriage, especially, seemed to bother him. But at least they could argue about it and find some mutual measure of respect, and once when Boyer was at a bar, some man made a remark about Gibson. "The trouble with that goddam Gibson is he's a racist," the stranger had said. Boyer gave him a long cold look. "You don't even know the man," he said with contempt. (In the early sixties, Cassius Clay, not yet Muhammad Ali, became pals with some of the Cardinal players who were staying at the same segregated motel, and Clay convinced Curt Flood and Gibson to come to an early Black Muslim meeting. The speeches that night, Flood recalled, largely seemed to be about taking some form of vengeance on the white man. Gibson was not impressed: "Sounds as if black power would be white power backwards. That wouldn't be much improvement," he said.)

One of the key players in helping to create the culture of the new Cardinal clubhouse was a man few people knew. George (Big Daddy) Crowe was gone from the team by 1964, but he played a vital role in bridging the gap from one era to another. Crowe was physically imposing, six feet two inches and about 210 pounds, and a man of immense pride and strength who was, without ever trying to be, a powerful presence in the clubhouse. If you were casting him in a movie, the writer Robert Boyle once said, you would want the young James Earl Jones. His influence on the team was vastly disproportionate to his actual contributions on the playing field. He had arrived with the Cardinals in 1959, an aging player, his skills on the decline, his legs and his feet causing him constant problems. He had played for a number of years in the Negro leagues, and the integration of major-league baseball had come more than a little late for him. He first moved into the world of white baseball in 1949, two years after Jackie Robinson had played for Brooklyn. Though his listed age was twenty-six, his real age was perhaps twenty-nine or thirty, and he played very well from the start. But the Boston Braves had been in no rush to bring him to the majors. He played for three years in the minors, hitting .354 with 106 runs batted in for Pawtucket in the New England League in 1949, .353 with 122 runs batted in for Hartford in the Eastern League in 1950, and .339 with 24 home runs and a league-leading 119 runs batted in for Milwaukee in the American Association in 1951. Only then had he made it to the majors.

What Crowe had learned in so unusual a life, filled as it was with so much success gained at so high a price, commanded the respect of his teammates—white and black. He was someone who had a history, and that invested him with authority. He seemed to imply in what he said, and in what he did not say, and even in his body language that whatever was happening, he had seen it all before. He was certainly not going to be undone by anything he encountered. He was, thought Bob Boyle, very calm, very quiet, but his silences had as much meaning as his words. By the time he played for the Cardinals he was primarily a pinch hitter. He would sit in the dugout waiting, an immense black man wearing slippers in order to make it easy on his feet, which were clearly older than the rest of him. On one occasion Carlton Willey, a pitcher who loved to throw sliders, was pitching against the Cardinals, and Big Daddy looked out at him, half bored, and said, "Sometime in the next three innings they're going to come to me and make me put on my shoes and go up to bat, and that young man out there is going to throw me a slider inside and I'm going to hit that pitch over the 354 sign." Two innings later that is exactly what happened.

He was a man to be listened to, and, most assuredly, not to be crossed. During spring training in 1960 Big Daddy was not pleased with the calls of Ed Hurley, the home-plate umpire, who came from the American League. Crowe started getting on Hurley early in the game, his voice strong, penetrating, and distinctive. There was no doubt when he yelled out his dissent that Hurley heard every word. Finally Hurley had enough, pointed at Big Daddy, and said, "Crowe, that's enough—you're gone! Now get the hell out of here!" That enraged Big Daddy, who started to walk the length of the dugout as if stalking Hurley. Finally, he pointed at Hurley, his words coming out now in real anger. "Ain't no meat too tough for me, Hurley." It was not a routine confrontation in baseball, where quick flashes of temper are the norm. Rather, it was something more threatening that seemed to suggest that if things went any further, if *Hurley* transgressed any further, his authority as an umpire might come to an end as Crowe's authority as a human being superseded it. The scene was more than a little frightening to some of the younger Cardinal players, and frightening, they suspected, to Hurley as well, who looked shaken.

In another era Crowe might well have been a manager, or even a general manager, and one of his protégés, Bill White, went on to become president of the National League. No one was going to abuse anyone or bully anyone on a team as long as George Crowe was there. And no one was going to toss racial epithets around lightly. He became, not surprisingly, the self-appointed judge of the team's kangaroo court, a job for which he seemed to have been ordained at birth. He loved setting fines on the players for their minor mistakes—missing a sign, or failing to move a runner ahead with either no outs or one out—and his commentary was a far more important part of the team's byplay than the fines collected. Almost unconsciously, he merged the culture of the two races, for he was a black man who had lived for a long time in a black man's world, and when he came to the white man's world he brought with him a distinctly black sense of dignity and pride.

6

The 1964 season began as something of a disappointment for Mel Stottlemyre. Until the 1963 season he moved with surprising ease up the difficult ladder of minor-league baseball. Success had come readily, if not exactly effortlessly, to Stottlemyre. A Yankee scout named Eddie Taylor picked up on him when he was pitching for Yakima Valley Junior College and had written to his superiors, "He has a good sinker and the courage and the control to use it right. I would recommend signing him for a small bonus or a larger bonus contingent on performance." Signed by the Yankees, Stottlemyre went to a rookie-league team in Harlan, Kentucky, where he was impressive, and where the scouts and managers quickly sat down to grade him. The highest classification they could give was "Yankee," which meant that he would end up with the big-league team; the next highest grade was "major leaguer," followed by "AAA," and then "AA." His first report card said, "He has no outstanding faults. He has a fastball that sinks, and a pretty good curve. He needs to develop a change. He is serious about baseball. I classify him Yankee." In his next season, 1962, at Greensboro in the Carolina League, he won 17 games and lost 9, with an earned run average of 2.50. Based on so promising a performance, he was invited to spring training with the major-league ball club in 1963, when he was only twenty-one years old.

From the start, Stottlemyre's best pitch was an unusually sharp sinker ball. How and why he was able to throw such a vicious sinker fascinated his teammates. He did not have particularly large hands, which might have been the answer, but he had exceptional flexibility in his wrists, which helped greatly with the sinker ball. That flexibility was in part natural, but when he was in college Stottlemyre had seized on it and done a considerable number of drills with light weights, drills that were designed to maximize his ability to give the ball such snap. He knew early on that this was his ticket. His ball always seemed to move. In the spring of 1963, working out with the big-league club, he was not particularly pleased with his performance, though unbeknownst to him, his superiors were quite impressed. Johnny Sain watched him carefully and thought for a time that Stottlemyre might be ready to go directly to the major leagues, skipping, as very few players do, the critical years of apprenticeship in either Double A or Triple A. Sain watched Stottlemyre with increasing admiration and at one point called aside Ralph Terry, one of his pitching protégés, the star of the previous World Series, and an aficionado himself of pitching technique. "Ralph, I want to show you something," Sain said, and they moved over to about fifty feet from where Stottlemyre was warming up. Terry looked over and saw a slim, young right-hander who was throwing a good but not great fastball with seeming ease. But every ball seemed to come in right at the knees of the batter, and then suddenly break down. "With most young pitchers who attract your attention in the spring," Sain told Terry, "it's because the ball comes into the catcher so hard and you hear this huge explosion in the catcher's mitt. But you think about it, Ralph—usually the catcher is jumping in all kinds of different directions trying to spear the ball because the pitcher's control isn't worth a damn. But look here at how sweet this kid is. Every pitch breaking down below the knees, right around where the strike zone is every time. Good movement too—every pitch has a wicked little break." Terry asked who the pitcher was. "A kid named Stottlemyre. Just out of B ball. Won sixteen or seventeen games there. I'm recommending him for the majors right now. I think he's ready," Sain said. But in the end the Yankee field staff decided that Stottlemyre was not quite ready and assigned him to the Yankee Triple A team in Richmond, Virginia.

There, for the first time in his career, Mel Stottlemyre hit a wall. He did not pitch as well as he expected. The roster seemed to be loaded with pitchers, and Stottlemyre thought for a time that he might be sent down to a lower classification, perhaps Double A. But they kept him on in Richmond. There he struggled and was not able to get into the starting rotation. In the past, he had always been carried by his sinker, which was virtually indistinguishable from his fastball, but he had noticed that at Richmond, in Triple A ball, the balance between hitters and pitchers was already changing. The hitters were better here, and they were smarter, and his ability to dominate them based on pure natural ability had disappeared. In the past his skill was such that he could afford to be almost careless with it. But if he made a mistake in Triple A ball, he quickly paid for it: if the pitcher fell behind in the count, the relationship between hitter and pitcher tilted dramatically in favor of the hitter, as batters started hitting good pitches. It was no longer a matter, as it had always been for him in the past, of merely throwing strikes, but of throwing *quality* strikes, putting the ball exactly where he wanted to whenever he needed to. He could no longer pitch by pure instinct.

He had to think about every pitch now. If he was to have a career in major-league baseball, he had to improve, particularly as far as his control was concerned. It was a frustrating year for him: he was used mostly in relief and his record was 7-7. He gave up a hit for almost every inning pitched and his earned run average ballooned up to 4.05. What made the season worse in his mind was that when it came time to get ready for 1964, he was not invited to spring training with the big-league club, the way the top pitching prospects in the farm system generally were. That was a shock for Stottlemyre, for it marked the first time in his career that he had not moved ahead. Perhaps, he thought, he was no longer one of the Yankee's top prospects. Perhaps he had fallen in their estimation. In 1964 he was still in Triple A, making $1,200 a month for five months, starting in April and going through August.

Stottlemyre was a young man of unusual confidence and maturity; he never really doubted that he would somehow make the Yankee team, but he decided in the spring of 1964 that it might take longer than he had expected. Back in Richmond for 1964, he started the second game of the season, and was cuffed around a good deal. His command of his pitches was poor, and he fell behind frequently in the count. After that he was sent back to the bullpen. At first his relief appearances were not very successful either, as he continued to have problems with his control. He did not start again until the Memorial Day doubleheader.

Though the Richmond team did not have a full-time pitching coach, it did have the equivalent of one, a thirty-three-year-old pitcher named Billy Muffett. Muffett was one of those men who form the very foundation of professional baseball: he was something of a career minor-league pitcher. He spent eight years in the minor leagues and had one great season with Monroe in the Cotton States League, when he had won 22 games, lost only 9, with an earned run average of 2.25. In both number of games won and ERA he had led the league that year, and he was rewarded for this splendid season with two years in the army. After coming back to pitch, this time for Shreveport in the Texas League with a record of 5-11, he finally reached the majors at the age of twenty-six. He won seven games for the Cardinals over two years, and then went back for three more seasons in the minor leagues before surfacing again with Boston in 1960, where he won six games—his high-water mark in the majors. By 1963 he was back in the minors with Richmond, pitching mostly out of the bullpen. When the Yankees encountered bullpen problems in the middle of the season, Muffett hoped the call would come for him. Instead it came for young Tom Metcalf, and Muffett knew then that he had reached the point in his career when youth began to outweigh experience. So, when Richmond manager Preston Gomez asked him to coach as well as pitch, he was glad to accommodate. He was a shrewd observer of the game and he had the rare capacity to pass on his knowledge to younger, sometimes more gifted men. Thirty years after that season he was still a big-league pitching coach.

What Muffett saw in Mel Stottlemyre was a young man of enormous talent, who had been carried in his early career by raw ability, and who was now facing the first major crisis of his career. Either he would learn to deal with this crisis, Muffett thought, and become a first-rate big-league pitcher, or his career would quickly decline. Part of the problem was simple mechanics. Stottlemyre was planting his feet too close together when he completed his follow-through, and that was diminishing his power and velocity. In addition, he was not getting the ball *down* enough, which was hurting his location. Muffett got him to work on coming up higher with his arms and using his legs more to drive through his motion.

The most important thing was location. Stottlemyre had marvelous movement on the ball, movement that the average pitcher would kill for, but sometimes it took place outside the strike zone, which helped no one but the hitter. Muffett began to tutor Stottlemyre in the bullpen. Pitching in the majors was all about concentration, location, and mastery of his pitches, he explained. Under Muffett's guidance, Stottlemyre quickly improved his mechanics. He was releasing the ball better, the ball was coming down more, and that helped his control. But what helped even more was a lesson that Muffett taught him on improving concentration. Muffett suggested that when Stottlemyre was about to throw a pitch, he think not of the larger strike zone, but that he refine it and aim for a much smaller part of it, on the inside corner to right-handed hitters. If he could hit the inside corner with right-handers regularly, then he was a sure thing. To allow himself the luxury of thinking of the entire strike zone, Muffett taught him, was the equivalent of being mentally lazy. Shave the strike zone, Muffett told him, fine-tune yourself, go for smaller and smaller targets. That way, even if you don't put it exactly where you want to, you still may be in the strike zone, and even if you miss the strike zone, you may be close enough to get the call. It was brilliant advice, and though it might not work for everyone, it was ideal for Stottlemyre. Actually, he was a coach's dream as a pupil, for he not only listened but had the ability to take advice and act on it successfully.

On Memorial Day the Richmond team played a doubleheader

and Stottlemyre was summoned out of the bullpen to start one of the games. It was a one-start call, and he was by no means back in the rotation. Able to fine-tune his work now and place the ball almost exactly where he wanted it, he stayed ahead of the hitters. His sinking fastball continued to frustrate them as it broke down six inches below the knees; they ended up not with the vicious line drives they expected, but with yet another grounder. On that day he turned around his career: Mel Stottlemyre pitched a shutout. He was still not back in the rotation yet, but because of his success he was given another start, and he pitched another shutout. With that, he was back in the rotation.

Jake Gibbs, a young bonus baby who had signed with the Yankees after graduating from the University of Mississippi, and who had been converted to a catcher, marveled at the poise and ease with which Stottlemyre was pitching. There was one series of at bats, Gibbs thought, that seemed to epitomize the young pitcher's newfound skills and confidence. It occurred in a game against Toronto when Ozzie Virgil, a former major-leaguer, and a good hitter, was at bat. Virgil was a right-handed hitter, and the first time he came to bat, Stottlemyre got him out by jamming him. So the next time Virgil came up, he backed off a little. But Stottlemyre ran the sinker in on him again, and Virgil swung and broke his bat, a sure sign that the sinker had triumphed. The third time Virgil came up, he turned to Gibbs, who was behind the plate, and said, "I'm not going to let him jam me again," and then moved a little farther off in the batter's box. But Stottlemyre jammed him again and broke his bat again. The fourth time he came up, Virgil was virtually out of the batter's box. Again Stottlemyre jammed him. That was amazing, Gibbs thought: four times a kid pitcher had tied up one of the better hitters in the league, and twice he had gotten broken bats. Stottlemyre threw what professionals call a heavy ball, which meant that it came into the plate hard and heavy. It was hard to catch and hard on the catcher's hands as it broke down. Catching Stottlemyre over a few games almost guaranteed that Jake Gibbs's hands would be swollen and the fingers would be a purplish blue with little circulation in them.

Gibbs watched as Stottlemyre went on a roll. He reeled off ten wins in a row. He was pitching like a major-league starter against minor-league hitters. There was talk in mid-season that he would be called up to New York to help the parent club, which was struggling. But Stottlemyre doubted that that would happen. The Yankees did not like to rush their young pitchers up from the minors in mid-season. They regarded it as a sign of panic in the organization and liked to think of themselves as an organization so professional that it never had to panic. Only in rare situations, such as with Bob Porterfield in 1948 and Whitey Ford in 1950, had the Yankees made exceptions. The sportswriters in Richmond began asking Mel Stottlemyre when he thought he would be going to New York, and whether it was true that the Yankees were getting ready to bring him up, but Stottlemyre was sure he would stay the season in Richmond. Which was just fine with him; he was happy in his work and sure now that he would be a major-leaguer in 1965.

7

There was a certain gallantry to Mickey Mantle as he pressed forward in the twilight of his career. By the start of the 1964 season he had already hit more than 400 home runs, and he appeared to be on his way to a .300 career average. He was the man who carried the team, and yet he played now in constant pain, reaching for physical skills that were no longer there. However, in some remarkable way, the athlete within continued to rebel against the pain and refused to accept the limits set by his body. Again and again he endangered himself. Watching him tape himself every day—for the ritual of taping his legs had been going on for so long that he could do it himself—his teammates were in awe of him. "He is," his teammate Clete Boyer once said, "the only baseball player I know who is a bigger hero to his teammates than he is to the fans." His teammates knew from their own lesser encounters with injuries how much pain he was playing with every day. Hobbled by a bad right knee for most of his career, he now had two bad knees. His right knee was his pillar of support when he swung from the left side, and it sometimes buckled on him. That was painfully obvious when, batting left-handed, he started to swing and then decided to hold up on a pitch. His right leg, trying to break the force of the rest of his powerful body, seemed to give, and the pain on his face was clearly visible to his teammates. Watching him that spring, his former teammate Jerry Coleman, by then the team's broadcaster, could hardly believe the deterioration of that once-great body in so short a time, for when Mantle had first come up, he was the fastest runner Coleman had ever seen. When he had raced down the first baseline, Coleman remembered, you could not see the right leg go down and then the left go down; what you saw instead was the blur of both legs as part of one relentless motion. His legs, Coleman thought, were like the spokes on a moving bicycle wheel. But that speed was destroyed by injuries that occurred in his very first season. Charlie Silvera, the backup catcher, carpooled with Mantle in the very early years and watched him, even as a young player, unable to get into a car properly: instead, he would have to slide his body onto the seat, and then use his arms to lift his legs over the seat. By 1964, Coleman thought, he had become a very great athlete somehow managing to compete at the highest level of professional sports, while being, in medical terms, very close to a cripple.

The question of Mantle's health cast a shadow over the Yankee camp that spring. The 1963 season had been a disaster for him: he had missed almost one hundred games because of injuries. The cartilage was wearing thinner and thinner on his right knee, and, indeed, he was perilously close to having *no* cartilage there. That meant bone was grinding against bone, guaranteeing that he would limp in some manner for the rest of his life, and that the limp would be accompanied by pain. He had torn up his right knee in his first World Series in 1951, when he caught his leg in a drainage ditch in the Yankee outfield while trying to stop at the last minute to avoid a collision with Joe DiMaggio. A series of injuries followed. In 1963, in a game in Baltimore, he ran into a wire fence in the outfield, broke his left foot, and tore the cartilage in his *left* knee. When the season was over, he immediately underwent surgery to remove cartilage from it.

Mantle's teammates and the sportswriters now wondered whether center field was the right position for him, with all the running that was demanded of a center fielder. Perhaps, some of his teammates thought, left field or right field might be better. But Ralph Houk thought center was better—that he was less likely to run into a fence as a center fielder, and that there was less stopping and starting. Playing first base was also a possibility, for many other outfielders had moved there once their speed had begun to go, but in Mantle's case it was not an easy solution. Playing first might involve too much starting and stopping and quick lateral movement, all of which would be hard on his right knee.

In the first days of spring training all eyes were on Mantle, and the reporting on the Yankees seemed more like the work of medical writers than sportswriters. Mantle, ever stoic, said he felt well, and for the first few days he even tried to play without bandaging his legs. But then, in an early spring-training game, his left knee began to hurt, and he was forced to sit the game out. When the Yankees played the Mets in an early-spring game, several of the Met players noticed that Mantle did not seem like the Mantle of the past. His swing, they thought, was more hesitant and not as powerful. Worse, when he was in the outfield, he could not make diagonal cuts going back on a ball. He tended instead to go straight back and then move either to his left or to his right as the path of the ball mandated. The main problem, he was discovering as the team played through its spring-training games, was not the left knee, but once again the right one, which had plagued him on and off for thirteen years now.

Yet there was never any doubt that this was Mantle's team. In the locker room early that spring, Johnny Blanchard, the backup catcher and pinch hitter, lathered up Mantle's body in a coat of thick suds, as if he were protecting this most precious resource. "We've got to take damn good care of Mickey," Blanchard said. "He's The Man." That spring training was more an ordeal than ever for Mantle. He was only thirty-two, a relatively young age for outfielders, but his body was an old thirty-two. Convinced by his family history that Mantle men died before they were forty, he had never taken care of himself. He had played hard and caroused hard during the season, and he had both caroused and loafed when each season was finished, letting his body slip out of condition by not doing even minimal exercise.

When Mantle was a rookie he roomed for a time with Jerry Coleman. Coleman, who was on the pension committee, had tried to talk to Mantle about what the pension meant. But Mantle was never interested. "I'll never get one," he said. "I'll never live that long." His father had died at thirty-nine of Hodgkin's disease, and his grandfather and two uncles had died at roughly the same age of the same thing. No amount of persuasion on the part of his teammates could convince Mantle he would not die young as well. Whitey Ford would argue with him that the other Mantles had worked all their lives in mines and that he enjoyed far better medical care than those who had gone before him, with an annual examination at the Mayo Clinic. But dying young remained an obsession of his. Many of his friends thought that the driving force behind his reckless behavior and his increasingly heavy drinking was the belief that he might as well have as much fun as he could while he could. Later, as he lived first into his fifties, and then into his sixties, he would say with a certain sadness that if he had known he was going to live so long, he would have taken better care of himself.

It was only three years since the memorable summer of 1961, when he and his teammate Roger Maris had chased Babe Ruth's record of sixty home runs in an exuberant display of youth, power, and audacity. Maris had won the chase, beaten the record, but only after Mantle succumbed to illness in the final two weeks after visiting a quack to get rid of a bronchial illness. He had been injected so crudely and incompetently that his lower body became badly infected. He had attempted to play in that year's World Series with blood running out of the abscessed wound, which was, in the words of Clete Boyer, the size of a golf ball. Nonetheless, he ended up with fifty-four home runs: it was to be his last great season of statistical glory. If there was an official asterisk alongside Maris's name in the record books, then there was, in the minds of many fans, an imaginary asterisk alongside Mantle's, signifying first what he might have done had he been healthy during the last few weeks of the season, and second what might have happened had he batted in front of Maris, instead of the other way around. Still, that season there had been a sense of immortality to both young men, as if they were invulnerable to the fates and would perform like this again and again. That, of course, had not been true. The following year, Mantle was voted Most Valuable Player just ahead of his teammate Bobby Richardson, but he had come to bat only 377 times, and in 1963, he came to bat only 172 times. The futility of his participation in that year's World Series—two hits in fifteen at bats in the four-game sweep by the Dodgers—emphasized the larger frustrations of the Yankees. Great pitching had been decisive, not great hitting.

His decline, the deterioration of his body and skills, was something noted but not talked about very much by teammates or even opponents. In 1963, Hector Lopez, the Yankee left fielder, noticed that sometimes when Mantle came to bat against right-handed pitchers who were not power pitchers, he did not bat left-handed, as he had always done in his prime. Jim Bouton watched when he came up to bat that same season and saw the pain on his face when he swung lefty and tried to check his swing. He would watch Mantle virtually stagger out of the batter's box. No one knew what was going on in his head as this deterioration took place, but Al Downing, the young Yankee pitcher, noticed something that seemed to reflect Mantle's growing mental exhaustion: just before the team went on the field for the start of a game, Mantle would pause as he reached the top dugout step, as if for one brief second he were pulling himself together and summoning all his strength and willpower in order to play one more day.

Mantle's buddy with whom he toured the cities of the American League after hours was Whitey Ford, each calling the other, in a name they had picked up from Casey Stengel, "Slick." Stengel, to be sure, had not used the phrase admiringly and had referred to them as being "Whiskey Slick," to imply that the whiskey they drank made them feel smarter and more audacious than they really were. "I got these players," Stengel once said of Mantle and Ford, partly in exasperation and partly in admiration, "who got the bad watches, that they can't tell midnight from noon." The dynasty years were the Mantle and Ford years; of the previous thirteen, the Yankees had gone to the World Series eleven times, and much of the reason had been the extraordinary abilities of the two friends.

Uncomfortable and ill at ease with the demands of stardom, innately shy for much of the early part of his career, Mantle had taken refuge in the locker room, where he was always comfortable, and where he was the undisputed king. His predecessor as the star Yankee player, Joe DiMaggio, had been distant and suspicious to almost everyone, and had remained aloof even from his teammates. The Yankees of that era had been proud to play on the same team with him, but they did not know him and they did not cross that invisible line he drew between himself and the rest of them. Each year DiMaggio summoned one minor player, usually younger, to be his confidant, so that he would not have to eat by himself at night and so that strangers would be less likely to approach his table.

Mantle was the opposite. Warm, funny, and gregarious, he was beloved by his teammates. His humor was raucous, sometimes crude, but joyous and without malice. (After he retired from baseball, Mantle went into a number of businesses, including a fried-chicken enterprise for which he thought up his own advertising line: "To get a better piece of chicken, you have to be a rooster.") He was remarkably generous to Yankee rookies (some thought in direct response to the studied coolness DiMaggio had shown him as a rookie), and when a rookie pitcher won his first game he was likely to find that, when he got to the locker room, the great Mickey Mantle was laying a row of towels from his locker to the shower, a baseball red carpet of sorts.

He quickly picked out the rising stars among the rookies. He once told Clete Boyer, against whose older brothers he had played as a boy in the Ban Johnson League back in the Ozarks, to take the number 6 because it was Stan Musial's number and he knew how much that meant in the Boyer family—even if Clete had strayed east to New York. "No, Mickey, I can't, that's Musial's number," Boyer said, for to wear it seemed almost a sacrilege. "Clete, on this team it's okay," Mantle replied. When Tony Kubek was coming up, Pete Sheehy, the clubhouse man, was about to give him a relatively high number. "No, Pete, give Tony a lower one. He's going to be around here for a long time," Mantle said. In every sense it was *his* clubhouse.

His teammates thought he excelled in all things that mattered. Once, whiling away time in the bullpen, Jim Bouton, Ralph Terry, and several of the other pitchers rated the different players in terms of their success with women, and they did it as if they were scouts rating baseball players in terms of talent. Joe Pepitone, the first baseman, got good scouting reports, more on commitment and attitude than on God-given ability—a kid, they decided, who really came to play, and who had a good attitude. He had great potential. Bouton himself got average marks: he was relatively good-looking, he was ready and eager to carouse, but he was young and unsure of himself with women. But Mantle was the scout's delight, clearly number one on the team, for his reputation preceded him, which helped, he was very good-looking, and he had a natural, unaffected country-boy charm. If he only had a line to use with women, they decided, he would have been sure Hall of Fame material.

If Mantle was born to rule the locker room, it was also where he was happiest. There he was among men who did the same thing he did, who understood the hardships that had been imposed on him physically and psychologically, and who never expected anything more of him than to be who he was. With his teammates he was in no danger of failing or letting them down, or of being in over his head. Even if he had been a marginal player, some of his teammates thought, he would still have been popular with his teammates because of his looks and his manner. The things he wanted to talk about were the things other ballplayers wanted to talk about. He also had the good sense to know where he was comfortable and where he was not. When invitations came in through the mail, it was the job of his mail assistant to select the most important ones and go over them with him. If an invitation did not interest him, if it seemed designed to lure him to a place where he would not be at ease, he would simply crumple it and drop it to the floor.

Mantle was not political, but his innate shrewdness and sense of fairness allowed him, when the other players were just beginning to form a strong union, to play it right, and not take the owners' side, the way some other highly paid players of the era did (Carl Yastrzemski, for instance). Rather, he watched the coming of the union with an essentially benign attitude. When he was about to retire after the 1968 season, and the issue of free agency was just coming up, Steve Hamilton, the team's player representative, asked him to keep the news of his retirement to himself for a bit longer. That would permit the union to benefit from his stature in its final negotiations with the owners before the 1969 season: the union could argue that the great Mickey Mantle was for the same things that ordinary players were for. He did what Hamilton asked, and Hamilton thought it was immensely helpful, though there was nothing in it for Mantle. (In fact, though he eventually drew what were for those years exceptionally large salaries, he was oddly indifferent to money. He made money and he spent it. Once, after spring training, when the Yankees returned to New York to start a new season, the players went into the inner part of the clubhouse, where a safe-deposit box was located for their valuables. There, to his amazement, Mantle found a check for ten thousand dollars from the previous fall. He had put it there and simply forgotten about it over the ensuing six months. "I'm not going to tell Merlyn about this one," he laughed as he found it.)

Somehow, even the goofiest things he did with his teammates always seemed funny; if he raffled off tickets for ten dollars each on a ham, and in the end there was no ham for the winner, no one got angry. "Well, I said you guys were taking a chance and you took a chance," he would explain. If the team returned to La Guardia at three A.M. after a long road trip and he and Whitey Ford offered to lead the other players to the bus but instead mischievously took them on an endless tour of the labyrinth of tunnels beneath the airport, it was considered by all to be some marvelous experience: Mickey and Whitey being Mickey and Whitey, and everyone else being allowed in as their pals. He loved inviting Joe Pepitone, who longed to be his buddy, to meet him at restaurants that were not only hard to get to, but which, on occasion, did not exist. If a young television reporter came to interview him before a game, Mantle might give a long, seemingly serious discourse on how, when the wind was blowing in, he would try to swing with topspin so that the ball would not hang up there for the outfielders to get, while *if the wind was behind him, he would hit with backspin so that the wind would carry it farther, over the distant fence.* It was all done for the benefit of his teammates, who he knew were watching in the clubhouse and were breaking up. If a young black rookie joined the team and he was in the shower for the first time, Mantle might give him a quick scan to see whether the reports of black sexual endowment were true, and he would yell to Ford, "Hey, Whitey, take a look. It's okay—he's just like us. No bigger."

Mantle's jokes were never mean or humiliating, for he had an instinct to include, rather than to exclude. When Jake Gibbs, the rookie catcher from Ole Miss, showed up wearing loud argyle black-and-orange socks, Mantle asked him if there were a lot of rattlesnakes in Mississippi. When Gibbs said yes, Mantle told him that it was okay to change socks now, there were no rattlesnakes in New York and he didn't need to wear those socks to scare them off— which at once had everyone laughing and at the same time managed to make Gibbs feel more a part of the team. Mantle's great gift, Phil Linz said years later, was to tell the worst jokes in the world but somehow make them seem enormously funny.

Only when he wasn't hitting well did he brood, and then the entire team would feel his darkness. His bad moods, in fact, could be very black. He was ever aware of the burden placed upon him as the greatest player on a team that historically was expected to win, and he took failure, even momentary failure, very hard. If he failed in a key situation, he would often smash at least one bat against the bat rack. During slumps he would go deep inside himself and become unreachable—a massive man filled with rage at himself and the world around him, a man very much to be left alone. To the beat writers, these moods were particularly ominous, because they were supposed to deal with him whether or not he was in a good mood. Their editors, who, after all, had their own bad moods, cared nothing about Mantle's. He was never at ease with sportswriters in those years anyway, for they represented something alien: they spoke in ways that made him uneasy, and he had suffered in the early days when some of them had mocked him as a hick in contrast to the seeming sophistication of DiMaggio. When he was hitting badly, he was cold to writers in a way that few ballplayers of that era were, and he could, on occasion, be quite abusive: Get the hell away from me, he would say, what the fuck are you bothering me for? His anger, his ability to look right through men he dealt with every day, men whose reporting had in general helped build the myth of Mantle as the greatest ballplayer of his era, could be shattering. Once when Maury Allen, the beat writer on the *Post*, was standing near the batting cage and Mantle was taking batting practice, Mantle turned to him and said, "You piss me off just standing there." That became something of a motto in the Allen household when one member of the Allen family was irritated with another.

Once some of the other sportswriters on the Yankee beat were amused when a young city-side reporter from *Newsday* came out to do a piece about Mantle, the man. The young reporter was talented, had a reputation on the paper as a rising star, and was a huge Mantle fan to boot. He was quite sure that the assignment would go well, because he was a walking encyclopedia of Mantle trivia. Unfortunately for him, he arrived at a moment when Mantle was not hitting well. He was warned in advance by his peers that this was not the most opportune moment to approach Mantle, but he proceeded onto the field anyway to talk to his hero. He made his introductory statement about how much he admired Mantle and outlined the purpose of the proposed article. While the beat reporters watched, half amused and half sad, Mantle fixed the young man with The Look—totally cold, totally withering—and for a terrible moment the young man ceased to exist: the story, which was to be so admiring of Mickey Mantle, was never written.

Yet he was a true baseball hero of that era, the athlete as mythic figure. In some way he was a prisoner of his own myth. The more he did and the better he played, the more others expected of him. American boys (at least white ones) who grew up in the fifties and early sixties and who loved baseball idolized him more than any other player. Everything about Mantle seemed to come from a storybook about the classic American athlete; he was the modest country boy with a shock of blond hair that turned the color of corn silk every summer, who became a superstar in the big city.

In those years, thought Marty Appel, who had been a boy growing up in Spring Valley, a suburb of New York City, at the time, there was a virtual cult of Mantle, and Mantle fans not only knew everything about him, all the trivia of his life, but because of television they could mimic his every move. They knew that if Mantle took his batting helmet off he *always* took it off from behind, never from the front, perhaps because in front there were two bills—and so they removed their batting helmets in the same way. If Mantle ran out his home runs always looking down while he ran, then a generation of young American boys ran out their home runs with their heads down. They ran out to their positions, too, Mantle-style, heads turned down, elbows behind them but slightly up, and they moved in that same curious half-run, half-jog—in truth, a kind of fast limp designed to conceal the limits imposed by his bad knees. They knew he had a size 18 neck, and that it took him 3.1 seconds to go from home to first, which was said by experts to be the fastest time ever. The fans, Appel noted, even took pleasure from his number—7—which seemed right for him, standing out as it did on that broad back, and being a lucky number as well, whereas 6, his original number, seemed wrong, too circular.

Once, *Life* magazine ran a cover photo of Mantle and his teammate Roger Maris, both unshaven, and it was jarring to Appel and his friends at the time, for no one had ever seen either of them unshaven and it violated the sense, in Mantle's case, that he was the all-American boy, which meant, at the very least, that he was somehow always clean-shaven. The fans knew everything about his life, Appel remembered, that he had been born in Spavinaw, Oklahoma, that his father was named Mutt, and because Mutt Mantle had wanted his son to be a professional ballplayer, he had named him after his favorite player, Mickey Cochrane. Mutt taught his son to be a switch-hitter early on. There had also been twin brothers, but they had not made the majors, even though Mickey thought they were as good as he was or better.

A highlight of the myth was, of course, the way in which he had been signed. The story sealed the image of Mantle as a country boy plucked out of the heartland to come east and perform legendary feats in the nation's largest city. He had been scouted and signed by Tom Greenwade, the greatest of contemporary Yankee scouts, and quite possibly the best scout in the country at that time. It was a classic scene, straight out of Norman Rockwell. Greenwade, a country man himself, spotted Mantle while on his way to Broken Bow, Oklahoma, to scout another player. Stopping by chance to watch a game along the roadside, he saw Mantle drive the ball with such amazing power that he decided this might be the greatest prospect he had ever seen, the one superstar player that every scout dreams of discovering. When Greenwade eventually returned to sign the boy, he negotiated with Mickey and his father in the backseat of his own car for a tiny bonus of about a thousand dollars. The signing took place on the night of Mickey's high school graduation. Here the myth of Tom Greenwade, the greatest scout of his age, blended with Mantle's myth to create a classic illustration of the American Dream: for every American of talent, no matter how poor or how simple his or her background, there is always a Tom Greenwade out there searching to discover that person and help him or her to find a rightful place among the stars.

The truth of the signing was very close to the myth: Greenwade had been scouting Mantle for more than two years, ever since he had set out to look at another player, but had seen instead a skinny young shortstop for Baxter Springs who had exceptional speed and, for someone so slight, unusual power. In addition, the boy had a good, if erratic, arm. That was what Tom Greenwade always looked for: power, speed, and a good arm. After that first game, he asked Mantle how old he was, and Mantle said he was seventeen and a junior in high school. (At fifteen, he had been so good that a coach for a nearby junior college had taken him off to play for his team, warning Mantle that if anyone came over to ask his name, he was merely to walk away from him as quietly as he could.) Greenwade said that he could not legally begin to talk to Mantle about signing a professional baseball contract, but he would be back to see him the moment he graduated from high school. Greenwade made a careful note of his graduation date. He was scared to death of losing him to another scout, and he also wanted to watch him play one more time. By chance, on Mantle's graduation night, the Whiz Kids were playing, and Greenwade called the high school principal to see if Mantle could be excused from the graduation ceremony so that he could play that night. The principal said yes, for everyone in the area knew about Tom Greenwade of the Yankees, who was an important man in the region. That night Greenwade watched Mantle play, although the game was called after a few innings because of heavy rain. Then the Mantles, father and son, and Greenwade raced to Greenwade's Cadillac, where the scout tried to sign the boy to a Class D contract with the Independence, Kansas, team.

Greenwade began his pitch by telling the Mantles about the advantages of signing with the Yankees—that they represented the best in baseball, and that the best players always wanted to play for them. He spoke of the World Series checks that came in every year. Greenwade and Mutt Mantle were in the front seat and Mickey was in the back. Greenwade turned around and asked, "How would you like to be a Yankee, Mickey?" "That's what I've always wanted to be," the boy answered. Then there was the question of money. Mutt Mantle asked how much the contract would pay and Greenwade said $140 a month. The boy, Mutt Mantle answered, could make more playing Sunday games at Spavinaw and working around the mines during the week. So Greenwade took out a pencil and a large manila envelope and figured out how much Mickey could make playing Sunday ball and working in the mines, and how much he could make on the Class D contract. The difference was $1,150 (Mantle later said that the bonus was $1,500, but Greenwade always insisted it was $1,150), and that became his bonus. It was paid by the Independence club, and until the club folded years later, the canceled check hung in a frame in that team's headquarters.

Tom Greenwade was an old-fashioned scout, a man of the Ozarks. He was a quarter Cherokee, a descendant of Chief Middle Rider, a legendary Cherokee who had led his people during the tragic Trail of Tears, when the Cherokee people were forcibly relocated from their homeland in the Southeast to the harsher land of Oklahoma. For most of his career, Greenwade never wore glasses. He was proud of his heritage and thought it might have given him his unusually sharp eyes and an ability to pick up quickly on things that other people did not notice. Though he was not a boastful man, he liked to say that he could look at a player walking up to bat and tell just from his build and the way he moved whether or not he was fast. Unlike other scouts, he did not keep any notes on the players; what he needed to know he filed away mentally. "Half the time the scouts have their heads down making notes and don't even see which way the ball is hit," he would say.

Greenwade was a frugal man. He had grown up poor in Willard, Kansas, and even later in life, when he became rather wealthy, he thought of himself as someone who grew up poor, in a poor era, in a poor part of the country. Life was a difficult and harsh experience, he believed. Everything was to be saved, and nothing was to be wasted. He started earning a living at ten, and he left school at thirteen. As a boy he had a good arm and great eyesight, and he could kill rabbits with one throw of a rock. Some people there paid him twenty-five cents for each rabbit, which they would salt down and ship up north in those days before refrigeration. Eventually he tried professional baseball, and he had one great year in the old Northern League; according to legend, he won twenty-two games and lost only two when he hurt his arm pitching during an unusually cold game in Montana. With that, his career was over. He returned to Willard, made a run for sheriff and came close to winning, and then drifted back into baseball, first managing a minor-league club for the St. Louis Browns, eventually scouting for them, and then scouting for the Brooklyn Dodgers.

His life had taught him to be careful. Every penny mattered, even when he was quite successful. The Greenwade women canned their own food and raised their own animals for pork and beef. He had an almost pathological fear of being poor again. Late in life, he would go to a neighboring farm where the men did not have time to pick all the corn and where it lay going to waste; he would pick up the loose ears to feed his own pigs and cattle. The dollars saved didn't matter, said one neighbor. It was the waste that mattered. In the Greenwade home every purchase was to be accounted for. If Tom Greenwade's wife and daughter saw a dress they liked in a store window, they were to study it carefully, then sketch it and make it themselves. There was to be no debt in the household. Everything was to be paid for in cash, including his car. The Yankees used to send him some of their old uniforms, presumably to hand down to likely prospects, but the Greenwade women took those uniforms, cut them up, braided them, and made rugs out of them. Years later Angie Greenwade McCroskey, his daughter, thought of those old uniforms and, knowing the astronomical prices fetched by baseball memorabilia, decided that they had quite possibly cut up millions of dollars' worth of old uniforms. Tom Greenwade's only indulgence was a new Cadillac, always a Caddy, which he bought every other year because he put thousands and thousands of miles on a car annually. In that vast territory, he knew every back road, every local coach, every player, and every bird-dog scout (that is, a local part-time scout). He dressed simply, always wearing the same outfit during baseball season—khaki pants, a long-sleeved white shirt, and a straw hat.

He was absolutely without pretense, so when he came to a prospect's home to talk with the parents, he seemed more a member of the family than the famous visitor he was. At the Boyer home in Alba, Missouri, he was well known, for he had scouted several of the Boyer boys, three of whom went on to play major-league baseball. He hunted and fished, and when it was October and World Series time, he would go to New York and stay at the Waldorf—both literally and figuratively a long way from Willard, Missouri—but he always brought with him a bunch of quail he had just shot. The Waldorf's chefs would cook some of them for him there, and there would be extras for the cooks to take home for their families.

He played an important role in the clandestine scouting that had taken place when Branch Rickey sought out baseball's first black major-league ballplayer. In 1944, Rickey told Greenwade to meet him at the Biltmore Hotel in Kansas City for an important but highly secret mission. Greenwade hurried over only to find that the hotel did not have a room for him. He insisted that a reservation had been made for him by his boss in New York. "You know that's odd—we already have a Mr. Greenwade registered here," the desk clerk said. The impostor turned out to be Rickey himself. What's going on? Greenwade wondered. But then Rickey explained his grand scheme. He was planning to sign the first black player in major-league baseball, and he wanted Greenwade to look at a black shortstop then playing in Mexico named Silvo Garcia. "They say DiMaggio can't carry his glove," Rickey said. Greenwade was not even to tell Mrs. Greenwade where he was going and what he was doing. Greenwade said he could not do that. So Rickey, whose alternative calling clearly would have been as a CIA agent, said that Tom could take Mrs. Greenwade with him—they could be two American tourists traveling in Mexico. A bank account was set up for him in Mexico City. All his telegrams back to the home office were to be in code. Greenwade found Garcia impressive physically, "a huge fellow who ran well, and had a great arm," he later said. But he was already at least twenty-eight or twenty-nine, which was not ideal for someone who would, in effect, be a big-league rookie. Worse, Garcia, a right-handed hitter, could not pull the ball. "Everything he hit went to right field," Greenwade said of him. If he could not pull the ball in this league, what would happen to him in the major leagues? Greenwade reported back to a very disappointed Rickey that Garcia was not his man. However, he had, he reported, seen a catcher on the Monterrey, Mexico, team that he liked named Roy Campanella. But working in his own territory, which included Missouri and Kansas, he soon stumbled on a player he thought a much better prospect, a young army veteran playing for the Kansas City Monarchs named Jackie Robinson. Greenwade had heard from a number of his bird dogs that Robinson was special, and he set out to follow him. Almost from the start he was sure that Robinson was his man. For a month, he later said, he did nothing but track Robinson. Though Clyde Sukeforth was often given credit for doing the early scouting on Robinson, it was Greenwade who actually did it, which was not easy since the Monarchs traveled by bus, and Greenwade was told to remain as inconspicuous as possible. He saw him play about twenty times, yet the two men never met or spoke (they met years later when Robinson was already a star with the Dodgers and Greenwade was scouting for the Yankees).

Greenwade was immensely impressed by Robinson. He had great speed, exceptional power for an infielder, and the rarest kind of competitive fire. He was mature, a college man, but still, at twenty-six, young enough to be coming into his prime, unlike most of the better known Negro league players who were now considered a little old. The one weakness was his arm. He was playing shortstop for the Monarchs because their regular shortstop, Jesse Williams, had hurt his arm. To make the throw from short, Robinson had to take a step and a half. He would make the major leagues, but he would play as a second baseman or a first baseman, Greenwade reported, not as a shortstop.

The Mantle legend, which began with his signing, grew during a special rookie camp the Yankees had held at Casey Stengel's behest in 1950. There, some of the old-timers in the organization got a sense that they were seeing something rare, a true diamond in the rough. Mantle's potential, his raw ability, his speed, his power from both sides of the plate, were almost eerie. If his talent were honed properly, they thought they were quite possibly looking at someone who might become the greatest player in the history of the game. There were some fast players in that camp, and one day someone decided that all the faster players should get together and have a race. Mantle, whose true speed had not yet been comprehended, simply ran away from the others. What had made some of the stories coming out of the camp so extraordinary was the messenger himself, Bill Dickey—the former Yankee catcher, a Hall of Fame player, and a tough, unsentimental old-timer who had played much of his career with Ruth, Gehrig, DiMaggio, and Henrich. He was not lightly given to hyperbole. Dickey started talking about Mantle to Jerry Coleman, the veteran second baseman, with superlatives that were unknown for him: "Jerry, he can hit with power righty, he can hit with power lefty, and he can outrun everyone here." "What position does he play?" Coleman asked. "Shortstop," Dickey answered, which made Coleman nervous, because that meant they were both infielders. "He's going to be the greatest player I've ever seen," Dickey added. A few days later Dickey grabbed his old teammate Tommy Henrich. "Tom, you should see this kid Mantle that played at Joplin. I've never seen power like that. He hits the ball and it stays hit. He's really going to be something." Even the sound of his home runs, Dickey said, were different, mirroring something

Ted Williams would say years later: the crack of the bat against the ball when Mantle connected was like an explosion. Henrich simply shook his head—it was one thing to hear about a coming star from an excited journalist, but quite another to hear it from someone like Bill Dickey.

So that had piqued everyone's interest, but the myth of Mantle as the superplayer really began the following spring, in 1951, when the Yankees brought him up to train with the big club. That spring the Yankees, as a favor to Del Webb, who had a contracting business in the Southwest, exchanged camps with the Giants, and trained in Arizona. Years later, Mantle believed that this change of venue helped him considerably, and added to the excitement he generated. For when he began to hit his home runs there, he was doing it where the air was lighter, so the ball carried farther, and the visibility was greater—all of which seemed to make each home run not only longer but more memorable. Rarely had a rookie been showcased as Mantle was that spring. The Yankees were a big draw on the West Coast as they might not have been on the East Coast. DiMaggio was near retirement (it was in fact his last season), so everyone was eager to see this new rookie about whom so many stories were already beginning to be told.

That spring Mantle had been awesome. No one on the team or in the league was stronger. His body was deceptive: he was not that tall. He was listed at five feet eleven inches, or indeed at five eleven and a half, but others thought he was closer to five nine. It was the width of the body that stunned such veteran baseball men as Henrich, who now were scrutinizing him carefully. Henrich, who had been assigned to work with Mantle on his defensive play in the outfield and on his throwing, believed he had never seen the kind of strength that Mantle possessed in the body of a baseball player. Normally, to be that strong, to hit a ball that hard, a man had to be bigger than normal; one envisioned an immense man—lean, wide shoulders, muscular, and perhaps six feet six inches tall for that kind of power. But in baseball, as a man's height increased, he was also made vulnerable, for the size of his strike zone expanded as well, giving pitchers too big a target. (The first time Whitey Ford looked at Frank Howard, the six-feet-seven-inch Dodger outfielder, all he could think of was what a wonderful strike zone Howard presented.) In baseball it was too easy for a smart pitcher to come inside and tie that kind of hitter up, and keep him from extending his arms. But with Mantle, Henrich thought, it was as if God had taken the ideal body necessary for a great hitter, and then simply made it wider and stronger, extending the power package, but not the strike zone. Mantle was stronger than everyone else, but just as compact. It was almost, Henrich thought, unfair. Mantle was powerful, but he was not a prisoner of his power; he was surprisingly lithe, with a quick bat and a good eye.

When Mantle hit a ball that spring, Henrich thought, it was often like he was hitting a golf ball. His home runs seemed longer and more majestic each day. And so as the Yankees moved north and west through California, Mantle began to hit as no rookie had ever hit before, home run after home run, drives that were soon to be known as tape-measure drives. Bolstered by the news reports from the camp, the crowds grew ever larger, and it was said that when the tour was over, the Yankees had played in spring training before more than 500,000 people, an astonishing figure. It was all about Mantle, about people wanting to see this amazing rookie hit one of his awesome drives. Even the players gathered when he took batting practice every day, and they were as awed as the people in the seats.

Wherever they played that spring, someone would point to a place where some player had hit the longest home run ever, and Mantle would proceed to hit one even longer. The consensus was that the longest one he hit came during a game with the University of Southern California, at the USC field. It was the longest home run that Tom Henrich had ever seen. Mantle hit it to right field, and it seemed to jump off the bat, and because the fence was made of wire, the fans were able to see where it landed. It was, thought Henrich, the length of *two* complete home runs—at least six hundred feet. Jerry Coleman thought it made the rest of the hits in the game look like those of Little Leaguers. Henrich, who had grown up on the mythic deeds of Gehrig, Ruth, and Foxx, thought mythic deeds always belonged to those who had gone before; now, right in front of him, this kid who was almost young enough to have been his son was entering not just the book of baseball records but the world of baseball myth.

It had all been too much for Mantle. He was "the Phenom." It was Stengel who gave him the nickname that spring. My Phenom, he called Mantle to reporters, a name that Mantle hated. He did not like all the attention, particularly when he had yet to play in a big-league game, and yet to earn those raves. That pressure to be the greatest ever was far more than any young player wanted or needed. He came to the big city carrying his meager belongings in a straw suitcase (actually, he said, it was not even a straw suitcase, it was just a sack). "What a hayseed," Whitey Ford remembered thinking the first time he saw Mantle. Even when he went out and got better clothes, he was still awkward. Taken out to dinner by his teammates on one of his first days in New York, he had watched them order shrimp cocktail and then admitted that he had never seen a shrimp before. In an early interview with Joe Trimble of the *Daily News*, Mantle was scared to death and apparently irritated Trimble with the limited nature of his answers. Trimble later wrote that Mantle was "a hillbilly in a velvet suit." To Dan Daniel he was a kid "in a bad haircut whose sports coat barely covered his wrists." The image of a hick stayed with him for quite a while and, his friends thought, caused him a fair amount of pain when he was young. Later on, he was good at making fun of the clothes he wore back then—the loud sports jackets, the cowboy boots and blue jeans, which were not then in fashion—and he liked to tell of how Hank Bauer, one of his first roommates, had taken him out to buy several suits at a local store favored by Yankee players.

It was, he said years later, a difficult orientation. He had been painfully shy at first, essentially still a high school kid who, in his own words, was afraid to smoke in front of his father. There was one memorable game in which he struck out again and again against Walt Masterson, a shrewd pitcher then with Boston who had given Ted Williams fits when he was with Washington. Masterson started Mantle high, just around the letters, and then threw him ever higher pitches, which Mantle kept chasing until finally the pitches were far out of the strike zone and almost unreachable. That first season the Yankees realized they had not done him any favors with that huge buildup, and Stengel soon called him in and told him they were going to send him back to the minors so that he could regain his eye. Both Stengel and Mantle were in tears. "Don't get down on yourself," Stengel said. "We want you to get your confidence and your timing back." They sent him to Kansas City, which was still their Triple A farm club, and, at first, still feeling the pressure there, he did badly—one hit in twenty-two at bats for the Blues. He called his father in tears, and Mutt Mantle drove up to see him. Mickey, desperate now, told his father everything was going wrong, but Mutt Mantle had little sympathy. He had worked all his life in the lead and zinc mines, like his father before him, and his baseball experience was restricted to a semipro league called the Lead and Zinc League, where, as his son would later say, they played for a keg of beer afterward. Mutt Mantle started throwing his son's belongings into a suitcase. "What are you doing?" the boy asked. "I'm taking you home," Mutt Mantle said. "I thought I raised a man, but you're nothing but a coward." So Mickey stopped feeling sorry for himself, got his eye back, and hit .361 for Kansas City before being recalled to New York in August.

A few weeks later, he found himself playing in his first World Series game. There was noise and pressure everywhere, and countless strangers, who seemed to know him, would come up to him and tell him what they expected from him in the coming days. It was all too much for him. In desperation he knocked on the door of Tom Greenwade's hotel room. Though Greenwade was out, Mrs. Greenwade was there, and Mantle asked if he might come in and just sit quietly for a while.

8

As the St. Louis Cardinals prepared to leave their camp in Florida, Barney Schultz, in the spring of what was to be his twentieth season in professional baseball, was told that he was going to be assigned to the Cardinal Triple A farm club in Jacksonville. For most men this would have been a terrible blow, for it seemed to mark, once and for all, the end of his major-league career. He had been optimistic about sticking with the big-league club, because he felt he had pitched well after being traded to them in mid-season in 1963. But any disappointment he felt was buffered by the rest of the offer—the Cardinals said that they hoped he would stay with the organization and eventually become a pitching coach either in St. Louis or with one of the farm clubs. In the meantime, he would begin the season as both a relief pitcher and a pitching coach for Jacksonville. The Cardinals, Schultz thought, were being eminently fair—his salary would remain the same. The more he thought about the prospect, the more it pleased him, because it meant that he could continue a career in professional baseball, which was the one thing he loved, and the only thing he knew. He was thirty-seven years old, and he had been in baseball ever since he had graduated from high school in 1944 at the age of seventeen. He was best described as a journeyman: of his previous nineteen seasons, some part of five had been spent in the big leagues. He had a total of 32 big-league decisions to his credit—17 wins and 15 defeats. He was literally king of the road, for among other cities and towns, he had played in Hagerstown, Maryland, Rock Hill, South Carolina, Terre Haute, Indiana, Macon, Georgia, Schenectady, New York, Utica, New York, Denver, Colorado, Omaha, Nebraska, and Charleston, West Virginia. He loved it all, and he was filled not with disappointment that his career had not been more brilliant, but rather with wonder that an ordinary man like himself, with something of a lame arm, had salvaged enough ability for a full career doing what he loved. He was grateful to have been able to share in the friendship and camaraderie that was at the heart of a baseball season. It was, he thought, a life to be proud of: "Barney," a friend once told him, "millions and millions of American boys grow up with one dream—playing in the big leagues, and you're one of the handful who actually did it—the handful out of millions."

By 1964, he was aware that he was different from many of the young players now coming into the game, whose expectations both of what they were going to accomplish and of how much money they were going to make were so much greater than his; for much of his career he had made three thousand or four thousand dollars a season. The truth was that his own career had been virtually over before it started. In 1945, in his second year in professional baseball, he was still a hard-throwing young right-hander with Wilmington in the Phillies' organization. Some fifty years later, he remembered with stunning clarity the fateful night when Wilmington played Lancaster. It was hot and muggy and he was more than a little tired. In the seventh inning he faced Nellie Fox, soon to have an exceptional career as a major-leaguer. Worn down by the heat, Schultz did what many young pitchers do when they are tired—he reached back and tried to throw too hard, and something happened to his arm. The next day he could not even tie his shoelaces and a roommate had to do it for him. Medical treatment in those days, especially in the minor leagues, was primitive. If an injured player was lucky, he might get a rubdown. What he had probably done, Schultz decided years later, was tear the rotator cuff in his pitching arm, which was perhaps the worst thing that could happen to a pitcher until the miracles of modern surgery began to help in the seventies.

It was usually a career-ending injury. He was told by the Phillies' organization to rest his arm in the off-season, and he did, but the following season he could barely get the ball to home plate. Gradually his arm loosened up during spring training, but it was obvious to Schultz that he would never again be a power pitcher. If he was to have a career, it would have to be one of throwing junk, particularly a knuckleball that had been taught to him by a neighbor. That kind of career could exist in an era when there were lots of minor leagues and the money paid to minor-league ballplayers was minimal. It was a life of finding temporary housing in new cities from which he would soon be gone, of figuring out how to live and save some money on a tiny salary, and of riding beat-up buses over long distances to the next town to play under lights that never would have been approved by any association of optometrists.

In 1955, the summer he turned twenty-nine, Schultz reached the big leagues with the Cardinals, as a reliever. He pitched in 19 games that season, always in relief, for a total of 29.2 innings. His earned run average was a hefty 7.89, and it did not surprise him greatly that the next year he was sent back to the minor leagues for four more years. In 1959, he made another appearance in the majors, this time as a reliever with Detroit (13 games, 18.1 innings pitched, and an earned run average of 4.42). Thereupon he went back to the minors again. That was pretty much the story of his life, but Barney Schultz not only survived, he persevered. It was far better than the alternatives; he had once taken a winter job working in a plant, and the people who ran it asked him to come back as a foreman. It might well have paid him more than he was making as a minor-league pitcher, but the work did not interest him. Baseball was what he loved. When he was told that he would eventually become a pitching coach, it was more or less how he hoped his career would end up.

As Schultz started the season pitching and coaching for Jacksonville, it was, he thought, a nice moment in his life. He was pitching well that spring. He was primarily a knuckleball pitcher and now he had his knuckler down cold. He could almost always throw it for strikes. In the previous season the Cubs had traded him to the Cardinals, and he had done what was probably the best pitching of his career. He had appeared in a total of 39 games, had won 3 and lost none; even more important, his earned run average was down to 3.59. He had become the classic knuckleball pitcher—no power, but rubber-armed—and the fluttering, dancing ball he threw was the bane of good hitters and catchers alike. (By this time Schultz brought his own catcher's mitt to the park for the catcher—it was more like a first baseman's glove than a true catcher's mitt.) Managers loved him, though, because he could pitch every day.

Just how fragile the world of baseball was was brought home to both the Cardinals and the Dodgers on the night of April 22. Sandy Koufax was matched against Curt Simmons, who had taken to calling himself "the poor man's Koufax." Three times in 1963 Koufax had beaten Simmons, including the 4–0 shutout he had thrown during the decisive late-season sweep of the Cardinals, one of eleven shutouts he had pitched that season. The night before the game, at the annual dinner of the Knights of the Cauliflower, which was an extended group of Gussie Busch's partying pals, the Cardinals' owner publicly challenged Simmons to beat Koufax this year. If he did not, noted Jack Buck, the broadcaster who was emceeing the dinner, the Anheuser-Busch beer truck might have a new left-handed driver.

The Dodgers came into Busch Stadium on a six-game losing streak. Koufax was having trouble with his left arm and was scheduled to have it X-rayed when he returned to Los Angeles. It was not a happy evening for him. He got the first two batters out, but Bill White went after a wild pitch and managed to reach first as the ball got away from the catcher. Ken Boyer walked on four pitches, and then Charlie James, one of the young players vying for a regular job in the outfield, homered. Koufax finished the inning, but then Walter Alston pulled him from the game. Koufax had not wanted to come out—his arm was obviously hurting him, and he kept shaking his head at John Roseboro, the Dodger catcher, whenever Roseboro called for the curve. Later, the Cardinal doctor examined him and said that he had an inflammation of the left elbow and a slight muscle tear in his left forearm. His arm had apparently been bothering him since spring training, but Koufax thought he could pitch through it. He flew back alone to Los Angeles, ahead of the team, and there the Dodger team doctor gave him a cortisone shot. There was talk of his going on the disabled list. His left arm was not merely an arm; for the Dodgers, for better or worse, it was a season. Curt Simmons won the game, 7–6, even though he gave up a mammoth home run to Frank Howard. He had finally gone against Koufax, albeit Koufax with a bad arm, and he had won. "The boys," he said of the Cardinal hitters, "kept me off the beer truck. It was close though—it was parked just outside." The Dodgers were now 1-7. With Koufax and Drysdale on the mound in every big series, they sometimes had seemed invincible to the other National League teams. With Koufax possibly injured, they suddenly seemed quite vulnerable.

9

With Koufax injured, it was possible that the hardest throwing pitcher in the league at that moment was Bob Gibson of the Cardinals, just reaching his full power that season. In late May, Gibson threw a masterpiece at home against the Cubs. He had won, 1–0, while striking out twelve men. The Cubs had gotten just four hits off him. He had not walked anyone. Gibson had been bothered by a stiff shoulder earlier in the season, and he was having trouble warming up, so he had polished his car before coming to the park in order to loosen up his right shoulder, and it seemed to work. As the game wore on, he only got stronger, and he retired the last seventeen men in a row. In the ninth inning, he faced and struck out Ron Santo and Billy Williams, and it seemed, said his manager, Johnny Keane, as if he were saying, "Hurry up and get out of there—I want to go home." His teammate Dick Groat said he had seen him display that kind of power only once before, in a game that Gibson pitched against Pittsburgh when Groat was still a Pirate. The Pirates had gotten three hits off him—two on sliders, one on a curve, none on a fastball. "I felt that for one given night Gibson was the fastest pitcher I ever faced," Groat said. Questioned by reporters after the game, Ron Santo of the Cubs said he thought that Gibson was now as fast as Koufax at certain times, and that Gibson's ball had far more movement than that of the other great power pitcher of the league—Jim Maloney of the Reds.

Gibson was talented, to be sure, with a high-velocity fastball and a very good slider, but it was his competitive fire, his intensity, and his willingness to fight every batter on every pitch that came to distinguish him. His ability in baseball did not exist apart from the rest of his being; rather, his ability as a player was an extension of his will as a man. When opposing teams prepared to battle Gibson (and that was the right word: *battle*), they were taking on not just Gibson the pitcher, but Gibson the man.

If anyone knew and had mastered the uses of adversity, it was Bob Gibson. He was born during the Depression in Omaha; his father died three months before he was born, and he was one of seven children. His mother worked in a commercial laundry. The family lived in a four-room shack on the north side of the city; as a boy he was bitten on the ear by a rat. He was small and sickly as a child, and nearly died once from pneumonia. Later, the Gibson family moved to a government housing project, and for the first time they had heat and electricity. His mother, a woman of great courage and determination, somehow managed to make enough money so that there were always food and clothes for her children.

Gibson was a man of unusual self-discipline. That came from his family, especially his brother Josh, the eldest. Fifteen years older than Bob, his legal name was LeRoy, but he was nicknamed Josh. He was a serious, ambitious man, with a master's degree in history. He had wanted to teach history, but given the ceiling on what an educated black man could do in those days, he had to settle for a job in a meat-packing house. He had always wanted to coach at a school or college, and he ended up coaching at the local black YMCA, where he touched many lives, most notably that of his younger brother. If he was hard and demanding on the youths he coached in those days, it was because he knew that the way was harder for them, that it was easier for them to quit, and that they had to be better than whites at all things. He was hardest of all on his younger brother, because Josh Gibson saw Bob's natural ability early on: he pushed him not merely to be good, but to be excellent.

When Bob was in high school, he was small for his age and the football coach turned him down. Josh was pleased because he did not want his brother's basketball and baseball careers jeopardized by a football injury. Even though Bob was relatively small, he was quick and a good all-around athlete, with a strong arm. By his senior year in high school he began to grow, and he was six feet tall and 175 pounds by graduation. He became a good high school basketball player, missing the All-State team, he believed, only because he was black. He was fast enough to run the 440 and the 880 in major track meets. He played baseball in summer leagues, under Josh's auspices, on a Y team that toured throughout the region, and was good enough at the end of his third year in high school to receive an offer from the Kansas City Monarchs. There was even a feeler from Runt Marr, the Cardinal regional scout, and some talk of a minor-league contract, but Josh Gibson insisted that his brother go on to college.

Josh made sure that his brother always played with kids several years older so that he had to reach for more. There were times when it was too much and Bob would on occasion burst into tears. But Josh did not back down. At all times Bob had to push himself to be the best. In addition, he was to handle himself with pride and dignity. It was important to dress well, to carry himself well, and to speak well. Small things, acts of social carelessness, which did not offend when they were done by white people, could easily be seized on and held against a black man. Among other things, there was to be no smoking in the Gibson household. Bob once got hold of a small silver pipe and figured out how to tear open cigarettes and use the tobacco from them in his pipe. He hid in a closet one day and was smoking away when Josh found him. His older brother whacked the pipe right out of his hand. "Don't you ever do that again!" he said. Bob had a small space between his front teeth, and as a boy he mimicked the way he had seen older boys spit; it was a way of showing that he was grown up. Josh put a stop to that as well. If he saw his brother spitting he would slap him. "Don't ever do that! That's not the person you're going to be!" He was going to be a man who knew how to comport himself and to gain the respect that was rightfully his.

Slowly over the years, certain qualities of toughness and resilience were instilled in Bob Gibson, which would enable him to play sports in a white-run world. Playing with Josh's all-black YMCA baseball teams against the all-white local teams, Bob saw that the all-white umpires were so prejudiced that Josh on occasion had to threaten to take his team off the field unless they were willing to give the visitors a break on calls. It was a given that Bob would go to college—he was not going to enter an unwelcoming white world without an education. He applied to Indiana University, hoping to win a scholarship to that basketball powerhouse, but was told in a return letter that Indiana already had its quota of Negroes for that year, which, Gibson later found out, turned out to be all of one. Josh thereupon talked his brother up to Duce Belford, who was the athletic director and basketball coach of Creighton, the local Jesuit college. Since Gibson was one of the best high school basketball players in the state, Belford eventually offered him a basketball scholarship, and Gibson went on to be an outstanding athlete at Creighton, where he was the first black to play on the baseball and basketball teams. Still, on occasion, he had to stay in a different hotel and eat at different restaurants because of local customs, even there, in the heartland of America. He was a good enough basketball player to get offers to play with the Harlem Globetrotters upon graduation, but he was attracted more and more to baseball, which in those days was the professional sport that offered the greatest and most immediate financial rewards.

As Josh Gibson had once talked up his brother to Belford, now, as Bob's college graduation approached, he began talking him up to Bill Bergesch, the general manager of the St. Louis Cardinal Triple A farm club, the Omaha Cardinals. The two were acquaintances, and Bergesch admired Josh Gibson considerably—Josh was always asking Bergesch for used baseballs, old bats, and used uniforms for his Y teams. In the spring of 1957, Bob Gibson's last year at Creighton, Josh started telling Bergesch, "I've got this kid brother who's going to play in the major leagues." Bergesch would ask what position and Josh would say he was a pitcher, but, then again, he was a hell of a hitter, and could also play the outfield. And the infield, too, as a matter of fact. And catch, by the way. The general manager of a Triple A farm team tended to hear that kind of thing from almost everyone he dealt with—legendary prospects being hidden away in a tiny town, or pitching for a sandlot team nearby—and those reports tended to be met with considerable skepticism. But Josh Gibson had a reputation for being a careful man, and he had never been boastful before about anyone or anything else. He was *very* persistent, and so Bergesch decided, both as a courtesy to someone whom he liked and because a good baseball man never knows when he's going to find a diamond in the rough, that he would watch Josh Gibson's kid brother pitch for Creighton. He went to two Creighton games, but he never saw Bob Gibson pitch. The first time, Gibson played the outfield, and Bergesch got a quick sense of the boy's speed and power and that he had a very strong arm. The second time, Gibson caught. This time, seeing the way he blocked the plate, Bergesch sensed his competitive fire. Bergesch asked Duce Belford about him. Belford, who, besides being the baseball coach, was a bird-dog scout for the Dodgers, was not impressed. "That kid's never going to make it," he told Bergesch. "He's much too wild. Why, he's not even our best pitcher." That, thought Bergesch, was the difference between coaching college baseball, where you wanted a finished product, and working in the minor leagues, where you looked for raw ability. As far as Bergesch was concerned, Bob Gibson was all potential—the only question was which position he would play. So he told Johnny Keane, who was managing the Omaha team, that young Gibson was a genuine prospect and suggested they bring him in for a tryout. At the tryout Gibson was awesome: first he took batting practice and showed exceptional power, driving a few balls over the fence. Then Bergesch had him throw to the Cardinals' regular catcher. Neither Bergesch nor Keane had ever seen a kid throw like that before, and, though they did not have the resources to clock him, years later Bergesch estimated that he must have thrown at about ninety-five miles an hour. In addition, his fastball already had movement. That meant they were likely to be able to teach him how to put more movement on it. "That's some arm," Keane told Bergesch. "Let's sign him and start him off as a pitcher. I'll guarantee you if he doesn't make it as a pitcher, he'll sure as hell make it as an outfielder." A few days later the signing took place, ironically at the end of the college World Series, when all sorts of scouts had gathered in Omaha and were eager to sign that year's hot prospect, Ron Fairly of USC. There was no small irony in that, Bergesch thought: all those scouts clustered around, waiting for the Series to end so they could make their pitch to Fairly. For if Bergesch was right, and he suspected he was, then he was about to sign someone who was a good deal more talented than Ron Fairly.

That did not mean that the Cardinal organization was going to shower bonus money on Bob Gibson. He was not highly touted, he had no reputation, he had played for a relatively obscure college, he was black (which was one reason he was not highly touted and had no reputation), and in those days black talent still came significantly cheaper than white talent. There was also a danger in giving Gibson too large a bonus, for it would mean they would have to put him on the big-league roster and not let him develop in the minor leagues. That had happened to Sandy Koufax, and it had almost surely slowed down his development. Gibson's case was similar, for he obviously needed time to learn to control and master his awesome talent. Going directly to the majors and sitting on the bench would be disastrous for him. Gibson, who always had a strong sense of his own value, had thought in terms of a bonus of thirty thousand dollars, and he was not pleased with the offer of a tiny bonus, even though it allowed him to go to the minor leagues for an apprenticeship; it seemed to him he got the short end of the stick, which he believed was the end black people inevitably got. As far as he was concerned, the small bonus, and the rationalizations that went with it, was just one more consequence of being black in America. The one player to whom the Cardinals gave a big bonus that year was a pitcher named Bob Miller, who won nine games in four years for the Cardinals, and who became a journeyman relief pitcher. Bob Gibson, in years to come, never ran into Bill Bergesch without reminding him of Bob Miller and comparing his own signing and his own Cardinal career with those of Miller's. "There's Bill Bergesch who got me for four thousand dollars, because he thought Bob Miller was a better pitcher," he liked to say.

Gibson was so disappointed with the first offer from the Cardinals that he hesitated for a time between professional-sports careers. He had not gotten a basketball offer from an NBA team, for Creighton was not yet a basketball power and the NBA teams did not yet throw out as fine a net for college prospects as they would later, but the Globetrotters were interested in him because he had once played well against them on a college all-star team. So he worked out a deal whereby he signed with Omaha for a $1,000 bonus and $3,000 in salary; that done, he negotiated with Abe Saperstein of the Globes for $1,000 a month for four months. That gave him $8,000, which was a lot of money for a ghetto kid in 1957, he thought. At his first full practice with the Omaha Cardinals, he was told to go out and throw batting practice. Though he was not throwing with full speed, the Omaha hitters were fouling the ball off and not even getting it out of the cage. Johnny Keane told him to throw some curves. No one seemed to be able to hit them either. "Should I start throwing hard?" he asked Keane. No, Keane told him, what he was doing was just fine. "I just knew I was going to make it," he later wrote of that moment. "As an outfielder. As a catcher. As a first baseman. As a pitcher. I would play wherever they wanted me to, but I was going to make it."

Gibson was a man who had to win, at baseball, at the daily bridge game with his Cardinal teammates (his bridge partner, Dick Groat, was very much aware that he was not supposed to let Bob Gibson down, that if they had a makable bid in the game and they did not complete it, there was going to be a price to pay), and, later, even with his young son in tic-tac-toe games—for letting his son win, he was sure, would teach the boy the wrong lessons. His teammate Mike Shannon, who watched Gibson closely over many seasons, first as a player and then as a broadcaster, decided that it was not so much that Gibson needed to win, but that he hated to lose, and above all, he did not want to be a loser. There was, others thought, more than a little truth in that, for Gibson was less demonstrative in victory, even in critical victories, than many of his teammates. He kept his pleasure in success oddly private; he did not sit around the locker room afterward soaking in the glory and the champagne and noisily proclaiming the triumph of the moment. Rather, he was, given the considerable nature of his own contributions, surprisingly quiet and almost distant from any celebration taking place around him. It was as if winning merely confirmed Gibson's role as a famous, admired, and well-paid professional athlete. *Losing*, on the other hand, threatened to reduce him to what he had once been, a poor, sickly black kid from the Omaha ghetto, always on the outside looking in.

He was not just a gifted pitcher, he was a gifted overall athlete. When his Cardinal teammates talked about him as a possible NFL player, most of them assumed that, because of his arm, he would have been a quarterback. But Lou Brock thought otherwise. "No way he's a quarterback with that mind-set," Brock said. "Bob plays only one position in football—linebacker." His teammate Roger Craig thought of him as being like a great heavyweight boxer, in part because he was so strong, but even more because of his determination—if he ever got a lead on you, Craig thought, if he put you down on the canvas, then you were almost surely finished because he was so single-minded, he would never let you back up. Sometimes, before a game in which he was not pitching, Gibson liked to work out at shortstop ("with more range there than Groat," Curt Simmons liked to joke); Frankie Frisch, the great former Giant infielder, took one look at him there and thought, with his speed and his great arm, he could have been the best shortstop in the league.

For a young, relatively untutored (even as he was trying out with the big-league club he did not seem to know the difference between a curve and a slider) power pitcher, Gibson developed surprisingly quickly. He pitched for a while in Omaha and then was sent to Columbus in the Sally League; he pitched well enough there and showed enough promise that the Cardinals raised his salary sufficiently so that he would quit the Globetrotters, thereby reducing the risk of injury and permitting him to concentrate on baseball. In 1958 he started the season at Omaha under Johnny Keane. Keane was the ideal manager for him—sensitive, steady, patient—and Gibson came to think that Keane was one of the best men he had ever met. He brought Gibson along slowly, never put him under unnecessary pressure. Rather, he focused on what Gibson could do, which was to throw hard, and not, as some managers might have, on what he could not do, which was to show great control. Keane was never negative. He understood that he was dealing with a proud young man who was a potentially great, great player. As a result, Gibson thought Johnny Keane was as color-blind as a man could be, not by liberal social conscience, but by innate human decency.

Johnny Keane was unusually sensitive to all young players, very much aware of the stress they were under. His own career was one that tested a man's love of baseball. He had been a career minor-league player, a marginal one at that, and then a career minor-league player-manager, and then, finally, a career minor-league manager. Starting in 1930, he reached the Triple A level twice: in 1932, after three years in professional baseball, for all of eight games and twenty-two at bats with Columbus in the American Association; and three years later, for three games and five at bats for Rochester in the International League. If any man was an expert on the anxieties experienced by young players in the lower rungs of baseball, it was Johnny Keane. While he was very strict about certain rules, he nonetheless never sought to denigrate his players, or, as some baseball managers did, to assault them about their weaknesses. Rather, he tried to reinforce their strengths, hoping that, over time, their vulnerabilities would diminish. He was essentially a kind man, surprisingly gentle in the relatively crude world of baseball in those days. He had studied for the priesthood, had spent six years as a seminarian, and when he switched professions, he managed to retain his humanity. Bill Bergesch, who worked closely with Keane, thought Keane's younger players were like part of an extended family to him.

To Gibson, Keane made a world filled with all sorts of pressures and dangers seem a simpler and less threatening place. What Keane offered him was basic and essential: a belief in Gibson's future. During the 1958 season, Gibson did well enough to be sent to Rochester, which was also a Triple A team. In 1959 he spent a part of the early season with the major-league team, and then was sent back to Omaha, this time under Joe Schultz's management. Gibson's job was to work on his control, and to some degree he succeeded. His record was 9-9, and in 135 innings he struck out 98 and walked 70. He threw hard enough to start gaining a reputation as a fireballer, and later in his career, when major-leaguers started to complain about batting against him, players in the minors would remind their teammates what it had been like to go against Bob Gibson where the lights at the ball parks were so much weaker and when his control over his fastball had been less certain.

Gibson was certain that 1960 was going to be his year, when he would finally make it with the big-league club. He did go to the majors that season, but it quickly became the worst moment in his professional career. The manager at the time was Solly Hemus, replacing the recently fired Fred Hutchinson, and as far as Gibson was concerned, Hemus was the absolute opposite of Johnny Keane as a manager. Hemus, he thought, needed to show the world the kind of self-conscious toughness that seemed to come with being a small man in a world of bigger men. "Mighty Mouse" was his nickname. Hemus had been a marginal big-league player himself, fighting hard to maximize limited skills and compensating by being fiery and combative; some thought he was the kind of player who wore his uniform too large because he figured that he might get a couple of calls each year on tight pitches that might otherwise not have hit him. As a player, he was a holler guy, making up for his size with his noise. When he and Curt Simmons had played together on the Phillies, Simmons had once been in a minor jam out on the mound, and Hemus, the second baseman, came over to the mound to give him a pep talk. That irritated Simmons, who felt the crisis not that grave and did not want a boost from his second baseman, so he brusquely waved him off. Hemus seemed almost apologetic. "If you can't hit, you can't run, and can't throw, then you've got to holler at them," he said as he retreated back to second base. As a manager, he was a product of the Leo Durocher school, raging at umpires, opponents, the world, and, of course, his own players. He was absolutely determined, thought Jack Buck, the Cardinal broadcaster, to show that he was tougher than everyone else. He seemed not merely to lack the flexibility to deal with different kinds of players, but also to lack the ability to let go of defeat, to get over the anger and frustration created by whatever it was that had gone wrong that day on the field. In 1961, when Hemus was still managing the Cardinals, he used Curt Simmons, a good all-around athlete, as a pinch runner in one game. Johnny Keane was then the third-base coach, and he flashed a sign a little late, and Simmons ended up being picked off at second. Simmons returned to the dugout disgusted with himself, with the play, and with Keane. He knew he was going to be ripped by Hemus in the dugout and he was—the manager was out of control. When the game was over, the Cardinals had lost by one run, and Hemus exploded at him again. Simmons took a shower, Hemus walked into the locker room, and the sight of Simmons sent him into another tirade. By this time Simmons had had enough. When the team arrived back at the hotel, Hemus started in *again*, but Simmons shouted back: "Solly, if you can believe it, I'm more pissed off than you are. The goddamn fault is Keane's because he was late with the sign, and besides, I'm a pitcher and I don't want to be used as a pinch runner in the first goddamn place. Now get off my ass." Hemus, Simmons thought, was not cut out for managing—a manager had to know, above all else, when to let go.

In his combatitiveness, Hemus was not unlike Eddie Stanky, who had already been phased out by the Cardinals. But he lacked Stanky's great eye for judging talent, which made Stanky a valuable part of the Cardinal organization after his managing days had ended. Hemus had not been Bing Devine's choice for the job, for Devine had not wanted to fire Hutchinson. Devine thought it was harder to go from being a player to managing than most people thought, and he was uneasy with Hemus's confrontational style. There was a gift to being a successful manager, Devine thought—the ability to understand and motivate different men in different ways while earning their respect. Fred Hutchinson, tough as nails in his own way, had been like that, and Johnny Keane in Rochester had the gift as well, he was sure. If Hutch had to go, Devine had wanted Keane for the job, but Gussie Busch was very much taken with the letter Hemus had written him in 1956 after being traded away.

The Hemus years were not happy ones for many of the Cardinal players. Hemus had damaged his authority by his inability to handle the decline of Stan Musial, the great Cardinal icon who was then about forty. Hemus tried benching Musial, to the astonishment of the other players: Musial was still a great hitter, although he was slipping a little, and the idea of *Solly Hemus* benching *Stan Musial* seemed to violate every axiom of the baseball universe. "Hey, Stan," Curt Simmons, the veteran pitcher, said to Musial, "he can't do that. All you have to do is go and see Gussie, and you'll be in the lineup and he'll be gone." "Don't worry," Musial answered with the assurance of a true legend, "I'll be back in a week." But it was a hard time for him. Curt Flood could remember Musial, usually calm and easygoing, kicking the huge container that contained the dirty towels in the locker room at least thirty times.

The younger white players thought the problem was a generation gap of considerable proportions, but Gibson thought Hemus was a racist. Curt Flood heartily agreed ("He acted as if I smelled bad," Flood later wrote of him). Flood thought that Hemus used others with significantly slighter gifts in center field, while he languished on the bench. Not every other player on the Cardinals accepted the idea that Hemus was racist—for it is always hard to know what is in another man's heart. Perhaps it was just a failure on his part to understand what black players needed at the time. Tim McCarver, who was white, had problems with Hemus as well, for Hemus once dressed him down so brutally in front of the rest of the team, telling him that the play he had just made was *the stupidest goddamn thing that Hemus had ever seen in the game of baseball*, that McCarver was on the verge of tears. Bill White was not sure whether Hemus was a racist or simply a man of limited vision who did not handle young players very well.

Still, there was no doubt that the first two years under Hemus were terrible ones for Gibson. As far as Gibson was concerned, Hemus looked down on him, rarely giving him starts, pulling him too quickly when he did start, and using him all too often to mop up in hopeless games. Yet Gibson's sheer talent was so dazzling that the only person who seemed to doubt it was Hemus. Gibson hated Hemus as much as anything else because Hemus told him to work on his control, but then did not seem to give him enough chances to do it. Hemus, the other veteran pitchers thought, was jumpy and invariably too eager to pull a pitcher. Gibson felt there were too many games in which he barely got into a rhythm when Hemus would appear at the mound ready to take him out. Once, when a fly ball almost killed Bill White, a natural first baseman playing out of position in the outfield, Hemus somehow blamed Gibson. There were angry exchanges between them, Gibson asking Hemus what the hell he was doing when he went out to the mound, and Hemus saying that if Gibson could get some goddamn body out, he wouldn't be out there. "He'll never make a big-league pitcher," Hemus liked to say about Gibson. "He throws everything at the same speed." That was certainly true, thought Tim McCarver, who caught Gibson, but the speed was matched by few in major-league baseball.

Of the many things Hemus did and said that bothered Gibson, what stung the most was when the manager would discuss at a team meeting how they would pitch to hitters on an opposing team. He would tell Gibson not to pay any attention, that this did not concern him, implying, as far as Gibson was concerned, that he was some kind of lesser person, not as smart as the white pitchers. It was the ultimate insult to an extremely sensitive, highly intelligent young black man. Gibson never forgave Hemus for his predictions that he would never make it in the big leagues, or for failing to put him in the rotation, or for the fact that Hemus once mistook him for Julio Gotay, the soon-to-be-traded utility infielder who played better in practice than in games. Gibson thought that when Solly Hemus looked at him, he saw not a man but a stereotype. There was a game against Pittsburgh in 1959 in which an incident occurred that angered all the black Cardinals players. Bennie Daniels, a black pitcher, was on the mound for the Pirates. Hemus inserted himself in the second game of a doubleheader as a player. In his first at bat, Hemus edged his leg into a Daniels pitch and got a free ticket to first base. On the way down to first, he shouted over to Daniels, "You black bastard . . ." The next time he came up, Daniels threw at him, and in time Hemus swung and managed to throw his bat at Daniels. Both benches were ready to explode. The next day, Hemus called a team meeting. The black players were sure that he would apologize for what he had said to Daniels. There had been no apology. Later, Hemus said that he had done it to fire up his team and went on to praise Daniels as a pitcher to his players. Daniels was unmoved by the gesture. "Little Faubus," Daniels called Hemus, in honor of the governor of Arkansas, who had recently made a national reputation for himself by trying to block the integration of the Little Rock schools. The entire Hemus-Daniels incident left a bad aftertaste with the Cardinals. Bill White, slower to make judgments than many, agreed that a bridge had been crossed on the Daniels incident.

Hemus himself later felt he had been at the wrong place at the wrong time in those years with the Cardinals. Gibson, he believed, had been on the verge of becoming a great player, but was not yet there. He had constant control problems, and Hemus had wanted Howie Pollet, the pitching coach, to work with him on keeping the ball down. Hemus had been dubious about Flood's hitting ability and felt the Cardinals needed more bats in their lineup; later Hemus decided that he had been completely wrong about Flood, more so than about any younger player he had ever dealt with, and he wrote Flood a letter to that effect. He did not think he had been racist. He had grown up poor in San Diego, in a neighborhood where the other kids had been poor as well, some black, some Mexican, some white. In the baseball world in which he had come up in the forties, harsh ethnic epithets had still been used: dago and Guinea, Polack and kike. When he had first broken in, he would get a scratch hit off Warren Spahn or Lew Burdette, two of the toughest men who ever played baseball, and they, apparently believing he was Jewish because his name was Solly, would scream, "Hemus, that's a goddamn cheap Jew hit and you're a goddamn Jew hitter!" When he had called Daniels a black bastard, he had done it because that was what you shouted in a confrontation like that, he thought. He had not meant to offend his own players. Instead, he had been the one, he felt, who had pushed the hardest with Bing Devine and Gussie Busch to end the segregated facilities in St. Petersburg because he had disliked the idea of splitting his ball club up, and he did not think that white players should be favored over black players. He was saddened that years later Gibson and Flood still thought of him as a racist. He accepted the blame for what had happened: the world had been changing but he had not, he later decided.

Gradually, the other men in the Cardinal organization had reluctantly come to Devine's view that Hemus simply could not adjust to the complexities of managing modern baseball players. Moreover, they thought there were simply too many confrontations with umpires, too many days when he lost his temper, and too much energy being used up for matters that did not win baseball games.

Gibson's control was the only thing standing between him and success as a big-league pitcher. He had made progress as he came up through the minor leagues. What he wanted in the Hemus years was to make the rotation and be given a chance to pitch regularly, or be traded. The other players were sympathetic to his dilemma. Bill White, the senior statesman among the black ballplayers, knew how frustrated Gibson was, and counseled him not to blow it. When Gibson would rage at Hemus, it was White who would counsel him not to explode, not to challenge Hemus, not to make the problem into something larger. By asking to get out of a good organization, he would quite possibly pick up the reputation of being a difficult, hot-headed young black man. "Don't blow it now when you're so close," White would say. "Don't burn yourself out on things you can't change. Work on the things you can change." As Gibson would continue in a fury, White would counsel him, "Your time will come. Believe me, it will come. What you want to do is be ready for it, so when they come to you and tell you to pitch, you know damn well you can go in and do it."

Gibson was sure he was ready to pitch in the major leagues; he had an awareness of his fastball—that it was big-time major-league heat—and that his ball had exceptional movement. (Midway through his career with the Cardinals Gibson pitched in an All-Star Game against Joe Pepitone of the Yankees. With one strike on Pepitone, Gibson delivered, and Pepitone swung and missed. "Throw me that slider again," Pepitone shouted out to the mound, and so

Gibson threw the exact pitch again, and Pepitone swung again and missed. What amazed Joe Torre, who caught the game, was that it was not a slider, but a *fastball*. It simply moved so much that Pepitone thought it a breaking ball.) He was economical on the mound: his mechanics had a certain purity to them—a simple, fluid warm-up, and then the explosion.

Harry Walker, the hitting coach who had been around baseball all his life—his father had been a big-league player and a minor-league manager—thought Bob Gibson the greatest *athlete* ever to pitch in the major leagues. With that arm, that athleticism, and that passion, there should be no stopping him. Walker was puzzled by Solly Hemus's inability to understand Gibson's great potential. He did not think it was racial prejudice so much as Hemus's failure to understand people who were different from him. Still, Walker watched with surprise as this great young player smoldered with resentment. One day when Hemus lifted Gibson early in a game, Gibson finally snapped. He went into the locker room and decided that that was it, he had had enough. He started to pack his things. Just then Harry Walker walked in on him. "What are you doing?" Walker asked. Gibson answered that he was no longer going to be jerked around, and that he was going. "I just can't take it anymore," he said. Walker gave him a long, appraising look. "You'll be here a lot longer than he will," said Harry Walker, whose brother Dixie was known almost as well for his reluctance to play with Jackie Robinson as he was for his ability as a hitter. Walker was right. By the middle of the 1961 season, Hemus's third as the Cardinal manager, the team was playing below .500, and it was rife with tension and bad feeling. The problem now was in getting Gussie Busch to admit he had made a mistake in hiring Hemus. That was not easily done, but Dick Meyer worked steadily on him, and seventy-five games into the 1961 season, Hemus was fired and replaced by Johnny Keane.

At the moment of Hemus's firing, Keane had been a coach on the team for more than a year. Initially, he had resisted it. He wanted to be a big-league manager, and he believed that the right path to that was to manage in the minor leagues. Bing Devine had argued with him, telling Keane he needed time as a big-league coach. In 1959,

Keane finally agreed and left Omaha. So when Hemus was fired Keane was not only ready, he knew the talent better than Hemus did. Keane did a number of things immediately. He told Stan Musial he wanted him on the field. "You may be coming to the end of your career," he told Musial, "but I want you to do it on the field and not on the bench," and Musial's final seasons were successful, even exuberant—in fact, the following season he hit .330 and came close once again to winning the National League batting title. Keane also told a very frustrated Curt Flood that he was the regular center fielder as of that day. Then he told Bob Gibson that he was in the rotation. "Bob, you're going to start every four or five days. I don't want you to worry about anything else. Just go out and pitch," he said. Those were the words Gibson had wanted to hear. Gibson interpreted them to mean simply: You don't have to worry about being pulled if you get in trouble in a bad inning. Just pitch. We'll give you a real shot. The rest will take care of itself.

It was hard, Bob Gibson later thought, for white players of that era and for black players who arrived later to understand how much Johnny Keane meant to the black players of that team, how much they liked and trusted him. If they were not the black players of the pioneer generation, they had come up right behind them: most had grown up in ghettoes, and their way into the big leagues had often been difficult, often through a still-segregated minor-league system. This obstacle course remained the foundation of big-league baseball, and it was rife with prejudice. Playing on minor-league teams in tiny Southern towns meant the crowds—even the home crowds— were usually hostile. Worse, most of their fellow players were rural country white boys, who, more often than not, seemed to accept the local mores. Some of Bill White's teammates rallied to his side when he had been abused by fans. But Curt Flood, who started in the Cincinnati organization, had a harder time. He had endured an unbearable season in the Carolina League, which he later came to call the Peckerwood League. In the Carolina League, the kindest epithet yelled at him was "nigger"; it got worse after that. The more they yelled at him, the harder he played. The next year, in Class A, with the Savannah Redlegs, it was not much better. One of the few white teammates who befriended him, Buddy Gilbert, thought he had never seen anyone as lonely as Curt Flood. Here he was, Gilbert thought, intelligent, sensitive, talented, a good teammate who played hard all the time, by far the best prospect on the team, and yet he lived completely apart from his teammates. By Georgia law, Flood and Leon Cardenas, a black Hispanic teammate, could not even dress with their teammates; they had to dress within a separate cubicle in the locker room. Gilbert, a Tennessean and a seriously religious man, thought this prejudice loathsome. He had invited black players to his home in the past, and had been upbraided for it by some teammates. He tried to bring Flood food on occasion, when he could not eat with the team. At park after park they would walk on the field together, Gilbert to center field, Flood to third base, and the epithets would rain down, the crudest and most brutal language Gilbert had ever heard. "I don't know how you stand it," he would tell Flood again and again. Even his simple acts of friendship were considered offensive by some of their teammates. "You know what you are, Gilbert?" more than one teammate said to him. "You're a goddamn nigger-lover." "No," he would answer, "I just like people." Sometimes Gilbert thought he did not know who was worse, those teammates who went through the motions of being friendly with Flood but made cruel racist remarks when he was not around or the ones who refused to talk to him at all. "I don't understand you," he told one teammate. "You pat him on the back when he's here, and then you say terrible things the moment he's gone." Gilbert knew that there was a lot of prejudice in America, but he thought that in sports a person could overcome it, that his teammates would respect Flood for his abilities and see past his color. But in Savannah, Flood was playing hard and extremely well, and yet that did not win over his teammates. For Flood, the worst part of that year were the bus rides; after a long doubleheader in the brutal heat, he would get back on the bus, but when it stopped and everyone else got off to eat, he would have to remain behind. Flood later decided that if he could stand those two years, he could stand anything.

Nor did blacks always receive kindness and instruction from the

representatives of the big leagues, who were there ostensibly to help
them develop their skills. Many of the minor-league managers were
tough men whose own careers had been disappointing. What was
especially hard about it, the black players believed, was that those
who were supposed to be on your side—your teammates, and your
manager—rarely were; the organization that was supposed to be behind them did not appreciate the ordeal they were experiencing.
Baseball's executives had clearly decided that they needed black
ballplayers in the game, that the talent was too great to ignore. But,
the young blacks of that generation wondered, did they really belong? Were they really wanted? Or were they to come, make their
contribution, and then be gone as quickly as possible when the game
was over? They experienced a spiritual loneliness, a sense of being
apart from those who were supposed to be teammates, and of doubt-
ing the loyalty of the men for whom they played. For many of them
the worst moment came when they showed up for spring training at
the hotel where the rest of the team was staying only to be told that,
no, they were not to stay there, they were to be taken instead to a
seedy hotel in the black section of town, or to a home that had been
turned into a boardinghouse where the black players from several
different teams stayed. It was a slap in the face. In fact, nothing high-
lighted the differences between the white and black experiences in
the major leagues so much as spring training. Almost all veteran
white players loved spring training—it was a chance to be in the
sunshine with their families, to go fishing, and to recover from a
long, difficult winter. They thought of it as a kind of paid vacation.
The black players, by contrast, hated it. Bob Gibson disliked the
boardinghouse in St. Petersburg in which he and other black players
stayed and the overbearing black woman who ran it, who, he
thought, charged the players too much for their room and board.
She was someone, he believed, who was making a good thing off
other people's pain and humiliation. Years later he would talk about
her with scorn and anger as if all this had happened only the day
before.

It was against that background that Johnny Keane was so special.
As far as the black players were concerned, there was not an ounce of

prejudice in him. They sensed that he cared for them not just as ballplayers, for what they could do for him on the field, but he cared for them as men as well. He had a rare empathy with young players. His own reasonably promising professional career had been cut short when Sig Jakucki had beaned him in a Texas League game in 1935 when he was twenty-three. There was a fracture in his skull that was seven inches long, and he had come very close to dying. He remained unconscious for almost a week, and his temperature had stayed steady at 105½. When he made his comeback the next season with the same team, the Houston Buffaloes, his manager had made him stay in the batting cage for a very long thirty minutes against a wild young pitcher on the Houston roster. Only then had he proven that he was still man enough to play baseball.

His friends thought his sense of what life was like for a young player had stayed with him from those days. He thought that the macho managers of his own era, those men who verbally brutalized their own players and used fear as their primary weapon, were not particularly effective back then, and he knew that in the new, more affluent America of the sixties, their tactics were even less effective. The new breed of players, reflecting the changes in society at large, were better educated and better informed and had more options from which they could choose in life. Johnny Keane was a complicated man—religious, sensitive, occasionally authoritarian. In his early days as a manager, the expletives needed to engage in proper dialogue with the umpires had come hard to him. It was said that when Keane was a young man managing in the Texas League, he had been thrown out of a game by an umpire named Frenchy Arceneaux. He had been furious, but was virtually at a loss as to how to express his fury. Finally he yelled from the dugout, "Arceneaux! You know what you are, Arceneaux? You're just a mean man is what you are!" Gradually, he expanded his vocabulary to meet the requirements of his profession, however, and by the time he surfaced as a major-league manager, he could, if need be, swear like a longshoreman.

There were certain things Keane would not tolerate as a major-league manager. For instance, he hated the Cardinal poker games, because there was never any silver on the table, just bills, and he thought the young players needed to save their money. Some players were losing two hundred dollars a game, which was nearly a week's salary. As such, the poker game was inevitably bound to create resentments among the players. One of the first things he did when he became manager was to end the poker game. "I felt like an old mother hen, but I knew what I was doing was right, so I told 'em no more poker. There was a little grumbling, mostly by a few players who were getting rich off the game, but they came around," he said later.

He did not intend to fail as the Cardinal manager. He was forty-nine when he got the job and he had waited a long time for it. The pressure on him to win was enormous. He did not drink unless he had to, for he had seen alcohol as the most destructive vice in baseball when he was young, the crutch all too many players and baseball men seized on when their careers began to fade. But if he had to, he would nurse a drink through an evening as a courtesy to others. He smoked four packs of cigarettes a day, and even though smoking in a major-league dugout was technically forbidden, he smoked right through the games. He was not a man who smiled very much, and he seldom laughed. There was also a certain rigidity to him. Some of the young white players thought he loved the rules too much. By contrast, the young black players thought that if there were too many rules, at least they were employed fairly.

If Gibson and Flood had encountered problems early on in their careers, he believed, it was because they were too wired, and because they put too much pressure on themselves. His job, Keane felt, was to reduce, not increase, the pressure on them, to reduce extraneous distractions. That did not mean Keane and Gibson always had an easy time together. They had their own private war over the use of Gibson's breaking pitches. When Gibson had a batter down 0-2, he wanted to go for the kill, because he hated to waste a pitch, but Keane would argue that the hitter was on the defensive and that this was a moment when Gibson should go to a location just outside the plate, making the hitter reach for a bad pitch. Then there was the question of the curve: Gibson loathed his own curveball, but Keane wanted him to go to the curve more, particularly when he was behind in the count. They squabbled long and hard over that, and there had been one close game when, in a tight situation, Keane demanded that he throw the curve. "All you do is throw that goddamn fastball. Now I want you to throw a curve and if someone hits it out on you, I'll eat my fucking hat." Gibson threw the curve, the batter hit a home run, and both Gibson and Tim McCarver looked over at the bench to see if Keane was taking off his cap. He never touched his hat. If Keane liked Gibson's curve more than Gibson did, then Gibson liked his own slider more than Keane did, and he went to it more often than the manager thought he should. In one game against Cincinnati, the Reds hit his slider hard, and when Gibson returned to the dugout after one tortuous inning, Keane told him, "Gibson, you ought to take that damn slider and shove it right up your ass." They were epic battles, the other players thought, and great fun to watch. There was Gibson, a physically intimidating man, and there was Keane, only five feet eight inches tall, going head to head, shouting at each other, Keane wanting nothing but to make Gibson an even greater pitcher, and Gibson, despite the heat of their arguments, somehow always aware of that.

Almost from the moment he went into the rotation Gibson began to pitch as everyone had hoped. In 1960, Hemus's last full season, Gibson started 12 games and his record was 3-6. Then, in 1961, his record was 2-6 at the moment when Hemus was fired, a little more than a third of the way through the season. From that point Gibson began to show the strength and willpower—if not yet the mastery of his pitches—that would mark his career, and he was a winning pitcher from then on, ending up with a record of 13-12 overall for the season. His control was still a problem, and he had led the league in walks, but even with his control problems, and perhaps because of them, he was an intimidating figure on the mound, and his earned run average was only 3.24 by the end of the season. The following season he started 30 games, won 15, and, even more important, finished 15, a vital statistic as far as he was concerned. His strikeout-to-walk ratio improved dramatically. He struck out 208 and walked 95.

Beyond the statistics, he jumped to a high place on the list of pitchers that National League hitters least liked to face. From the moment that Keane put him in the rotation, it was clear to the Cardinal management that a big-league fastball pitcher had finally arrived on the team.

Gibson and a number of other fastball pitchers got a significant break in 1963 when the National League changed the strike zone, expanding it to incorporate the high fastball. Until then anything above the belt buckle had been a ball. That season they brought the strike zone up to the letters. For those pitchers who threw a high or a rising fastball, such as Gibson, Koufax, and Jim Maloney, it was a huge advantage. Koufax, already in the process of mastering his control, jumped from a record of 14-7 to 25-5 and a walk-to-strikeout ratio of 58 to 306; Maloney went from 9-7 to 23-7 with 88 walks and 265 strikeouts. With Gibson the results were not quite so dramatic—he went from 15-13 to 18-9; but there was a general belief around the league that the change had empowered these pitchers, that at the very least they had gotten a major boost in their confidence, because they were now pitching to a much bigger strike zone, and therefore they had far more flex in tight situations.

For Gibson the timing could not have been better; he was on the threshold of greatness. In 1964 he was not yet the great pitcher he soon would be, so dominating that, among other things, the pitcher's mound had to be lowered to make things a bit easier for the hitters, but he was already a force, with a great fastball and a good slider, and he was beginning to improve his control. He was learning how to hold the ball on the seams or against the seams in order to make his fastball run in or run out on a hitter. If he was not yet a great pitcher, he was capable of pitching great games. He did not have a change, as Solly Hemus, now departed the big leagues, had noted, and he did not have a good curve or the full assortment of pitches that other great pitchers, such as Juan Marichal, had—for Marichal seemed to be able to throw every pitch in the book from every arm position and with vastly different speeds. But Gibson's determination usually made him harder and harder to beat as a game progressed. Already it was being said of him, as it was said of very few other pitchers, that if the opposition wanted to beat him it had better get to him early, because he got tougher as a game went on.

He was a physically talented man, but what set him apart was his determination. There were wrongs to avenge, the prejudice that had kept down millions of black men. All those dumb things that white people still said about black athletes—that they were gutless, that they folded in the clutch—had to be disproved. It was the most personal of struggles. To Tim McCarver, Gibson was someone who carried an immense amount of anger with him, and with good reason: he was a young black man in a society that was just beginning to deal with centuries of prejudice. But, unlike so many other angry people who were defeated by their rage, Gibson mastered his anger and turned it into a positive force.

10

Americans raised during the Depression had known real poverty, while those raised after the war knew far more comfort and affluence; by the mid-sixties sociologists were beginning to talk about a generation gap in American society. If Johnny Keane was more tolerant, and more sensitive to the problems of young players, than most managers of his generation, that did not mean that the Cardinals were different from most other baseball organizations of the day in their attitude toward their young ballplayers. Though he was gentle, Johnny Keane was a fairly strict disciplinarian and a quite conservative man. He had strong ideas about how his younger players should behave. He was still very much the seminarian, and some of his young players thought him almost prudish in some respects. The Cardinals under Keane seemed to know a great deal about what their young players were doing, and there were many warnings about proper behavior. The organization did not like it when Ernie Broglio took an apartment in Gaslight Square, the Bohemian section of St. Louis (Don Blasingame and Joe Cunningham had lived in the same apartment before, and the ball club had not liked that either). If a ballplayer bought too much liquor at a local store, somehow the ball club always knew, and the young player was warned. If a young single player, such as Tim McCarver, not only stayed out ten minutes past curfew but was seen with a girl, he might be called in to Keane's office and reprimanded, not so much for missing curfew by a few minutes but for being with a *girl.* "But, Johnny, I'm single, and I'm twenty-one," McCarver protested, but to no avail. The organization was, in some ways, virtually omniscient. (A reporter covering the Cardinals for one of the local papers was believed by the players to be reporting to management on their off-field behavior. That irritated the players no end. Indeed, it was said that the reporter's wife sometimes hung out with the switchboard operators at the motel where the team stayed during spring training, and that she tried to pick up such information from them as to which players were calling numbers other than those of their wives.)

The issue was, thought such younger players as Ray Sadecki, Ernie Broglio, and Tim McCarver, about control. This was hardly unique to the Cardinals—it reflected the attitudes of most front-office executives. The Cardinals, like other ball clubs, stressed self-confidence as a key quality for their players, but they did not really want truly self-confident young men, McCarver thought. What they wanted instead was a very limited version of confidence, molded to their particular needs and uses: they wanted their players to be fearless and aggressive from two to five P.M. during day games and from eight to eleven P.M. during night games. But at other times, McCarver thought, management wanted players utterly dependent upon and responsive to management, to trust utterly in the goodwill and abiding wisdom of the club, and to believe that what was good for the Cardinals (and The Brewery) was also good for the players.

The young players chafed at the paternalism, none so much as Ray Sadecki, a confident, talented young left-hander who had been a success almost from the start. At the age of twenty, he had already won fourteen games and seemed well on his way to becoming the ace of the staff. Sadecki was a rare young man in baseball in that era, a bonus baby who was actually worth the money he had been paid. As early as his sophomore year in a Kansas City high school, the scouts had started coming to his games, and by his junior year there were four or five bird-dog scouts at each game he pitched. By his senior year, there were often two full-time scouts from each major-league team present, and his team went 18-0 and won the state championship. A professional career seemed to be a sure thing. The most amazing thing about Sadecki's performance, his high school coach, Doug Minnis, thought, was that it had never gone to the young man's head, that he had remained remarkably balanced throughout, committed to his teammates, never drawing attention to himself at their expense. That made him most unusual, Minnis thought, because by his junior year in high school he was already being promised a good deal of money and a bright future. Most young men would have been caught up in all the attention, but Sadecki seemed to reject it as if it were somehow an unwanted by-product of what he really wanted to do, which was to play baseball.

As his high school graduation approached, the pressure on Sadecki to sign began to mount. On the day of his graduation, the Sadecki house was like a landing field at an overcrowded airport, with scouts assigned time slots to make their appeals. The Milwaukee Braves, then drawing 2 million fans a year and able to throw a good deal of money around, were said to be readying an offer of $100,000. The Cleveland Indians, where Frank Lane had landed after his unhappy tour in St. Louis, were also interested. Ray Sadecki had flown to Cleveland for what turned out to be a memorable tryout. He usually dealt with the scouts accompanied by his father, who ran a small grocery store, but on this occasion he had gone up there by himself. He worked out virtually alone in that giant empty stadium, pitching in front of thousands and thousands of empty seats, with just a handful of older men standing around watching him. Sadecki handled the pressure of that eerie tryout quite well, and afterward Frank Lane called him into his office and offered a contract for $50,000. Lane knew there were other comparable offers on the table for this accomplished young man, and he tried to bully him into signing. The idea of paying $50,000 for an untried player who had not even pitched one inning in the minor leagues enraged Lane. He began shouting at Sadecki. "I'm going to offer you fifty thousand dollars," Lane shouted, "and you've got one shot at it! You can have it by agreeing right now! But if you walk out that door, it's gone and you'll never get it again! I'll pull it off the table and if you tell anybody I offered it I'll deny it!" For a seventeen-year-old boy it was an amazing scene; he had ventured there without his father (and therefore could not sign the contract anyway), and as he tried to explain this to Lane, the Indian general manager only became angrier. "Who the hell do you think you are! Nothing but a goddamn kid!" Ray Sadecki had never seen a grown man so completely out of control.

Lane's tantrum hastened the decision in the Sadecki house to expedite the signing process, and not to have Ray fly all over the country doing one-day exhibitions, a procedure that might end up costing him a large part of a season that could be more profitably spent in the minor leagues. Rather, the Sadeckis decided to choose quickly from the teams that had shown the most interest. That most certainly did not include the Yankees, though Tom Greenwade had given Sadecki the traditional Yankee pitch: sign for less now, but play with the best and make more money in the long run with all the World Series checks. Milwaukee was very hot early in the chase, but pulled back to go after another pitcher, Tony Cloninger, and an infielder, Denis Menke. Cincinnati was interested, and made what was possibly the highest offer, and the Cardinals were right in there at $50,000. Kansas City, with a new franchise, was interested, but in the end did not make an offer. The Cardinals then sweetened their offer and said they would give Ray three years' guaranteed salary at $6,000 a year, a good basic wage in those days, for a total package of $68,000. The pull of the Cardinals was considerable, for Sadecki had been weaned on the exploits of Stan Musial and the voice of Harry Caray, the famed Cardinal broadcaster. He signed with the Cards, and his father, Frank Sadecki, an immigrant's son who had not been permitted to play baseball by his father, took the $10,000 check for the first part of the bonus and showed it to his own father. The old man looked at it and broke into tears of both pleasure and anguish; the boy, he said, is making that much money just for playing a game, while he had had to work so hard all his life for so much less.

Sadecki went right into the minor leagues, and at first he had felt some resentment from the career minor-league players because he had made so much more money before he had even thrown his first pitch. He sometimes thought it was as if his first two names, as far as the newspapers were concerned, were "Bonus Baby" and his nickname was "The $50,000 Left-hander," as in "Bonus Baby Ray Sadecki will pitch tonight," or "The $50,000 left-hander pitched another complete game." He was well aware that by the time he arrived in professional baseball, it was a two-tiered society, and that by dint of big bonuses, he and a few others, such as Tim McCarver, were part of an aristocracy. The chasm between the bonus babies and the others was particularly great in the minor leagues; Sadecki and McCarver talked of one of McCarver's teammates in Keokuk, a middle relief pitcher named Warren Rodenberry, who had a wife and two children and a third child on the way. Rodenberry made $250 a month, not an uncommon salary in those days, and he supplemented it by driving the team bus for an additional $50 a month. Sadecki pitched well in the minors, and in 1960 he made the starting rotation with the Cardinals, arriving with the big-league club even sooner than expected. He won 9 and lost 9, with an earned run average of 3.78. He was a young man of exceptional poise and confidence, and he had a maturity beyond his years. "The rest of us who were roughly the same age as Ray," Tim McCarver said years later, "were very unsure of ourselves, and very immature, and by contrast, Ray was very mature and grown up for his years, and extremely independent in the most natural and unpretentious way." And, added McCarver, "management most assuredly did not like that degree of independence." The Cardinal management was very ambivalent in its attitude toward Sadecki, McCarver thought, like a parent with a too-precocious child. This independence particularly irritated Johnny Keane, who was only a coach when Sadecki joined the club, but soon became the manager.

No one was ever entirely sure why Keane was so down on Ray Sadecki. Perhaps, some of the players thought, it began with the team poker games on the back of the plane. Solly Hemus had played in them, as did some of the veteran players, such as Musial (who was considered by his teammates a terrible poker player, always drawing to inside straights, but who nonetheless always seemed to win, favored in this, it seemed, as in all else). Sadecki, the same age as one of Musial's sons, joined the game almost as soon as he joined the team. Clearly, neither Keane nor Harry Walker, one of the other coaches, liked the idea of someone so young being in the poker game. Walker never said anything directly to Sadecki about it, but he kept saying little things to some of the other players: "He's too young to be in it"; or, "Suppose he loses—he can't afford to lose the money it takes. It's going to get him in trouble."

There was clearly something about Sadecki that put Keane off. Sadecki might be pitching hard, but he did not seem to give off the usual signs that he was pitching hard. Bob Gibson on the mound grunted so hard on every pitch that his throat was parched at the end of a game, but Sadecki pitched so fluidly and with such ease that he did not reveal the effort behind it. Soon after Johnny Keane took over as manager, Harry Walker began telling Sadecki he had to look more fierce when he was on the mound. He was supposed to put on some kind of grim game-day face, much the way Bob Gibson did. But Sadecki was not Gibson, and he did not want to do anything that felt false. These requests struck Sadecki as childish, and he answered that that was the way he looked, and that that was the way he pitched, and he was not going to go through false histrionics or try to look tougher. Sadecki was still, in his own words, primarily a thrower with a good fastball, but not yet, in the complete sense, a pitcher. He did not yet understand the process of how to set up hitters. Yet when he was on the mound, the ball seemed to zip into home plate with surprising speed.

In 1961, Sadecki pitched very well, and at 14-10 he owned the best win-loss record of any starter on the team. He was still only twenty that year, and his future looked bright. There was no tension, as far as he was concerned, between himself and Keane. What happened next was (and some of his teammates agreed) a textbook example of how the hierarchical system worked in baseball in those days, even with men as decent as Bing Devine and Johnny Keane. With his early bonus money Sadecki bought his parents a small restaurant in St. Petersburg, and he spent the winter there after the 1961 season. He had been paid around $7,000 for his first season, and about $11,000 for his second season, and now, after a successful full year, he was asking for $18,000. It was a big jump in salary, but he was also aware of how well he had done, that he was becoming something of a hot property, and that baseball, when it needed to, had in fact a good deal of money with which to reward talent. He was very optimistic about the coming season, and he had high hopes of winning twenty games at the age of twenty-one and becoming one of baseball's elite pitchers. The ball club, he recalled later, answered his demand of $18,000 with an offer of $13,000 a year. Throughout the winter he and the ball club haggled, and there was very little movement on either side. As spring training approached, it became clear to Sadecki that he was in danger of becoming a holdout. Since he was already in Florida, he went to talk to Johnny Keane about the salary stalemate, hoping that Keane would take his side, turn to Bing Devine, and say something along the line of, "Hey, this kid pitched well for us. Let's do something for him."

That turned out to be a considerable misperception on his part, thinking there was any difference between the front office and the field manager, who dealt daily with the players. Bing Devine and Johnny Keane were very close, so much in synch with each other that each, it often seemed, spoke not only for himself but for the other. The meeting went very badly. Sadecki barely began to talk when Keane quickly disabused him of the notion of getting his help. "I know everything that's going on," Johnny Keane said. "Bing Devine is a very fair man—I've known him a long time and we've worked together and there isn't a better or more decent man in baseball. I want you to sign the contract that he's offering you, and I want you to be with the team tomorrow." It was a stunning moment for Sadecki. It was one thing to have the front office play down what he had done, but it was quite another thing to have the manager, the man for whom he had played for an entire season, stonewall him as well. "I'm sorry," he answered. "I don't feel that way, but I hope we can work it out." Not very long after that, Ray Sadecki signed. In what was the accepted practice of the day, they had split the difference, and he signed for about $15,000, which was probably the figure the ball club had penciled in in the first place. But in the process, two things had happened: Ray Sadecki had transgressed in the eyes of Keane and shown himself to be arrogant and ungrateful, and Keane had proven himself a company man in the eyes of a talented young player.

It was clear to Sadecki that everything that happened from then on was about discipline and that he was being taught a lesson. The ball club still had complete control over a player's life. It could, if it so chose, send a quality player back to the minors. And that soon happened with Sadecki. In the spring of 1962 he did not pitch particularly well, but he had never been a good spring pitcher. As spring training ended, he was not in the starting rotation. Instead he was in the bullpen, which puzzled him, for it was a clear demotion, and yet he had not been driven there by opposing hitters in real league games. This was a hard time for Sadecki, for he was not accustomed to failing. He was in the bullpen, he did some spot starting, and then he and Keane had a major confrontation. It came after a June relief appearance against the Reds and their ace, Bob Purkey. Sadecki had come in and given quite possibly the worst performance of his career. He faced five batters, gave up a single and two home runs, and put two runners on base with his own errors. He left the ball game trailing, 9–1. Eventually the Cardinals came back to win, 10–9, and so the clubhouse was jubilant after the game, but Sadecki was not one of the players taking part in the celebration. Nonetheless, he was surprised when Johnny Keane called him into his office. "That's the worst effort I've ever seen," Keane began. That, as far as Sadecki was concerned, was the wrong phrase to use, and soon both men were shouting at each other. It was one thing to question his performance—he freely admitted that he had been terrible—but it was another thing to question his effort. "I pitched lousy and I fielded lousy—but don't ever question my effort," he said. "I always play hard." Both men were in a rage, and Keane said that he had intended to fine Sadecki $500 because he had done so poorly, but because the Cardinals had ended up winning, he was only going to fine him $250. If anything, that made Sadecki even angrier. "Are you going to fine me every time I lose?" he asked. "Are you going to fine the other pitchers when they lose? Do you think Cincinnati is going to fine Purkey because he blew a big lead today?" Then Bing Devine walked into the room and suddenly Sadecki felt that he was taking them both on. It was, he thought, an unfair match, and the culmination of a frustrating period. He told Devine, "Why don't you do us all a favor and trade me? I'm sure there's some value out there. You don't seem to want me, and I don't like it here anymore." That angered Devine. He said, "The players don't run the club. We run the club and we decide who we'll trade." Things went downhill from there, and by the end of the meeting Devine talked of suspending Sadecki. In fact, Sadecki believed he had been suspended, and so he did not show up at the ball park the next day, and thereupon the club *did* suspend him. That produced yet another meeting, this time at The Brewery with everyone but Gussie Busch there. A great deal of talking was done, some by Devine, some by Keane, none by Sadecki, and there was a general consensus that everyone had overreacted, that too much had been said in the heat of battle, but Sadecki was still unhappy, and remained $250 short because of the fine, which in those days was the equivalent of almost a week's pay.

Things did not get better for Sadecki. He thought he could pitch well if only they would put him in the rotation. There was a meeting in Bing Devine's office at which Devine and Keane said they wanted to send him back to the minors and Sadecki said no way, he wanted none of that. Devine answered that he had not pitched well, and besides, there was no argument about it, he was going back to the minors. So he went back and pitched well with the Triple A club in Atlanta, going 12-2 including play-off games. That winter, when Sadecki was doing his six-month army service in Minnesota, Bing Devine flew up to see him and suggested that they try to put the entire thing behind them, that it had been a long and difficult season and things had not worked out the way anyone had hoped. That was fine with Ray Sadecki, who quite liked pitching for the Cardinals, but there was no doubt that a certain coolness had developed between him and his manager.

Sadecki did not think that Johnny Keane ever quite forgave him, and two years later, as the 1964 season was unfolding and he was pitching very well, he and some of the other players were aware that when Johnny Keane talked to reporters, he was significantly less generous in his mentions of Sadecki than he was of other players. Even when Sadecki was doing well, Tim McCarver thought, it seemed to irritate Keane, as if it showed that Sadecki could flaunt management's vision of how a young player should behave and still win, which was in some ways worse than flaunting it and losing.

What was clearly happening was a kind of generational tension. Johnny Keane, who had been produced by a less affluent America, and who did not get his chance to manage a major-league team until he was fifty years old, believed that professional as well as financial success had come too quickly to Sadecki, and that somehow he had not paid his dues. Keane, without realizing it, probably resented Sadecki, because the pitcher, as a successful young bonus baby, was somehow a little beyond his control, unlike a poorer young pitcher in another era or in the lower minor leagues might have been. In 1964, Sadecki started the season poorly. He was 0-3 in early May, which did not bother him that much because he never pitched well in the cold weather. But then he began to hit his stride. In May he won four games and his record was 4-4. "Hey," he said to one of his teammates, "all I have to do is win four games in June, July, August, and September and I'll be a twenty-game winner," which in fact is what happened.

None of his success, though, changed Johnny Keane's attitude toward him. In early June he pitched an important game against the San Francisco Giants in Candlestick Park. In the ninth inning, with the Cardinals leading, 1–0, Jim Ray Hart led off for the Giants with a single. Sadecki got the next two batters, only to find the immensely dangerous Willie McCovey coming up as a pinch hitter. With a 2-2 count on McCovey, he went to his curve and struck him out. After the game the players were in the locker room washing up, and Sadecki was shaving. Right next to him, also shaving, was Dick Groat. Bob Gibson and Tim McCarver were standing nearby. Everyone was in a good mood because it was a big win against a tough team and Sadecki had done it by striking out one of the most dangerous hitters in baseball. Just then Johnny Keane came over. "Hey, Sadecki," Keane said. "What did you get McCovey out with?" "A curveball," Sadecki answered, not picking up that there was a certain edge to Keane's voice, and that Keane did not seem to be sharing the pleasure of the big win with the rest of the team. "And if you had missed with that, what would you have thrown him on the three-two count?" asked Keane, who had a running argument with some of his pitchers because he wanted them to come in on a 3-2 count with a breaking ball. "A fastball," said Sadecki, whose best pitch was his fastball. "Yeah, you do that and you'd have gotten beat," Keane said, and only then did Sadecki and the others realize how angry the manager was. It was a truly weird moment, Sadecki thought, being told that this pitch that he had not even thrown was going to be hit for a home run. Beside him, Gibson and Groat were breaking up. It was funny, Sadecki thought, and yet it was not funny.

11

In mid-June the St. Louis Cardinals were struggling. The high hopes generated by the strong finish in the previous season seemed to be dissipating. The team was not playing well. It hovered near the .500 mark, sometimes going a little above, and then slipping below it. The confidence and the cohesion that had been there late in the 1963 season had disappeared. In addition, there was a gaping weakness in left field where Stan Musial, for so long the best hitter in the National League, had played. His retirement had been announced in late August of the previous season at an emotional ceremony after which, for the final month of the season, just to show that he was not being forced out, Musial concluded one of baseball's greatest careers by seeming to hit nothing but line drives. Ernie Broglio, the pitcher with the best record on the team in 1963, 18-8, was convinced that the Cardinals were only one player away from winning the pennant: a talented young outfielder. In spring several young players had been tried in the outfield, and there had been much discussion in the press about who was to be Musial's successor. Musial himself was interviewed regularly about which of the candidates seemed likely to take his place. (STAN'S MAN, CLEMENS, LOOKS GOOD, read a headline in the *Post-Dispatch* during spring training, referring to the chances of Doug Clemens, one of the many outfield hopefuls.)

That the team was so flat in early 1964 was an immense disappointment to Bing Devine, whose job was obviously on the line. So, starting in late May, Devine called other National League general managers looking to make the trade that would jump-start his team. By this time, Devine would not hesitate to trade a starting pitcher for an outfielder. He was sure that a good farm system in working order would always keep enough strong-armed young men in the pipeline to deliver first-rate pitchers. In putting this Cardinal team together, he had been guided by that philosophy; several years earlier, he had made an important trade of that kind, giving up Toothpick Sam Jones, quite possibly the best pitcher on his team and a man who always pitched with a toothpick in his mouth, for Bill White, a promising outfielder–first baseman, who had played for only one full season in major-league baseball, and who had been away for two years in the army. It was not a popular trade at the time in St. Louis, or even in Devine's own household, and he had come home that night only to find his wife and daughter at the dinner table, both of them with toothpicks in their mouths.

Now Devine felt the pressure mounting on him as the June fifteenth trading deadline approached. What he wanted was a quality hitter who could play the outfield every day. He began to push harder to make a deal. Devine and Johnny Keane had long ago agreed that, given the changing nature of major-league baseball, particularly in the National League, which had more and better black players coming in, speed was increasingly important. They talked often about the diminishing chances of finding a great new superstar in the rough, a young DiMaggio, Williams, Mantle, Mays, or Aaron. Again and again they talked late into the night on this one theme: How do you create a winning team if you aren't fortunate enough to have a superstar in the lineup every day? Coming up with a superstar was always, to some degree, a matter of luck, and it was becoming tougher all the time with more and more teams spending increased amounts of money on scouting. Now, in the sixties, even those teams that had once not deigned to search for black talent were scouring the back roads of the Deep South. In fact, the region was now crawling with scouts. Therefore, they decided, if you had to narrow your expectations on finding super talent, you had to set other priorities. They both decided that speed was the one thing you could spot early on, and it was something that could not be coached. If a young player had speed, there was a chance that the other qualities—the ability to hit consistently, and to field a position well— might come later. The other aspects of what might constitute a great player—the ability to hit for power, the hunger to improve, the ability to play well under pressure—were harder to gauge. But speed was an elemental ingredient for success, particularly as the nature of the game was changing.

If anything, Keane believed even more passionately in the idea of speed than Bing Devine. The player he had wanted for more than a year was a seemingly undistinguished black outfielder for the Chicago Cubs named Lou Brock. Brock was twenty-four years old at the time, and he was not a particularly good outfielder, he had not hit very well in his brief time in the major leagues, and he had an erratic arm. Worse, after two full seasons, he was nothing more than a .260 hitter. An outfielder who was a defensive liability and who hit only .250 or .260 was not exactly a gem. Still, there was the matter of Brock's speed. He was obviously one of the two or three fastest men in the major leagues, perhaps the fastest. In addition, the Cardinal executives were privately convinced that his talents were being poorly showcased in Chicago, and that the Cubs were the wrong team for him. Because of the nature of their small ball park, the Cubs were not a running team. They tended to wait for the wind to blow out in Wrigley Field and go for the big inning. Stealing bases was considered a high-risk art form for a team like that, thus Brock had never been set loose as a base runner. Nor was Wrigley Field an easy place for a young man to play the outfield, because the sun came right in on the right fielder.

The Cardinals had scouted Brock carefully while he was in college at Southern University in Baton Rouge, and been quite interested in signing him, but then had managed to blow their chance. But that meant they knew a lot about him. He might, for instance, look slim, but, in fact, he was so powerfully built that he had the ability to hit a long ball. He once hit a home run to dead center in the Polo Grounds, a ball that carried at least 485 feet. At six feet and weighing 170 pounds, he was almost devoid of body fat. It was a body, said his teammate Tim McCarver, that looked as if it had been chiseled out of marble. A few years later Senator Eugene McCarthy, a former minor-league ballplayer himself, signed on to cover the 1968 World Series for *Life* magazine. Being in the clubhouse with someone as muscular as Brock, he said, was like being in the clubhouse with a superior species of being. "I was ashamed to be in the same locker room with him," McCarthy later said.

Keane had been pushing Devine to get Brock for more than a year, and Eddie Stanky, the former Cardinal manager who was now a Cardinal scout and instructor, appraised him carefully in his Chicago incarnation and remained very high on him as well. Brock was a player, both Keane and Stanky felt, who might blossom on the Cardinals, a far more aggressive team on the base paths than the Cubs. The Cardinals did not play for the big inning, they fought and scratched for one run at a time. They not only ran more often than the Cubs, they tended to use the hit-and-run and other plays that used speed on the bases to pressure the opposition.

With the trade deadline approaching, and the Cardinals in the doldrums, the team went on a trip to the West Coast. On June 11, St. Louis played the first of three games with the Dodgers. It went on to lose all three games. Suddenly there was a sense of mounting desperation on the Cardinals. The third loss to the Dodgers, with roughly a third of the season gone, had put them under .500, 28-29, tied for seventh place. Devine now felt an even greater urgency to make a trade and beat the deadline. From Los Angeles he telephoned John Holland, his opposite number in Chicago, to whom he had been talking over a period of months. The Cubs too were slipping. "I'm glad you called," Holland said. "We're doing poorly and I see you're not doing very well. Let's talk about doing something together quickly." The Cubs, it turned out, badly wanted a starting pitcher. At the time Ernie Broglio, one of the previous year's big winners for the Cardinals, was struggling. Broglio had lost one of the three games in Los Angeles, and that made his record 3-5. Johnny Keane had never been a very big fan of Broglio's. Keane felt Broglio's attitude was not intense enough, and from time to time

Harry Walker would tell Broglio, as he had also told Ray Sadecki, that he did not look fierce enough when he was out on the mound. "You've got to look meaner when you're out there," Walker would say.

Bing Devine finished his conversation with Holland, and boarded the plane for Houston with Keane and the team. "We can get Brock for Broglio if you want," he told his manager. "Then what are we waiting for?" Keane asked. "For this plane to land in Houston so I can call John Holland," Devine answered. And so the deal was done. It was an immensely risky deal. Broglio was twenty-eight, just coming into his prime as a pitcher. He had won 60 games in the last four years and had been 18-8 in 1963 with an earned run average of 2.99. Brock was an unknown. What the veteran Cardinal players knew about Brock did not impress them. The trade inspired considerable resentment and a good deal of grumbling among them. Broglio was a talented and extremely popular player. Bob Gibson, the Cardinal pitcher, who was as powerful a force within the locker room as he was on the field, thought it was the worst trade he had ever heard of. Broglio was a twenty-game winner, he said. Who knew what Brock was or could do? Brock later told Gibson that he had, in fact, batted against him, but Gibson had no memory of him as a batter. Gibson was angry and, as always, quick to express his anger. Bill White, the first baseman, also thought it was a bad trade; Dick Groat, the veteran shortstop, was sure that the team had panicked. There was so much complaining that Johnny Keane called a team meeting. "Who we trade for is our business, and you guys have no right to criticize what we do. This trade is none of your business," he told them. The Chicago sportswriters, by contrast, were jubilant. "Thank you, thank you, oh, you lovely St. Louis Cardinals," wrote the same Bob Smith who had placed Brock's name in contention for the title of worst outfielder in big-league history. "Nice doing business with you. Please call again anytime."

The irony of the trade, Lou Brock always thought, was that it came just as he had finally begun to feel confident about playing for the Cubs and had begun to hit well. In the weeks just before the trade he had gone on a roll as one of the hottest hitters in the league.

There had been a game against Cincinnati early in May when he had felt he belonged in the big leagues for the first time. Vada Pinson had been up and hit a shot toward right-center that looked like it might carry over the fence for a home run, or at the very least hit the fence and come back for a double. Brock, with his exceptional speed, had gone after it, jumped at the last moment, and made a sensational stab at the ball just as he and the ball reached the fence at the same time. Brock had come down hard after the catch, so jarred by the collision with the wall that he had no idea whether he had caught the ball, and he started to look for it on the grass. Finally a fan in the bleachers yelled out, "Look in your glove, Brock—you might just find it." He was elated by the catch and had returned to the dugout grinning, quite possibly for the first time, he thought, as a Cub. He had started laughing with that, and he had spent the rest of the day grinning, almost uncontrollably. His teammates were puzzled—it was a good catch, to be sure, but his pleasure seemed out of all proportion to what he had done. To Brock it was different, it was as if with that catch, the weight of the world was finally off his shoulders. It was shortly afterward that he was traded to St. Louis.

If the prevailing wisdom was that the Cardinals had been snookered, not everyone agreed. One baseball man who was sure that the Cardinals had made a good trade, and quite possibly a great trade, was an older black man named Buck O'Neil. O'Neil had played in the Negro leagues, had for a time managed the famed Kansas City Monarchs; then, late in his life, with the Negro leagues in collapse after the integration of more and more black players into the big leagues, he had become a scout for the Cubs. Buck O'Neil had scouted Lou Brock for three seasons in Baton Rouge, and had been absolutely sure Brock was going to be a great player. He thought it was a shame that the Cubs had neither the time nor, it seemed, the place for this exceptional young man. He was pleased with the trade for Lou Brock's sake, for he believed that the Cardinals were the perfect team for him: they liked to run, and they liked to put constant pressure on the other team.

Brock's Cub teammate and close friend Ernie Banks was not the only one who thought that Brock's problem had been that he was trying so hard, he was tying himself up in knots. Bob Kennedy, the Chicago manager—actually, one of nine managers, for the ownership had created a bizarre system of nine coaches who rotated as coaches and managers—once asked Brock to write his name on a piece of paper. Brock had done it easily, without thinking. Then Kennedy asked him to write it again, slowly this time, thinking carefully about each letter. Brock did and produced an entirely different signature, so pinched and unrecognizable that no bank would have cashed a check with it. That, Kennedy told Brock, was what he was doing at the plate.

Unfortunately, neither Kennedy nor the rest of the endless parade of Chicago coach-managers were able to create an atmosphere in which so ambitious a young man could relax. There were too many people in charge, too many different people telling Brock different things—to choke up, to swing all out, to pull the ball, to hit to the opposite field, to hit the ball down and beat out his infield hits, to relax, to play harder. Brock had become so frustrated and so despairing that when the front office called him in to tell him they were transferring his contract, Brock was sure he was being sent down to Tacoma, a Cub minor-league team. The most interesting thing about all those managers and coaches, Ernie Banks thought afterward, was that somehow they did not see or understand Brock's passion, and some of them thought the problem with him was that he was not trying hard enough. Banks hated it when he heard about the trade. He thought the Cubs were giving up on a great talent and a great human being much too early.

Ernie Broglio, the pitcher who thought the Cardinals were one player away from a pennant run, was called in and told he had been traded to Chicago. He was not told whom he had been traded for. He was stunned by the news. Though he gave the requisite interviews, saying that he was delighted to be going to the Cubs, he was, in truth, very upset. He loved being a Cardinal, and he liked his teammates and wanted to stay in St. Louis. Lou Brock flew immediately to Houston to join his new team. When he arrived in Houston he was greeted with a certain amount of teasing. Curt Flood welcomed him by saying that he had heard that Bing Devine was going

to pull off another brilliant deal: Bill White for two broken bats and
a bag of peanuts. Well, Curt, Brock thought, it's nice to be welcomed to the Cardinals. He played for the first time on June 16. The
Cardinals had lost seventeen of their last twenty-three games and
seemed headed straight for the cellar. In his first game Brock appeared as a pinch hitter, and struck out on three pitches. Bing Devine was sitting right behind the Cardinal dugout when he struck
out. Some Houston fans were behind him, riding the Cardinals.
"Brock for Broglio! Who would make a deal like that?" a fan yelled.
"Yeah," Devine said to his assistant Art Routzong, "what kind of
general manager would make a deal like that?"

Brock soon discovered that the Cardinals were very different
from the Cubs. When the Cubs lost, everyone sat around pondering
the game, and the players who had made mistakes were particularly
penitent. In no way did that help the team, Brock thought, and if
anything it seemed to reflect the power of negative thinking, making
each defeat all the heavier. With the Cardinals, by contrast, the
sense of defeat did not linger long in the clubhouse. If they lost,
there were vows to go out and get them the next day, and someone,
usually Bob Gibson or Bob Uecker or Tim McCarver, would play
some prank. If Brock had made an error, he was likely to find Gibson imitating him with astonishing fidelity in the locker room after
the game, and asking everyone, "Who do you think this is?" Gibson
could do a brilliant imitation of Brock, especially Brock misplaying a
ball in the outfield. Nor was he being singled out—for Gibson did it
to everyone. The Cardinals, he realized, knew how to play hard, and
better still, they knew how to get a bad game out of their system as
quickly as possible, as the Cubs did not.

He quickly came to like Johnny Keane, the manager, who was
protective of him at first, very much aware of the pressure he had
been under in Chicago, and of the great pressure he faced in St.
Louis because of the trade. A few days after Brock joined the Cardinals, Bob Broeg, the veteran St. Louis sportswriter, came to the
clubhouse before the game. He motioned toward Brock and told
Keane that he thought he would do a piece on the newest Cardinal.
"Bob, why don't you wait a bit," Keane suggested, "until he gets a

better feeling for this place, and there's less pressure on him. There'll be plenty of time to write about him later." That did not mean Keane was a particularly sentimental man. (With Sandy Koufax pitching for the Dodgers, a left-hander who was unusually hard on left-handed hitters, Brock would look over at the dugout to catch Keane's eye, as if to say, *Get me out of here and get a right-handed hitter up here*, but Keane would always avert his eyes instead of offering encouragement.) Early on Keane called Brock over and talked to him about his role on the team. "We've seen you hit the ball and we know you have power. We don't care how you hit the ball as long as you hit. Be as natural as you can," Keane said. The other subject was stealing. "Since you've got the speed for it, I guess you're going to want to try stealing bases," he said. "Hell yes," Brock answered. "Well, go for it when it strikes you as right," Keane said. "You make the call." That was all. For Brock it was a stunning moment. On the Cubs there had been all kinds of rules about when he could go and under what conditions he could go, all of them in some way inhibiting him, and all of them in some way making him go against his instincts and limiting his natural ability. Not only were there rules, but had he run and been thrown out, there would have been endless recriminations after the game in which his mistake would have been scrutinized and corrected. Now Johnny Keane was telling him what he needed to hear more than anything else—just trust his instincts.

There was also a team meeting in which Keane got up and said that there was a new element in professional baseball, that it was speed, and that the Dodgers had become the leaders in this new game with Maury Wills. "Now," Keane said, "we're going to run the bases too. We're not just going to match the Dodgers, we're going to go right past them." So far he had not mentioned any names. But as Keane continued to talk, Brock began to wonder if he was going to be traded again, this time, perhaps, for Maury Wills. At that point Bob Uecker, the backup catcher, a slow runner but the team comedian, raised his hand and said, "Okay, Johnny, it's a hard job but I'll do it—I'll steal those bases for you." No, said Keane, they did not need to trade for another player and they did not even need Uecker to steal, in the unlikely event that he got on base. They had their thief right here in this meeting. "Brock," he announced, "you're going to do it for us." So his role was clear. "Brock, I want you to keep running. If I don't tell you to stop running, then no one else on this team does either, and if someone tries to stop you, then you can tell them where to go."

Brock came alive as a Cardinal. With Johnny Keane giving him the green light to run, he stole 33 bases in what remained of the season and hit .348 as a Cardinal. It was the trade that changed the season for the Cardinals. A team that had been one key player short of making a run for the pennant had not only gotten the right player, it had gotten something more, a veritable ignition system for its offense. Still, the Cardinal players had been right about Brock in one sense: his talent was raw, and unrefined. Here he was, now in his third full season, and for the first time, with the help of Curt Flood, he was learning how to use his sunglasses—how to flip them down, to keep the sun from being an enemy. He had spent precious little time in the minor leagues, and he was still unsure as an outfielder. A few games after he had joined the team, the Cardinals were playing Milwaukee. With a runner on first, Rico Carty was at bat. He hit a ball to left field, and Brock, playing in left, broke the wrong way, toward center. Suddenly he reversed himself, put on the brakes, broke back for the line, and made a magnificent catch near the line. "Brock," Bill White told him when they were back in the dugout, "you're either the best outfielder in the game, or the worst."

If his new teammates had been unhappy with the trade at first, their attitude quickly changed. It was not just his speed on the bases that brought them around—and, most certainly, most of them had never seen speed like that before—but also the determination with which Brock came to work every day. This young man, his teammates decided, was *driven*. He was quiet, he kept to himself in a world of rather gregarious teammates, but he was one of the most focused players any of them had ever seen. Whoever had been in charge of him in Chicago and thought that he was passive had completely misread him. He was wired to play baseball; he existed as if for no other purpose than to play hard. He not only wanted to justify the trade, he wanted, it seemed, to be the best ever. If Gibson

wore anger openly on his face, almost as a weapon against the opposition batters, Brock smiled constantly, but the rage to succeed was
always there. The joy boy of the Cardinals, Bob Broeg, the St. Louis
writer, once called him in print because of his ready smile. "Bob, I
know you don't mean anything negative when you use that phrase,"
Brock told him afterward, "but you have to understand the implication of the word 'boy' to a black man."

 If he was just learning how to harness his great ability, he nonetheless had an immediate impact on the Cardinals. As he was aggressive, so his teammates became more aggressive. They already played
a hard-edged game that emphasized baserunning, but now, with
Brock on the team, they were more aggressive than ever, and within
a week, it was clear that Brock's speed was going to pay off. On June
23, a week after he joined the team, Brock gave the Houston Colts
an exhibition of what he might do, not just in stealing but in putting
pressure on an opposing team and forcing it to make mistakes. He
dragged a bunt in the first inning and beat it out. Then he broke for
second. John Bateman, the Houston catcher, tried to throw him out
but threw the ball away, and Brock went on to third. He scored
when Bill White singled, and White scored when Ken Boyer hit a
home run. Two innings later, Brock opened the inning with an op-
posite-field double to left. With White up and no one out, Brock
thought he had timed the pitcher, Dick Farrell, and broke for third.
He was sure he was safe, and the other Cardinals thought he was
safe, but the umpire, Jocko Conlan, called him out. (Part of the
problem, Brock said later, was that he was using his distinctive pop-
up slide, in which even as he slid in, he popped up to be ready to go
to another base in case there had been an error. The problem was
that the umpires were not used to it, and he was not getting the calls
on it; indeed, it appeared as if he were popping up into the tag.) It
had not, he said later, been a particularly smart play, stealing third
with no outs and the heart of the order coming up. But in the seventh inning, the Cardinals saw the perfect illustration of what his
speed could do, and how much pressure it placed on an opposing
team. Brock came up with two outs and Tim McCarver on third. He
hit a little chopper in front of the plate. It was Bateman's play, and

the catcher rushed the ball and rushed the throw, which went off the glove of Rusty Staub for an error. McCarver came in to score the winning run, to make it 5–4. It was just the kind of win Keane wanted: when the teams had been seemingly even, the winning run had come not off a home run or a double, but rather because of the pressure that Brock's great speed had put on the Colts.

After the game, Keane was euphoric. Brock had forced the key mistake, he told reporters, and had scared the Colts so much that they had unraveled. "With anyone else it's an easy play," he said. "But Brock hurried the defense and thus increased the chances for an error." Keane was sure now that the trade, only one week old, was a brilliant one, and that it had given the Cardinals the missing piece for the kind of team he wanted. Brock, he decided, was not only going to be a good player, he might well become a *great* player. Brock was only going to get better, he told the assembled sports-writers after the game. For the moment he was stealing through sheer speed, and he lacked technique. Look at Maury Wills of the Dodgers, then the leading base runner in baseball, Keane said. Wills had spent *nine years* in the minor leagues and had been able to work on his technique during that prolonged apprenticeship. By contrast, Brock spent only one year at the Class C level, and he had been given little time to work on how to measure and time both pitchers and catchers, how to maximize both his lead and his start. "Maury Wills is a good runner, but he can't run with this kid," Keane told the writers.

In Chicago Buck O'Neil heard about what his young protégé had done in his first week with the Cardinals and he felt at first a certain relief, and then a rush of pride. He was almost embarrassed to be that proud of the young man he had helped bring to the majors. The trade of Brock to the Cardinals, thought O'Neil's other protégé, Ernie Banks, had at first been a bitter disappointment to O'Neil. If Banks and Brock were not exactly the children of Buck O'Neil, they were, at the very least, athletic and spiritual extensions of him. O'Neil had seen in Brock not just a potentially great ballplayer but something more, an athlete so exceptional that he would bring to the world of white baseball skills and dazzling speed rarely seen there in the past. O'Neil had become very close to Brock, and for a brief time when O'Neil was one of the nine Cub coaches, they had even roomed together. O'Neil had loved teasing Brock, trying to get him to be a little looser. Brock would get ready to go into the batter's box and he would hear Buck's voice saying, "Good eyes, Lou . . . you got the good eyes . . . good eyes . . . now open them up so you can see . . ."

Buck O'Neil was a traveling man, fifty-two years old in 1964. His territory extended from Florida to Texas, and his job was to find every talented young black player in' that vast region. He had watched Lou Brock for three years before he had signed him off the campus of Southern University, in Baton Rouge. He had been far ahead of all the other scouts in picking up on Brock, and he was so much of a celebrity himself within the black athletic world that well into his pursuit of Brock, and absolutely sure of his prospect, O'Neil decided to spend less rather than more time on the Southern campus, for fear that the other scouts, most of them, of course, white, would become aware that Buck was up to something—and therefore the ante on Brock might be raised, and he might even lose him. O'Neil's life was a fascinating reflection of the black American baseball experience. He had had the misfortune, or at least the poor timing, to be born in 1911, during the era when the major leagues were closed to black players. O'Neil grew up in rural Florida near Sarasota, and in those days, the Yankees, the Giants, and the Athletics all trained there. As a boy he had been allowed to watch them practice. These were the Yankees of Ruth and Gehrig, the greatest baseball players of their time. He had watched them with awe, though their world was unattainable to him. He could watch and admire them, but he could not dream about being like them. But then an uncle, a railroad man, and therefore a truly cosmopolitan figure, came down from the North and told him that he had not seen the greatest players in the world; there were great teams made up exclusively of *Negro* baseball players, and *they* were the best players in the world. O'Neil argued with his uncle, but his uncle took him to Palm Beach, where two great black teams were training—

Rube Foster and his Chicago American Giants for the Breakers, and
C. I. Taylor and the Indianapolis ABCs for the Poinciana Royal.
The games were known as Maids Day Off Baseball, because they
were played on Thursdays and Sundays. That was when the maids
and other domestics, chauffeurs and cooks, who had been brought
down to Florida by their wealthy employers, had half-days off. The
spectators were a fascinating blend of the very, very rich and their
servants. It was a different kind of baseball than Buck O'Neil had
seen before. It was all about speed and aggressiveness. A man would
draw a walk, and he would steal second and then third. There was a
lot of use of the hit-and-run. There wasn't a slow man on the field,
he thought.

With that Buck O'Neil decided that he would be a baseball
player, even if it meant playing within a segregated world. At first he
spent several years in the rough and scruffy substratum of black
baseball that existed just beneath the Negro leagues, then he finally
made the famed Kansas City Monarchs, one of the great teams in
the leagues. He became manager of the Monarchs just as Jackie
Robinson was breaking into organized baseball. O'Neil had been an
eyewitness to the historic process in which the Monarchs had gone
from being a great baseball team that played within a segregated
world before segregated audiences, their players' exploits written
about only in Negro newspapers, to a team that had become a de
facto Triple A farm club for the all-white teams of major-league
baseball. By the early fifties, many of the older players were gone,
replaced by younger players, who were playing not for the thrill of
beating a rival black team before a crowd of black fans but rather for
the chance to play in the big leagues. That was brought home to
Buck O'Neil in 1953 when he watched the Chicago Cubs sign one
of the sweetest young players he had ever handled, a young shortstop named Ernie Banks. Banks had wondrously soft hands, extraordinarily quick wrists, a quick bat, the rare ability to drive a low pitch,
plus a wonderful disposition. He had come to the Monarchs in 1950,
on the recommendation of one of the greatest black players of all
time, Cool Papa Bell, who was running the Monarch's B team that
year. (After Jackie Robinson had played for the Monarchs and gone

to the Dodgers, Buck O'Neil's phone started ringing off the hook—every black high school, college, and recreational coach in the country was calling to tell him of some great player he had just seen. Because of that—because they were so overloaded with young talent—the Monarchs had created the B team.) When Cool called and said that he had just seen a great-looking young shortstop, Buck O'Neil immediately signed him, because Cool always knew what he was talking about. Banks had played for the Monarchs in 1950, and then gone into the service for two years. It was clear in 1953, when he returned, that his future was in the big leagues. The Cubs were pursuing him, along with the White Sox, the Reds, and, much less ardently, the Yankees. Near the end of that season O'Neil was told by Tom Baird, the Monarchs' owner, to bring Banks and an eighteen-year-old pitcher named Bill Dickey to Wrigley Field for a tryout. He arrived to find Wendell Smith, the prominent black sportswriter, and Wid Matthews, a Cubs executive, waiting for him and his young players. Matthews had told O'Neil that Baird was going to sell Banks to the Cubs that day, and that since Buck O'Neil had signed Banks to the original Monarchs contract, why didn't he participate in the signing?

O'Neil had said nothing beforehand to Ernie Banks about signing with the Cubs because he did not want to put any additional pressure on the talented young player. Of course, there had been rumors that scouts were interested in Banks. The day before, when the Monarchs happened to have finished their season, Banks and Dickey talked about what they were going to do in the off-season. Dickey thought he would go back to Shreveport, Louisiana, and work in a grocery store, and Banks thought he would go back to Dallas and work at the Adolphus Hotel as a busboy. Just then the phone rang and it was Buck O'Neil, who told them to meet him in the lobby the next morning at 7:00 A.M. He did not say why, nor did they question him. They simply showed up in the lobby at 6:45 so that they would be on time. O'Neil hailed a cab, and they got in. They did not ask where they were going, and Buck O'Neil did not tell them. Eventually they arrived at a ball park where a huge sign announced in giant red letters that it was Wrigley Field, the home of the Chicago Cubs. There they both signed contracts with the Cubs. Then Wid Matthews took O'Neil aside. "Buck," he said, "your kind of baseball is just about finished. Right now we're still getting these young players from you, but it won't be long before we go out and get them out of the high schools and colleges ourselves and put them right in our farm system. And it isn't going to be very long before Tom is going to sell the team, and then you might be out of a job. So why don't you go to work for us as a scout when that happens." So in a way it had been a double signing—Banks went to the Cubs as a shortstop and O'Neil agreed to sign on later as a scout; in 1955, Tom Baird sold the Monarchs, and the year after that, Buck O'Neil went to work for the Cubs for six thousand dollars a year plus expenses to scout young black ballplayers.

So O'Neil devoted the rest of his life to gaining for younger, more fortunate black men the opportunity that had been denied to him: to play major-league baseball. That did not bother him greatly, for Buck O'Neil was a man who felt he was rich within his own life. He knew that the world was changing and he believed the changes were, by and large, for the better. Ernie Banks thought O'Neil was not merely a great baseball man, but that he could have been successful at *anything* he undertook—medicine, law, or politics. Banks believed that O'Neil could spend an hour with you, and, thanks to a lifetime of his wide experience, he would not only know who you were at that moment but who you had been, what had formed you, and, even more important, who you were going to become. O'Neil was determined not to be bitter because he had played in a segregated age, for he knew that bitterness was a problem with some of the black players of his generation. Bitterness could easily lead to drinking, and then you would be undone by the forces arrayed against you—when they got inside you like that. He had decided long ago to live by an ethic of hard work and he taught his younger players to do the same. Things were going to change in America, he said, for someday soon, baseball, like many other aspects of American life, was going to open up. When that happened, you had to be ready, and the only way to be ready was to work harder than anyone else. According to Buck O'Neil's code, if you had a headache, you went to work and got rid of the headache through hard work; if you had personal problems, you went to work and tried to lift yourself above your problems, and in time the success you achieved would solve them. He believed that there was almost nothing in life that could not be solved by hard work.

Buck O'Neil did not think of himself as a victim. He had been a star player in black baseball, a celebrity of no small proportions in his own world. Even if white people had not known about it, and even if his name had not made the pages of the white newspapers, the people who counted in his world knew how good he was. For the men who played in the Negro leagues were true black celebrities, as important and prominent among their own people, though less well known to whites as the black entertainers of the period. There was a black world in Kansas City that white people knew almost nothing about. It was centered at Eighteenth and Vine, where the famed Streets Hotel, a grand hotel where all the best people stayed, was located. It was a beacon to the celebrities, politicians, and entertainers of black America who came through Kansas City in those days, and it was where the Monarch players who did not have their families with them stayed. On a Sunday morning Buck O'Neil would wake up in his room at the Streets and go down to have a late breakfast. There would be Duke Ellington or Count Basie or Louis Armstrong, and he might join them for breakfast. He could remember years later the Duke teasing him, "Hey, Foots, you going to go easy on our New York team today?" It was a curious, bittersweet life, he thought, to be denied so much and yet to have so much. The booking agents tended to bring in the great black musical artists to Kansas City when the Monarchs were at home, so that the black upper class would come in from all the surrounding towns, like Wichita and St. Joe, to make a weekend of it: baseball during the day and music at night at a place called the Subway, which did not open until midnight, when the rest of the city was closing down.

The black players had a strong loyalty to each other because they had all been subjected to the same discrimination and the same indignities. They even had their own slang, the language of Negro baseball, designed, at least in part, to give their world some distance and some privacy from that of the whites. There were words like *hog cutter* (to cut a hog meant to embarrass yourself publicly, to participate in conduct dramatically unbecoming, such as cursing in front of a woman, particularly the owner's or manager's wife); *mullion* (a player who always seemed to be taking out unattractive women); *monty* (an ugly-looking ballplayer); *drinker* (a fielder so good that he seemed to drink in every ball hit to him); and *foxy* (a sharp-looking woman). Buck O'Neil was too much the gentleman to cut very many hogs, but he was a drinker, for sure, an exceptional fielder who always seemed to inhale the balls hit to him.

When he was serving in the Pacific at the end of World War II, O'Neil had been thrilled to hear that the Dodgers had signed Jackie Robinson. O'Neil became a great Robinson fan, and he hated it, then and later on, when he heard people say that Jackie had not even been the best player in the Negro leagues, that there were others who were better. It did not matter whether Jackie was the best baseball player in the Negro leagues, O'Neil knew; what mattered was that he was the best *man* for the job. Jackie was younger, stronger, tougher, and better educated than the others, and even if some of the older players had been to college, the colleges had been such black colleges as Grambling, where young men were taught, among other things, to swallow their anger. Jackie had been to UCLA, where black people had a more modern outlook. Even in his brief time in the Negro leagues, he had been different and had impressed his teammates with his courage and independence; he had brought with him new and better ways, and he had represented the dawning of a new day. When Robinson joined the Monarchs, O'Neil believed, the Monarchs started learning from him very quickly. Previously, they had always traveled by bus, and as they swung through the South, there were certain places they always stopped for gas and food. There was a place in Muskogee, Oklahoma, where they had always gassed up, but where the owner never let them use the rest rooms. Robinson had not known that, so when the bus pulled in, ready to fill up its twin fifty-gallon tanks, he got out to go to the men's room. "Where you going, boy?" the owner said, and Robinson answered that he was going to the men's room. "No, you're not," the owner said. "You boys know that." Robinson never even hesitated. "Take the hose out of the tank!" he said immediately, and that was no idle threat, for one hundred gallons of gas was a big sale, a fair percentage of the amount of money the man might make on a given day. The man looked at Robinson and saw the anger and the strength in his face. He was not the first, and certainly not the last, white man to see that conviction, and he immediately backed down. "You boys can use the rest rooms," he said. "Just don't stay there too long."

It would have been nice, Buck O'Neil thought sometimes, if times had changed a little more quickly. He knew he was good enough to play in the majors with white boys because he had done it often enough barnstorming with their best players at the end of the regular season. He would have played first base, he thought, and would have hit around .290 to .300, with 20 home runs and 90 runs batted in. Not only a good big-league player, but a consistent one, right at the All-Star level. He saw himself honestly, he believed: as good a hitter as the famous Hank Greenberg, but certainly with less power, though just as certainly, a better fielder. He always had wonderful feet. But that was all in the past; it was important now to find young men who had talent, inner strength, and the conviction to excel in the majors, the ones who would not waste this most precious opportunity.

For a time he was the only full-time black scout working the region, the others being white scouts aided by black bird-dog scouts, both black and white. The white scouts who worked the area might, if they even bothered to come over to Southern, stay two or three hours, then head over to LSU, and from there go to New Orleans, where they were more comfortable. If O'Neil had always felt somewhat uncomfortable in a world that was largely white, now the white scouts were having to work in a world where they were the outsiders, a world that was predominantly black. Buck O'Neil had his own itinerary: he would start in Florida when it was still cold and then move north and west as the weather changed. He would, more often than not, stay at the home of the president of the university or the school's baseball coach or its athletic director. As a celebrity in the black athletic world, he was almost never allowed to stay at a hotel, or to eat in a restaurant. He was *always* in someone's home, the food was better, and he would learn a good deal more. Often he was asked to give a motivational speech to the school's baseball team and sometimes to the other teams. If, for the first forty-five years of his life, he had lived in a world where white people had always had all the advantages, he was astonished now to find that he had the inside track.

In the spring of 1958, two years after O'Neil joined the Cubs, he arrived in Baton Rouge and saw a young freshman playing baseball for Southern named Lou Brock. No one had ever mentioned the name before, and there had been no hint that Southern had a hot young prospect, for in fact Brock was not a hot young prospect—he was a green kid out of a backwoods Louisiana high school. Brock had been born in El Dorado, Arkansas (Arkansas, Brock liked to say later, billed itself in those days as the land of opportunity, and at the very first opportunity he had gotten the hell out of there). The child of sharecroppers, he never knew his father. His mother moved to Louisiana, and as a child he watched the annual exploitation of his family by the plantation owners: year after year, despite their hard physical labor in the cotton fields, and whether the crop was excellent or terrible, his family always seemed to end up owing the plantation owner three hundred dollars. Because of that, when he was lucky enough to get a scholarship to Southern, Brock chose math as his major so that he would never be duped in the future. It seemed to him the most basic of subjects, and if he mastered it, he at least could stop the cheating each year when his people came to settle up their bills. He came to Southern not on an athletic scholarship but on an academic scholarship, and in order to stay in school, he held a number of term-time jobs. He went out for baseball, he later said, not so much to be a baseball star, but simply to stay in school, and an athletic scholarship made that a great deal easier. Brock also wanted an athletic scholarship for another reason: without one, he wasn't a real athlete in his own eyes and in those of others.

If at first he did not have the reputation as an athlete, he always had speed. Everyone at Southern seemed to know about how fast he was except Brock himself. Back where he came from in rural Louisiana, he thought, he was the slow one, and everyone else was faster. In Collinston, everyone could *run*. But at Southern he soon found himself at the center of a debate over who was the fastest person around. Some of the jocks argued for a young man named Harry Keyes, who was the conference sprint champion, but some argued for this young guy named Brock, who was not even a real jock. They woke him up around midnight and told him that he had to come down to the football field and race against Keyes. "If I do it," Brock asked, still half asleep, "will you guys let me go back to sleep?" They said yes, and so he went over to the football field, where all the lights had been turned on, raced against Keyes, and smoked him.

Word of his speed got around, and there was even some talk about him trying out for football. While he was still at Southern one of the baseball coaches said that football might now be the sport for young black athletes, even more so than baseball, because the pro receivers had to be fast, and more and more of them, therefore, would be black: this meant that the players who could catch the fastest runners in the world, the defensive players, would also be black. Brock was given a quick inspection by one of the football coaches, who asked him to do one of the most basic drills in the football manual, a kick step. "What's a kick step?" asked Brock. "Go back to baseball," said the coach. Baseball would have to be his sport. He loved it; he had played it as a boy and in high school. He sometimes thought that the sound of the bat hitting the ball was the most beautiful sound he had ever heard. He was drawn to the game by its pace, at once languid and then fast. When he tried out for the team, he made it as a walk-on athlete. How good a player he was no one knew. The first thing Buck O'Neil saw was Brock's speed, the kind of blinding speed he had not seen in a long time. O'Neil thought immediately of Cool Papa Bell, his old friend and teammate, who was by consensus the fastest man in a world populated by very fast players. Of Cool's legendary speed, his roommate Satchel Paige once said that Cool was so fast, he could turn off the light and be in bed before the light was out.

Cool had been a little bit taller and a little slimmer than Brock, but this young man was already more powerfully built than Cool, with big shoulders and a tiny waist. A body built for power and speed, O'Neil thought. Even in the baggy old uniforms that Southern wore, you could tell he was strong and going to become even stronger. Buck O'Neil sensed that he had a great prospect, and from then on he watched Brock carefully as his talent began to surface. O'Neil also noticed the hunger in Brock. Whenever O'Neil was around Southern, talking with either Bob Lee or Emory Hines, the baseball coaches, somehow Lou Brock was always there too, a little shy, not unlike the young Ernie Banks when he joined the Monarchs. Banks had been full of questions, wanting to know everything about all the great black ballplayers of the past: Buck, tell me about Josh Gibson, Ernie would ask. Banks had always wanted to get better, and he would demand that O'Neil hit fifty grounders to the right of him and fifty to the left of him, and when that was done, he would demand that O'Neil hit more. "You got a few more in you, Skip?" Banks would ask. "I'm going to wear your hands out." In a way, Banks had been a revelation. He was thinking not about being the best there was in the Negro leagues, he was thinking about playing in the major leagues and being the best *there*. Brock had that same drive, O'Neil soon decided.

Brock had not played particularly well in his freshman year—he hit only .140 and struck out frequently—but then he began to blossom in his sophomore year, when he hit .545 with 13 home runs in 27 games. Suddenly other scouts began to materialize. Southern became the first black school to win the NAIA title, and Brock became a member of the American baseball team at the Pan Am games in 1959. The Pan Am games became his first big showcase, and there was no way that O'Neil could hide him now, but he knew he had the inside track, for he had been there from the start. Besides, Brock seemed in no rush to sign. He would sign with a National League team, O'Neil was sure, for the scouts from each league were using the racial makeup of the other to their advantage: the National League scouts were pushing the more integrated quality of their league to young black prospects, while the American League scouts were quietly emphasizing to white prospects from the South that if they signed with an American League team, they would play with fewer blacks. O'Neil knew that little game well—he had played it himself whenever there was a young talented black prospect he was interested in.

The real move on Brock came after his junior year, when he was finally eligible to sign. That year had not gone as well as his sophomore year. It had been cold and rainy much of the time, and a number of Southern games had been canceled. The scouts were quick to move on to other cities. It was not a good season in which to be showcased, though he hit well over .300. There was still interest in him, though, most of it from the two Chicago teams, the White Sox and the Cubs, although, ironically, the Cardinals were interested too. A Cardinal scout named Charley Frey scouted him with unusual eagerness, and arranged, Brock believed, for him to come to St. Louis for a tryout. Brock, with almost no money to his name, got on a bus from Baton Rouge to St. Louis, thinking he had an appointment for a Cardinal tryout arranged and chaperoned by Frey. He paid for the ticket himself and had only ten dollars left in his pocket. When he got to St. Louis, there was neither a tryout nor Charley Frey. Frey turned out to have gotten his wires crossed, and was off in the state of Washington signing a pitcher named Ray Washburn. Brock found himself almost broke and friendless in St. Louis. It was a low point in his life. He felt terribly foolish and alone. But he still had the ten dollars in his pocket and one friend from back home in Chicago named Noah Pates, with whom he might stay. With the last of his money spent on the ticket to Chicago, Lou Brock boarded a bus and headed there. He stayed with Pates and worked washing walls and floors at the local YMCA while trying to get a big-league tryout. At least, he thought, he wasn't quite as green as he had been a year earlier, when he had been invited to join the Pan Am team and had taken his first airplane flight, flying first class. When they had brought him the menu for lunch and asked him which selection he preferred, he had been terrified. There was no price attached to the menu, and he assumed it cost a huge sum, and with only three dollars in his pocket, he told the stewardess that no, he would skip the meal. "I never eat on planes," he told her, and he arrived in Chicago absolutely starved and determined not to look like some hick in the big city. So, during the entire Pan Am games, whenever he was unsure how to behave, he would say, "Oh, hell, no, we didn't do it that way at Southern." Just like never eating on an airplane.

He got one tryout from the White Sox, but their interest seemed to have waned. The Cubs, well primed by O'Neil, were more serious. At the first workout, a player named Eddie Bouchee, the Cubs' first baseman, took pity on Brock, so young and scared, and noticed that he was wearing what was quite possibly the shabbiest pair of spikes in baseball history. "Hey, kid, this is the big leagues, and to hit like a big leaguer, you want to feel like a big leaguer," Bouchee said and handed him a pair of his own shoes. The only problem was that Bouchee wore a size nine and Brock a size ten, so Brock's feet were badly cramped during the entire workout. The Cubs were impressed with his play, nevertheless, and they scheduled him for a second workout. In the meantime, Brock went out and, with the help of Pates, bought a pair of decent spikes that actually fit. The next workout went very well. Rarely had he seen the ball so clearly and hit it so hard. The Phillies were in town that day, and Gene Mauch apparently told one of the Cub coaches, "I don't know what you guys are going to do, but that kid is not going to get out of here unsigned. Either you do it or we do it."

Buck O'Neil was still sure he had the inside track on Brock, for early on he had gotten a promise from him that would allow O'Neil and the Cubs to make the last offer in a bidding war. By 1960 he was absolutely sure of Brock's ability. Brock did favor the Cubs because of O'Neil: of all the scouts, O'Neil was the one who hung around after a game, and would take him out for dinner, and would talk to him as a man—about what life in the big leagues was going to be like and how he was supposed to dress, and act. Brock thought that Buck O'Neil was the most elegant and graceful man he had ever met; he seemed to be the embodiment not only of the real world but of the rarest kind of success achieved by a black man. That summer O'Neil was on the road in Memphis when he got a call from John Holland, the Cubs' general manager, saying that Brock was up in Chicago having a tryout with the White Sox and was going to have one with the Cubs as well. O'Neil flew there immediately. After his second Cub tryout, Brock signed for $12,000 with the Chicago Cubs. The Cubs gave him a check for $5,000, the first installment on his bonus, and he, a young man without a bank account, found a place to cash it in downtown Chicago and was handed back $5,000 in small bills, which he stuffed into his pants pockets as he headed for the Greyhound Station to go back to Baton Rouge.

The first stop in his pro career was in Class C ball in St. Cloud, Minnesota, and he did well. He thought he should be at a higher level, because he had finished his junior year in college, and most of his teammates seemed to be eighteen-year-old boys just out of high school, away from home for the first time, and desperately homesick. He burned up the league, and for a long time that season he even hoped to hit over .400 and perhaps record the highest batting average in the minor leagues. But no matter how well he hit, there was always this one other player who managed to stay a few points ahead of him, whom he could never catch, and about whom he often wondered. A few years later he was at spring training, and the Cubs were supposed to play the Twins, when someone called him over and said, "Lou Brock, I'd like you to meet Tony Oliva." "How do you spell Oliva?" he asked the slim young man in front of him, who was to win three American League batting titles. Then Brock said, "I'm glad to finally meet you, Tony. I've thought about you a lot in the past."

Because he did so well in his one season in the minor leagues, the Cubs brought him up at the end of 1961. He was in the outfield playing against the Cardinals when Stan Musial came to bat. With one out, Musial hit a rocket to right-center. Brock raced for the ball and made a great catch, but then he held on to the ball. Richie Ashburn came over from center, and Brock was still holding the ball. "Kid, throw it back," Ashburn said. But Brock continued to hold the ball, as if it were some kind of souvenir, which for him it was, for he had grown up listening to the exploits of Stan Musial. "Kid," said Ashburn, "sooner or later, you've got to throw it back." So that was it, he was in the big leagues, and the next season, when the Cubs played against Milwaukee, Warren Spahn hit him with a pitch, and as he ran down the first base line to take his base, he thought, *I've been hit by the great Warren Spahn*, for he believed it a point of honor that Warren Spahn had wanted to take him out. Then he heard Spahn's voice yelling, "Fall down, fall down . . . Goddammit, fall down so it will look like I'm throwing hard."

12

It was not a historic moment. The hitter came up in the fourth inning and drove the ball off Bill Monbouquette into the right-field stands for the first run of the game that the Yankees won. It was his tenth home run of the season, in the fiftieth game of the season, and it was also his third home run in three games in Boston. For many hitters, that might have been encouraging, but for Roger Maris, who had once broken Babe Ruth's record for home runs in one season, it seemed to show only how much his power had declined in the three years since he and Mantle had chased Ruth's record.

The year of the record was hard enough, but the year after it was worse; Maris found that, having pursued Ruth, he was now pursued himself by a press corps he did not want to talk to and by adoring fans whose adoration he did not seek. He responded by retreating deep into his shell, increasingly unhappy with how he was perceived by the fans, the writers, and even his employers. He became convinced that no matter what he said or did, he couldn't win: if he played poorly the fans would get on him for failing, but if he played well they would criticize his presumption in playing well.

From the start he saw New York City as an alien and inhospitable place. He had been upset by the news of the trade that had brought him from Kansas City to New York. "I'm not all that happy about coming to New York," he told the New York writers on his arrival for his first spring training as a Yankee in 1960. "I liked Kansas City.

I expected to play out my career there." On his arrival in New York as a Yankee he was met at La Guardia Airport by a man named Big Julie Isaacson, a wheeler-dealer who seemed to be right out of the cast of *Guys and Dolls*. Isaacson had been assigned by their mutual friend, Irv Noren, by then playing in the National League, to pick up Maris and help him find a place to live. Big Julie had been appalled by Maris's clothes. There he was, this newest Yankee, without a sports jacket, and wearing a sweater, a polo shirt, and what appeared to Isaacson as a pair of inexpensive Pat Boone white bucks. "Roger," Isaacson tried to explain, "the Yankees don't dress like that. They wear jackets and shirts and ties. You've got to change the clothes." "If they don't like the way I dress they can send me back to Kansas City," Maris said. "At least," Isaacson suggested, "get rid of the Pat Boone shoes." The next day Isaacson picked up Maris at his hotel to see if they could find a place for him to live, and Isaacson continued his assault on Maris's wardrobe. First and foremost the shoes had to go, he said. "Roger, you just can't dress like that in this city—it's too hick." "Where's the nearest Thom McAn store?" Maris replied. "Why?" Isaacson asked. "Because these are the only pair I have and I want to buy another pair, and Thom McAn is the only place that carries them." So off they went to Thom McAn, and Maris bought *two* pairs. That, Julie Isaacson decided years later, was the definitive Roger Maris story. The moral of it could have become his epithet: Don't tell me what I have to do, don't lean on me.

Life is filled with self-fulfilling prophecies, and, fittingly enough, the longer Maris played in New York, the less he liked it. He was a small-town boy raised in Fargo, North Dakota, and he remained a small-town boy the rest of his life. He did not lightly accommodate to anything that was different, nor was he ever anxious to change his ways. He was what he was, and the world of New York owners, New York sportswriters, New York fans, and even New York baseball players would have to take him for that or find someone else. The more he was pressured to change, the more he resented that very pressure, and the less flexible he became. Confronted with any kind of resistance, he tended to bristle and pull in. He was a player, said one teammate who never heard the cheers but always remembered the boos. Late into his tour in New York, he bought a memento from a novelty store which he placed on the stool by his locker: it was a plastic hand with the middle finger extended upward into the air.

It was part of the irony of Maris's celebrated but painful career in the big city that he was made to order for Yankee Stadium and its short right-field fence. He was a great pull hitter—in fact, Mike Shannon thought that he never saw a hitter who was as good at pulling an outside pitch as Roger Maris. A lot of hitters, Shannon thought, could pull the inside pitch, but pulling a ball outside was much harder; it demanded a very good eye and a very, very quick bat and no wasted motion in the swing. Maris was not a particularly big man at six feet tall and 190 pounds, but he was a superb all-around athlete and he had a short, sweet swing. Few baseball players channeled their power and muscle through their bodies as successfully as Roger Maris did. To this day the photos of him swinging at a ball are unusually striking, because his entire body is fused so perfectly: shoulders, arms, and legs, leveraged as one piece, nothing wasted. Because his swing was shorter and more compact than Mantle's, his home runs were not as majestic; instead of being carried ever higher and higher, going toward the third tier, they were line shots that had extra distance but not that much loft to them. The difference in their swings can be measured by their strikeouts in 1961: in that season Maris came up 590 times, hit 61 home runs, and struck out only 67 times, whereas Mantle came up 514 times, hit 54 home runs, and, with that huge swing, which surrendered contact for power, struck out *112* times.

Maris, who had thought for a time of playing college football, was fast and had an exceptionally strong and accurate arm. Baseball professionals in those days rated him as almost the equal of Al Kaline, then considered the best defensive right fielder in the league. The threat his arm posed to enemy base runners was considerable, and it had kept Matty Alou on third in the crucial play of the 1962 World Series. Maris also ran the bases exceptionally well; in 1961, even though he was pursuing Ruth's record, he still played hard on defense and went into second base hard, risking personal injury for the good of the team.

He was quiet and reserved, far more introverted than Mantle, with whom he was invariably compared. His had not been an easy childhood; his father had worked for the railroad for small pay and was a hard and unsparing man. Boyhood friends thought Maris's childhood had never been easy, and there was a time when he had even lived with another family for part of a year. He had none of Mantle's exuberance, gregariousness, or, for that matter, his mood swings. In the locker room, he was never the show that Mantle was. Mantle, for all his reservations about the press, his moodiness and his modesty, was always aware of his role in baseball history as the star of the Yankees. Even if on occasion he felt burdened by it, he quite liked being on center stage at Yankee Stadium, the heir to the tradition of Ruth and Gehrig and DiMaggio, with all the challenge and all the glory implicit in that role. Mantle was, thought Jim Bouton, like a long-running Broadway show all his own—funny and tragic, difficult and engaging, but always well acted. It was a rare performance by a player who always understood the special glory of being the star. If Mantle had any regrets about his role, they were momentary, and in the end the glory far outweighed the burden.

Maris was completely different. He liked to play baseball, and he was good at it, but he pulled back from the theatrics associated with the game. Most ballplayers, thought Maury Allen, a talented sportswriter who covered Maris in those years and knew him exceptionally well, liked to *say* that they did not care about getting their names in the papers or their faces on television; but Roger Maris, more than any other player Allen knew, truly felt that way. He liked playing the game, but everything else was extraneous. He disliked dealing with the media—not necessarily the media people themselves but the daily byplay. "I'm not a good talker, get someone else," he would usually say when reporters tried to grab him for interviews. He was a physical man, not a verbal one: he was skilled in the use of his body, not in the use of words. Social encounters were difficult for him and left him distinctly uncomfortable. In that 1961 season, when he hit his twenty-seventh home run and seemed to be on a record pace, a reporter asked him the big question for the first time: did he think he had a chance to break Ruth's record. His answer was pure Maris: "How the fuck do I know?"

Since he was a man who did his job, he understood to some degree that the beat reporters had their jobs to do as well, and he would try to be reasonably accommodating with them. He was better with reporters he knew than with strangers, and he had a reputation with the Yankee beat reporters as being unusually fair, straight, and consistent in his moods. But his answers were always as short as he could make them. He would talk about what pitch he had hit and how he had played a hitter, but he never allowed the writers to get inside his mind or his personality. When they tried to do that, and in 1961 they tried little else, a curtain came down immediately. There was a certain edginess and defensiveness about Maris. He was quick to find and, on occasion, to hold resentments, and even those men who were fond of him were aware that if, for some reason, Maris felt he had been let down, he never forgave it. In his first two years on the Yankees, most of the reporters, especially some of the younger ones, quite liked him. They felt themselves outsiders in the world of the Yankees, and, thanks to his competition with Mickey Mantle, Maris was always going to be cast by the fans and even his teammates as an outsider as well. There was to him, thought the writer Larry Merchant, who quite liked him, a wonderful kind of indigenous American populist sourness, handed down in a family that had never known success or wealth, and where there was an innate conviction that those who had wealth and power always screwed those who did not. Maris reminded Merchant very much of men he had met in the army, constantly griping, constantly irritable, and yet surprisingly tough and good at everything to which they were assigned. In 1961, Whitey Ford had joked that he was going to form a cabinet just like Jack Kennedy's, except he was going to assign his ballplayers to the cabinet positions. Maris's job, he noted, was going to be Secretary of Grievances.

Maris gave his trust slowly and reluctantly. He was much better in one-on-one interviews than he was when a group gathered around his locker, for then he was sure reporters he did not know would quote something out of context, or in some way cause him harm. "Shit-stirrers," he and some of the other players called such reporters, that is, men who were out to cause trouble by exaggerating some small tension or problem in their articles. What an irony, then, that Roger Maris involuntarily became one of the first modern athletes caught in the glare of the new media society. As the power of television grew in the late fifties and early sixties, those who were propelled forward in sports and other walks of life began to find themselves under a new, relentless scrutiny. In many cases they loved the fame, in some cases they were indifferent to it, and in some cases, such as that of Roger Maris, they truly hated it. In the past, sports had been sports, and while it is true that it was also a form of entertainment, the athletes themselves, with few exceptions, were first and foremost athletes, not entertainers, and by and large that was the way they thought of themselves. They were supposed to go out there, play hard, and win, and if they did, that was enough. But with the coming of television, things began to change: the *show* was now as important as the event—the athlete was supposed to be not just someone who did his job but someone who was a star as well.

Maris, a man of old-fashioned values and loyalties, an honorable man who tried to live within his own code, was completely unprepared for this new definition of the athlete. Unfortunately, his assault upon Ruth's record was probably the first great sustained sports story in the age of modern media. At first print reporters seized on it, which soon whetted an appetite for television coverage, and as television coverage followed the chase with an ever more watchful eye, that inspired even greater print coverage. In addition, it had continuity, something the media loved, and became, day after day, a great running story. As the interest in him grew, he encountered a changing definition of what his fellow Americans wanted to know about him. They did not, it now appeared, care whether or not he had hit an inside curveball or a low fastball; instead, they wanted to know what he thought and what he felt about a vast number of things, including a good many about which he had no thoughts or feelings at all. Millions of Americans wanted to know what Roger Maris was really like, and they wanted to know every day for more than two months. It was a sea change in the nature of media, and it foretold the coming of a media-obsessed society, a society that would culminate almost three decades later when *People* magazine sold more advertising than its older and more traditional sibling, *Time* magazine.

Perhaps even three years earlier, he might have chased Ruth's record with far less commotion, and he would have been covered under the old rules, the simpler rules of print. But in 1961, Americans were watching live televised press conferences of their president, dazzling performances really, and they watched Alan Shepard, the first astronaut, lift off live from Cape Canaveral. In the next year the networks, responding to better and better technology and a great hunger for news, went from fifteen-minute news shows to half-hour ones. For John Kennedy the coming of television was a great boon, and it had greatly aided his campaign; when Kennedy had debated his opponent, live, on television the year before—the first time that had ever been done—it had greatly enhanced his candidacy. In addition, it made him a star. The American people wanted to know not just about his policies, but about his family, and what he ate, and what he wore, and what he read. Kennedy was perfectly comfortable with this new entertainment-driven definition of politics, certain always that he could use it to his advantage. At about the same time, a brilliant young heavyweight boxer named Cassius Clay understood intuitively that he was as much star and entertainer as boxer, and that he was engaged in theater of a high order. He gloried in his new role and orchestrated the show as no athlete had ever done before him. His weigh-ins became as exciting as some of his fights, and he began to write poems in which he predicted when his opponent would fall.

What Clay and soon Joe Namath pursued with zest and brilliance, Roger Maris pulled back from with fear and loathing. He was being pulled before a spotlight he never sought, the likes of which had never been turned on a baseball player before. It permitted others, strangers, to examine him in a way he did not want to be examined. So it was that he faced a terrible dilemma in that fateful season, for every time he hit a home run, and every time he came a little closer to breaking Ruth's record, he lost just a little more of his most precious commodity, his privacy. As he neared the record, the crowd of reporters grew larger, and the questions became more and more personal. "Do you play around on the road?" a reporter from *Time* magazine asked. "I'm a married man," Maris answered. "I'm a married man, too," said the reporter, "but I play around on the road." Worse, there were to be heroes and villains in this, as in every great story, and Maris, somewhat to his surprise (for he was only doing what he was paid to do), became a villain. Not everyone, it turned out, wanted Babe Ruth's record broken, especially older fans. Many younger fans, on the other hand, were quite willing to see it fall, but only if it fell to Mantle, whose team this rightfully was.

In 1960, Maris had played in the Stadium regularly for the first time, and he had hit 25 home runs in less than half a season; at one point he was slightly ahead of Ruth. For the first time there had been mention of his name in connection with the Ruth record. Even though he injured himself, he had still ended up with 39 home runs in only 136 games and had been the Most Valuable Player in the American League. Mantle had led the league with 40 home runs in 153 games, and 28 more at bats. Maris later told his friend Mike Shannon that the ambition to beat Mantle in 1961 had been a calculated affair. He had been goaded into it, he told Shannon, by the fans. In 1960, they had begun to cheer Mantle and boo him, and he decided quietly to get even by beating Mantle out for the club home-run championship. If they wanted to boo, he would give them something to boo about. He set out to lead the club, an amused Shannon said years later, as much as anything else, out of spite. This was a rare admission by Maris, for again and again, both during and after that season, when the subject of the home-run derby came up and reporters asked about the apparent competition with Mantle, Maris would shrug it off and say that he was just having a good season. In truth, he thought he could do it because of the short right-field porch, which was a target for him far more often than it was for Mantle. So it was that both of them had gone at the home-run title with a vengeance that season. If Mickey was going to hit two, Maris told Shannon, then he was damn well going to hit two as well. As far as he was concerned, it was all about home runs, and his batting average (for he was a .260 to .280 hitter in those days) did not matter. That offended some purists, who favored Mantle, in part, because he was a .300 hitter as well. Theirs was an unspoken competition, for Mantle, proud and every bit as competitive, understood the game from the start. For Maris, it was a year in which everything went right for him on the field. He seemed to be in a groove for most of the season, he saw the ball exceptionally well, and it just seemed to jump off his bat that year. His health was good for the entire season, which was rare for him. Because Mantle was hitting behind him, Maris knew he was likely to see a lot of good pitches, and it became clear early in the season that he had a genuine shot at the Ruth record.

A great sports team is always a surprisingly delicate mechanism, because it includes all kinds of egocentric, highly motivated people with a common objective: to win. Yet, at the same time, great teams demand enough talented players with similar goals and drives whose egos may very easily clash. On a great team such tensions are resolved because the idea of winning is so powerful. But they remain just beneath a thin veneer of unity, and they often surface when the idea of winning is not so powerful. With the Yankees in 1961, those tensions abounded even though both Mantle and Maris handled their personal rivalry with exceptional maturity. This was Mickey Mantle's team, and Roger Maris never had any illusions about that. Mantle was a far greater player certainly than Maris, who saw himself quite realistically, and knew his own strengths and limitations better than most of his critics did. The two players were friends, it was true, and for a few months that season they even roomed together, along with Bob Cerv, who was a close friend of Maris's. But it was, in the words of Julie Isaacson, a cool friendship, one of men who at once liked each other but were not close, and the fierce, unspoken competitiveness hovered always. There was no animosity, though, and no hard words. Later, when sportswriters claimed there was a considerable bitterness between them, they were wrong. The bitterness was between Maris and the fans, and subsequently the

Yankee management. Though it should have been the easiest thing in the world to root for both men, that was not what happened. Everyone, it seemed, had to take sides that year, and almost everyone, of course, favored Mantle. Maris was made to feel the interloper, even by the Yankee organization. The problem, as Julie Isaacson later said, was that the wrong guy had broken the record.

Maris lacked the skill and the desire to win the fans over. His greatest sin, as far as the media contingent covering him was concerned, was that he not only was boring, he liked being boring. Worse, the larger the media contingent grew, the more determined he became to seem, if anything, even more boring than he really was. He was a man absolutely without pretense, and he wore no face save his own. He was not graceful or subtle. He was almost always blunt, sometimes unspeakably so. Late in the assault Al Kaline, the Detroit right fielder, retrieved a ball that Maris hit off Frank Lary for home run number fifty-seven—it had bounced back on the field and Kaline tossed it into the Yankee dugout as a souvenir for Maris. After the game, one of the Detroit writers suggested to Maris that what Kaline had done had been a very nice thing, and Maris, blunt as ever, curiously obtuse about how his words would later appear to readers, said no, it was something that anyone would have done, and that he would have done the same thing for Kaline. To the New York beat writers, that was simply Maris being Maris, but the Detroit writers were offended.

At the end of the season, when Maris wrote his authorized account of the home-run chase, he chose for his co-author Jim Ogle of the *Newark Star Ledger*, one of the least known beat reporters, but a true Yankee loyalist. He did this because he liked and trusted Ogle. The result was exactly the kind of book Maris wanted, almost completely devoid of color and humanity; it was written statistically, home run by home run, as if by an accountant. Maris could never summon up the heroic words and images to go with his heroic deeds. Writers described him in desperation as a meat-and-potatoes kind of guy who got along well with his teammates and wanted his team to win. So the reporters would gather around his locker and he would say that he had hit a low inside fastball or a hanging curve, or that he was just doing his job as best he could, or that he liked Mickey and they were good friends, or that he revered Babe Ruth and knew he was not as good a player as Ruth. (When he did that people wrote in complaining, Who was Maris to compare himself with Ruth?)

As the pressure closed in on him, he became more and more superstitious. Early in the season he had Julie Isaacson drive out to Queens to pick him up, and they went into Manhattan and ate a late breakfast at the Stage Deli, a famed New York Jewish deli in the theater district. Maris, who loved eggs and baloney, forced Big Julie Isaacson to have eggs with chopped-up baloney in it. "Roger, Jewish guys don't eat baloney and eggs," Isaacson protested, but Maris insisted that Isaacson eat his eggs in what he claimed was Fargo style. Isaacson, knowing how stubborn Maris could be, surrendered and ate his eggs with baloney. That day Maris hit two home runs. Clearly the eggs and baloney were an omen, and so from then on, they had to go to the Stage every day when the Yanks were home, and they had to have the same table, and the same waitress, and Big Julie had to eat his eggs with baloney.

As he got closer to the record, the reporters Maris knew and trusted became a minority, greatly outnumbered by others from publications he had never heard of, and who clearly had no interest in baseball. The more he became the story, the warier he became. The Yankees, completely unprepared for the media circus, gave him no help, offered him no protection, and set no guidelines. They let him, stubborn, suspicious and without guile, hang out there alone, utterly ill prepared for this ordeal; they never gave him a press officer to serve as a buffer between him and the media, or even set certain times when he would deal with the reporters, so that it would not be a constant burden. They did not filter requests, or tell him whom he might trust and whom he might not or which requests were legitimate and which were trivial.

Under all this pressure, Maris grew more and more irritable. He found that he could go nowhere without a phalanx of journalists. When, late in the season, after he had hit more than fifty home runs, a reporter asked him about the record, he answered, "What record?

Am I close to it? I don't want to talk about it. Do you want me to concede defeat? If you do, I'll concede, all right?" But he tried all season to be a good teammate. On days when he did nothing, and when Elston Howard or another player won the game for the Yankees, the crowd of reporters would swarm around his locker anyway, and he would try to guide them to Howard's locker instead. "Talk to Ellie," he would say. "He won the game for us." No one, of course, moved toward Howard's locker. It got worse and worse: Maris's hair began to fall out because of nerves, and he developed a number of rashes. His wife came to visit him in New York, looked at his hair, and told him he looked like a molting bird near the end of the season. The chase was made more difficult because the commissioner, a former Ruth ghostwriter, Ford Frick, noted that Ruth had set his record in a season of 154 games. Therefore, there should be an asterisk beside Maris's name, Frick suggested. In effect, that left him with two deadlines: he could break the record within 154 games and enter the record book clean and unsoiled, or he could do it in 162 games and enter the book with an asterisk.

When he finally broke the record, it was extraordinary; hitting sixty-one home runs was a remarkable accomplishment under the best of circumstances, and Maris had done it under the worst of them. Ruth had never dealt with the comparable pressure. After the last game, when he had hit number sixty-one off Tracy Stallard, a radio reporter asked him if he had thought of Mickey Mantle while rounding the bases during his home-run trot. That struck him as the weirdest question of the day. That night he went to dinner in the city with a few friends, and when he saw a nearby Catholic church he left the dinner party to go over and pray. The priest noticed him in the back of the church, and announced to the other parishioners that Roger Maris was among them. Even here there was no moment of privacy, and he quickly fled the church.

As the Yankees did nothing to protect him during the assault, they did nothing to reward him after it was all over. "You know what I got from Topping for hitting those sixty-one homers that year?" Maris said to Maury Allen years later. "Nothing. Not a cent. Not a gift. Nothing. I don't know what the Yankees drew [they had their largest attendance in ten years], but they gave me nothing." He was bitter about that. He felt that, at the very least, he should have gotten a one-shot bonus of $50,000. When it came to contract time there was the usual squabble. Maris, who had made $37,500 the year before, wanted to double his salary to $75,000. The first contract from the club called for a salary of $50,000. Maris was enraged. The Yankees did not like the idea of doubling a salary, no matter how good a year a player had enjoyed: it was a dangerous precedent, but they were also nervous about being in an ugly negotiating war with a player who had just broken Ruth's record. That gave Maris rare leverage in his contract talks. After some haggling, management came in at $72,500. But all in all the Yankee management had not behaved well; financially and emotionally it had not been generous and a huge wound had been left at the end of the season. In the following years, when he did not play at that level again, in part because he was often injured, in part because it had been a special season, one not easily recaptured, he was berated for not being Ruth or Mantle.

Maris's frustration with the Yankee organization continued to grow. He felt they had signaled to him in a variety of ways that he was not a true Yankee, not a member of the inner group, and he resented that. He felt club officials minimized his injuries, and sometimes did not even seem to believe he was hurt. A year after the home-run assault Jake Gibbs, the young catcher, came up to join the team, and was with Maris on a swing through Boston. Gibbs was stunned to hear Maris suddenly utter a prolonged and bigger diatribe against the club, its medical practices, and its lack of trust in its players. Maris had been hurting and it was clear that management did not believe him, and suddenly it all poured out, etched in bitterness: "Jake, the next time I'm hurt, I hope the bone comes right through the skin and shows and there's lots of blood so they'll finally believe me. I'm so damn tired of being hurt and them thinking I'm faking it."

The problem with the media, Maris said years later, was not in 1961 but in 1962. It would have been easier for him, given his nature and his love of privacy, if he had come close and just missed it. Then he would have been cast as an ordinary man who had come close in one magical summer to living the great baseball dream. In that case he would have been seen as a sympathetic figure who had just fallen short of an elusive goal. Instead, he was cast as an ordinary player who had the temerity to break a record of which he was not worthy. There was nowhere to go but down. The sports world was primed for his failure, that is, for him to fall short of that great season, and to prove himself unworthy of his extraordinary accomplishment. The spotlight followed him relentlessly. If, during the off-season, he left a sports dinner a little early to catch the last flight out to the next night's dinner, that was news. If he did not handle an autograph session with young boys well, that was news. In spring training there was an incident when he was asked to pose with Rogers Hornsby, a great hitter but a notoriously churlish man from another age, who had frequently demeaned Maris during his home-run chase. Each man thought the other should come over to pose, and in the end, the picture was never taken. There were other incidents: a column by Oscar Fraley belittling Maris (because Maris had been unwilling to give his side of the Hornsby story), and then one by the very influential Jimmy Cannon, ripping Maris for having missed an appointment with him. Cannon had been very close to DiMaggio and was wary of Maris anyway, and his column widely influenced other writers in the press corps, not only in New York. Its ripple effect was considerable, and in other cities that the Yankees visited, Maris now found that sportswriters were prepared to judge him unsympathetically. His relations with the media, always fragile, grew bitter.

It was hard to believe in 1964, as the Yankees struggled to stay near the top of the American League, with Mantle, Maris, and Ford all coping with various injuries, that only three years earlier, the Yankees had been the mightiest team in baseball. Maris was still a good line-drive hitter, but his home-run power was in sharp decline.

13

To the New York writers there was something schizophrenic about New York players. They wanted the glory of playing in New York, and they knew playing there made them more famous and affected their income, but they were innately suspicious of dealing with the press. Such stars as Hank Aaron, playing in other cities, often felt they were shortchanged because they did not get the benefit of the New York media machinery. Part of the problem was the nature of the game itself, for even the best player hit only about .333, which meant that he went out two out of three times; in turn, that meant that no matter how enthusiastic a writer was about a player, he was, more often than not, describing the player's limitations or even his failures. Casey Stengel was very much aware of that, and would point out to the writers that ballplayers were the only professionals who had their every mistake and failure scrutinized the next morning in print. It didn't happen to Hollywood actors, Stengel said, no one wrote that they had done a bad take on a scene; and it didn't happen to reporters themselves, no one graded them each day on their stories or published a list of their journalistic mistakes. "You guys wouldn't like it if you had a box score on yourselves every day," said Stengel.

Another part of the problem was cultural. The writers were, by and large, urban and college-educated; many of them were Jewish. They were verbal, not physical, men. The players were country boys, high school graduates, and often not even that. The writers sometimes seemed to be making fun of them at their expense. There was on occasion a resentment, albeit an unconscious one on the part of the writers, of being part of the instrument that brought fame and glory to men who did not even read books, and who in fact often did not read the stories written about them each day. If anything, the complaints that the players passed on to the writers seemed more often than not to be triggered not by what the players had read but by what some friend of theirs had said after reading a story. It was an ongoing complaint of the writers that if they wrote a long, essentially praiseworthy story about a player, they never heard about it. But if they wrote one negative sentence, a friend of the player would call him up, and there would be an unpleasant confrontation the next day. It took a rare athlete, such as Whitey Ford, tart and cocky, both ballplayer and New York City kid himself, to know the rhythms and the voices of the city and its newspapers. He, as far as most of the working journalists were concerned, was a model of what an athlete should be like in dealing with the press. Available to reporters on bad days as well as good, he was candid, often funny, and, above all, straight. There was a general feeling among the reporters that the one player on the Yankees who might have pulled off being subjected to the scrutiny that Roger Maris underwent was Whitey Ford.

In years past the press corps had been remarkably reverential, and the most important sportswriters tended to reflect the views of management as well as to sanitize accounts of tensions that existed on teams. Later there was much talk about the good old days, when the writers and the players had gotten on better, but the truth was that even in the good old days, the players often hated the writers. By the sixties those tensions were steadily exacerbated by a new and very different kind of media approach, one decidedly less reverential toward athletes. Some of that had been obvious during the Maris ordeal, but it was becoming clear that that was no mere fluke. The changes taking place were driven by two distinct forces, first by the coming of television, and second by the rise of an increasingly iconoclastic and eventually confrontational press corps.

The impact of television on the sports scene was already immense. Fifteen years earlier baseball had been a radio game; now it was a television game, and teams played not so much in cities as in markets. The Milwaukee Braves, once enormously successful after their move from Boston, were already completing negotiations to go to Atlanta, where they would have a market all to themselves, instead of sharing the greater Chicago market with two Chicago teams. Television was making the sport ever more an instrument of big-time entertainment, and it was also changing the nature of fame for the players. Because of television, not only were the stars recognizable now, but so were the backup players. Greater celebrity led, almost certainly, to greater ancillary money, all of this gradually undermining the traditional hold of management over ballplayers based on salary. Television was making other sports as popular as baseball, and it was creating a different kind of athlete; within the year the New York Jets, an upstart team in an upstart league (but an upstart league with a network television contract) would sign a quarterback out of Alabama named Joe Namath for more than $400,000 a year, based on the belief of the team's owner, a former agent and promoter named Sonny Werblin, that Namath had precisely what Roger Maris lacked: star quality. At Namath's signing there was a press conference befitting the size of the contract. Lou Effrat of the *Times*, one of the more senior sportswriters, asked Namath what would happen if after all this promotion and furor he did not make the grade as a pro quarterback. "I'll make it," Namath said quietly and confidently, and there was an immediate sense that Werblin had bet on the right man.

If television was creating the athlete as star, it was also applying pressure on the press corps for a new kind of story. Newspapers were going out of business in the late fifties and the early sixties in New York under the pressure created by the rise of network and local television as a more dramatic and accessible alternative. Not only were a number of tabloids dying, but so was a great paper like the *Herald Tribune*. That meant that the competition among the surviving papers, particularly the surviving tabloids, had become fierce. The *New York Post* was the prototype of an afternoon paper

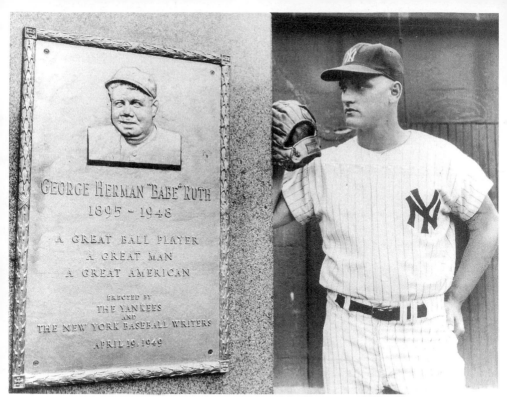

Roger Maris looks at Babe Ruth's plaque in center field at Yankee Stadium. His successful pursuit of Ruth's single-season home-run record in 1961 found little favor among New York fans, who booed him and rooted instead for Mickey Mantle to break the record.
(UPI/Bettmann)

It was the summer of his discontent: Ralph Terry had been a mainstay of the Yankee pitching staff in the past and a World Series hero in 1962, but an injury to his shoulder and back in the spring ruined his 1964 season. He watched, frustrated that he could not contribute more and aware that the Yankees would trade him after the season.
(National Baseball Library, Cooperstown, N.Y.)

Pete Mikkelsen hurt his arm in the minor leagues just as he was sure he was on his way out of baseball. That turned him involuntarily into a sinker-ball pitcher and helped him make the big-league club that spring. *(AP/Wide World Photos)*

Bobby Richardson was probably the most underrated player on that team. A fine fielder and an exceptional clutch hitter, he got thirteen hits in the 1964 World Series. *(National Baseball Library, Cooperstown, N.Y.)*

The key to much of the Yankees' success, their opponents thought, was their exceptional middle infield, with Tony Kubek (left) at short and Bobby Richardson at second. When injuries wore Kubek down in 1964, opponents thought the Yankees lost a critical part of their strength. (*National Baseball Library, Cooperstown, N.Y.*)

il Linz and Tom Tresh, as rookies in 1962, take some instruction from Frank Crosetti, the rd-base coach. (*AP/Wide World Photos*)

The trade for Lou Brock in mid-June was the turning point of the season for the Cardinals. He gave them not only far more speed, but a new degree of aggressiveness. No player worked harder at the game, and none studied his job more closely than Brock.
(Sam Onyon)

Curt Flood was, by 1964, probably the premier center fielder in baseball and a key player on the Cardinal team. His decision to fight a trade to Philadelphia started a legal-political process that changed the face and salary structure of baseball.
(National Baseball Library, Cooperstown, N.Y.)

Dick Groat was a classic old pro who came over from the Pirates to anchor the Cardinal infield. He was slow afoot, but he had quick hands and a quick bat and was an exceptional hitter and a very smart player. (*National Baseball Library, Cooperstown, N.Y.*)

Curt Simmons, a shrewd veteran left-hander, was cut loose earlier on by the Phillies, even though it turned out he had several years of good pitching left. Had the Phillies stayed with him, they might have won the pennant. Instead, he was a crucial factor for the Cards down the stretch and took particular delight in tormenting his former teammates. (*AP/Wide World Photos*)

Bill White, the Cardinal first baseman. Thoughtful and judicious, he somewhat reluctantly left Hiram College and a possible career as a doctor for baseball because it offered immediate financial advantages. Eventually he became a broadcaster and a baseball executive. (The Sporting News)

Elston Howard, who had played in the Negro leagues for the Kansas City Monarchs, was the first black player to make the Yankees. A thoughtful, careful man, Howard handled with great skill the pressure of being a pioneer in a reluctant organization. He had a good bat and was an excellent receiver, and his pitching staff greatly admired him. In 1963 he became the first black MVP in the American League. Nine out of the previous ten National League MVPs were black.
(*National Baseball Library, Cooperstown, N.Y.*)

This is The Look. Bob Gibson, on his piece of territory, brought intimidation to an ever higher level. He could throw tight to hitters, and he never talked to opposing hitters, lest his ability to dominate them be weakened by even the smallest show of humanity.
(The Sporting News)

Roger Craig (right) came over from the Mets in an off-season trade and gave the Cardinals a number of critical wins, including a great performance in the fourth game of the Series. Here he is with pitching coach Howie Pollet.
(*AP/Wide World Photos*)

The two left-handers who were to start the opening game of the Series, Whitey Ford of New York and Ray Sadecki of St. Louis, pose before Game One. Neither finished the game. *(UPI/Bettmann)*

Yogi Berra posing with Johnny
Keane before the start of the
Series. These were the last
games for either manager in
the uniform he was wearing,
despite the fact that each
had won a pennant.
(The Sporting News)

The brothers Boyer of Alba,
Missouri, pose before the first
game: Ken of the Cardinals
and his younger brother
Clete of the Yankees. Both
were exceptional fielders,
although some observers
thought Clete had the edge
on the field while Ken
was the better hitter.
(The Sporting News)

Lou Brock scores the first run of the World Series. He had singled and then gone from first to third on Dick Groat's single to right while Mantle did not even try to make a throw. Then he scored when Ken Boyer flied out. The play reflected the Cardinals' more aggressive baserunning and convinced them that they could run on Mantle. *(UPI/Bettmann)*

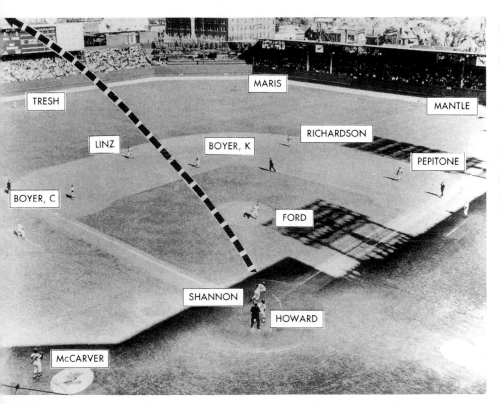

Mike Shannon helps drive Whitey Ford from the mound in the first game with this enormous home run to left field in Busch Stadium. The score is 4–2 New York, and Ken Boyer is at second as Shannon swings. McCarver would follow with a double, and Ford, the winningest pitcher in World Series history, would leave the mound for the last time in a Series. *(National Baseball Library, Cooperstown, N.Y.)*

Bill White of the Cardinals (left) poses with Joe Pepitone of the Yankees before the second game. White was one of the steadiest influences on the Cardinals and went on to become the president of the National League; Pepitone, one of the shakiest of the Yankees, squandered most of his talent as the Yankees began to slide. *(UPI/Bettmann)*

This is pure power against power. Bob Gibson threw as hard as he could, and his follow-through seemed to carry him to first base. The batter is Roger Maris, who leveraged his body as completely as Gibson did. Here Gibson strikes him out in the first inning of the second game, which was won by the Yankees. *(UPI/Bettmann)*

Jim Bouton was a power pitcher, but a relatively small one—he once compared himself to a Volkswagen at the Indy 500. He had to use his entire body on every pitch, but he played well in all three of his World Series starts before his arm finally gave out. Here he pitches in the first of his two wins in the 1964 World Series.
(AP/Wide World Photos)

When Mantle hit a ball, it made a sound distinctly louder and sharper than that made by other hitters. Here is a rare picture of Mantle as he absolutely crunches the knuckleball thrown by Barney Schultz in the third game. A moment earlier Mantle had told Ellie Howard, the on-deck hitter, that he was going to drive Schultz's knuckler for a home run.
(UPI/Bettmann)

Mickey Mantle trots home after his massive home run off Schultz in the ninth, and a delighted Frank Crosetti follows. Notice that Schultz is almost to the Cardinal dugout by the time Mantle reaches home. *(UPI/Bettmann)*

Mickey Mantle poses with winning pitcher Jim Bouton after the Yankees' 2–1 victory in the third game. Mantle holds up the ball he hit for his home run off Barney Schultz. It was his sixteenth World Series home run, which not only won the game but broke Babe Ruth's record. The ball may not actually be the one Mantle hit, but a bogus one foisted on him by his pal Whitey Ford. *(UPI/Bettmann)*

This is the play that helped seal the Yankees' fate in the fourth game. Bobby Richardson has trouble digging the ball out of his glove and getting it to shortstop Phil Linz (34) in time, and the ball arrives after he crosses the bag. Curt Flood (21) comes in hard on Linz, knocks the ball loose, and the Yankees fail to get a double play or the slow Groat for even one out at first. This brings up Ken Boyer with the bases loaded. *(UPI/Bettmann)*

With the bases loaded after the misplay at second, Downing shook Howard off and went to his change; Boyer, swinging on the change here, expected a fastball, but adjusted in midswing for his grand slam. *(AP/Wide World Photos)*

Ken Boyer, the National League MVP that year, crosses home plate after his grand-slam home run off Al Downing in the fourth game. Waiting for him are (from left) Curt Flood, Dick Groat, and Carl Warwick, while a disconsolate Ellie Howard looks on. In what was probably the decisive moment of the Series, Boyer has just turned a 3–0 Yankee lead into a 4–3 Cardinal one. *(UPI/Bettmann)*

Ken Boyer (left), Tim McCarver, and Mike Shannon all hit home runs in the World Series. Here they pose for photographers before the sixth game. *(AP/Wide World Photos)*

The look of pain on his face is one that his teammates had become accustomed to and opposing pitchers had begun to recognize: Here in batting practice before the sixth game, Mantle grimaces after a swing. *(National Baseball Library, Cooperstown, N.Y.)*

was one of the last manifestations of the famous Yankee power in a World Series. Roger Maris, ickey Mantle, and Joe Pepitone all hit home runs in the sixth game, which evened up the ries, 3–3. (The Sporting News)

n Boyer, the Cardinal third baseman, rushes over to hug Bob Gibson er his gritty performance in the seventh game of the Series. Running t to the mound is catcher Tim McCarver, while fans are already hurdling e fence and coming down onto the field.

ational Baseball Library, Cooperstown, N.Y.)

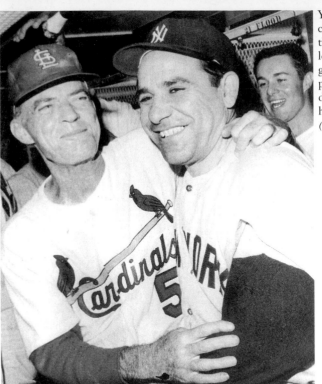

Yankee manager Yogi Berra congratulates Johnny Keane of the Cardinals in the St. Louis locker room after the seventh game, without realizing that the people he works for have already decided to fire him and replace him with Keane. *(UPI/Bettmann)*

Johnny Keane (right) with Gussie Busch, owner of the Cardinals (center), and Bob Howsam, the team's general manager, as he announces that he will not accept a contract renewal and a large raise. Keane was furious over the way Busch had fired his close friend Bing Devine, and, besides, he was on his way to manage the Yankees. It was a rare moment when the imperial Busch did not get his way, and it shows on his face. (The Sporting News)

trying to survive in those days. Still liberal, and still trying to get by despite an ever weaker advertising base, it relied heavily on liberal columnists in the front of the paper and boasted an exceptional sports page. Though by the early sixties the great Jimmy Cannon had departed, the paper still had Milton Gross, Maury Allen, and, for a time, all the Leonards (Leonard Shecter, Leonard Lewin, and Leonard Koppett), as well as Vic Ziegel. The *Post* gave its writers a free hand, but it had to, since so few papers in the country paid so poorly. Larry Merchant, summoned from a Philadelphia tabloid to go to work for the *Post*, had to take a pay cut in order to do so. In the past the beat reporters covering such teams as the Yankees had tended to be men in their fifties and their sixties and had held the beat much as Supreme Court justices held their jobs, until death did them part. Now that was changing, spurred by changes in society, and by the harsher demands of more travel and late games on the West Coast, a new generation of younger reporters was taking over. They were called the Chipmunks, a name given them by one of their own heroes, Jimmy Cannon (who was not at all sure that he wanted to be one of their heroes). Cannon had come into the press box one day and had seen them all gathered and, it seemed to him, chirping together. Because one of them had teeth that protruded, he called them the Chipmunks.

The Chipmunks (who liked being called Chipmunks) gloried in the fact that they were part of the new breed. Not only were they younger than their predecessors, they were generally better educated, definitely more iconoclastic, certainly more egocentric, and probably less grateful to be covering the great New York Yankees. Leonard Koppett, a traditionalist who worked for the *Post* and then went to the *Times*, thought that the Chipmunks were different in one additional way: the older writers had written for their readers. The best of them all, Dick Young, was the most irreverent of baseball writers when he was younger, and widely admired by his peers as the best baseball beat writer who ever lived. He was considered brilliant because he had an unerring instinct for exactly what the fans wanted to know each day. By contrast, Koppett thought, the Chipmunks often wrote for each other, admiring each other's leads and different takes on stories. There were other differences. They did not go to Toots Shor's and drink with the ballplayers and managers as their predecessors had, which was a major change, one dictated by the endless night games and harder road trips. They often drank wine instead of whiskey. They were more likely to hang out on the road at nightclubs like the hungry I, where Mort Sahl was playing; when they were in New York, they were to be found at the Lion's Head, a bar in Greenwich Village, where novelists and poets gathered. Nor did they necessarily intend to spend their whole lives covering baseball. The older reporters had regarded their jobs as the best ones on the paper, and they thought of themselves, consciously or unconsciously, as an extension of the team. Once, in a Detroit-Yankee game, Al Kaline of the Tigers made a great running catch to rob Roger Maris of a home run, and the next time up Maris drove the ball much deeper, some four hundred feet into the bullpen, far over Kaline's head. One of the old guard stood in the press box, shaking his fist at Kaline. "Let's see you try and catch that, you son of a bitch!" he thundered down at the Detroit right fielder. The Chipmunks looked on with contempt.

The Chipmunks deliberately put distance between themselves and the players. They found Mantle intriguing but difficult, an occasionally brooding, occasionally joyous figure who clearly did not value what they did. Told by the more senior figures how exceptional a man DiMaggio was, they were often puzzled when they found him to be unusually suspicious and uncommunicative. "For a time," reflected Maury Allen, one of the most talented men of that era, and an early Chipmunk, "I was puzzled because I had heard how wonderful DiMaggio was, and I always found him unpleasant, and for a long time I thought it was my fault, and then gradually I found out that the older writers felt much the same way, but that they were afraid to admit it because it would reflect badly on them." One of the Chipmunks, Stan Isaacs of *Newsday*, arrived on the field as a young reporter when DiMaggio, by then a coach in spring training, was instructing for the Yankees, and he went over to interview him. DiMaggio seemed irritated by this impertinence, and later Isaacs was told by Joe Trimble, a more senior figure on the

Daily News, "You don't just go over and talk to Joe—you wait for him to give you a signal that he's ready to talk."

Stan Isaacs, knowing of Ralph Houk's complete fidelity to the Yankees and their cause, once asked him if he wore the Yankee logo on his pajamas. If a young reporter from a small newspaper came to a postgame interview with Houk and Houk did not like his questions, he would look at the traditionalists and roll his eyes to try to diminish the young man, but Stan Isaacs, Maury Allen, and Leonard Shecter would just repeat the questions. Of Isaacs, it was said that he asked the definitive Chipmunk question after the seventh game of the 1962 World Series. Ralph Terry, the winning pitcher, was being interviewed in the locker room by a bunch of reporters when he took a long-distance phone call. He spoke over the phone for a few minutes and then returned to the reporters. Who called? one of them asked. My wife, he said. What was she doing? the reporter asked. Feeding our baby, he answered. "Breast or bottle?" Isaacs asked.

The first Chipmunks were Isaacs and Leonard Shecter. Shecter started covering the Yankees in 1958; it was a hard assignment at first, and he had felt very much the outsider, isolated by the older reporters, who would not let him in on the stories they shared—such as the fact that George Weiss had put private detectives on his players, and a gumshoe had followed Bobby Richardson and Tony Kubek instead of the carousers. Then, on the train coming back from the game in Kansas City in which they had clinched the pennant, there was a more serious incident: Ryne Duren, the relief pitcher who had been drinking, squashed Ralph Houk's cigar in his face, and Houk, then a coach and the manager-in-waiting, swatted Duren with the back of his hand, cutting him near the eye with his World Series ring. Shecter had asked the veteran writers what they were going to do with the story, and they said they were not going to do anything with it. By chance he got off the train at the next stop, and in a phone call to his editor, Ike Gellis, he mentioned what happened. Gellis, in turn, mentioned it to Paul Sann, the operative editor of the paper, and the *Post* not only went with the story but greatly overplayed it. The small incident was described as a vast, ugly brawl. (Years later Shecter asked Gellis what he would have done if he had been the reporter on the train, and Gellis answered candidly that he had pondered the same question and decided he would have given it a pass.) That turned Shecter, already an outsider, into something worse: a leper. For much of the rest of that season when he was on the team train, he carried with him the new novel by Jerome Weidman, *The Enemy Camp*. The next year Shecter spent an evening with Jerome Holtzman, the distinguished Chicago sportswriter, and poured out his unhappiness about how much the players hated him and how lonely his assignment was. To Holtzman it was a stunning confession, because while there had always been incidents between players and writers in the past, there was a new and frightening dimension to what Shecter was saying. A few years later, when the Yankees clinched yet another pennant, one of the few players on the team who liked Shecter warned him to stay out of the locker room because some of the Yankee players were out to get him. What had made the isolation bearable, he later told his colleagues, was the fact that he had waited for so long to get a beat. He had been a desk man working inside the paper for more than fifteen years, and every time he asked to go out and cover a story he was told he was too valuable to the paper as a desk man. Now, finally unleashed on a beat, he could bear the loneliness.

It was a volatile time in America, with a dramatically changing consciousness about race and the beginning of an unwinnable war in Vietnam. Many of the Chipmunks not only reflected the greater alienation of young journalists, they were determined to bring the issues of the real world into the closed world of sports. They wanted to know how the baseball players reacted not just to the daily games but to the larger issues being posed by society. They were determined not to do what Red Smith thought his old friend Grantland Rice had done—go around godding up the ballplayers. Their hero was not Rice, the role model to the previous generation, but A. J. Liebling, the famed press critic of *The New Yorker*, who wrote wonderfully about food and boxing, and who railed against those aspects of the press that they themselves were rebelling against. They judged some athletes not just on how they played ball but on how they dealt with social issues, which did not endear them to many of the players.

Gradually, as other young reporters arrived, Shecter felt less isolated. At the 1960 World Series, a group including Larry Merchant, Isaacs, and Shechter got together and pulled a famed Chipmunk stunt. Irritated by a writer named Joe Reichler of the AP, who they thought was the inventor of endless trades that never took place, they decided to invent a trade for him, making it at once both outlandish and yet credible. The Giants always seemed to be on the verge of trading a pitcher named Johnny Antonelli. But to which team and for what player would he be traded? Since the Giants at the time were looking for a manager, what about Yogi Berra for Antonelli, with the idea that Yogi would become the player-manager of the Giants as well? That seemed perfect—it was just ludicrous and improbable enough to be true, the idea of Berra as a manager funny enough to make an ideal prank. So they went their disparate ways putting out the rumor, and though, to their great annoyance, Reichler did not bite, a number of other writers did. Needless to say, floating a false rumor did not please the older writers, and the lines between the generations were drawn that much more sharply.

Jimmy Cannon, whom the Chipmunks admired, was not entirely appreciative of them; he thought they were too noisy and they did not always focus on the subject at hand, which was baseball. Once he came in and found them all talking about football when below them a baseball game was unfolding. He was very disturbed about their transgression: "Baseball, gentlemen! Baseball!" Cannon was considered a talented writer, and a very funny man, and it was he who had said of Howard Cosell that if he were a sport he would be a roller derby. Hearing that the summer house of one colleague, Gene Ward, whom he did not consider a very good writer, had burned down and that arson was suspected, Cannon muttered, "Probably a professor of English." Yet those were not easy days for Cannon; he had given up drinking and was fighting terrible loneliness. He was not as close to the younger athletes as he had been with those like

DiMaggio. As one of the most elegant writers in sports, he seemed to suffer from the fact that in 1956 the Pulitzer Prize had been bestowed upon Arthur Daley of *The New York Times*, widely regarded by his colleagues as an affable man but perhaps the most pedestrian writer of the period. Cannon was wont, late at night, to slip into prolonged soliloquies on the injustice of Arthur Daley's winning the Pulitzer Prize. "It was stealing," he would say.

More and more, the afternoon papers, barely hanging on, pushed for the angle on a story. Even such morning papers as the *Daily News* started looking for a human-interest angle each day, and were behaving as afternoon papers once had. Shecter had written thirty Roger Maris stories during that momentous summer, which was regarded by his peers as a herculean achievement, just short of Maris's own, and after the season ended he wrote a quickie paperback called *Home Run Hero*, for which he was paid the grand sum of one thousand dollars. For the start of 1962 Shecter had been with the Mets, a preferred Chipmunk assignment, and by the time he joined the Yankees at the All-Star break, the relationship between Maris, the fans, and the press had deteriorated terribly. Shecter picked up the Yankees in time to watch Maris collide with the fans during a doubleheader on July 30 at the Stadium. Some fans had thrown golf balls out on the field at him, and Maris responded by throwing them back into the stands. That made it worse and more debris was thrown at him. (After the game Maris reacted predictably and said that he was through trying to win friends and influence people.) Before the day was over, the umpires had to escort him to the outfield. Shecter was appalled by what was happening; he talked to one of the umpires, who did not seem very sympathetic to Maris, and who seemed to think he was doing a poor job of handling his fame. They thought that with the money he made, it was imperative to learn how to deal with the fans, even if the fans were difficult and provocative. Shecter wrote of the incident, of the cycle of growing mutual hostility between Maris and the fans, and quoted Maris in the end as saying that as far as the fans were concerned, he no longer gave a damn. To

Shecter's surprise, Maris absolutely hated the story. "You fucking ripping cocksucker," Shecter quoted Maris as saying. "Look, Rog, isn't that the way it happened?" Shecter had asked Maris, trying to appease him. "That's got nothing the fuck to do with it," Maris said. We settled our problem, Shecter later wrote, by never talking again.

14

July 3 was a terrible night for Ralph Terry. He had been one of the mainstays of the Yankee pitching staff for the last three years, winning a total of fifty-six games during that time. But in 1964 he was not only struggling, he was failing. As July arrived his record was an egregious 2-7, and his earned run average resembled Mickey Mantle's slugging average more than anything else. That summer he was discovering a state of anxiety peculiar to pitchers. As they grew older, regular ballplayers worried that their abilities would gradually wear down, and their reflexes would slip just a fraction. It was the rare regular player whose career ended overnight. Pitchers were different: they lived constantly in fear that one physical mishap might cause the arm injury that would finish them. Ralph Terry had plenty of time that summer to ponder the fragility of a pitcher's life. His arm bothered him most of the season, and he was well aware that if it did not get better quickly, his major-league baseball career was over.

Terry thought he knew exactly what had gone wrong. It had happened almost as soon as he had arrived at St. Petersburg for spring training. The Yankees had built some new mounds for their pitchers, and they were far too steep; when Terry went out to pitch for the first time, he came down on his follow-through, and the mound threw him off. Where he expected his foot to hit the ground, there was no ground, and he overextended his shoulder and his back. Then, he later decided, he made a rookie mistake and tried to come back too quickly. His back had bothered him through May and June, and now it was July and he was still having problems. The injury had cost him location as well as power.

He simply could not find his rhythm, and he continued to falter. In one brief stretch he pitched sixteen innings and gave up eleven home runs. His record reached 2-8. It was a terrible time for him, and there were days when he wondered whether Yogi Berra had lost confidence in him completely, and, worse, why Berra should not have. He was immensely frustrated with his own performance. His team was in a pennant race and the pitching was not up to expectations, principally because of him. He had seen this happen some five years earlier to teammates of his, Don Larsen and Bob Turley. Turley had lost something on his fastball and for a time he managed to hold on, throwing a sinker instead of a fastball in tough situations; but the hitters caught on, realizing that they did not have to face Turley's feared fastball, and his effectiveness declined quickly.

Making it even harder for Terry was the absence of Johnny Sain. Sain had been the Yankee pitching coach for the last few years and was adored by most Yankee pitchers, including Jim Bouton, Al Downing, Steve Hamilton, and Terry. Sain, a former star pitcher for the old Boston Braves, had come over to the Yankees near the end of his career, as a reliever and spot starter. As much a psychiatrist as a coach, he was immensely skilled, his many protégés thought, at getting the pitchers to figure out what it was he wanted them to do. Sain's commitment to the nonpitching members of a baseball team always seemed minimal; he was interested only in pitchers. A manager who signed him on as a pitching coach did so at his risk, for it was almost as if Sain ran a completely independent organization, a separate team of pitchers whose loyalty was only to him. He seemed to feel that his pitchers were on loan to the *other* manager—that is, the manager of the team—for two or three hours a day. If a manager, as they were wont to do, tried to tell *his* pitchers what to do and what to throw, Sain would quickly intercede. He was likely to ask the manager how many pitches he had thrown as a big-leaguer. His success with pitchers who had not been successful before was truly phenomenal. Friends would tease him about this, and he would reply, with a paraphrase of Will Rogers, that he had never met a pitcher he didn't like.

Other pitching coaches were concerned with the physical condition of their pitchers; Sain was more concerned with their minds. He wanted his pitchers to think positively and to be at peace with themselves at all times. Pitching was all about confidence and concentration, Sain thought. More than most other pitching coaches, he worked on having his pitchers come up with moves to first and second, not so much to pick off base runners but to minimize the distractions that base runners posed. Unless a pitcher was prepared to deal with him, a runner was likely to be a larger psychological distraction than most professional baseball people realized. The better prepared you were for runners on base, Sain believed, the less distracted you were in game situations. Part of his strength, the pitchers thought, was that he did not play to the manager's whims or favor the players who were doing well at the moment; rather, he spent more time with the players who were in trouble than the ones who were the stars. Once during the 1963 season, Jim Bouton stopped him and asked him, "John, how come you're not talking to me anymore?" "How are you doing these days, Jim?" Sain answered. In fact, Bouton had been on a considerable roll for several weeks, keeping the ball down and winning low-scoring games. "Fine, John," he answered. "Then you don't need me, do you?" Sain answered.

Sain's lessons were not just psychological in nature, for he was a very good practitioner of the art as well, always trying to give his pitchers an additional pitch as one more weapon against their true enemies, the hitters. He would sit with the pitchers in the bullpen and together they would experiment on different pitches and how to hold the ball for them, along the seams or across the seams. He could explain how a particular ball, held in a certain way and thrown in a certain way, was likely to break. He gave almost every pitcher on the staff an additional pitch. He was not, thought Downing, a velocity man, he was a location man.

If he saw a pitcher make a mistake during a game, he would not say anything during the heat of the game or immediately afterward, when the pitcher was down on himself. Instead, he would wait a couple of days. Then he and the pitcher would grab gloves, and they would begin by playing catch, at first throwing at thirty feet, and then at forty-five feet, and soon at sixty feet. Suddenly, without anything being said, in order not to make the pitcher tense, and without a single word of criticism having been uttered, he would be well into a lesson on mechanics and on trying to correct the error. There was never anyone, thought Al Downing, better at getting inside the head of a pitcher than Johnny Sain, and of seeing the game as the pitcher saw it.

Just before Downing came up to the Yankees for the second time, Bill Yancey, his scout and sponsor, a man who had played in the old Negro leagues, took him aside and said that when he got to the majors he was to make no judgments about people and their racial attitudes unless they showed prejudice. Downing was going to be surprised by the people he met, Yancey said; for example, a big old country boy from Arkansas named Johnny Sain. His accent might be heavy and off-putting, but he would prove to be, Yancey predicted, one of the greatest people Downing ever met in his life. If Downing worked hard, Sain would work equally hard for him, and he would make him a much better pitcher. Sain would not see Al Downing as an upstart young black man in what had once been a white man's game, but as a young man with a good fastball, good curve, and good change, who needed to work on his control, his confidence, and, finally, his reason for throwing each pitch. It all turned out to be true, Downing later thought.

No one, including Sain himself, was ever sure about the chain of circumstances that caused Johnny Sain's departure from the Yankees after the 1963 season. Part of it was that he thought the organization didn't appreciate him. Certainly it took a very strong manager with a very strong ego to put up with his independence, which sometimes seemed to border on out-and-out disobedience. Some of the Yankee pitchers thought it was because Ralph Houk and Sain no longer got along. Certainly Sain was surprised that he had not been notified in advance of the switch by which Houk would become general manager and Berra manager. He heard about it first from an outsider, a close friend of Mickey Mantle's. That was jarring to him because it meant that he was somehow outside the inner circle of the organization. It was true that after the 1963 season Sain had asked Houk for a two-year contract at $25,000 a year, which was a raise of $2,500, and had been turned down. "Mr. Topping won't go for it, John," Houk had said, which also meant that Houk was not going for it. After four years of helping to create a championship pitching staff, Sain thought it was a shame; the organization had not been very direct with him. He also thought the appointment of Whitey Ford, an immensely popular player, as his successor was a skilled move politically. Now no one would criticize the management publicly for letting him go. But most of the pitchers thought his loss was a major one. The problem with Ford as a pitcher-coach was that he was in the process of fighting his own overwhelming physical ailments, his body and arm were both wearing out, and he had little time to work with his teammates.

Almost every pitcher on that staff felt indebted in some way or another to Johnny Sain, but none more so than Ralph Terry. Terry had had a good but not great fastball, and a fair curve. Even for a right-handed pitcher who had good location, that was not quite enough to win in a home ball park that so heavily favored left-handed hitters. Knowing that Terry needed one more pitch, Sain taught him how to throw the slurve, a small breaking ball, half curve, half slider. He did it in time for the 1961 season and it proved so successful that Terry had gotten off to a 5-0 start at the beginning of the season. But a few weeks into the season he experienced arm trouble for the first time, and he suspected it had come from throwing the slurve. But the slurve had taught him the value of having an additional pitch, and he started experimenting with what was in effect a slider off his fastball. Later known as a cut fastball, it did not break in as large an arc as his curve, but instead had a small but very sharp break to it. He had badly needed that pitch because when he had to go to the breaking ball, the good hitters in the league would not just sit around and wait on what might otherwise have been nothing but a big old curve. With its acquisition Terry suddenly jumped from being a mediocre pitcher to a top-line pitcher who came close to winning twenty games a season.

During the 1962 World Series, Sain handled Terry with exceptional care. He pitched in the second game and lost, 2–0, although he threw a six-hitter. There was an undercurrent of feeling among some of the Yankee people, going back to a home-run ball Terry had thrown in the 1960 World Series to Bill Mazeroski, that he might not be able to win the big games. Terry was scheduled to pitch the fifth game too, and as the players got ready to go on the field, one after another they came by Terry's locker and patted him on the back. "Go get 'em, Ralph," they said. Sain stood aside watching this, thinking this was not exactly what a control pitcher like Terry needed just before a big game. He did not need to reach for something extra, he needed to be exactly who he was, to pitch to spots. So when all the others were out on the field, Sain sidled over to him. "Don't try and be sensational, Ralph," he said. "Just be yourself. That's good enough. You'll win." Sain was not even sure that Terry had heard him, but Terry beat the Giants that day, and the next day in the clubhouse he came over and told Sain, "See, John, I didn't try to be sensational." Then he came back and beat them again in the seventh game, 1–0.

Now, in 1964, Terry needed a mentor like Sain who might have been able to understand how much of his problem was physical, how much was mental, and who just might have told him to take his time recovering.

On that night of July 3, Terry was called into a game at the Stadium against the Minnesota Twins, at the time the hardest-hitting team in the American League. The score was 0–0 after nine innings. Stan Williams, a pitcher recently acquired from the Dodgers, had pitched the first nine innings and given up only two hits. Even as Terry made his way out of the bullpen and started walking in from right field, the booing began, and then, when the public-address system announced his name, more boos thundered down. It got worse a moment later when Don Mincher drove his first pitch over the head of Mantle in center field for a triple. Jerry Kindall came in to run for Mincher. The booing increased. It was so harsh that it reminded one sportswriter of the booing reserved in the past for Roger Maris. With Kindall on third, Earl Battey, the catcher, bunted and was thrown out without advancing Mincher. But the next batter, Jim Snyder, flied out and Kindall scored the winning run. Terry reminded himself that night that these same fans had booed Maris in recent years, and had only switched to Maris after devoting so many seasons to booing Mantle. He knew that fans were fickle—he had pitched in Fenway Park one night when Ted Williams had let a pop-up drop in left field, and the boos had been as loud as any he had ever heard. Then, only a few moments later, Williams made a great running catch and the same people gave him an ovation. Williams had responded to this by placing his left hand on the muscle of his right arm, which he extended toward the crowd. Still, it was painful to be booed, and to know that as the Yankees continued to flounder, he was part of the problem.

For Terry there was irony in the fact that the Yankees were coming up short on pitching. Sometimes in the past they had had so much of it, there had been almost an arrogance in the way management handled its pitchers. Like other Yankee pitchers, Terry was convinced that late in certain seasons, when the pennant seemed a lock, the Yankee management had on occasion tried to suppress the statistics of the team's starting pitchers, lest the pitchers become too demanding at contract time. It wasn't necessarily deliberate, and it certainly wasn't personal. It was just smart business. In 1963, with less than two weeks to go in the season, Terry had led the league in complete games and in innings pitched, and then suddenly he had pitched significantly less—for the good of the team, he was told, so that management could look at other pitchers. He had still managed to lead the league in complete games, but Whitey Ford ended up pitching one more inning than he did, which made it easier for management to maintain the pecking order in salaries.

Terry was only twenty-eight in the summer of 1964, and he found it hard to believe that his career was in decline already; for him the glory years were only yesterday, and by all rights he should still be enjoying them. It was only two years ago that he had been the star of the 1962 World Series, when the Yankees had taken on the San Francisco Giants and he had started three games. He had pitched brilliantly in the entire Series against what was arguably the hardest-hitting lineup in baseball, and his control had never been better— when the Series was over, he had pitched twenty-five innings, given up only two walks, and struck out sixteen in three games. He lost the second game of the Series, 2–0, to Jack Sanford, although he had pitched extremely well. In the fifth game he came back and beat Sanford, 5–3. Then, in the seventh game, he took on Sanford once again in one of the greatest World Series games ever played. Jim Bouton was supposed to pitch the seventh, but there had been a three-game rain delay when the teams had gotten to San Francisco, and so Terry was able to go once more, fully rested. The seventh game, he thought, was the best game he ever pitched in his life. The weather was still harsh; the field was still so wet that helicopters had been called in to hover over and help dry it off. On the day of the game a formidable wind blew in from left field, and Tom Tresh, the Yankee left fielder, caught six balls, though it was a hard day's work for him, as he battled the gale on every one.

That kind of wind, though, helped Terry, who felt razor-sharp anyway. He pitched a perfect game into the sixth, when Sanford got a hit. The Yankees scored their run in the fifth. They had loaded the bases with no one out and Alvin Dark had played the infield back for the double play. Tony Kubek hit into the double play, but Moose Skowron scored from third. That meant Terry had taken a 1–0 lead into the bottom of the ninth inning. Matty Alou was the first man up; he fouled a ball over near the Giant dugout and Ellie Howard got under it, but just as he had been about to gather it in, he was jostled by two people in the dugout—Bob Nieman, a reserve out-fielder, and Dark, the manager, he later said. With that reprieve Alou beat out a perfect bunt. That made Alou the runner with no one out. Both Chuck Hiller and Felipe Alou tried to move him along, but Terry managed to strike them both out. That brought up Willie Mays, to be followed by Willie McCovey and Orlando Cepeda—the heart of the order, a new black Murderers' Row. That gave Terry pause, and a quick flash of sympathy on his part for those pitchers who in recent years had faced a Yankee batting order that contained Maris, Mantle, Skowron, and Howard.

Of the three, Mays was the toughest hitter, a man without a single weakness. Terry came inside twice trying to jam him, and he just missed the call both times. On the 2-0 pitch Mays hit what Terry thought was a good pitch—a fastball low and away—and laced it to right field toward the corner. Roger Maris then made the crucial play of the World Series. He got a good jump on the ball, and despite the wet, slippery field he got to it quickly, got a good bounce, and whirled to throw a strike to Bobby Richardson. Richardson thought that Maris's throw was perfect and he took it and fired a strike to Howard. Alou held at third. Without that perfect fielding (and the threat posed by Maris's great ability as a defensive outfielder with one of the best arms in baseball), the Giants might have had the tying run. As it was, thought Terry, if they had sent Alou from third, he would have been out by ten feet.

That brought Willie McCovey up, with Cepeda on deck. Out to the mound came Houk. "I don't know why I'm doing this," Houk told Terry. "How is your control?" Terry said his control was fine. "Do you want to go after McCovey," Houk asked, "or walk him and go after Cepeda?" Terry said he preferred to go after McCovey rather than walk him and have to work against Cepeda with the bases loaded. Cepeda was a very good hitter, and he was having something of a career year. There was a margin of error in working on McCovey with a base open. Earlier in the year, in a play-off game, Stan Williams, the Dodgers pitcher, had walked in the winning run, and Terry was aware that the home-plate umpire was from the National League, which meant you could be a little less sure of what the strike zone was. So Terry told Houk, "I'd like to take a couple of shots at McCovey high and tight, and then low and away, and if we lose him, then we lose him, and we go after Cepeda." So Terry decided to give Willie McCovey pitches just off the strike zone. Behind the mound Tony Kubek walked over to Bobby Richardson, his roommate, and said, "I sure hope McCovey doesn't hit it to you." Why, Richardson asked. "Because you've already made a couple of errors," Kubek said. If nothing else, thought Richardson, Kubek got Willie Mays to laugh.

The Yankees were playing McCovey like a dead pull hitter. Terry checked his infielders just before he threw his first pitch and noticed how far over in the hole toward first base Bobby Richardson was playing. Terry was worried about McCovey going up the middle, and for a moment he thought of calling Richardson over and moving him back more toward second, but then he checked himself—he was playing with Tony Kubek and Bobby Richardson, and they were the best infielders around. National League hitters or no, they knew more about how to play batters than he did. His first pitch was a slow curve, just outside, and McCovey swung and hit a soft drive down the right-field line, which the wind carried foul. The next pitch was an inside fastball, and the moment Terry threw it, he was pleased, because it was a very good pitch, just where he wanted it, and by all rights it should have tied up a big powerful hitter like McCovey. But he watched as McCovey did a brilliant job of hitting. Almost by instinct and in the fraction of a second allotted to him, McCovey bent his immense body slightly backward in order to get more arm extension, and he hit the ball like a rocket, a vicious smash right at Richardson. For a moment Richardson thought it was a base hit, a ball that would go over his head, and then, because McCovey had hit it so hard, with topspin, the ball began to come down. Years later at his induction into the Hall of Fame, McCovey said that he never hit a ball harder. Many fans were later left with the image that Richardson had jumped and speared it, but, in fact, even as Richardson caught it, he was moving his hands down to match the sharp downward trajectory of the ball. Ralph Terry not only won but in the process obliterated the ignominy of being the pitcher who had thrown the home run to Bill Mazeroski in the 1960 World Series. The ball McCovey hit went to the Hall of Fame, as in time did McCovey himself (Terry would eventually go back to Larned, Kansas and play on the senior golf tour). Now not even two years later he was struggling for his career.

He was one of the most popular players on the team, a country boy who loved the big city. Relaxed, tolerant, highly intelligent, he had come from a small town in Oklahoma to the biggest city in the country. Unlike many of his teammates, he came not with the fear and anxiety about things that were different, but with anticipation and curiosity. In the locker room, more than most players, he was able to cut across the different groups, finding something of value in almost all of his teammates, and always accepting them for what they were. If some of the other veteran players were made uneasy by the new breed of players, Terry was different. He quite admired them, and thought that in some ways they might even be tougher than the old-time ballplayers because they knew a world outside baseball, and therefore were not so torn apart by a single defeat.

He was one more of the Tom Greenwade boys on the Yankees. He had even played on the same Baxter Springs team that Mickey Mantle had once played on, and in time Greenwade showed up at Terry's home—a lean, older man driving a black Cadillac. Tom Greenwade, Terry thought, had a pretty good line when he dealt with country boys. "Ralph," he said, "how would you like to play baseball in the biggest city in the world?" Terry liked that idea immediately, and he liked it even better when Greenwade told him that Terry's timing could not be better. "Why, son, the Big Three [Raschi, Reynolds, and Lopat] are getting a little old. You'll be coming up just in time." And Terry not only loved the sound of Greenwade's words, but with the confidence of the young, he believed them as well. He signed with the Yankees for a small bonus and was sent to Binghamton, New York, to play with one of the Yankee Class A teams. Since Cooperstown was not very far away, he got permission from his manager to go over and watch the annual Hall of Fame game there, where the Yankees were playing that day. Jim Turner, the Yankee pitching coach, recognized him and, because it was not a league game, told him it was all right to sit down at the end of the Yankee dugout. Terry walked down to the end of the bench, where he found three very old men sitting together. Very full of himself, and sure that the big leagues were just around the corner, Terry introduced himself to the nearest of the men. "Hi, I'm Ralph Terry, and I'm pitching for the Binghamton Yankees," he said, and the tone of his voice, he later decided, was more than a little cocky, implying that within a year or two he would be with the big-league club. The older man, one of the most courteous people Ralph Terry had ever met, said, "Well, Ralph, it certainly is a pleasure to meet you. Now, my name is Cy Young. And these fellas over here next to me are Zack Wheat and Ty Cobb." Just as Terry decided that he was the youngest and biggest fool in professional baseball, Cy Young moved over a little closer, to sit next to him, and he talked pitching with him for the rest of the day.

Terry knew that the Yankees were not a particularly altruistic organization. In 1961 he had won 16 and lost only 3, even though he had missed six weeks with a sore arm and shoulder. In the spring of 1962 he had been ordered to fly to Florida and prove to management that he was healthy before he was even offered a contract. By August 1964 he had heard rumors of trades, and there was one report that the Yankees were going to trade him to the Mets for Frank Thomas. Then, later on, when the Yankees picked up Pedro Ramos from the Indians for a player to be named later, he heard that he was the player to be named later, that the Yankees had to submit five players, and that the Indians had demanded that his be one of the names. As the summer moved along, his back began to feel better and he began to pitch better. Someone in the Yankee management came to him at that point and asked him to tell reporters that he did not feel well and that his arm still hurt, as a way of decoying Cleveland and getting the Indians not to pick him up.

15

The Cardinals were a troubled team at the All-Star break. The addition of Lou Brock had added a badly needed spark and given them a new dimension of speed, but as a club they still were faltering. They were one game under .500 and ten games behind Philadelphia. At the beginning of the season the Cardinal players had felt that they could beat the Phillies in head-to-head competition, and that they were a better team. Yet here were the Phillies doing everything right, with Johnny Callison making a bid to become the National League's Most Valuable Player and a young player named Richie Allen looking like he might be the Rookie of the Year. The Phillies were looking harder and harder to catch. For St. Louis it was turning into a season of disappointment: the Cards would go on a small streak of three or four wins, and then they would slip back and match it with a comparable losing streak. The Cardinals decided they had to make their move at the All-Star break. They had started the season needing to fill two positions in the outfield. Curt Flood and Lou Brock were set, but they were still looking for an everyday right fielder. They were still, Bing Devine thought, incomplete as a team; both their power hitters were infielders, and they were falling short in getting sufficient power from the usual source—the outfielders. They were using something of a patchwork combination in right, so Devine decided to call up a young outfielder named Mike Shannon. He was twenty-four, a big, strong local boy who signed with the Cardinals in 1958 after playing quarterback with the University of Missouri freshman football team. Football was his game of preference, and he was probably better suited to it physically than he was to baseball, but baseball not only offered more money, more important, it offered its money up front—in his case, a fifty-thousand dollar signing bonus. Because he was a local boy, the Cardinals had watched him grow up, and they took him into Busch Stadium for a tryout. It was a day on which Shannon, who was built more like a tight end than a quarterback, simply hammered the ball. Devine had asked Hutchinson what he thought, and Hutch had said, "Lock the goddamn door and don't let him out until we sign him."

The Cardinals, Shannon thought, were very good to him; they moved him up quickly, letting him skip a classification every year. In 1963 he went to spring training with the big-league club, one of several players trying to crack the outfield. He showed up only to find George Altman's name written in on the board for the right-field job. He immediately went in to see Johnny Keane. "Hey," he said, "I hit .300 in the minors and I may be the best defensive outfielder you have, and I'm not getting a chance here." It was more than a little audacious, he later decided, but Keane was not put out. "You're right," the manager said, and thereupon gave him a very good shot at the right-field job, but Shannon did not hit well that spring and found that he was not yet ready. He went in to see Keane to thank him for giving him the chance. "That's okay," Keane said, "we'll give you a couple more days, and we don't want you to lose confidence in yourself. We think you have a place here one day." It was a very nice way for a manager who had a lot of other things on his mind to treat a kid who was not even a rookie, Shannon decided.

In fact, Shannon was very much in the Cardinals' plans, and in 1964 they called him up, Bing Devine said, to make their outfield complete. They were not thinking batting average, for he was hitting only .278 in Jacksonville, but he was a very good defensive player, with one of the best arms in the league, and he would hit for power, they thought. But the Cardinals were still far back and had not shown any signs of making a pennant run. There was no doubt that the tension and frustration on the team was mounting. As far as

Johnny Keane was concerned, the source of this was Dick Groat, the shortstop. Groat was a good player, professional, smart, *and* very heady, but someone to be watched, Keane thought. He had a tendency to be something of a clubhouse lawyer, a man who always seemed to be whispering something to other players, often, Keane was sure, words of discontent. That, in fact, was true—"Whispering Smith," his teammates called him, after a fictional character of the day—but whether he was the true source of dissidence was another thing. It was true that Groat was down on Keane at this point. Groat liked to use the hit-and-run play and he was very good at it, which was no small achievement, since he was one of the slowest players in the league. That meant Groat had to call for the hit-and-run himself when he was sure the opposing team was completely unprepared, since he could not do it in situations that normally mandated it. Keane had given him permission to do that earlier in the season, but in one game it had backfired, and Keane was so irritated that he had taken away the right to call the play. That, in turn, had angered Groat—it limited his freedom at the plate, and he thought it a too-severe rebuke by an untested manager of a senior player. There was no doubt that he sulked after Keane restricted his freedom, but his teammates did not think he was truly sowing dissension—it was just Groat being Groat. There was always a touch of the shadow manager to him, which was almost inevitable in a player with his exceptional baseball knowledge and whose mind was always in the game.

Still, Keane was angry. Not only was the team playing below expectations, but with the pressure mounting on him to win and his own job in jeopardy, he saw Groat as a challenge to his control. He became determined to flush out the shortstop as a malcontent at a team meeting in New York, where the Cardinals had gone to start the second half of the season after the All-Star Game. The meeting unfolded as a sort of theatrical play in which Johnny Keane had written all the lead parts: Keane got up and told the team that he knew what was going on, that there was someone out there who was always second-guessing him and he was damn well tired of it. It was a curious scene, this normally mild man in a genuine rage, prancing back and forth with his odd little pigeon-toed walk in front of a room of silent players. Whoever was doing it was damn well under-mining the team as well, Keane continued, and he was not going to stand for it. "Maybe I'll lose my goddamn job, but I'll promise you this—I'm going to take some of you with me," he said as he finished up. Then he went around the room asking each player if he had any criticism of the way the team was being managed. "Flood, you got anything to say?" Flood said he did not. "Brock, you got anything to say?" Brock said he did not. Eventually he came to Groat. Groat stood up and said, "Well, John, I think you're talking about me." *"You're goddamn right I am,"* Keane said. "John," Groat continued, "I did not mean to undermine you or to hurt the team. So let me apologize to the team if you think I did."

Mike Shannon, just called up from the minors, nudged Bob Skin-ner, a veteran player, who was sitting next to him. "What the hell is this all about?" he asked. Skinner answered, "Mike, whatever you do, don't say anything. Just keep absolutely silent." Though Keane had cleared the air, it was not a particularly pleasant experience. All the players, one Cardinal remembered, were looking down at their shoes as Groat's apology took place, and for many it seemed overkill on the part of Keane, a man whom they quite liked. It was some-thing that should have been settled in private, between the two men. Some of the younger players felt uncomfortable being at a meeting where a grown man had to humble himself so completely when his sins were so small. If anything, some of the players thought, the meeting was more divisive than it was unifying, and it obviously re-flected the mounting pressure on Keane and his awareness that, if things continued the way they were, he was on his way to becoming a minor-league manager or a major-league coach once again. Nor did the team rush out later that day and crush the lowly Mets. With two outs and a 3–2 lead in the ninth inning, Curt Simmons threw a change to Frank Thomas, who jumped on the ball and won the game for the Mets, 4–3.

That day Bob Broeg, who was the sports editor of the *St. Louis Post-Dispatch*, was traveling with the team and, since it was the mid-point of the season, he decided to ask the Cardinal players what they thought was wrong. Some of them did not want to talk, and some talked reluctantly, only off the record, but Bill White, the first base-man, was quite willing to talk for the record. What was wrong with the team, he said, was himself. He was supposed to be one of the two power hitters on the team, along with Ken Boyer, and he was not doing the job—knocking in 100 runs as he was supposed to. A year earlier at this time, he said, he had already knocked in 60 runs; this year he had a measly 30, which adjusted for the entire season would come only to 60. Boyer was doing his job, he said, but he, Bill White, was not.

There was a reason for White's problems. He had hurt his left shoulder during the off-season doing exercises, perhaps, he decided years later, inflicting some damage to the rotator cuff. His shoulder had yet to heal, and since he was a left-handed batter that was ex-tremely damaging, because it robbed him of his power shoulder, the one he used to drive the ball. He had been getting regular shots from the Cardinal doctor, Dr. I. C. Middleman (of whom he was not a great fan, saying in private that the good doctor's initials stood for I Cut), but none had given him any relief. In a way Bill White was the lineal descendant of George Crowe, though he had not played in the Negro leagues and had not lived through two different ages of black baseball history, as Big Daddy Crowe had. But from the start, in part because of his intelligence and his inner strength, he had been a leader among the black players, and not merely on his own team. When other teams came to St. Louis, the black players tended to check in with Bill White and talk with him about whatever was on their minds. White, too, was an impressive man physically, well muscled, so powerfully built that some of his teammates marveled that someone so big and strong and potentially muscle-bound could get around on the ball so quickly with his bat. White had not really wanted to be a professional baseball player, and had actually entered college, hoping to become a doctor. However, his athletic skill and the early offers to sign a baseball contract were too good to refuse.

He was exceptionally fair-minded and, as such, an immensely val-uable teammate, for he had the ability to rise above his own prob-lems to comprehend the complex feelings and motivations of others, instead of merely reacting with his emotions. He understood almost perfectly the historic moment when the black players had finally arrived, how much was invested in them on the part of those who had never had a chance to succeed and those who might come after, and he was determined that he and those blacks around him would use this great moment not just to play well but to make an even larger statement about black purpose and black ability. He was unsparing in his judgments about himself and the other black players. Long after Solly Hemus had been fired, he was capable of getting on Bob Gibson, if Gibson was having trouble with his control. There had been one game in 1962 when Gibson was pitching with the bases loaded and had walked a weak-hitting batter to force in a run. White had yelled at Gibson (as probably no one else on the team would have dared to), "Come on, Bob, you got on Solly for not using you, and now you got your chance and you're not doing the job. Maybe Solly was right. Maybe you don't belong here."

Nor did his demand for excellence, for playing hard and doing your best, extend merely to his own teammates. The previous year there had been a young black player with Cincinnati who was obviously irate about not playing enough, and he had come up as a pinch hitter late in a game. He dogged the at bat, standing at the plate and taking three straight strikes, the bat never leaving his shoulder. After the game Bill White sought the player out and told him, "Listen, you cut that crap out. We can't afford to do stuff like that. You're hurting *everybody* when you do that. A lot of people worked very hard for us to be here and we're not going to blow this chance." Bill White seemed to know how to handle not just baseball but life, gaining the respect of everyone he met. Barnstorming with black players in 1960, Bob Boyle, a writer for *Sports Illustrated*, had been intrigued by the black baseball slang. "Was there any one of the black players who never cut a hog [and thereby never disgraced himself]?" he asked a couple of black players. "Only Bill White," one of them said.

Bill White was one of those forceful and determined men who seemed strengthened by the adversity he had faced growing up. He was born in the Florida panhandle in 1934, but came north to Warren, Ohio, as an infant. His family had been sharecroppers who picked cotton for generations and became part of the great migration north that began in the earlier part of this century. Six brothers and three sisters, along with their mother, eventually moved to Ohio. The young men in the family found work in the steel mills, first one member arriving, and then another, each living with the other for a time and then finding a place of his own. In time, seven of Bill White's uncles were in the Warren steel mills, which was hard and demanding work. The family matriarch was his maternal grandmother. Tamar Young was a dominating figure, called "Mother" by every one of her children and grandchildren. She ruled the family with an iron hand and a strong belief in the value of the switch to discipline children. Bill White's father was not a presence in his life, for he had left the family early on; White's mother was a sensitive woman who should have gone to college, but had lacked the money even though she had been the best student in her high school class.

Growing up, White remembered the singular forcefulness of his grandmother. In her politics and her attitude toward white people she was, he recalled later, not unlike the Black Muslims who surfaced in the sixties. Her hostility toward whites was uncompromising: she blamed them for stealing black people away from their native land, and for selling them into slavery; she blamed them for passing on their vices and diseases to blacks; and she blamed them for the alcoholism she saw all around. She was at once very antiwhite and very religious, a true believer in the literal word of the Bible. She was determined that no one in her family was going to slip into the failure and degradation that she believed whites had deliberately inflicted on black people. No one in her family was going to drink. No one was to use profanity. Everyone went to church. No one was to steal. The grandchildren had to be in the house by sundown. On one occasion when Bill White was five years old and his mother was reluctant to spank him for some minor infraction of the house rules, his grandmother took up a switch and punished both her daughter and her grandson. The essential code of the family was simple: life was filled with prejudice and injustice, and it was each member's individual job not to succumb but to succeed, despite the efforts of those who would denigrate them.

In some ways his experience with racial prejudice was slow in coming. In elementary school black and white children socialized, but later, he realized, as they entered junior high school, the socializing ended; parties were now segregated, and the black children were no longer invited. Similarly, at school dances he realized that the black children were on one side of the room and the whites on the other. As a football star and a boy with a powerful presence he had seemed likely to be voted student-body president, but the opposing forces deftly entered another black student as a candidate, the black vote was split, and he lost. He was, however, elected senior-class president, but at the class dance the adults chaperoning arranged things so that for the first time in recent history the class president did not dance the first dance with the queen of the class, who was white. His athletic ability in high school helped get him into college, and though a number of larger schools were interested in him, he chose Hiram College in Ohio, because it was said to prepare students well for medical school and it seemed to be a comfortable place. He got a grant of $250, which was to be applied against an annual bill of $750.

In 1952, when he was eighteen, Bill White caught the eye of a scout named Alan Fey at an amateur tournament and was recommended to the New York Giants. Their early sorties into the black world had yielded, among others, Willie Mays, and with that success the Giants decided to double their efforts in that direction. Soon Tony Ravish, who was further up in the Giants' hierarchy, showed up and smiled his approval on White as a prospect. Ravish took him to Forbes Field in Pittsburgh, where the Giants were playing (and which later turned out to be one of his favorite parks to hit in), and they signed him that day for $2,500 plus a new pair of baseball shoes, given him by Leo Durocher, the manager. They promised to let him come to spring training in Phoenix, and also that he would make the big leagues in three years. Cleveland was after him at the same time, but he preferred the Giants because the massive Luke Easter was playing first base for Cleveland, which seemed to eliminate his natural position. Ironically, by the time he arrived in the major leagues, in 1956, Luke Easter was gone from the Indians, and both Orlando

Cepeda and Willie McCovey were moving up in the Giants' farm system, potentially ready to challenge him for the Giant first-base job.

White mentioned to Tony Ravish that there was a catcher on another team who he thought was a very good ballplayer, but Ravish, having seen the catcher, was not interested. "That guy has a little bitty skinny neck," he said, reflecting the physiological biases of the time, "and we never sign a player with a turkey neck. Those guys never grow and fill out." Size and power were the critical parts of the new Giant mandate, and that became clear to White when he showed up at his first instructional camp in Melbourne, Florida. Over the next few weeks, he played with Willie McCovey, then tall and somewhat skinny, but still awesomely strong—when White would hit a home run of 350 feet, McCovey would seem to answer with one of 370 feet. In other camps they were joined by Leon Wagner, Orlando Cepeda, Willie Kirkland, and, at different times, various members of the Alou family. The godfather of the nonwhite players in those days, both American blacks and Hispanic blacks, was an intriguing figure named Alex Pompez, who had owned a black baseball team; he was unusually proud of his ability not so much to scout black talent as to spirit it out of the Caribbean countries, which was not always easily done. Pompez was designated to baby-sit these young players in Melbourne, and he became something of a cult figure to them, telling them what was expected of them in the big leagues, and what life in the Negro leagues had been like, and how he had existed in the numbers racket until the mob had squeezed him out. His favorite story was how he signed the great Minnie Minoso in Cuba for his team in the Negro leagues. He arrived in Havana to get the man who scouts said was the best player in Cuban baseball at that time, but his early advances toward Minoso were not successful. Depressed at his failure, Pompez was about to return to New York when he was having his shoes shined at his hotel. "You're Pompez, the baseball man from New York," the shoeshine man said. Pompez said he was right. "You're here to sign Minoso, our greatest player," the man added. Pompez said that that too was right and asked how the man had known. "Because I am a *brujo* [pronounced broo-ho]," he said, using the local word for witch doctor. Then the witch doctor made a prediction: if Pompez went to Minoso's house the next night at six P.M., Minoso would be ready to sign. Pompez did that, and found a rather terrified Minoso waiting eagerly to sign a contract. "How did you know he would sign?" Pompez asked his friendly *brujo* the next day. "Because if he did not his leg would have been broken," the *brujo* explained.

At his first spring training in Phoenix, Bill White quickly learned that he was not as gifted as he thought, that he could not hit the curve or the change, and that he had problems scooping balls out of the dirt. If he was going to make the big leagues, he was going to have to work harder than anyone else, he decided. He was going to have to make himself into a big-league ballplayer. So he went off to play with the Burlington-Graham team in the Carolina League. It was Class B ball, and it was a testimonial to the insensitivity of the men who ran baseball in those days that they did to Bill White what they did to so many young black players at that time; instead of letting him play on one of their farm teams north of the Mason-Dixon line, they sent him not merely to the South but to a tiny town with not even the marginal protection offered by an urban setting. White was not just the only black player on his team, he was the only black player in the *league* that year. It was 1953, the year before the *Brown* v. *Board of Education* decision. The South was already afire with much angry talk about the coming of northern integrationists, but the only integrationist around that year was Bill White. It was very hard for him, for his team played in small factory towns, and he became a kind of beacon to local rednecks, who would come out to the ball park and, for a tiny amount of money, yell at this one young black player, who symbolized to them a world beginning to change. Somehow he survived it, and managed to hit 20 home runs and bat .298. There was one day that summer when he got tired of being the recipient of all those cruel and ugly slurs, spit out of mouths as if they were machine guns; he yielded finally and gave them the finger. He and his teammates grabbed bats and had to fight their way back to the bus. There was another game in which a fan had gotten on him and yelled, "Bill, Bill White," and when White turned toward him, the fan unloaded a staggering list of racial epithets. White, enraged, hit the next ball *through* the wooden fence, and as he crossed home plate he heard the fan yell out, "Okay, after that I'm going to call you Mr. White."

Somehow after that season it seemed to get easier in his career, perhaps because he had been through the worst. He was no longer afraid. It was not about him, he knew, it was about them, and somehow he had managed to rise above it. Besides, some of his teammates, even the Southern boys, had been very good; if they had not understood all the problems he was facing, they understood a confrontation by a redneck mob, and they realized in some basic way that this was unfair, that it was a them-and-us situation, and they rallied to him. More than thirty years later, Bill White, an immensely successful man who was the president of the National League, violated his own rules about not getting involved in politics by going down to campaign for a man named Charlie Allen, a catcher on that Burlington-Graham team, who had stood by him in those early, dark days, and was running for sheriff.

After the Carolina League he played the next season with Sioux City in the Western League. That was, by contrast, a laugher, and there he hit .319 and 30 home runs. He came up to the New York team in 1956, and did well. He was making $4,000 and was called in by Horace Stoneham, the team's owner, who told him he was going to get a $1,500 raise, which White thought generous until he learned that it merely brought him up to the major-league minimum. After 1956 he went into the army for two years, and when he came back Orlando Cepeda seemed installed at first after he had been voted Rookie of the Year. At the same time, Willie McCovey was burning up the farm system and was about to arrive midway through 1959 for an equally sensational rookie year, and he too would be voted Rookie of the Year; between the two of them they would hit exactly 900 regular-season home runs. The Giants seemed to have an abundance of big, powerful black first basemen, all three of whom would be National League All-Stars, and it was time, White decided, for him to go. He asked the Giants to trade him. The only two places he did not want to be traded to, he said, were St. Louis and Cincinnati, cities with reputations among the black ballplayers in those days as being difficult to live in. ("Bill, you're my second best player on the team behind Mays," Chub Feeney told him. "I'll find a place for you." "And he did," White noted years later, "in St. Louis.")

Eddie Stanky had scouted him for the Cardinals before the trade and enthusiastically endorsed the idea of picking him up. Stanky was a huge Bill White fan. White had played for him at Minneapolis in 1956, and he was the rare modern player whose work ethic satisfied the demanding, old-fashioned Stanky. If anything, White had been known among the other Minneapolis players as Stanky's bobo—that is, his pet—the only player on the team whom Stanky never chewed out, and who even dared to talk back to him. Once Stanky caught White doing a crossword puzzle. "White, put that goddamn thing away and study a rule book," Stanky said. "If I got a rule book we wouldn't need you as a manager," White answered as his dumb-founded teammates looked on, for no one talked to Eddie Stanky like that.

If White was apprehensive about St. Louis, he soon found that the city was changing. The people in the Cardinal organization made an effort to ease his way. Bing Devine was helpful, as was Al Fleishman, who did public relations for The Brewery and thought the integration of the Cardinal team one of the most important things on his agenda. Bob Hyland, general manager of KMOX—the powerful radio station that broadcast the Cardinal games—soon became a friend. Certainly the fiasco of the St. Petersburg breakfast meeting had been an early lesson to them, but they were all, in their ways, exceptional men and, more than most men in baseball in that era, understood the social problems of integration. They helped Bill White to find better housing as the size of his family increased; when he bought his third house in a white suburb, Bing Devine asked his lawyer to represent White in completing the sale, which gave it the imprimatur of the Cardinals and removed many potential racial difficulties. Hyland, as a gift, landscaped the entire grounds, and Johnny Keane, by then the manager, gave him a tree as a house-warming present. Those were, Bill White thought, generous acts at a time when few white people did things like that. Jack Buck, the broadcaster, had also tried to help him buy a house in his neighborhood—but houses there cost about $60,000 at the time and Bill White made only $12,000 a year. These men wanted Bill White to feel that he not only played for their team but was a friend and a part of their world as well.

He did well in St. Louis. At first he tried to power every ball. He had, after all, hit 22 home runs in the massive Polo Grounds as a Giant rookie, and he was sure he could hit 40 in the smaller Sportsman's Park, so he swung for the fences every time. After a few weeks he was hitting .091, so he turned to Harry Walker, the hitting coach. Walker was a pure baseball man, and he could talk about the science of hitting for hours. He was an exceptionally talented, albeit demanding coach, a relentless perfectionist. When, either in a game or in batting practice, a hitter did something that displeased him, he would instantly yell out. He hated wasting a single at bat.

It struck Bill White in his first encounters with Harry Walker that the old racial attitudes might still be there. But Walker was a professional above all, and he was going to teach this big, strong young man how to hit, whether *either* of them liked it or not. It was obvious to Walker that White needed to learn how to discipline himself, and he had to learn that he could not pull every pitch. Walker had watched Bill White during spring training and thought he was potentially a very good hitter. He sensed White's problem then: a man that strong on a team that lacked power hitters might be tempted to muscle the ball all the time. White had enjoyed a very good spring and had hit something like seven home runs in the preseason. That early success, Walker thought, would almost surely push him even more toward trying to be a pure power hitter. Spring training, Walker believed, was a deceptive time: the pitchers were not yet ready, and they did not go to their full repertoire, particularly their change-ups. Walker decided that he would not push White, but that he would let him start the season, and if things went wrong, then he would talk with him. But before that could happen, White, by then hitting below .100, came to Walker. "Harry, if we don't do something, I'm going to be out of this league," White told the coach.

They were in Los Angeles at the old Coliseum, and Walker suggested they go out early each day before the other players were around, to work on his hitting. "You're trying to hit a home run every time up," he said. "Don't do it—just try and hit the ball up the middle." Walker taught Bill White to use his hands; to go inside out on his swing, but still to swing hard, in order to hit to left field; and, above all, how to use the entire field. "Damn it, Harry," Harry Caray the broadcaster said, watching their workouts one day, "you're going to take a power hitter and turn him into a Punch and Judy hitter." No, said Walker, he was going to make him into a good hitter who could hit to all fields but who still had power. He was still to swing hard, Walker emphasized, but if he would wait just a fraction of a second instead of trying to pull everything, and if he would go with the pitch, he would not lose all his power.

Despite the immense social, cultural, and generational gaps that lay between them, there developed just the slightest glimmer of friendship. Harry Walker was born to teach; as a coach he had an almost maniacal need to pass on to others *everything* he had ever learned, and there were few more apt students in baseball than Bill White, a world-class listener. "You have to have one very good year to know what you can't do," Walker kept telling White, "and when you have your very best year, then you've learned your limitations. Then and only then you can understand what you can and can't do." When they discussed subjects other than baseball, such as race, the gulf between them was enormous. Harry Walker would talk about what he thought was wrong with blacks as he knew them in the South—that they were shiftless and lazy, that they did not take care of their property. It was not easy for Bill White to hear such things, but he came to respect Walker's honesty and fairness; in some ways, at least, his mind was not closed. By July of that first year White was hitting over .360 and he made the All-Star team. He knew he owed a considerable debt to Harry Walker and he came to believe that he never would have lasted thirteen years in the big leagues if it had not been for Walker.

White's bat was critical to this Cardinal team. During the 1963 season he dove for a ball along the first base line and bruised his shoulder. Johnny Keane took him aside and said, "From now on don't dive for any balls. It's not worth it. And don't go into second base trying to take out the second baseman. It's too big a risk. We need you for all one hundred and sixty-two games." That season, his best year in the majors, he hit 27 home runs, knocked in 109 runs, and hit .304. But the 1964 season, to which he had looked forward, was turning into a disaster because of his shoulder injury. He hated feeling weak and knowing that his physical condition was directly responsible for the team's poor performance.

While he was in New York he spent some time with Bob Boyle, who had become a friend when Boyle had written a wonderful piece on the last black barnstorming tour for *Sports Illustrated*. White told Boyle of his problems. Boyle thought that perhaps White was not getting the absolute best medical treatment available (in fact, Boyle thought that most team doctors in that era got their jobs by dint of being drinking buddies of the owners, an assumption that was sometimes not far from wrong). He suggested that perhaps White might see a specialist in New York. Boyle sent him to a distinguished orthopedic surgeon named Hans Kraus, who had helped Boyle with his severe back problems. Kraus was famous, having helped treat John Kennedy for his chronic back problems. White went to see him and Dr. Kraus immediately gave him a shot. Unlike the team doctor, who had targeted an area in the front of the shoulder, Dr. Kraus went after a spot in the back and White felt immediate relief. A few days later, in a doubleheader in Pittsburgh, White celebrated by getting six hits, including two home runs, and knocking in five runs. The Cardinals swept the series. It was the kind of day a power hitter should have and which he had not had all year. A critical piece had been restored to the Cardinal lineup.

16

Jim Bouton was having a hard time pitching in the early summer. His back had been hurting constantly since the spring, and he was not able to throw his fastball with full force. Bouton was a power pitcher without a power pitcher's body—too small by the usual standards to be a big-league fastball pitcher; in his own words, he was a Volkswagen at the Indianapolis 500. His fastball was, at best, in the low nineties, and if he lost anything on it, then he was immediately vulnerable. Other, bigger, stronger, pitchers might encounter physical problems, but they would be strong enough or experienced enough to pitch their way through them; with Bouton there was no buffer zone, everything had to be perfect. Here he was, in his second big season, after winning twenty-one games in 1963, and he was without his real strength, which meant increasingly that balls hit off him were home runs. Curiously, Bouton was not in unbearable pain. He went to see Dr. Sydney Gaynor, who told him, "Son, if it hurts, just don't throw." It didn't hurt, but he just could not throw as hard as he wanted to. He kept wondering what he was doing wrong. In June and July he experimented with his mechanics, but things only got worse. He was adjusting, except that his adjustments were the wrong ones.

Then, in mid-season, his shoulder and back began to feel better. His body was somehow healing itself. Later he was diagnosed as having had a low-grade chronic strain of the brachialis muscle, which attaches the biceps to the bone; this injury would, in any real sense, end his career as a power pitcher the next season. In retrospect, the fact that he had chronic arm and shoulder problems was not surprising, because he threw as hard as he could on every pitch, with a delivery so ferocious that his cap often flew off. He was well aware of his tenuous position as a star major-league pitcher. When he was pitching well he was able to get seven or eight strikeouts a game, but the line between being a star major-league pitcher and being out of the business entirely was a thin one for him, and he was well aware of it. He was, as much as anyone, the first fan as player, as a teammate once told him, someone for whom being a major-leaguer was an unlikely, indeed almost giddy, experience. It was not surprising that in some sense at least he always remained an outsider, able to see the frailties and vulnerabilities of big-leaguers in a way that most players, who had always expected to play in the majors, did not. It was not surprising that when his career was over he became not a coach but a writer. He had always had to work hard at being a baseball player. He barely made his high school team. Only in his senior year had he been able to pitch, and until then his nickname had been "Warm-up" Bouton. He was a walk-on player at Western Michigan, and he did not do well there, but then one summer he played for a very good team in an amateur league in Chicago, the Cook's Sportscraft. Even here his career did not look bright (he was their number-four pitcher) until the National Amateur Championship in Battle Creek, Michigan, a double-elimination tournament. His team went up against a famed team from Cincinnati, which, it was said, never scored fewer than fifteen runs. The place was loaded with scouts, and that day Bouton pitched the single best game of his life, striking out ten, and after the game the scouts swarmed over him. His parents, who were middle class, thought the world of professional baseball a perilous place, and his father had made him agree that he would not sign unless he got a $30,000 bonus. The Yankee offer was considerably under that: a $6,000 bonus and three years guaranteed at $500 a month for five months, plus an additional $10,000 bonus if he made the big-league team. As far as Bouton was concerned, that was $30,000 and more, and his

father, knowing how much his son wanted to try professional baseball, finally gave permission.

He found himself starting the 1959 season with the Yankee Class
D team at Auburn, where very shortly thereafter he was hit in the
right hand with a line drive and broke the thumb on his pitching
hand. That finished him at Auburn, where his record was a less-
than-inspiring 1-4 and his ERA was 5.73. Things were not looking
good. After the accident he was sent out to the Yankee rookie team
in Kearney, Nebraska, and told to work as hard as he could to keep
his right arm from atrophying. His arrival in Kearney was inauspi-
cious; he checked into his hotel, went immediately to the hotel room
of the manager, Jimmy Gleeson, and announced eagerly that he was
Jim Bouton, the new pitcher who had been sent out by the Yankees.
Gleeson looked up at him, shook his head, and said, "Young man,
I'm going to give you a great piece of advice. Don't ever knock on a
manager's door without first calling from the lobby. It just so happens that it doesn't matter to me, but there may be other managers,
if you go higher up, who may be entertaining guests. So I'd be careful about it in the future." In Kearney he worked out and pitched in
a few games, and his record was 2-4 with an ERA of 5.40. For most
young players in Bouton's position, this would have been a dark moment. But Bouton was curiously optimistic. From Kearney he wrote
his father a letter that began by saying that he was at the absolute
bottom of the barrel, that he had a broken pitching hand, that he
was still listed with the Class D team, the lowest ranking one of the
thirteen teams in the Yankee organization, and that since there were
ten pitchers per team, he ranked himself as the 130th pitcher in the
Yankee organization. "But I think I'm going to make it," he concluded. Years later that confidence astounded him, and he often
wondered where it had come from.

It came, Bouton later decided, from an intuitive sense of how to
deal with adversity. In high school, when he had not made the team,
his love of the sport had kept him going. Now, he thought, as he
grew stronger and a little heavier, perhaps his body was catching up
with his hunger for the sport. In addition, he had begun to notice
that, although the other young pitchers with him were taller,

stronger, and far better credentialed, they seemed emotionally vulnerable. That vulnerability, he thought, came from the easy, early successes in their lives, when they had almost always been the biggest and strongest players among their boyhood peers, and therefore inevitably chosen as pitchers. As such, few had had to deal with adversity before. Now, for the first time, they were being subjected to physical and emotional stress. They had been sent to large, impersonal rookie camps where they were given numbers to put on the backs of their uniforms—and by this act alone, they were shorn of their individuality and perhaps their confidence. In addition, for the first time, they were pitching against other kids who were big and strong, and who had also always been the best. Bouton noticed something else about the other young men: because they had been high school stars, life in general had always been relatively easy for them. They had been invariably treated by their communities as local heroes; good usually not just in baseball but in basketball and football too; captains, it seemed, of all three sports, and thereby catered to; and always favored by the society around them. Now, starting out in these lower rungs of baseball where the amenities of life were quite marginal, they were dealing with being away from home for the first time. They missed their families, and they missed their girlfriends, and they missed those coaches who had been dependent upon them and who had treated them as if they were their own children, and in some cases better than their own children. They became homesick and their confidence had begun to desert them. When things went wrong they did not have the inner resilience to deal with their problems. When things went wrong in a game and their anger flared, they had a hard time controlling their tempers because this had never happened before. When they lost two games in a row, they got down on themselves, and it was harder for them to control their disappointment and depression. When their talent alone no longer carried them, they were not as smart about making adjustments, about listening to older pitchers who might teach them a new pitch. Whatever else, that was not Jim Bouton's problem. He was by nature mentally tough. Hardship and disappointment had come early for him.

His career seemed fluky from the start. In 1960 he was sent to Greensboro in the Class B League, expecting that as the players moved downward in the beginning of the season (a few pitchers released from the major-league team would go to Triple A, and they in turn would move the Triple A pitchers to Double A, etc.), he would end up in Class C or perhaps Class D again. But right before the cut, a pitcher named Dooley Womack, who was supposed to pitch a game, had a sore arm, so Bouton pitched and won. A few days later, with Womack still unable to pitch, Bouton won again. They kept him in the rotation and he was 4-0 when it was time to make the cut, so he stayed with Greensboro and made the All-Star team. He pitched well there, winning 14 games and losing only 8, with a league-leading earned run average of 2.73, and that won him a chance to go to spring training with the major-league team.

No one was more surprised than he at having gone so far in so short a time. He was nothing if not a quick study and an eager student. In 1961 he already possessed at least a fair fastball, a good curve, a slider, and a knuckler, and he went over to Johnny Sain during spring training and asked him what he needed to do to become a big-league pitcher. Sain told him he needed to define himself better—that he had a good selection of pitches, but that he had to figure out which was his best pitch and then devote a disproportionate amount of time to developing it. He had to make that basic pitch his strength, so that the people in charge of the team knew what kind of pitcher he was. "What they look for down here is potential—that is, velocity and movement," Sain said. "That can't be taught. The other stuff, location, finesse, how to work against the hitters, they figure they can teach you. But the speed of the fastball—and whether it has movement—that's what matters and that's what you have to show them from the start. That's what they'll look for in the very small amount of time that you have to work with them watching." Then Sain told him his own highly idiosyncratic philosophy of how the body behaves, that the body was all about memory: "It wants to do today what it did in the last few days. If you've run a lot in recent weeks, it wants to run today. If you've been throwing hard, it wants to throw hard. If you've been sitting down and doing nothing, it wants to sit down and do nothing." Therefore, he said, the best thing Bouton could do for his body was to throw hard, because in the end that was what his body would respond to. So Bouton worked religiously on his fastball that spring and summer, experimenting with how he held the seams of the ball to see which grip allowed it to move the most. Told as well that he needed a change, he studied how Pete Mikkelsen threw his exceptional palm ball—Mikkelsen reared back and seemingly threw as hard as he could, but despite the violent arm motion, the ball traveled very slowly to the plate—and got Mikkelsen to teach it to him.

During the 1961 season he pitched at Amarillo in the Texas League, which was Double A ball. There he played with Pepitone and Linz. That was a good team and, even more, a wild team. The Texas League was so grim, the bus rides so long and so rarely air-conditioned, that they all played hard, in fear of being returned there for the next season. Then, exhausted by the bus rides and the heat, they played hard both on and off the field. In the middle of the season their manager, Sheriff Robinson, was called home, and for a time it was as if the inmates truly ran the asylum. Then one day they were at the pool next to their motel, practicing dives, and Bouton was on the diving board when he heard a voice saying, "Bouton—you hit the water, and it will cost you fifty dollars." The Sheriff was back, and the party was over. It was a good season: he had made the All-Star team and, in a brutal hitter's league, where the ball always seemed to carry, he won 13, lost 7, and kept his earned run average at 2.97—a major victory of sorts.

In 1962 he went back to spring training, hoping to make it to Triple A or even, in his secret wildest dreams, the big-league team. There he picked up an additional bit of advice, ironically from a pitcher he did not particularly like named Jim Coates. Bouton thought Coates was shrewd about one thing in particular, and that was what to do when they called on you to pitch batting practice—"The Jim Coates Theory of Spring Training Batting Practice," Bouton later called it. The managers traditionally told the rookie pitchers to go out there and throw soft, so that the veteran hitters could work on their timing without being bothered by wicked curves and sliders. Coates said that was nonsense. Be selfish, he said. Go out there and throw as hard as you can and throw your best stuff. The pitchers who threw soft were soon gone. "Listen," he told the younger pitchers, "It's your ass and your career and you aren't going to get many chances. The veteran guys you're pitching to—they've already made the team." It was, he said, about the survival of the fittest. That made eminent sense to Bouton, and so he threw his best stuff, and the other pitchers noticed that Maris, Mantle, Yogi, and some of the other veteran players were quietly cursing him during batting practice, but that only made him throw harder and harder. Ralph Houk, on the other hand, was quietly smiling.

Bouton made the major-league roster in 1962 by the skin of his teeth, and early in the season he was given a start against the Senators. A good deal depended on that start, he was aware, for the major-league roster cutback was still coming, and he was a likely nominee to depart for Richmond. He barely made it past the first inning, walking the first two batters he faced without throwing a strike. With the bases loaded, the count 3-0, and Ralph Houk, poised on the top of the dugout to come out and relieve him, Bouton threw ball four. Houk began to come out of the dugout when the umpire called the pitch a strike. Given that reprieve, Bouton got the hitter out, and then he retired the side. From there he went on to pitch what was surely the most inartistic shutout in recent Yankee history. Giving up seven walks and seven hits, wearing out the Yankee bullpen, and helped by some spectacular catches by Hector Lopez in deep left-center, he won that game. When he came into the locker room after the game, Mickey Mantle had strewn towels from the entrance clubhouse to his locker.

In spring training 1963, still sure that he needed to improve even though he had spent a year in the majors with a record of 7-7, he sought out Ralph Terry to ask what he needed to do to improve his chances. Bouton considered Terry one of the most thoughtful players on the team. Terry thought for a moment and told him, "Well, Jim, I don't feel like you've really decided what kind of a pitcher you are yet. You have several pitches and you have enough talent, but you haven't decided whether you're a side-arm pitcher or an overhand pitcher. Let me give you one bit of advice. Forget about side-arm. You're not six-five or six-six and you're sure as hell not Ewell Blackwell. You're six feet, and you've got a good fastball. Get up on top and throw everything as hard as you can from up on top."

The first part of the season had ended up immensely frustrating for him. Bouton had evened his record at 7-7 just before the All-Star break in a game in which he had been very lucky to get a win. He had taken a 4–3 lead over the Twins into the eighth, but walked Tony Oliva to start the inning. Then Harmon Killebrew had hit an enor-mous home run to give the Twins a 5–4 lead. Berra had left Bouton in, largely because he was to be the first batter up in the bottom of the eighth, and Johnny Blanchard had batted for him. Blanchard struck out, but he had got to first because it was a wild pitch. Phil Linz bunted and got to first on a wild throw by the pitcher, Al Worthington. Bobby Richardson sacrificed the runners to second and third, Hector Lopez struck out, and then Mantle hit an enor-mous home run into the upper deck to win the game for Bouton.

At first the second half of the season seemed to be more of the same, a win and then a loss. Then, on July 21, with his record 8-8, Bouton pitched against the Senators. His arm had begun to feel stronger, and on that day he gave the Senators only four hits. It was the first of a mini–winning streak, and he ran four victories in a row, three of them complete games. Starting with that game, he went 10-5 for the rest of the season, feeling healthy and pitching as well as ever.

17

Late July was a bad time for the Cardinals, a time when the long baseball season seemed even longer. Bill White had begun to hit, and Lou Brock was playing so well that Bing Devine had already decided that the Broglio-Brock trade was the best of his life. But they were still playing .500 ball. On July 21 they played a three-game series at home with the Pirates and lost all three games. Worse, none of their three starting pitchers had gotten past the fifth inning. The next night they went to Philadelphia to open a four-game series with the Phillies. Bob Gibson pitched the opener against Chris Short and was hit quite hard, losing 9–1. It was not the way a team wanted to open a series against the league leaders, particularly with a man who was supposed to be its ace on the mound. The defeat gave the Cardinals a record of 47-48, and left them tied for seventh place, ten games behind the Phillies.

But they went on to win the next three games in Philadelphia. It was the beginning of what at first seemed like the slowest of comebacks. In Gibson's next start against the Cubs, he was hit hard again, lasting only six innings and giving up ten hits and six runs. Only the fact that the Cardinals absolutely hammered the Cubs' pitching for nineteen hits, and came back to win, 12–7, eased Keane's frustration. Keane told reporters afterward that he had no idea what was wrong with Gibson. "He's just not pitching," Keane said. People who should not have been hitting him were hitting him hard. There was some talk that he might have a sore arm and was stoically trying to hide it, but Gibson himself waved that speculation aside. "Why should I hide it? If I'm hurt I can't help the team and I can't do the club any good, I can't do myself any good," he said. The manager and the coaches studied him, and checked out his motion to see if there was a hitch, Keane said, but they couldn't find any. They tried giving him extra warm-up time because there were indications in the past that he needed more time than other pitchers to loosen up. They also, Keane noted, tried giving him less warm-up time. They tried to figure out if he was understriding or, for that matter, overstriding. Keane wondered if Gibson's arm was tired, something that occasionally happened to power pitchers without their knowing it, but Gibson insisted that his arm was not hurt and not tired. Tim McCarver, who was catching Gibson in those days, thought that his fastball was as sharp as ever, and that most of the hits were coming off the slider. By late July Gibson was very edgy. His record was now 8-8, and his earned run average was ballooning upward.

Finally, in desperation, the Cardinals sent for Clyde King, the top pitching instructor in their minor-league system. Bing Devine thought that King, who had a good eye for any hitch in a pitcher's motion, might be able to pick something up. King flew in, studied Gibson, and decided that he had found a slip in Gibson's motion on his slider: it was a barely detectable deviation that made the ball come in, if not slower, certainly fatter, with a significantly less sharp break as it reached the plate. It was the difference that baseball men said existed between the dime spin and the quarter spin on the slider. What they were talking about was the tightness of the spin as it was formed by the pitcher's release: a dime spin, delivered with the proper release and snap, was smaller and tighter, and the break that accompanied it was sharper and more abrupt when it reached the plate, thus it was much harder to hit; the quarter spin was bigger and lazier, offering a better target to hitters. Gibson, like many pitchers who had slipped out of their groove, was coming under the ball slightly with his hand as he released it, thus *pushing* it somewhat, rather than positioning his hand and wrist correctly and driving the ball to get maximum break.

King's visit helped. Gradually during the month of August, Gibson began to work back toward his groove. It was a hard time for him, his friend and battery mate McCarver thought. He was not so much angry as he was frustrated, and a frustrated Gibson was not an entirely pleasant phenomenon; weakness was the enemy of all athletes, and far more than most, Gibson resisted giving in to weakness. He hated the fact that he was burdening his teammates, rather than leading them.

How Bob Gibson felt on any given day mattered greatly to the St. Louis Cardinals. His was a towering presence on the field and in the clubhouse as well; his peer influence was all the more remarkable because he was a pitcher, not an everyday player. He played only every four or five days, and yet somehow he was gradually becoming the heart and soul of this team. If George Crowe had been the dominating figure in the past, and among the black players in the present it was still Bill White, then clearly the future belonged to Bob Gibson. McCarver watched his friend struggle that month, and kept his distance; he learned early on when to approach Gibson and when not to. A troubled Bob Gibson approached you; you did not approach a troubled Bob Gibson. They were becoming in that season not just teammates but friends. How Gibson worked out his relationship with McCarver was important not just to the two of them, but to the team as a whole. They were two of the strongest players on the team, and each was just coming of age. McCarver was the white son of a policeman in Memphis, one of the most segregated of cities. He was a raw and passionate athlete, driven to succeed no less than Gibson was. Ted Simmons, who came into the Cardinal organization a few years later, as the team was deciding to phase out McCarver, was intrigued by the two men. Simmons thought of Gibson admiringly as Wolf: predatory, loyal, powerful, dominating, single-minded, and with a singular instinct to find the weakness in others. Simmons equally admired McCarver, whom he thought of as Dog. The nickname Dog was not pejorative, for Simmons thought of McCarver as a fierce junkyard dog, utterly fearless, almost violent in protecting his territory, scrapping for every inch of turf, contesting everything on the field, reaching again and again beyond his natural abilities because he was so competitive.

They were to become the best of friends, McCarver and Gibson, with an enduring mutual admiration and trust. Baseball friendships could often be casual, based on whether a team did or did not trade a particular player to another team. But there was nothing casual about Bob Gibson; he had no choice over whom his teammates were, but he had a great deal of choice in his friendships. Generally in the baseball locker room, the better the player, the more popular he was and the more friends he had. That was not true of Gibson; if he was, as some teammates thought, a kind of samurai warrior on the mound, he was equally rigorous in his life. For him, friendship was based not just on ability, it was based on what kind of a *man* a teammate was; how he treated others, what he really believed in. McCarver, six years younger, was just establishing himself as Gibson's catcher. Their relationship did not start well. There was from the start the powerful but invisible difference in the way that the white society in those days treated a white boy like McCarver as a local hero, while a comparable black youth of perhaps even greater ability rarely got any journalistic attention; as he did not get journalistic attention, he did not become a star, and that had a direct impact on his price as a bonus baby. McCarver, a heralded schoolboy athlete, signed with the Cardinals for a bonus of $75,000 and moved up quickly through the Cardinal organization. Gibson, a few years older than McCarver, and most assuredly as gifted an athlete, resented that—in the light of his signing bonus of $4,000. When McCarver first came up in 1959, young and unsure of himself, fresh out of a world of Southern white boys, he was raw meat for Gibson, someone to be tested, and Gibson had an early go at him. The Cardinals were on their bus, and McCarver sat sipping an orange soda. "That looks really good," said Gibson as he went by him on the bus. "Can I have a swig?" Gibson knew, of course, that a young Southern white boy's mind was filled with ideas that black people carried more and different germs and yet he knew McCarver would be afraid of angering an important pitcher on a team he had not yet made. McCarver, who had never shared anything with a black man, let alone something as intimate as a soft drink, looked at the bottle of orange soda, and then at the deadly serious face of Bob Gibson, and mumbled something. "What was that?" Gibson asked, as if he could not hear. "I'll save you some," McCarver said. Gibby was just checking him out, McCarver realized later.

Gibson was always acutely aware of the different reactions of people to Bob Gibson the professional baseball player, and Bob Gibson the black man. White people often craved the friendship of the former, and sought his autograph and his friendship at dinner. But how would the same people treat him on the street? He *hated* it when white people made assumptions about him, when they noticed his careful dress, jacket and tie, and assumed that a black man that well dressed must be a minister. He never lost his wariness, and indeed, the more successful he became, the warier he became. In McCarver's case, there were lessons and cultural habits to be unlearned. There was a terrible day in spring training one year that McCarver long regretted, when a young black kid slipped over the fence and stole some baseballs, and McCarver yelled something at him. Years later McCarver thought he had said, "Hey, stop that, you little cannibal," while Gibson thought he had used the word *nigger*. McCarver looked up to see both Bob Gibson and Curt Flood studying him. He was embarrassed and later tried to apologize to Gibson. Gibson told him there was no need to apologize to him. But what he was really saying was: What you have to do is figure out why you said it. There was also the time McCarver was about to leave the locker room when he noticed a black man waiting for Gibson. He went back in to tell the pitcher, "There's a colored guy waiting for you. He says he's got a date with you." "Oh," said Gibson, "which color is he?" It was, McCarver came to understand, Gibson pushing him to be a better man and therefore a better friend as well.

As the distance between the two men closed, their relationship became tinged with humor. "Hey, Timmy," Gibson once asked, "do you know how a white boy shakes hands with a Negro?" McCarver said he did not. So Gibson trotted out Curt Flood as his straight man, and they shook hands—Gibson the white boy, Flood the black. Afterward Gibson looked down at his hand a little self-consciously and wiped it against his pants. "You've done it before, haven't you, Tim?" Gibson asked, and McCarver thought to himself, *Goddamn, he's right*, and he admitted that he *had* done it before. The more Gibson teased McCarver, the more secure their friendship became.

Gibson did an exceptional imitation of McCarver, particularly on those occasions when the ball popped out of his glove. "Gigub," he would yell, like a frog on a lily pad before he jumped into the water. Soon the rest of the team would yell it too, and McCarver became known as McGigub. By the middle of the 1964 season McCarver knew that he had earned Gibson's respect as a professional baseball player. There were more and more occasions when the Sadeckis, the Gibsons, and McCarver and his fiancée went to dinner together. The signs of acceptance from Gibson were often subtle. He did not lightly go over to people and tell them that he liked them a lot, or that he thought they were great ballplayers. One had to be skillful in knowing how to read him. One year McCarver had led the league in triples, and the following spring he hit a triple in an exhibition game. Gibson said to him after the game, "Hey, you like to hit triples," and it was something of a magic moment, McCarver thought. It was as if Gibson were saying, McCarver, you're all right and you're a pretty good ballplayer, and you may be all right as a man as well.

18

The Yankee scout first saw the young pitcher in 1959 at a high school all-star game in New Jersey, and he liked what he saw: an incredibly smooth delivery, and an exceptional natural fastball. He went over to the boy, who was soon to be eighteen, and who turned out to be well spoken and thoughtful. The boy had pitched only two innings and had been somewhat disappointed that day in his own performance, but the scout reassured him and started checking in regularly—how he was doing, where he had pitched, whether he still intended to go to college, as he had first said. It was a scene almost as old as professional baseball, but now there was a new twist to it: both the boy and the scout were black, and the scout was working for the New York Yankees, one of the last teams to get around to entering the chase for talented black players. The boy's name was Al Downing, and in time he would become the first black pitcher for the Yankees. The scout's name was Bill Yancey, and he would one day enter both the Negro Baseball Hall of Fame in Kansas City, Missouri, and the Basketball Hall of Fame in Springfield, Massachusetts. Denied the chance to play in both sports, Yancey, like Buck O'Neil, had become a professional scout, first for the Milwaukee Braves, who had been quick to seek the best young black players. Yancey developed a strong relationship with Roy Hamey, the general manager of the Braves in the fifties. In the late fifties, when Hamey worked for a brief time as the general manager of the Yankees, Yancey continued to scout for him, though he remained wary of the Yankees as an organization.

Yancey believed he had found in Downing the young man who might become the first black pitcher for the Yankees. Aware of the pitfalls ahead for any talented young player, but particularly for a talented young black player who bore the burden of being the first at anything, he was extraordinarily gentle and careful to nurture his recruit. He called him often and dropped by the Downing house regularly. Soon he became Uncle Bill to Downing, and his wife, a stunning woman who had once been a dancer at the Cotton Club, became Aunt Louise. She was also the standard by which Yancey compared disappointing prospects, as in "Louise can hit better than that," or "Louise has a better arm than that young man." Aware that Downing was thinking of going to college on a basketball scholarship, Yancey encouraged him to try college, telling him that baseball would always be there for him. When, after a year of college, Downing decided he wanted to try professional baseball, Yancey brought him to the Yankees. "I won't sign anybody," he told Downing, "that I don't think can pitch in the major leagues."

The Yankees were the right organization for him, Yancey thought, not just because they were ready to correct their lack of black players, but also because Downing was a left-hander and the Yankees always needed left-handers in that park; at that moment there were precious few talented ones in their farm system. He got Downing a bonus of sixteen thousand dollars. He could have gotten him a little more, he told the boy, but he preferred to use his extra leverage to start Downing a little higher in the Yankee farm system. It was better to begin in Class B rather than D, because if he started in D, he would have to burn up that much more time and energy climbing up the minor-league ladder. Only later did Al Downing realize how shrewd Yancey had been, thinking from the start in long-range terms. In addition, Yancey was trying to minimize the years Downing would have to play in small Southern towns. A few weeks after he signed, Downing was at Yancey's house and they were watching a game together. Juan Pizarro, a gifted left-hander from Puerto Rico, was pitching for Milwaukee. "You see him?"

Yancey asked. "You think he's a good pitcher?" Downing said yes, he did. "You'll be better than him," Yancey said. That was thrilling, the fact that Bill Yancey thought he would be better than Juan Pizarro, who was already pitching in the big leagues.

Yancey, Downing later thought, was an uncommon man, who was determined to make sure that Downing had some sense of the past as well—of his roots, and of those who had gone before him. So as Yancey became closer to Downing, he would come by on Sundays to pick him up and take him to the homes of some of the old-timers from the Negro leagues, such as Judy Johnson and Pop Lloyd, and he would introduce Downing to them. "Hey, Yank," they would say as they met, "is this the kid?" There was something thrilling in that, that he was "The Kid," and that these legendary men of the Negro leagues knew about him, talked about him when he was not there, and in some way were counting on him to make it. There was, Downing thought, something wonderful about watching Yancey with his old teammates from the Harlem Rens or the New York Black Yankees. Very few of them had money and most of them lived simply. But they had the gifts of laughter and camaraderie. They had shared a great deal: bad bus trips, being cheated on their promised pay by shady local promoters, white and black, and being run out of certain towns if they dared to beat a local white team. They *knew* they had been good enough to play in the major leagues, and they had often barnstormed on all-Negro teams against white All-Star teams from the majors; they would mention a white player of considerable reputation and would laugh and say, "Hey, we hit him, we hit him good"—though it was true that they retained a very considerable respect for the fastball of Bob Feller. It was clear to Downing that Yancey was taking him on these jaunts to show him there were men who had gone before him and who had not had the chance that Al Downing was getting. He owed it to them to succeed.

For all his gentleness and kindness, Bill Yancey was a tough man. One of the points he liked to make to Downing was that the players in the Negro leagues had been very tough. They might have been friends, but they played hard, because it was a rare opportunity in the America of the thirties and forties for a black man to make a

good wage, and the competition for places had been fierce. The
players had come at each other, spikes high, he said. Yancey sold
beer from the brewery to taverns in the black area of Philadelphia in
the off-season, which was not a calling for the faint of heart. He
was also a strict disciplinarian. "If you ever get too big for your
britches," he would say, pointing at his ass, "I'm going to get a
fungo bat and hit you right here." In his own universe of heroes two
men stood apart: Jackie Robinson and Jesse Owens. Everyone in this
era knew how hard it had been for Jackie because it had been reasonably well documented by the modern media. But very, very few,
Yancey liked to say, understood what Jesse had done, out there
alone in an earlier age. "Jesse," Yancey liked to say, "had been alone
in the most final and complete sense that a man could be alone, and
he never said anything to anyone." He had never complained. He
just worked harder and he never showboated. He was a man as
tough on the inside as he was fast on the outside. Those were the
black men that other black athletes should measure themselves
against.

Yancey warned him that it would not be easy in the South, but
even so, segregation came as a shock to Downing. When he arrived
at the Yankee minor-league center at Bartow, Florida, he somehow
thought, despite the warnings, that the Yankees, being the Yankees,
would not permit their young players to be so gratuitously humiliated. Somehow, fourteen years after Jackie Robinson's debut, he
had not expected to be separated from his white teammates as if he
were a lesser being. There was a terrible moment that he would long
remember when he first arrived and had gone up the steps of the
hotel. Someone stopped him and said, "No, no, you don't belong
here," and Downing answered that he did, that he was with the
Binghamton Yankees. But then they explained it to him—that the
white players stayed at the hotel and he and a few other players
stayed with a black family. Eventually he got past that memory, but
it never entirely went away.

He pitched for the first time in 1961 in Binghamton, and did very
well, though a certain wildness was there. He had far too much talent and too much raw power for that league, and he was striking out

a batter in almost every inning. In mid-July, with his record 9-1, he was called up to the major-league club. Downing called Yancey to tell him what he thought was the good news, but Yancey was furious. As far as he was concerned, it was the worst thing that could happen to a gifted young player. "I'm very much against it," he said. "You're not ready for it yet. You've got to learn to pitch in these leagues level by level." Yancey wanted him to spend at least half a year in Double A ball. As far as Yancey was concerned, Downing had succeeded merely by overpowering weak competition, and he had not passed the most critical hurdle of all: he had not learned to deal with adversity. He had not reached the moment when pure talent was not enough. Downing was not that good, he thought, because no one was that good.

Everything Yancey predicted turned out to be true. Al Downing pitched against Washington, and got knocked out in the second inning. It had nothing to do with talent; it was all about his knowledge of pitching. He had never been in real trouble in the minor leagues, so when he got in trouble in the majors he did not know what to do. In the past his answer had always been to reach back and simply throw harder. That had never failed before, but it failed him now. As he tried to throw harder he kept missing the plate. He had no capacity to change speeds, or to go to different pitches. In the minors, there were at most two men on any team who could hurt a pitcher, so when a pitcher got into trouble, he always tried to overpower them, figuring he would either strike them out or walk them. Then he went right back to his power against the other hitters. The game against Washington was a nightmare for Downing, and he lost his confidence. He was thereupon sent to the bullpen, but he was terrible there. He hated to get up when the call came from the dugout. He was throwing pitches all over the bullpen, and was something of a danger to the other bullpen pitchers. For the first time, he hated going to a ball park. Years later, Ralph Houk told him that they had wanted to send him down almost immediately after his performance in Washington, but they had been afraid they would damage his confidence even more, and so they had let him stay on.

Later in the year he was sent down to Richmond, and for a time he struggled. In 1962 he spent the year at Richmond, and for a while things went poorly. Slowly his confidence came back. In the last month of the season he began to get back his sense of self. He was 9-13 with Richmond, and by the end of the season, he felt he was ready for the major leagues. After all, there was a small difference between hitters in Triple A and those in the big leagues, and with the arrival of expansion even that difference had been blurred a good deal.

Yancey thought he was ready now, and his lectures began to change somewhat. Now they were more about how to handle himself in the big leagues. He should dress conservatively, like a gentleman. It was the sign of a quality person and it did not cost very much more to dress well as it did to dress poorly. With his clothes he would be saying important things about himself to people who would be watching him very carefully. In addition, he was to show respect to everyone and to have good manners, and indeed, in his rookie year, Yogi Berra went out to the mound to talk to Downing and later came back to the dugout shaking his head. Someone asked him, "What's the matter, Yogi?" "I was trying to tell him what to throw next," Berra said, "and he kept calling me Mr. Berra." In addition, Yancey emphasized, he had to understand the new pressures on him in terms of friendship. Suddenly he was going to be a celebrity, and therefore he had to be wary of instant friendship. As the first black Yankee pitcher, there were going to be all kinds of people coming after him, wanting to befriend him, some out to get something, even if they did not know what it was. Nor was he merely talking about the pressure of New York City. In every city the Yankees visited there would be people eager to get a slice of Al Downing, and they would know what hotels the Yankees stayed at and where the ballplayers went to eat. They would be quick to make moves on him, and they would be subtle and seductive. Stay with your old friends, and stay with your friends on the ball club, Yancey told Downing. Watch what Ellie Howard did, Yancey said. Howard had been through it all, as the first black on the Yankees, and he knew how to deal with the pressure both off and on the field.

During that rookie season of 1963, Downing truly arrived and went 13-5. As a celebration Bill Yancey took him to one of his favorite hangouts in Harlem, the Red Rooster. It was a celebration, an acknowledgment by Yancey that Downing had not only made the big leagues but was ready for his coming out. The Red Rooster was a famous place, and when they got there, Downing could feel Yancey's pride as he introduced the young pitcher to the owner: "This is Al Downing, the new pitcher for the New York Yankees." A fuss was made over him, and a book was brought over for him to sign. It contained the autographs of all the great celebrities who had visited—Louis Armstrong, Sugar Ray Robinson, Bill (Bojangles) Robinson, Cab Calloway, Duke Ellington, Count Basie, Earl Hines, Lionel Hampton, and Ella Fitzgerald, among others. The pages were so crowded with such celebrated names that it took Downing a long while to find a page with only one name, and he prepared to sign his own name there. "No! No! No!" said the owner, "That's Willie Mays's page! No one else signs on that page!"

The Yankees were sure that Downing was ticketed for greatness. Everything about him seemed right. He had a world of talent, and it was quite possible that in terms of pure ability he was one of the two or three most gifted young pitchers in the league; in addition, he was unusually mature, highly intelligent, and a model citizen. There were games when his control was near perfect and he was unhittable, and then days when he seemed to be trying too hard and missed the plate, getting in his own way. They were waiting for him not just to flash the greatness they were sure could be his, but to add to it a level of consistency, so that when he went out on the mound they could be sure they were going to get seven or eight strong innings. But it was not a process that could be rushed. So far this had been a reasonably good season for him. On August 9 he had pitched against Baltimore in a big game, and had won, 2–1, giving up only four hits. That made his record 9-4. Then, four days later, he beat the White Sox. Just when he seemed in a groove, however, he slipped out, losing his next three starts.

19

The old Yankee magic wasn't working. The other American League teams no longer rolled over and played dead for them. Indeed, the older Yankee players noticed something new: one of the key Yankee weapons—intimidation—no longer worked. Other teams, for instance, the up-and-coming Baltimore Orioles (managed by ex-Yankee Hank Bauer), not only had talented young players such as Boog Powell and Brooks Robinson in their regular lineups, but their pitching staffs might well have been better than that of the Yankees. The Chicago White Sox had fine young pitchers, and even the once-lowly Minnesota Twins (only so recently the parsimonious Washington Senators) had added the wondrous Tony Oliva that year. The ownership of other teams was getting better and more professional, their systems were better, with better scouting, while meanwhile the Yankee system was in decline. The old Yankee recruiting pitch—that if you signed with the Yankees you got less money in the short run and more in the long run as well as the chance to play with the best—had less and less appeal. Young men were signing with the team that offered the most money, and after the Yankee scouts made their pitch, rival scouts whispered that if you signed with the Yankees, you remained buried in their farm system.

George Weiss, the unpleasant but skillful creator of the great dynasty, had been aware by the late fifties that Dan Topping, the more involved of the Yankee owners, wanted to get rid of him, so Weiss had begun to cut back on his investment in the farm system and in signing young players. Whether Weiss had cut back to improve his own numbers, for his bonus was based, in part, on the profits each year, or to show two increasingly disenchanted owners who took the team's success for granted that he could still run a professional baseball team, no one was sure, but there was no doubt they had cut back.

Moreover, they were paying much more heavily for Weiss's racism than anyone had realized at the time. That racism was an unfortunate reflection of both snobbery and ignorance: Weiss did not think that his white customers, the upper-middle-class gentry from the suburbs, wanted to sit with black fans, and he did not think his white players wanted to play with blacks, and worst of all, he did not in his heart think that black players were as good as white ones. He did not think that they had as much courage or that they played as hard. That, thought Leonard Koppett, who had covered the team for many years for the *New York Post* and in 1964 for *The New York Times*, was his single biggest mistake. For in the past a key to the Yankee success was that in addition to signing such superstars as Di-Maggio and Mantle, they had always been able to sign a prototype player who was at the core of winning baseball—a very tough kid, wildly aggressive, who played hard, and who often signed with the Yankees for less money than he had been offered elsewhere because the Yankees were the Yankees and always won and these kids wanted to *win*. They were hungry, and they were driven for success: for them, being in the big leagues was not enough; they wanted to excel once they were there. These were players, Henrich, Bauer, or Kubek, who maximized their ability, who played above their level in pennant races and World Series games, and who helped give the Yankees their special advantage of playing well in tough games. They were tough kids, red asses or RAs, as they were known in the baseball vernacular. Here, more than anywhere else, thought Koppett, Weiss's racism had egregiously blinded him, for he did not see what was in front of him every day: that young black players coming into the big leagues exemplified the mental and spiritual toughness now that the Yankees had once demanded. Their lives had been strewn with far more obstacles than the white players'; since owners monitored how many black players they carried, there were very few black benchwarmers or backup players then. Either you were a starter or you did not make it. George Weiss did not understand the rage to succeed that drove so many of these young men, the passion to make up for so many years of racism and segregation and to avenge wrongs inflicted on those who had gone before them and who had been denied the chance. The harshest judgment on George Weiss, thought Leonard Koppett, was that he did not understand that the kind of player he had always sought out in the past, the tough kid who was at heart as much warrior as baseball player, was now, more often than not, black, and that among the new generation of red asses, a great many were black.

The Yankees were not a team that would have signed a Bob Gibson, for Gibson would have been too threatening to many of the people in management. It was no surprise that when the Yankees had finally brought up a black player, it was Ellie Howard, a talented, immensely hard-working player without the speed that marked the new generation of black stars (when Howard first arrived, Casey Stengel pronounced, "I got the one who can't run," and then, when Hector Lopez arrived, also black and also slow, the joke was amended to: "We've got the *two* who can't run"). If Vic Power, the great black Puerto Rican player, who had shown a quick bat and a great defensive ability in the Yankee farm system, had been somewhat different in his temperament, he might have been the first black Yankee, but Power did not fit the Yankee mold. He fielded with an un-Yankeelike panache and exuberance, playing first base not unlike a shortstop, one teammate noted (he was to win six Gold Gloves in the American League); in addition, he insisted, while in the minor leagues, on driving a Cadillac convertible, not only with the top down, which was bad enough, but accompanied by a white woman in the front seat. Of the many things forbidden to the first black Yankee, that was the most forbidden of all. On several occasions representatives of the major-league team went to him and urged him to change his ways, telling him they were not going to bring him up unless he did, but Power merely said to his roommate at the time, Hector Lopez, "They [the Yankees] can tell me a lot of things. They can tell me to play first base or the outfield, and how to hit, and whether they want me to pull or not, but they cannot tell me which women I can go out with." So Power languished at the highest level in the Yankee farm system: he hit .294 with Syracuse of the International League in 1951, which got him to the Yankee farm team in Kansas City in 1952, where he hit .331, which got him *another year* in Kansas City, where he led the league with a .349. That got him traded to the Philadelphia Athletics in December of the same year—a deal in which the Yankees got back very little. The Yankees, he told reporters years later, were waiting to see if he could turn white before they brought him up, but he could not do it. In succeeding seasons he loved to play against his old club, pronouncing it not "the Yankees," but "the Jankees." "The Jankees do not like me very much," he would say, but "I like to play against the Jankees and I like to beat them."

Ellie Howard came up in 1955, two years after Power was traded. He was the perfect player to break the Yankee color line—he had a sweet disposition, and he had the capacity to bury deep within himself the racial wounds inflicted by society. He had decided long ago that that was the path he was going to take. He was a man of the older generation, and his strength manifested itself not in rage at the injustices around him, as Bob Gibson's did, but in his ability *not* to show his rage. He had learned as a boy to walk away from provocations, and he did it for the rest of his life. He had grown up in St. Louis and went to Vashon High, a school famous for its black athletes. When he was still in high school in the late forties, the Cardinals used to have tryouts for local kids, and one year he went. Day after day he made the cut, and it was soon apparent that he was the best player there, the one who hit the ball most regularly and the hardest. At the end the people running the camp apologized and told him they were sorry, that he was the best prospect there, but that the Cardinals did not sign black players. He went instead to the Negro leagues, and inevitably to the Kansas City Monarchs, where Buck O'Neil thought him an exceptional player and an uncommonly strong man. A few years later, a number of teams came after Howard, including Cincinnati. Buck O'Neil carefully shepherded him away from the Reds and to the Yankees. Tom Greenwade talked to O'Neil about a great slugger named Willard Brown. "You don't want Willard," O'Neil said, for he feared that Brown was now a little old and it was very important that the first black player on the Yankees be successful. "You want a young kid that I've got here who's getting better and better named Ellie Howard." Within the world of black baseball, the honor of being the first black to play for the Yankees was considerable, and O'Neil wanted him to be a Monarch. He thought Howard was both mature and strong and was sure he could handle this demanding role as the first black Yankee.

Howard was the most polite of men. As Dan Daniel, one of the senior New York correspondents, wrote in *The Sporting News:* "Howard, the first Negro to gain a place on the Bomber machine, was chosen for that situation sui generis because of his quiet demeanor, his gentlemanly habits and instincts, and his lack of aggressive attitudes on race questions. He came to the Yankees determined to achieve the position he now occupies, not as a crusader." He was a man who kept everything in, and he never lost his temper. Years later, after Howard died quite young of a stroke, his widow, Arlene, would rage about the injustices of those years, and how she believed that repressing his rage had damaged his health. They both hated the fact that he was *always* under scrutiny, always being watched, that his behavior and his manners had to be so much better than those of everyone else. Both of them disliked it when people would tell them what an attractive couple they were, what a gentleman Ellie was, and sometimes say and sometimes imply that *if only all the rest of them could be like Ellie and Arlene, how much better it would be for everyone.* On occasion she could feel him stiffen just a little. The hardest thing was the loneliness of it all, the endless dinners and occasions at which they were the only black couple and everyone was watching them, to see if they were different, or if they would misbehave in some way. She knew that it was even worse for him, that day after day he was virtually alone at the ball park, where everyone was watching to see if he would blow it. Several years after he had joined the Yankees, they were at a dinner with Jackie and Rachel Robinson, and Jackie, who had no love for the Yankees, said he thought they were a terrible racist organization and that in some ways what Ellie was going through was as hard or harder than what he had endured. Robinson, at least, had always known that the front office was behind him, whereas Ellie knew that the front office had brought him up reluctantly.

His wife alone knew the price he paid. She would watch when things had not gone well at the ball park. He would withdraw, not talking to her or their children. He became very moody in those years, putting an unnatural pressure on himself to succeed. He was very much aware of the short curve of his career, that he had gotten to the big leagues later than most players and that, even then, he had been slowed down because Yogi Berra was in front of him. Arlene Howard liked to say that she was the one who got his ulcer. She was enraged when, rather late in his minor-league career, when he was twenty-four and already in Triple A ball, the Yankees decided to turn him into a catcher. She was convinced that would slow down his big-league career, for not only would he now have to learn to catch, a difficult adjustment for any player, but he would have to play behind Yogi Berra, only four years older than he was, a sure Hall of Famer. She felt that it was a racist decision, in some unconscious way, at least. She yelled at him, telling him that he had to demand a trade, that what the Yankees were doing was terribly unfair, and that, after all these years, someone else could learn to catch. "Let the Yankees trade for a catcher! They were able to trade for everything else. Let it be someone else's turn!" But he merely waved her objections aside, for he wanted to be a Yankee, he loved the aura of the team—"the great pinstripes," she later called them when she was angry. The Yankees were different, he would say, when she protested—they were special. She remained unconvinced. He never said anything when Stengel referred to him as a nigger or as an eight ball, or when Rudy York, scouting another team for the Yankees, described the color of what he said were a nigger's hands. Ellie Howard always held it in. Whatever ethnic slurs he heard in the major leagues, it was never going to be a problem, he once said, for whatever it was, he had already heard much worse. Stengel had wounded him, he had not expected words like that from a manager, but he understood that the manager was an older man and that similar quirks showed up in the way he treated some of the white players. Stengel never apologized for the use of ethnic slurs, for he was not the kind of manager who apologized to his players. However, as the years passed, there were certain small kindnesses from him directed at Ellie Howard, in part, the catcher thought, to apologize for his earlier insensitivity.

By and large, his teammates were a great deal better than the front office and the manager. At first, he had felt alone; he did not have a roommate because the Yankees did not yet have a second black player and were terrified of the idea of rooming a black player with a white one. On certain occasions he ate alone as well. But in general they accepted him, and accepted him quickly. Phil Rizzuto and Bill Skowron were particularly helpful, and the Fords—Whitey and Joan—seemed oblivious to color. Mickey Mantle was Mickey, generous to all, although not by temperament destined to live as conservatively as Howard. The one player on the team who articulated racial resentments was Jim Coates, a middle-inning relief pitcher from Virginia. In the past Coates had made little secret of his racial attitudes and that irritated some of the players. In 1961, when the Yankee team made its annual trip to West Point, Whitey Ford decided to settle the issue once and for all, and he arranged a boxing match in the army gym between Coates and Howard. Suddenly the two men were in the ring and it was a very serious business; no referee, no rules, just two men—one white, one black— slugging away as a lot of resentment came to the surface. Howard flattened Coates, and that ended Coates's racial sniping.

All of us, white and black, Arlene Howard later said, were part of an age in which everything was changing and all the rules were different; one society, which was segregated, was coming down, and another, ostensibly integrated, was replacing it. Everyone was trying to do the right thing, and at the same time everyone was very tentative. Howard himself had been amused by a trip the team had taken to Japan, on which most of the wives had gone as well, but which

Arlene had missed because she was pregnant. When they got back to the United States and the group was breaking up, everyone was kissing and embracing and saying good-bye, but no one knew how to treat Ellie: did they embrace him, did they kiss him, or did they shake hands. Suddenly everyone seemed flustered.

Management seemed not to care about his problems. The Howards always had difficulty finding housing, first when they came to New York and needed an apartment, and later when their family grew and they wanted to build a house. In 1959 they found a vacant lot in Teaneck and decided to build there. Arlene was not sure she was fond of the neighborhood, but Ellie liked it—he could hop into his car, go over the George Washington Bridge, and be at the Stadium in a matter of minutes. Just to make things a little easier, their builder bought the lot for them. Suddenly a neighborhood meeting was called about whether the Howards should be allowed to build and whether the neighborhood would accept them. Arlene was enraged: *Who are they to judge us!* she thought. *We are good people, we are responsible, we are a good family with good children. My husband is the first-string catcher for the New York Yankees, if that matters, which it should not, and these people are proposing to sit in judgment on us.*

The irony was that by 1964 he was probably the team's best player, admired and respected by all his teammates. The year before he had been the league's Most Valuable Player. If it had not been for the issue of color, he would have been a far better choice to succeed Houk as manager than Berra, for he had earned the respect of his teammates in a larger social sense, as Berra had not. But major-league baseball, let alone the Yankees, was still more than a decade away from letting a black man manage white players.

The Yankees were clearly in trouble. Mantle continued to shuffle in and out of the lineup, his great talent only sometimes showing through his injuries. More often it was not so much his talent that one saw now but a memory of that talent—the wounded hero, struggling with his body, looking old and vulnerable in the outfield, looking almost awkward at the plate, and then, as if in a moment seized out of the past, one swift, powerful swing and the ball jumping off the bat into the deepest part of the stands. A day or two later, though, reporters would be clustered around his locker asking about the latest leg pull or hamstring injury and whether he was going to be able to play that day. His right leg, one teammate said, seemed to be made not of muscle and cartilage but jelly; it was as if there were nothing there to control the leg until it was wrapped, but tape was no substitute for his cartilage. By mid-August he was batting .458 against lefties, and only .235 from the left side against right-handers. Those on other teams who watched him play, such as Jim Bunning, when he pitched for the Tigers, were puzzled as to why he did not give up the switch-hitting and simply bat right-handed all the time.

Maris was having problems too, and by early August Berra was not playing him against left-handers. Maris said he simply could not pick up the ball well against them. He was still a good all-around baseball player, but with two thirds of the season gone, he had only 14 home runs and 40 RBIs. At one point the starting Yankee outfield of Mantle, Maris, and Tom Tresh was so banged up that all three were limping. Once, when they came into the dugout from the outfield, Mantle looked around and said, "All we need now is a flag and a drum."

Ralph Terry was still bothered by a sore arm and was largely ineffective. Bouton, whom they had counted on to win 20 games, was bothered by his arm, which hurt just enough to limit his effectiveness, but not enough to keep him out. At mid-season his record had been 8-8. They had hoped before the season that Bill Stafford or Roland Sheldon might win 15 games, but neither was having a good year, and they ended the season with a total of only 10 wins between the two of them. Stan Williams, for whom they had traded Moose Skowron, was proving a disappointment. He had seemed like a 15-game winner when they had made the trade, and in 1963 he won 9 games for the Yankees, but in this year his record was 1-5 for the season, and he would be gone the next season, sold to Cleveland in a cash transaction.

In some ways the bullpen had done reasonably well. The two young relief pitchers working out of it, Steve Hamilton and Pete Mikkelsen, had given the Yankees much more than they expected.

Mikkelsen, with his heavy sinker, more than justified Berra's decision to choose him over Metcalf as far as the other pitchers were concerned. But by mid-season Berra already had a reputation for misusing his bullpen, for getting his pitchers up too early and too often and having them throw too much. That was proving not merely a physical drain on the pitchers but an emotional one as well, for relief pitching was an unusual part of the game. It demanded instant adrenaline—a pitcher half-dozing in the bullpen, then suddenly called into action in the middle of the game, had to jump-start himself emotionally as well as physically. But to get up, to get the rush of adrenaline, and then to sit down was very hard on the bullpen pitchers. Most of them thought Sain would have done a better job protecting them. By mid-season Hamilton, who had had a record of 7-0 at one point, largely as a reliever, had a sore arm and was unable to pitch for almost a month. He had been used too often. Hamilton was a breaking-ball pitcher, and he depended primarily on his curve. But when he got tendinitis, his breaking ball became a partial slider, a slurve.

Most ominous of all, the other pitchers suspected, was the condition of Whitey Ford. That year Ford was pitching on guile, control, and pure courage. His arm hurt all the time, and on occasion, when he would go out to warm up he would have *nothing*—his ball had no movement and little speed. Then he would go out and, with the guts of a burglar and the help of his reputation and a little doctoring of the ball, he would somehow manage to go seven or eight innings and win. For much of the season Ford's courage and shrewdness worked, and his record at the midway point was 12-2. But he was beginning to have circulatory problems in his left (pitching) arm, where the muscle was so developed that it cut off the circulation in the arm (Ford would later joke that because there was no circulation there, he did not sweat on his left side and he was the only player in the league who could get ten days out of a five-day deodorant pad). More and more he depended on experience and tricks now. No one in the league knew better how to use a hitter's strengths against him than Whitey Ford. He had been taught by the best, Eddie Lopat, a great Yankee pitcher of similar skills who had triumphed on the basis of intelligence more than God-given talent. Lopat had made it his business to know every hitter's strengths and weaknesses and had always managed to keep even the best hitters off balance. When Ford was young and new in the league, Lopat sat with him in the dugout on the days when neither was pitching and gave him a running tutorial, talking through every game, studying every batter, anticipating what each pitch should be, teaching Ford that each pitch helped set up the next pitch.

Now Ford would go to the bullpen on days when he did not pitch and work on doctoring the ball—seeing how it would move when he cut it in certain ways and held it either with the seams or against the seams. For a time Ford kept a tiny sharp-edged blade in his ring, but eventually the umpires caught on and made him stop. So the job of cutting the ball had fallen to Ellie Howard, who sharpened one of the clasps in his shin guard. By early August, not only was Ford's arm giving him trouble but so was his right hip. He was pitching in terrible pain and was not sure he could continue. Some sportswriters suggested that his career might be over. Against Kansas City on August 4, he told Berra that he would try to pitch, but he was not sure he could make it. Berra let him try, but had Stan Williams warming up simultaneously. Ford went seven innings and lost, 5–1. The next day, frustrated and in pain, he put himself in the bullpen. He tried again four days later, and could go only four innings. The doctors examined him and told him that what had been considered a minor ligament pull was in fact a calcium deposit on his hip. Yogi Berra, wrote one of the sportswriters, had better learn how to spell Stottlemyre, the name of the young pitcher playing so well in Richmond.

20

For the first five innings on July 29, Curt Simmons was pitching a no-hitter. Then, in the sixth, with one out, Lew Burdette, the Cubs pitcher, bunted. Ken Boyer at third charged the ball. Tim McCarver, behind the plate, yelled for Boyer to let it go, that it was going to go foul, but almost by instinct Boyer tried to make the play, and Burdette beat it out. That broke up the no-hitter, but Simmons coasted to victory. It had brought his record to 11-8. He was going to lose only one more game during the rest of the year.

Simmons was a vital part of the team, the veteran pitcher who had seen it all on a staff where both Sadecki and Gibson were still defining themselves. Baseball was life and life was baseball for him: Curt Simmons saw life through the prism of baseball. If someone was coming on hard times, maritally or had a lot of debt, the count in life was 0-2. If things were going well for him and he was on a roll, if he had a good-looking wife and a generous new contract, then he was going through life with the count on him 3-0. If Curt Simmons walked into the hotel coffee shop to have lunch, he ordered what he called a Baseball Special and seemed surprised if they did not know what it was, for a Baseball Special was the most basic of meals to be eaten on the road, a cheeseburger.

There was nothing mysterious about what he was going to do when he pitched. He was going to keep the ball low and away, or up and in, and try to keep the hitters from seeing anything good. Why?

someone asked him. Because God had attached the arms to the shoulders instead of the hips. Otherwise it would have been low and inside, and high and away. The correct ratio of pitches, he added, was four low and away to one up and inside, because if you missed high, the hitter was likely to do more damage than if you missed low. Simmons no longer had his blazing fastball, but he had a good fast curve, a good slow curve, a good change, and just enough of a fastball to keep hitters off balance. In addition, he had the kind of lovely control that delighted managers, catchers, and his own infielders. To beat Curt Simmons in 1964, when he was thirty-five and in his seventeenth season, a hitter had to be very smart and very patient. He had a great herky-jerky motion that threw hitters off, and because he did not throw that hard anymore, there was a perception that he was beatable. He was, but it was harder than it seemed. He was a manager's dream—six or seven quality innings on every start, a pitcher who performed well even when he did not have his best stuff. Good hitters had a hard time with him because he seemed particularly good at throwing their timing off. He irritated the great Henry Aaron no end. Once when the Braves were playing the Cards, Curt Simmons's young son wandered out on the field and was introduced to Aaron. Aaron looked at the young boy and told him, "Why don't you tell your dad to pitch the way everyone else does?" In one season Aaron got so irritated by Simmons's slow stuff, his off-setting motion, that he lunged at a pitch and drove it for a long home run. The only problem was that he had jumped out of the batter's box to do it, and he was called out. (Aaron had, in fact, jumped out of the batter's box on the previous at bat, popping the ball up, and the umpire, Chris Pelekoudas, had told one of the Cardinal infielders that if he did it again, he was going to have to call him out for leaving the batter's box.) A man who could torment a hitter as good as Henry Aaron was valuable to have on any team.

The last thing Simmons thought he was going to see in this season was a pennant race. He had been one of the top pitchers in the game for almost two decades, and it struck him that his best chance for a World Series had come and gone in 1950, when he was a star on the Phillies' Whiz Kid team of that era. As a twenty-one-year-old that season, pitching in what was for him an abbreviated season, he had won 17 and lost 8 with an earned run average of 3.40, but it was during the Korean War and he had been in a National Guard unit that was called up late in the season. He was not shipped overseas and there had been talk that he would be allowed to come in and pitch during the Series, but the army authorities had been reluctant to let him do it, fearing they might be criticized for favoring a young athlete.

The Cardinals had picked him up for nothing. During spring training in 1959 something had popped in his elbow, and he observed Opening Day of that season by having his arm operated on. That season was, to all intents and purposes, a washout. He came back late in the season trying to work himself into shape with the team's farm club in Williamsport. He felt good about his arm in 1960, but Eddie Sawyer, a manager he liked and trusted, quit almost as soon as the season opened, apparently because Bob Quinn, the general manager, was telling him whom to play and whom not to. He was replaced by Gene Mauch, who was young and smart—quite possibly the most intelligent man ever to manage a baseball team, some people said—but for a variety of reasons he seemed to have no interest in using Curt Simmons. Weeks passed and Simmons did not pitch and finally he was given his release one night around midnight in San Francisco. That was the low point of his career. Whether the Phillies had ever tried to trade him he was not sure, but ostensibly his career was over; he had won 115 big-league games, but it appeared that he now had no value in his chosen profession. Yet he remained confident about his future. His arm had felt good during spring training and he was sure he could still pitch.

Ken Silvestri, a former catcher and now a coach with the Phillies, told him that he had been screwed, that he could still pitch, and that he ought to send a telegram to every major-league team asking for a tryout. But Simmons was disgusted, and for the moment all he wanted to do was to go home. "No, damn it, do it," said Silvestri, "send out a bunch of telegrams." Simmons went home for a few days, pulled himself out of his funk, and then began to make a few calls. By chance the Cubs were in Philadelphia the week Simmons called Lou Boudreau, their manager, and asked for a tryout. Boudreau said yes, and he pitched to Del Rice, the Chicago bullpen catcher. Rarely had he felt so in command of his pitches, and he was throwing better than he had in years. "How the hell did they ever release you?" Rice asked. The Cubs were interested, Boudreau told Simmons, and they wanted to make some kind of a deal, but first they had to make some roster moves, so it was going to take some time.

The Cardinals were also interested in him; Solly Hemus and Bing Devine decided that he was well worth flying in for a tryout. Even as he was working out with the Cubs, Hemus called Simmons to ask him to fly to St. Louis. "He's down at the park trying out with the Cubs," Mrs. Simmons told Hemus. At that point, Devine and Hemus decided to skip the tryout and sign him blind. He turned out to be a great pickup; he was still a gifted pitcher—in 1963 he won 15 and lost 9, and a number of his defeats had come when the Cards had either failed to score a run or scored only one run. Now, in mid-season, he was pitching as well as he ever did, and he specialized in tormenting his old team, going 16-2 against the Phillies as a Cardinal (he would beat them four times without a loss in this season). A few days later he shut out Houston on five hits for his twelfth victory. Curt Simmons did not agree with others that Gene Mauch was the smartest man in baseball. He thought Mauch was too much like a drill sergeant who wanted to run everything, and who thought he was smarter than everyone else. He thought men like that could get other people in trouble.

On July 30, Johnny Keane gave the call to bring Barney Schultz back to the parent club. Barney Schultz was doing the best pitching of his life in Jacksonville, with an earned run average under 1.00. Frustrated by his bullpen, Keane had started asking for him in late July. "I want Barney," he told Bing Devine. "He's my man. He can pitch every day." It was Keane, after all, who had converted Schultz to a bullpen specialist when he had managed him at Columbus ten years earlier. So Schultz came up in August when it was not yet a pennant race. On August 1 he pitched for the first time in relief of

Bob Gibson. Of the remaining fifty-nine games left on the Cardinal schedule, he pitched in thirty of them. He was an odd figure, a young old man, more like a rookie than a veteran, extremely experienced on the field and equally tentative off it. All those years of meager salaries in the minor leagues had made him somewhat uneasy in the big leagues. He wanted to behave like a big-leaguer, to eat and tip like a big-leaguer. Big-leaguers tipped 10 percent, but Barney Schultz, from all those years when his salary was around three thousand dollars, calculated it exactly instead of rounding it out as some of the others did.

Curt Simmons had known him on the Phillies, had hung out with him in St. Louis, and seemed to be in charge of him. It was as if he were the much older player and Barney was the young rookie, though in fact Schultz was three years older than Simmons. He was constantly asking Simmons questions—Curt, how long to the ball park from the hotel? What time do we leave for it? Where do we eat tonight? Simmons loved it. "Barney," he would say, "this is Twenty Questions, and that's eighteen of them down, and you've only got two left." There was a constant byplay about where to eat: Simmons and a few others ate together regularly, and Schultz, new in town, joined them now. Where should we eat? he would ask each night, and Simmons would tell him it was his turn to pick the restaurant, which would bring on more questions about what kind of place they wanted to go to. "Barney, it's *your* turn to pick the place," Simmons would say. The next day there would be more questions about what to do, and then Simmons would say, "Barney, this is the big leagues." The Mother Hen, they called him. There was something very poignant, they thought, about a man getting a shot like this so late in his career, and from the start he was helping the club with his knuckler, which seemed unhittable this season.

The call from New York for Mel Stottlemyre came on August 10. By this time Whitey Ford had gone to the bullpen. Jim Bouton was fighting pain in his throwing arm, and Al Downing was still somewhat erratic, brilliant when he had his control, self-defeating when he didn't. When Yogi Berra had started pressing Ralph Houk to

bring Stottlemyre up from Richmond, Houk had held back. Stottlemyre was supposed to be the jewel in the crown for the extension
of the Yankee dynasty, and, all things being equal, it was better for
the Yankee organization if he finished the season at Richmond. But
Berra was insistent. Since Houk was the man who had asked Berra to
be the manager, now he owed Yogi a chance to call up the best
young pitcher the organization had in the minor leagues, and who
sounded from all reports as if he was ready to pitch in the majors.
Stottlemyre was hardly surprised when the call came. The problems
of the pitching staff were hardly a secret, and he was aware that there
had been representatives of the big-league team watching him work
in recent games. "Hey, Mel," a teammate would say, "all those big
men from New York—they're here to watch *you.*" At first he did not
believe them, but then he realized they were probably right. Even
so, the extra attention did not bother him, and it did not add to the
pressure when he went out to pitch. He had an unusual ability to
shut out the crowd and keep his mind in the game. That was one of
his trademarks—the ability to shut out everything else and concentrate. It was the bane, he later noted, of his wife's existence. One day
with the New York brass watching, he won, 2–1, his tenth victory in
a row. It made his record 13-3. His earned run average at Richmond, which had been 4.05 the year before with virtually the same
team in the same league, had dropped to 1.42. He was told to get to
New York as quickly as he could. He got a room at the Concourse
Plaza near the Stadium, and almost immediately he was called by a
New York writer who wanted to do a story about him. Stottlemyre,
the writer, and a photographer ventured down to Times Square,
where the rookie was dazzled by the sight—so many people, so
many tall buildings. He had come from a town of about one thousand people and did not believe that there could be so many people
in the world; the article about the country boy dazzled by the sights
in the big city was duly published. When Stottlemyre went to work
for the first time as a New York Yankee, the Yankees were in third
place, three and a half games out of first. No one reached out to him
more readily in those first days than the catcher, Elston Howard.

"Pitch the way you did in Richmond. Don't change anything. Don't try and do more because you're here and you're pitching against major leaguers. Don't try and throw faster. Do what you did there and you'll be fine," Howard said. Then he did something for Stottlemyre that he did for other pitchers: before a game Howard took the few last pitches squatting right over the plate instead of squatting just behind it; this allowed the pitcher to see exactly what was happening as the ball broke over the plate.

The Yankees had lost a doubleheader to the White Sox the day before, with both Bouton and Terry losing. They were three and a half games behind Baltimore and two and a half games behind Chicago when Berra decided to pitch Stottlemyre for the first time in an afternoon game at the Stadium. That day in his first major-league appearance he was everything management and his teammates had hoped for. He was the coolest rookie the others had ever seen. The other players, particularly the other young players, were in awe of him from the start. Here he was, a kid just out of the minor leagues, walking into the starting rotation of a defending championship team in the middle of a pennant race, and he was as relaxed as could be. Stottlemyre's was, thought Jim Bouton, the most economical motion he had ever seen in a pitcher. He would stand on the mound, go into a miniature windup, and take a small stride toward the plate. The ball would come in, nice and fast, but not *that* fast, and then it would explode downward, dead flat down. He had great control and he never seemed to throw a ball that was above the knees. Watching him that day, Jim Bouton thought, was like a scene out of a great western movie. It was as if the Yankees were the good guys but in desperate trouble, and the other teams were the bad guys, and then into town walks this tall, slim U.S. Marshal, who doesn't talk too much, but who is absolutely fearless and who doesn't know he is supposed to be scared. Quietly he starts cleaning up the bad guys, or at least, Bouton decided, getting them to hit into ground balls. In that first game against the White Sox, twenty-one batters hit ground balls, and he walked only one batter. The Yankees won, 7–3. He was going to be around a long time, Steve Hamilton, the relief pitcher, thought, and so Hamilton, unofficial monitor of the daily baseball-signing speed records, tried to talk Stottlemyre into changing his name to Stott.

Stottlemyre's first victory was a lovely blend of the old and the new. In the fourth inning Mantle came up with the right-handed Ray Herbert pitching for Chicago, and hit a tremendous drive to center field. The wind was blowing out slightly, and at first Mantle did not think he had quite gotten all of it. A look of disgust came over his face; he had, Stottlemyre thought, come very close to throwing his bat down. (Earlier in the year he had hit a ball and thrown his bat down, and then the ball kept carrying and went out for a home run, and Mantle had felt like a fool. Though he normally ran the bases with his head down, on this occasion he had angled his face down even more out of embarrassment.) Gene Stephens, the center fielder, thought at first that he could make a play on the ball, and then as he went back he saw the ball carry over the monuments, over the 461 sign, and over the screen, which was thirty feet high there. It landed fifteen rows back, and since each row was judged to be two feet, the ball was officially judged to be 502 feet. It may have been the longest ball Mantle ever hit to center field in the Stadium. Stottlemyre was in awe. Since he had seen the quick expression of disgust on Mantle's face, he wondered, *If that's not far enough, what is?*

Mantle was relaxed after the game, almost boyishly happy. "I'm glad I didn't bang my bat down," he told the assembled reporters. He loved the tape-measure home runs—they were his secret delight in the game. The reporters who covered him were aware of this, and knew how relaxed and affable he would be in the locker room after he hit one. The measuring of Mantle's home runs began in 1953 when he hit a tremendous drive against the Washington Senators that had gone out of Griffith Stadium. Red Patterson, the Yankee press officer, decided to measure it, which he did by walking it off, rather than using a tape, and he estimated that it had gone 565 feet. "You could have cut it up into fifteen singles," said Bob Kuzava, the bullpen pitcher who had watched it go soaring by. Again and again when Mantle was younger, Stengel had tried to get him to cut down on his swing, telling him that he was so strong, the home runs were going to come anyway, and they did not need to be such mammoth shots; if he cut back on his swing, his batting average would go up dramatically. That made no impression on Mantle, for he loved the tape measure drives; he loved just knowing that every time he came to bat he might hit a record drive; he loved the roar of the crowd when he connected, and was equally aware of the gasp of the crowd when he swung and missed completely, a gasp that reflected a certain amount of awe, as if the crowd was as disappointed as he was.

The home runs separated him from the other great power hitters of that era, as his pure statistics did not. The inner world of baseball was very macho; the clearest measure of macho for a pitcher was the speed of his fastball, and for a hitter, it was the length of his home runs. The players themselves were excited by the power hitters' extraordinary drives, and they cataloged them—who had hit the longest drive hit in a particular ball park—and spoke of them reverentially. More than thirty years after the event, Dick Groat could remember playing against the Yankees in the 1960 World Series and being out with a broken wrist. He was inside the clubhouse in the whirlpool bath when his roommate, Bill Virdon, rushed in looking stunned. "Roomie, you just missed the granddaddy of all granddaddy home runs!" he hollered. This was a drive Mantle had hit off Joe Gibbon, one of two he had hit in a 16–3 rout, and long after the game had passed into history, Groat still had the moment filed away in his memory, that the ball had gone over the iron gate in old Forbes Field, well over it and well past it.

There was a constant unspoken competition for the reputation of being the man who hit the longest one, and once in the early fifties, while Mantle was waiting in the on-deck circle, Joe Collins hit an enormous home run, one that had traveled way, way back into the upper deck in right field. When Collins finished his home-run trot, he looked over at Mantle and said, "Go chase that." Mantle did precisely that, driving the ball even farther back into the upper deck. When he returned to the dugout he took a drink of water and went over to Collins. "What did you think of that one, Joe?" he asked. "Go shit in your hat," Collins answered.

One of Mantle's great goals was one that mortal men dared not even think about: to be the first player ever to hit a fair ball out of Yankee Stadium. That would set him apart for all time. He never did it, but he came very close on at least two occasions. He hit one off Pedro Ramos of the Senators on Memorial Day in 1956 that was still rising as it hit the roof, just eighteen inches, by subsequent measurement, below the top. Ramos later said that he thought the ball was going to continue on to Connecticut. Then, in 1963, what people believe was the hardest ball he ever hit was a drive off Bill Fischer of the Athletics; the ball was still rising when it hit the top of the façade and bounced back down on the field, a drive that some people estimated might have gone 620 feet if the façade had not stopped it. He had been exhilarated after that game because it showed not only that it could be done but that this late in his career he still had the power to do it. The distance had been right, but he had been slightly off on the angle. If he had only gotten under it slightly, perhaps a millimeter or a centimeter more, he thought, it might have gone out. Now, in 1964, his body badly worn down, he still believed that one day he might drive a ball out of the Stadium.

21

In mid-August Bob Gibson started to find his groove, but whatever run Gibson and the Cardinals made now, it was going to come too late to help Bing Devine. From the start he had been vulnerable to Branch Rickey, and the slow start of a season they had all looked forward to so much spelled the end of Devine's reign. Rickey had continued to go after Devine relentlessly but subtly, using velvet scissors, as one colleague noted. "Now, Bing Devine is a fine, fine man," he would say to Busch of his adversary, "a wonderful family man, one of the best family men in our business, doesn't drink, doesn't smoke, doesn't carouse," knowing that Busch, who *did* drink, *did* smoke, and *did* carouse, did not trust men who were too fastidious in their personal habits. ("Now, Bing," Gussie Busch would say when they gathered in the late afternoon for a meeting and a drink, "did you get your Coke?") Rickey had recently found a new and persuasive line, which he used again and again with Busch: that he, Rickey, could be doing a better job with players who would cost only half as much.

As the season progressed and the Cardinals, failed to make their expected move, Rickey gradually increased the tempo of his drive against Devine. Rickey's secretary, Kenny Blackburn, stayed at the same hotel as some of the single players, and he was always telling them how close Busch and Rickey were becoming, and how Rickey now had Busch's ear. The veteran players, who liked Devine, and who did not think the team needed two general managers, were not amused. They knew that the more senior they were, the more likely Rickey was to get rid of them at the end of the season. "The Twig," they called him.

What finally blew it, ironically, was the Groat affair, which unfolded in August in a bizarre series of events. In those days Eddie Mathews, the Milwaukee third baseman, was going out with Elizabeth Busch, one of Gussie's daughters. Groat and Mathews were friends, and at one point Groat said something to him about the conflict over the hit-and-run play. Mathews, in turn, said something to Elizabeth Busch about it, and Elizabeth told her father. At the next meeting with his baseball people, Gussie Busch asked Devine and Keane if they had any problems on the team. In their minds the Groat affair was something they had already dealt with back at that meeting in New York right after the All-Star Game, and it was hardly that important in the first place. So they said they did not. For reasons that completely mystified Devine and Keane, Busch thereupon decided they were hiding crucial problems from him. He had learned about *something pertaining to baseball only from his daughter*. He was more than a little paranoid anyway: it seemed to go with the territory with a man who had so much power in, but knew so little about, the high-profile business of baseball. In Busch's curious scenario Devine and Keane were disloyal, and since he placed loyalty above everything else, this was a serious betrayal. Within days, Bing Devine was summoned for another meeting at The Brewery. That morning Al Fleishman, Busch's public-relations man, called Devine at home. "You have a meeting this morning with Gussie, don't you?" he asked. Devine said he did. "Do you know what's going to happen?" Fleishman asked. Devine said he did not know. "You're going to be fired," Fleishman said. "I hate to have to tell you like this, but I don't want you going in there unprepared and getting hit with a baseball bat." So, thought Bing Devine, that is how you learn that the world is about to be cut out from underneath you. He had fired people himself, of course, it was part of the game; he remembered having to fire Fred Hutchinson on Busch's order when he didn't want to. It had been a painful moment, but Hutch, who was a truly tough man, had handled it very well. Devine had been fumbling for words, and Hutch had said, "Hey, Bing, I know what you're trying to do, and why you have to do it. It's okay. I know it's not you. These things happen."

Devine went quietly. It was something he had always expected. He had been dealing for the last seven years from a position of limited strength, and the pressure to produce a winner had grown every year. Life under as volatile a man as Gussie Busch was like living on a precipice, he thought. He knew that Busch was surrounded by pals who were always asking him why he could run so great a brewery with such skill and yet could not win a pennant in something as simple as baseball. He believed that another man who had undercut him was Harry Caray, the broadcaster, who gloried in his close relationship with Busch and had never been a fan of Devine's. The only question in Devine's mind was whether Johnny Keane would go too, or whether he could last out the season. In the end, Busch decided to let him finish out the season, because firing both the general manager and the manager would be too disruptive.

Devine was replaced by Bob Howsam, Rickey's partner in a recent attempt to start a new baseball league. When the firing took place, the Cardinals were nine games behind. That they began to make a run at the pennant now was bittersweet for Devine; suddenly all the pieces had come together and all of the players were playing up to their full potential. It was his team, his players, and yet he was out of the picture.

At this point there was an exceptional balance between the younger and older players on the team. The younger players were all coming of age in those years, Tim McCarver later noted, harnessing their abilities, learning to deal with their frustrations, and coming to terms with what they could and could not do as big-leaguers. If you were going to grow up in baseball, then the opportunity to do it with older players such as White, Boyer, and Groat was a great advantage, McCarver came to believe. They typified the best of the older generation. Devine, he thought, had built well.

For the young pitchers looking for a role model there was Curt Simmons. If he had a single goal in life, it was to keep the game simple. When the Cardinals were about to start a three- or four-game series with another team, there was always a meeting of the pitchers to review how they would pitch to the opposing hitters. Simmons did not like his outfielders to shade hitters even to the slightest degree. He wanted them to play the hitters straight away. Someone would go down the list of opposing hitters, many of them pull hitters, and Simmons would respond, Alou? "Straight away." Crandall? "Straight away." Torre? "Straight away." Then he would give his own uncomplicated thesis: "Big guys, play deep," he would say; "Little guys, play in." To which he offered only one small addendum: "If you think they're going to hit it over your head, back up a little."

At this meeting the manager and coaches would use a projector to show a chart of where the opposing hitters tended to hit and where the outfielders were supposed to play them. The pitchers would go over the opposing hitters and set the positioning for the coming series. "Looney Tunes," the pitchers called these sessions. When it was Curt Simmons's turn to tell his fielders how to play the opposing hitters, Gibson would put a sign over the screen that said in huge letters: STRAIGHT AWAY.

If someone asked Simmons why he wanted his outfielders to play straight away, he would answer, "Because that's where Abner Doubleday put them, and he knew what he was doing." Only with Hank Aaron, one of the most murderous pull hitters of his time, would he adjust slightly. "Step to pull," he would say of the great Aaron, who pulled, it seemed, everything. Once, when Gus Triandos, the huge catcher then with the Phillies, was up with a runner on third, Mike Shannon, in right field, had started creeping in, in order to be able to make a play at the plate on a fly ball. Triandos drilled the ball over Shannon's head for extra bases, and Shannon knew when he came into the dugout that he was going to get a tongue-lashing. Simmons just shook his head. "Goddamn it, Shannon," he said. "Simple game. Simple instructions. Little guys, shallow. Big guys, deep. Triandos is a big guy."

In years to come Tim McCarver realized that the players of his generation were growing up in an unusually strong and highly professional environment. The Cardinals' system still emphasized serious teaching in its instructional leagues and camps. It stressed fundamentals, and Cardinal players knew how to play the game, how to run the bases, and how to do the little things that added up over a season; they had been trained to play in pressure games without even realizing it, so that when the time came they would instinctively make the right play. They were also being taught not just to be baseball players but how to be honorable men. Codes were learned, rules of conduct were enforced. The lessons were often basic: a young player, after a victory, might be chirping away in the locker room because he had gotten two hits; then a veteran player like Dick Groat would go over to him and ask him deadpan how many hits he had gotten that day, and the player, without thinking, would say two. There would be a long silence. The lesson was in the answer, and it was painfully clear to the younger player: in a season as long as this, with as many ups and downs, don't be that high when you get two hits, and don't be that low when you go hitless—be a true professional.

The lessons were, more than anything else, about how to deal with the adversity of playing in the big leagues and how to deal with so long a season, which might easily wear down even the most talented younger man. McCarver watched Gibson learn this as he worked to become a big-league pitcher, striving to master his pitches. He could also see it in the growing confidence with which Curt Flood began to play center field, as he came to terms not only with his own immense talent but also with his limitations—that he was to be a contact hitter, not a power hitter; that his job was to get on base and to move runners around and, if need be, to give himself up for the team, which he did constantly.

Most of all, McCarver came to understand how the growing-up process took place in his own case. The older players worked deftly to teach him how to control his anger and discipline himself and his ego, so that he managed to keep his competitive fire without becoming self-destructive. There was no doubt, the older players thought, that McCarver had a chance to become a great catcher. He was tough; he had a good but not great arm, but he was quick behind the plate; he was highly intelligent and had a fine instinct for the texture of a given game; and he had surprising speed for a catcher, who, as a breed, were notoriously slow. Above all, he had an obvious love for the game, and in many ways, the veteran players thought, was a throwback to the tough, gritty players of the past. What stood in his way was his temper, and perhaps, like many other young players, his ego. So, very quietly they set about trying to teach him to find what was best in himself, refine it, and at the same time discipline that part of him that was self-destructive.

There was, McCarver decided later, nothing that unusual about him in those years; he was a talented young player with a drive to excel, who had met nothing but success in sports all his life, and who was now, for the first time in his life, as a major-leaguer, dealing with the fact that there were other players as good (and some who were better). McCarver had always been the best, in high school in both baseball and football, and he had been an immediate star in the minor leagues, hitting .360 in Keokuk and .347 with Memphis, and somehow he had always assumed that he would be a comparable star in the major leagues. But it was harder than he had thought, the talent level was better, and he played every day against other people who, like him, had always been the best. When McCarver's batting average hovered around .270 in his early years, he raged against his fate, and did not readily accept the limitations of his place among more talented and experienced hitters. He was at war with himself. (Later in his career, when he caught Steve Carlton, he was impressed by the fact that Carlton did not want to find his limits; Lefty thought it a mistake to know his limits, and he thought it critical to enter a game as if there were no limits, as if by accepting them even theoretically was to accept the possibility of failure.) At first when McCarver reached his own limits, it seemed like failure. That meant he was often out of synch, and his anger was in the way. It was all right to play with fire, his teammates tried to teach him, but there was a line there between playing with passion and slipping into rage. He had to learn to draw the line, or his passion would become self-destructive. So when he tried to smash a bat against a wall after making an out in a big game, it was not Johnny Keane who talked to him, but the veteran players who took him aside gently and made him understand that the tirade jeopardized not just himself, but by risking injury he was jeopardizing his teammates.

In one important lesson, Curt Simmons had taught him how to deal with a pitcher. McCarver had called for one pitch from Simmons and Simmons shook him off, and the batter lined the ensuing pitch for an important hit. McCarver had returned to the dugout in a rage. He ripped off his shin guards and slammed them down. Simmons watched him out of the corner of his eye and did not say anything to him at the time, but the next day he took him aside. "Tim, when you behave like that, when you throw your shin guards down like that, don't you realize what it tells the other players on this team about our relationship?" McCarver was stunned and humiliated at that moment, appalled by his own behavior the previous day, but it had been, he later decided, an important lesson about getting outside his own selfishness, seeing the game as a team game, and understanding the respect teammates had to have for each other.

Ken Boyer helped him to come to terms with himself as much as anyone on the team. Boyer, as far as the younger players on the Cardinals were concerned, was a great role model, a consummate professional who played hard every day and never lost sight of his essential purpose. It was as if he had a God-given instinct about what was real and what was not real in baseball. Once Boyer made a great play at third base, moving almost all the way to shortstop to reach a hard grounder, and Dusty Boggess, who was umpiring, turned to McCarver and told him, "Take a good look, son, because you're not going to see anyone like him again." Later, after the game, McCarver mentioned what Boggess had said to Boyer. "Never get caught up in stuff like that," Boyer said, and that impressed McCarver even more, the unwillingness to put one's ego over baseball. It made Boyer very tough as a player: he never seemed to go up or down emotionally because of his performance. He had power, he had speed, and he could play any position in the infield and outfield. Bob Broeg, the St. Louis sportswriter, thought that if he was not the best player in the game, he might be the most versatile, and he liked to argue with his friend Bill Veeck about what he called the Eight Boyer Theory of Baseball. If the pitching was equal and eight Boyers were playing the other positions, could they beat eight Brooks Robinsons, or eight Eddie Mathewses, or eight Hank Aarons?

Once when McCarver went into a rage, it was Boyer who walked over to Lou Brock, who happened to be standing nearby, and said, "There are some guys who just have to learn that they're not going to get a hit every single time they get up." Then he winked at McCarver. It was Boyer who on occasion would take McCarver aside and say, "Have you ever thought about what would happen if you poured all of that energy you have when you're angry into actions that matter? Sometimes it seems that you put more energy into your actions after you hit than you do into hitting itself."

Boyer had come into the league as a kid when the best player on the team had been Stan Musial, and he had learned from Musial how to study the game (when the Cardinals traded for a pitcher from another club, the first thing Musial did was to amble over to the new pitcher and ask what the previous team's book on him was) and how to carry himself. Musial was a great player and a decent human being, and he treated everyone well. In some ways Boyer was passing on Musial's lessons to another generation. In 1968 Boyer, near the end of his career, was playing for the Dodgers, and Ted Simmons, a young player for the Cardinals, came up. Simmons singled and stopped at first base. "Is that your first big-league hit?" Boyer asked. Simmons said that it was. "That's great—I hope it's the first of twenty-five hundred," Boyer said, which somehow made the moment even nicer as far as Simmons was concerned. There was a stoic quality to Boyer. He played hurt all the time and he never complained about his injuries. Rather, he reminded the others that no matter how hard it might seem at the time, they were all still lucky in their vocation. Mike Shannon remembered Boyer coming into the clubhouse one day, clearly in such great pain that he was having trouble getting his arm into his uniform. When Shannon looked questioningly at Boyer, as if to ask if he could play, Boyer smiled and asked, "You know any other place where I can go and get a job that pays fifty thousand dollars a year?"

It was not always easy for Ken Boyer playing in St. Louis. The other Cardinal players believed that Harry Caray, the immensely popular local announcer, rode Boyer unfairly. For much of his career, Boyer was booed at home, and the source of that booing, the other Cardinal players were sure, was Caray. There was an edge there and Boyer's teammates and his brother Clete believed that it came from a moment when Caray was broadcasting a game on the road at the Los Angeles Coliseum and was doing it from field level. He had wanted to experiment by doing an interview with Boyer during the game. Boyer had said no, not during the game, perhaps when the game was over. They had apparently exchanged harsh words, and the Cardinal players believed that Caray had been hard on Boyer ever since. In fact, one of Bob Uecker's best early imitations was of Harry Caray sticking it to Ken Boyer: "Well, here's the Captain, Ken Boyer. Boyer haaaaaaasn't had an RBI in his last fifty-two games. . . . I don't understand why they continue to boo him here at Busch Stadium. . . . Striiiiiiiike one, he doesn't eeeeven take the bat off his shoulder . . . here's striiiiiiike two . . . and strike three. . . . He *nevvvvvver* even took the bat *offfffff* his shoulder. I don't know why they're booing him." None of this ever seemed to bother Boyer. It was as if, as far as he was concerned, the booing and the needling from Caray went with the paycheck.

It was easy for him to keep his perspective. The Boyers had grown up very poor in rural Missouri. They came from Alba, just outside Joplin in the southwest corner of the state, and a few miles from Mantle's Commerce, Oklahoma. It was said, Clete Boyer remembered, that you could go from Alba to Commerce entirely underground through the network of lead and zinc mines. It was an incredibly poor region; there was work in the mines, but it meant that you risked dying in your forties or fifties from lung disease. Ken Boyer was one of fourteen children, three of whom played major-league baseball. Vern Boyer, his father, was a carpenter by trade, but there was never enough work for a carpenter in Alba, so he also worked as a marble cutter in the local quarry. He rarely had a functioning car of his own, and often had to carpool with other men to get to the quarry in the morning. The price of the carpool was fifty cents a week.

Ken and his brother Clete, who played third base for the Yankees, were raised in a small house with no electricity and no plumbing. On occasion they would heat bricks in the stove at night to warm themselves in bed. As many as five brothers slept in one room in two beds. His mother decided to have one of her last children delivered in a hospital. Why? one of the older children asked her. "I just wanted to see what it was like," she answered. It did not seem to her to be a great improvement and so she had her remaining children delivered at home. Most of the older children had never eaten store-bought bread at home. Chicken on Sunday was the fancy dinner. Meals were mostly starches during the week—potatoes, beans, and fried baloney for dinner. It was a very strict home. If you were supposed to be in at 9:00 P.M. and you came in at 9:05, the strap awaited you. Vern Boyer was home by 5:15 and dinner was served immediately. You were not to be late to dinner. They were supposed to swim only once a day, but sometimes they swam twice a day and their mother tried to protect them. Above all, they were never to complain and never to whine. The Boyers played hard, worked hard, and accepted life as full of hardship and disappointment.

Baseball was at the core of the existence of boys growing up in tiny towns in that part of the country during those years. The connection to the larger world was not the voice of Edward R. Murrow and his fellow CBS correspondents so much as it was the voice of Harry Caray broadcasting the Cardinals. If there was a folk hero in the region, it was Stan Musial. The highest calling was to be a professional baseball player, but even better was to be a Cardinal. Tom Greenwade of the Yankees spent a lot of time in Alba eating supper with the Boyers at their home, but he was never there as much as Runt Marr, the Cardinal scout. Both Ken Boyer and his older brother Cloyd signed with the Cardinals, although within the Boyer family it was believed that the Cardinal organization had made a rare mistake by turning Cloyd into a pitcher instead of an everyday player. Somehow the Boyer boys and their father made their own ball park, rolling the field themselves, and they even managed to string a very simple lighting system around it. Clete Boyer thought that two more of his brothers could have played in the big leagues, his younger brother Len and his older brother Wayne. Wayne was major-league material but wanted to study dentistry. Their father was furious with Wayne for not going forward with a baseball career, and did not talk to him for several years. The Boyers practiced every day of the week, and they played three times a week: on Sunday afternoon, Monday night, and Wednesday night. Over seven years some twenty-one boys from the Alba team signed professional contracts, and at times there were as many as five Boyers on the Alba starting team, playing all the time, it seemed, against the Baxter Springs Whiz Kids, starring, as he was known as a boy, Little Mickey Mantle.

Slowly, over the previous few years, a certain culture had evolved on the Cardinal team, not unlike that which had existed on the great Yankee teams in the past—and men like Boyer, Gibson, Flood, Groat, and White were instrumental in creating it. The Cardinals were a strong team, and they played very smart baseball. Good defense and good baserunning were as important as good hitting. Individual statistics and goals were sacrificed for team objectives. Because it was a team that depended on speed and did not have many power hitters, moving a runner on first up a base when there was no one out or only one out was every bit as important as getting a base hit—particularly when Gibson, who gave up so few runs, was pitching. Players who seemed to be putting their own goals ahead of team goals were soon gone. A light-hitting utility player who was picked up only for his defense and who raged and threw bats in the dugout after he struck out was viewed with contempt. The other players knew the histrionics were false, because everyone knew he was there for defense and not for hitting. Curt Flood was greatly admired by his teammates because he was such a good team player, and because you could never tell from his attitude and the way he cheered his teammates whether he was hitting well or was in a slump. Dick Groat was admired not just because he was a superlative hitter, but because there was no one in the league who was better at moving runners up. Late in the 1963 season, when the Cardinals had lost their three games to the Dodgers and were finally eliminated from the pennant race, Groat was still in a race for the National League batting crown. Curt Flood went to him and told him to go for the batting title. "Think about Groat for the rest of the season," Flood said. "Go for the hits." That day there had been a man on first with no one out and Groat decided instead to move the runner ahead. "You just don't know how to do it, do you?" Flood said. It was a high compliment.

Years later, when Steve Carlton was voted into the Hall of Fame, he spoke of how much he had learned when he was young from Bob Gibson about how to concentrate and how to intimidate hitters, and how not to talk to hitters because it was part of the intimidation process. When Ted Simmons was just coming up as a catcher, Dal Maxvill had gone to Tim McCarver and told him to teach Simmons how to block the plate, even though Simmons's ascent might mean (and soon did) that McCarver would be traded. What was more interesting was the phrase Maxvill used to McCarver: "You owe it," he said.

When Simmons replaced McCarver in time, he too began to learn the rules that defined the culture of the team, and he learned it the hard way. Jerry Reuss pitched a strong game early in his career and Simmons had caught it; after the game, proud of Reuss, proud of himself, Simmons spoke to reporters and gave out some unusually enthusiastic quotes about how good Reuss had been, how much he had controlled the game. The next day he was in the locker room and had heard Gibson's unmistakable voice. "Hmmm," the voice was saying, "and what have we here?" Gibson began to read from that day's paper, and did so with a certain irony that made the quotes about how good Reuss had been seem both pompous and excessive. " '*One of the best pitched games of the year,*' " Gibson read aloud. " '*A very tough and gutsy performance,*' " he continued. "Well, I admit I am *impressed* by this," Gibson said, putting down the paper. And Simmons realized that he had been caught, that he had not been talking about Reuss, but that he had been staking out his own territory: *I am a big-league catcher, and I have caught a very good big-league game.* He started to defend himself. "Listen," he said, "I have a perfect right to say stuff like that . . ." And then he realized that he had been set up by a master, and that the entire locker room was laughing, and that this was part of the rite of initiation. "You take it very seriously, Ted," Gibson said, not unkindly now, and there was a lesson being directed at him, Simmons thought: you are a player, you are young, you would not be here and catching for the Cardinals if they did not think you were good, but you are not yet knocking on the Hall of Fame door. Wait your turn and find your place.

So, by the last third of the 1964 season, they had come together. That did not mean that everyone liked each other, or that they were all pals. A team did not have to be made up of friends. Everybody was dazzled by Brock, who had turned into a spectacular player, but Brock was somewhat apart, a true loner on the team. He was very comfortable in his own world, and enjoyed his privacy. He thought the Cardinals were a good team because you could at once be outside the inner group and yet still very much a part of the team. "Give me my nine selfish ballplayers anytime," Curt Simmons liked to say. Bob Gibson, a relentless competitor on the field, was a world-class comic off it, a true star of the clubhouse, with an unerring instinct for a person's weakness, which he would mime without mercy. He did a brilliant imitation of Bill White, normally a good fielder but not graceful under pop flies, looking very much like a dying robot—arms out, very stiff—when he was waiting for the ball to come down. He noticed that Ken Boyer had a tendency when playing third base to go to his genital area, and then somehow his hand would come up near his mouth. Gibson could do a great Boyer, ready to play, getting set at third, hands to crotch, hands to mouth. He and the others also could imitate Dick Groat, who, because of his baldness, was loath to take his cap off during a game. Gibson did Groat on the field when "The Star-Spangled Banner" was about to be played, waiting until the very last millisecond before taking off his cap. (On one road trip to San Francisco, Groat bought a new hairpiece for several hundred dollars, and when he had returned home to St.

Louis, he walked by his wife, who did not recognize him in it.) It was, however, generally believed that Gibson's single best imitation was of McCarver when he got hit on the fingers by a foul tip (he danced a little jig); Gibson would get into the catcher's crouch, mime getting hit on the hand, dance the jig, and yell, *"Trainer! trainer!"*

22

Johnny Keane knew from the moment Bing Devine was fired that he was hanging on by his fingernails. Gussie Busch had pointedly refused to offer any words of support for Keane when reporters had asked him about the manager's future, and in late August the Cardinals remained seven or eight games out. It almost did not seem to matter to Keane, some of his friends thought; he was so angry at the way Busch had treated Devine that he seemed to lose his taste for holding on to the job after the season was over.

In late August Gussie Busch found his new manager. The Dodgers came into town for a four-game series with the Cards. One of their coaches was Leo Durocher, then fifty-nine, a man who had first managed when he was thirty-three but had not managed a team in nearly ten years. He was the prototype of the ever-contentious, verbally fierce manager. "The Lip," he had been called, a man with roots in a very different era, where managers fought as regularly with their own players as they did with the opposition. Durocher was a flashy figure, and he liked to make the scene, whether it was the nightclubs in New York or the racetracks in California; there was some debate over whether the people he associated with were glamorous (such as Frank Sinatra, a man who, in Durocher's words, would give you the shirt off his back and always grabbed first for the check, and George Raft) or shady, or perhaps both. He had spawned such protégés as Eddie Stanky, Solly Hemus, and Gene Mauch, then managing the Phillies; after trying some of them, namely Stanky and Hemus, Gussie Busch decided to go for the real thing.

The intermediary, voluntary or involuntary, or perhaps a little bit of both, was the ubiquitous Harry Caray, broadcaster, beer salesman, and card-playing pal of Gussie Busch. Some of the players believed he regarded himself as the ex officio general manager. With the Dodgers in town, Durocher went on Caray's pregame show, and there was a good deal of talk about the fact that a number of Leo's boys were currently managing in the majors, among them Mauch and Al Dark of the Giants. "What about Leo Durocher?" Caray asked. "You're not a Number Two man. You're a Number One man." Was Durocher interested in managing again? Durocher gave a rather complicated answer in which he implied that, yes, he might be interested in managing again—it would depend on the circumstances, the city, and the club. "I'll tell you, though, if someone came to me and asked me to manage a team with some talent on it—*a team like the Cardinals here—well, I'd jump at it in a minute*. Because a team like the Cardinals should be winning." An answer like that could be viewed by some people as nothing less than a job application, particularly with Keane a lame duck. Among the people listening that day was Gussie Busch.

Busch immediately called Harry Caray and told him to bring Durocher out to Busch's residence the next morning for breakfast. Caray later wrote that he sensed what was going on at that point and tried to remove himself from the scenario because he liked Johnny Keane, but Busch would not permit him to. Instead, Busch arranged a clandestine pickup for Durocher by Caray early the next morning two blocks from Durocher's hotel, and Caray drove him out to Grant's Farm. Durocher and Busch talked together for an hour, and Busch then offered him the job. "You're the manager of the ball club," Durocher later quoted Busch as saying. "Don't worry about the salary." So it was done; Durocher would take over the team in 1965. It was not something that remained a secret for very long, and soon word began to slip out that Durocher had met with Busch and had been hired, and that Harry Caray had been the middle man. The Cardinal players were less than enthusiastic. Durocher had a reputation as a man who tended to overmanage, who got more from his players than one might expect early in the season and less than one might expect late in the season; when his team won, he used his considerable connections with the press, which tended to think of him as colorful, to get the lion's share of the credit, and when he lost, he always seemed able to blame it on his players. He liked to use the old-fashioned ethnic and racial epithets in his bench jockeying (in fact, when he returned to the Cubs in the late sixties, those epithets still spewed forth from his mouth, though the moment when they were considered acceptable in American life was long past, and he was criticized for it by some reporters and some of his players). In a curious apologia for his behavior, he wrote in his book *Nice Guys Finish Last*, published in 1975, that as long as he had been in baseball every Italian had been known as dago, and every Jew as Hebe, which was probably true in the sense that as long as *he* had been in baseball every Italian had been known by *him* as dago and every Jew as Hebe.

On August 15, the Cardinals played Los Angeles in Los Angeles, and Gibson lost, 4–3. It was a particularly frustrating game. He entered the seventh with a 3–1 lead. For the first six innings he had sailed along on a two-hitter, and the one Dodger run had come in the fourth when, with a runner on third, Ron Fairly hit a short fly to left and Lou Brock stumbled while making the play. He made the catch, but he was off balance when he made the throw, and Maury Wills was able to slide under the high throw. In the seventh with one out, Frank Howard and John Roseboro singled and Nate Oliver walked. Wally Moon came up as a pinch hitter for the pitcher Joe Moeller. Much to Gibson's irritation, Johnny Keane went to his bullpen and brought in Mike Cuellar. Walter Alston switched pinch hitters, going to Dick Tracewski instead of Moon. Tracewski hit a perfect double-play ball right to Groat at shortstop. The Dodger infield was one of the worst in the league, notoriously hard and uneven, and just as the ball came to the edge of the grass, it kicked high, well over Groat's head, and two runs came in to tie the score, 3–3. The Dodgers still had some luck in them. Cuellar picked Tracewski off first, and Tracewski in the rundown ran out of the base path. The umpire Tom Gorman was slow to call the runner out of the baseline, and though he eventually did, by the time he made the call, Oliver scored from third.

Gibson was furious. He had not been pitching well for much of the month, and then, on this evening, he *had* pitched well, and still lost. He had struck out eight men, given up four hits, and though there were four earned runs charged against him, they were all tainted. It was exactly the kind of game he hated to lose: he detested coming out of a game with a lead, turning over his work to a relief pitcher, and then seeing the game slip away. It evened his record at 10-10. The Cardinals, with 115 games down and 47 still to play, were in fifth place, nine and a half games behind the Phillies.

A few days later, in a game against Houston, Gibson lasted six innings and was not involved in the decision in a game the Cardinals lost, 8–7. Then, on August 23, the Cards lost, 3–2, to the Giants on the West Coast in the last game of a western swing. That left them eleven games out. The next day, August 24, Gibson pitched against Pittsburgh in the first game of a home stand. In that game he was completely in charge. Some of the Pirate players agreed that they might have seen him with better stuff, but none of them had ever seen him throw harder. He struck out twelve and walked only two. As in the game earlier against Chicago, it was one strikeout short of his personal record. He seemed to be getting stronger as the game went along, and in both the sixth and the seventh he struck out the side. He might have been a little sharper, he said afterward, in the 1–0 game he pitched against the Cubs earlier in the season, but on this evening he had been able to place the ball almost anywhere he wanted. It was, Dick Groat later said, like watching Koufax when he had a one-run lead and went to pure power, with Gibby saying in effect to the hitters: "Boys, now let's see if you can hit me." It was his first complete game in six weeks. How did he feel about it? a reporter asked him afterward. "About time," he said. That made his record 11-10. And with that he went on a roll and won his next five games, all of them complete, allowing on the average one earned run a game. That, he thought, was more like it.

He was glad to be back pitching as he was supposed to, somewhat annoyed that it had taken him so long to find his rhythm, especially because it was too late to help Bing Devine. With Gibson pitching well again, suddenly the Cardinals were a different team; because he was such a force, they became stronger. He brought an additional factor to each game now, and that was intimidation. Gibson was brilliant at intimidating opposing teams. His game face was a cold and angry mask, one that seemed to show no mercy to the batter. There was a mystique to him and he orchestrated it very deliberately. He did not want to be known as a good guy. He refused to socialize with opposing players, fearing that if he showed even the slightest sign of humanity, it might lessen his edge and make him seem less threatening. He hated it when his teammates fraternized with the opposing players before a game, and it was a fact of life around the Cardinals that there was a good deal less fraternization with the enemy when he pitched than when others did. He hated All-Star Games, where his sworn adversaries, the best hitters of the rival National League teams, cavorted as if they were not only his teammates but his friends.

At one All-Star Game it was the unfortunate fate of Joe Torre to catch him in the ninth. With no one out and Tony Oliva up and two strikes on Oliva, Torre wanted a particular pitch, up and in. He pondered the wisdom of going out to talk to Gibson, having heard of how Gibson devoured even his own catchers, and finally decided he should, since he was, among other things, the All-Star catcher. "Bob," Torre said, "I want it up and in to Oliva, not down and in." Gibson said nothing, but he looked at Torre as if he had no clothes on. The next pitch was of course *down* and in, since Gibson had more to prove to Torre than to Oliva—above all that he did not take suggestions, let alone orders. Oliva stroked it for a double. Thereupon Gibson struck out the next three batters. After the game they were among the last two players to shower, and Torre looked over to the next shower and said, "Nice pitching, Bob." Gibson said nothing in return, just turned away. Torre felt like a complete fool at this, an All-Star Game, which was supposed to be a celebration of excellence. A few years later, when Torre was traded to the Cardinals, the first person to welcome him was, of course, Bob Gibson.

"Hey," Gibson said, "it took me long enough to get you over here."
It was never personal, Torre realized, it was only about gaining the
extra edge and being the great pitcher he was determined to be.
These were his rules, this was his image, and he was unbending in
their implementation. Gibson once got into the players' elevator at
Dodger Stadium with a few teammates, and by chance Willie Crawford, a player from the opposing team, got on. Not knowing Gibson's personal code, Crawford made the mistake of trying to be
friendly, talking to him and the other players about how the Cardinals had just been swept by the lowly San Diego, and now wasn't it
just like them, they were up here and it looked like they were going
to sweep the Dodgers. Crawford blathered on, and as he did, Gibson's face grew colder and colder; there was no doubt as far as the
other Cardinals in the elevator were concerned about what was
going to happen when the game started—Gibson was going to
throw at Crawford with his first pitch, which, of course, he did.

Tim McCarver said that you could see the fire and the drive by
looking into Gibson's eyes, that the ferocity and determination
showed there more than anywhere else. The pitcher's mound was
his territory. Lou Brock remembered once when Dal Maxvill, who
was one of Gibson's favorite players, dared to come over and actually place a foot on the mound, at which point Gibson glowered at
him and said, "If you aren't a pitcher and you aren't prepared to
pitch, then stay the hell off the mound." He had his own rules of
what a batter could and could not do and the ability to deny and/or
punish a wayward hitter. He liked to work quickly, setting the pace
and the tempo himself; he did not like hitters who tried to disrupt
his tempo. If they stepped out of the batter's box, he would scream
at them from the mound to get the hell back in there, and if a hitter
ducked out too often, or if he got back in the batter's box too slowly,
there was a very good chance that Gibson would throw at him. It
was important for them to understand that they were on his turf. He
did not permit bunts—bunts, that is, by players who wanted a base
hit and were afraid to swing away at him. A bunt to advance a runner
was permissible; a bunt for a hit was not. He reciprocated by throwing at the player the next time he came up. There were certain parts

of the plate that belonged to him. If a pitch came in over the inside of the plate and the batter got a hit, he could accept that. But if a hitter got a hit on a pitch on the outside corner, an area that he believed belonged to him, the hitter was likely to have to duck the next time up. Bill White was a good friend, but when White was eventually traded to the Phillies and came up to bat against Gibson for the first time in a Philly uniform, he seemed to be trying, in Gibson's eyes, to gain the outside portion of the plate. Gibson hit him in the elbow. It was White's fault, he said, for not getting out of the way. "You're crazier than hell," White shouted.

He hated being beaten by a lesser hitter. Once in spring training he went out with a few teammates for dinner. After a few drinks he mentioned the name of a marginal hitter who had done well against him. The more he talked, the more agitated he became. "That son of a bitch has no right to hit me," Gibson said. They all had a few more drinks and, as they did, Gibson became even angrier. "I'm tired of it. He ain't shit and there he is hitting me like he's a real hitter." A few more drinks disappeared and Gibson was angrier still. "I'm going to knock him on his ass the next time we play." A few days later the Cardinals played against this hitter; Gibson knocked the hitter down with his first pitch and then came charging off the mound. "You son of a bitch—I'm tired of you hitting me the way you do. It's all over for you now," he said.

He respected strength in others: he knew another samurai when he saw one. Once in spring training when Gibson was getting a little older and Tom Seaver was in his prime, John Milner of the Mets hit two doubles off Gibson. The next time he came up Gibson nailed him in the ribs. A few weeks later, when the two teams played in St. Louis during the regular season, Seaver was on the mound for the Mets. It was time for Seaver to make a statement for himself and for his team. He chose his moment very carefully: Gibson was up with two outs, and Seaver would be the first Met up in the next inning, so there would be a chance for Gibson to retaliate if he so chose. Seaver threw three pitches inside at Gibson, driving him farther and farther away from the plate; the last pitch came in so close that Gibson had to spin around to get out of the way, using the bat more like a cane than a bat. Then it was Seaver's turn to bat against Gibson. The first pitch came in fast, and just over Seaver's head. The umpire had come out from behind the plate at that point to try and stop it, but Seaver pushed him aside. "Shut up," he said, "this is none of your business." At that point Seaver stepped away from the plate and yelled out to Gibson, "As far as I'm concerned this is over. But if you want to continue, we can keep going at it, and you better know that I throw a lot harder than you do now, you old fart." And that indeed ended it.

Gibson used the brushback pitch as a weapon: first to protect his teammates from other pitchers, and second to protect the plate as he saw it. He was rarely indiscriminate with this pitch, which was, in his hands, a frightening weapon. A confrontation with Dave Rader and Chris Speier of the Giants was memorable to Gibson's teammates. Rader was at bat. He was a talker, and started trying to talk to Gibson; worse, he started asking about Gibson's family at just the moment that Gibson was going through a divorce. Gibson hit Rader even though it endangered his own small lead at the time. Suddenly, from the dugout, Chris Speier, the Giant shortstop, started yelling at Gibson. In fact, he did more than yell—he started calling Gibson a gutless son of a bitch. His voice was clear and, as far as Gibson was concerned, insulting. Because Gibson had poor eyesight, he asked McCarver and Torre who was yelling at him. "It's Speier," they both said. At that moment Speier, realizing what Gibson had asked, turned his back to Gibson and pointed at his uniform number so that Gibson would know who he was. The game ended with Speier on base. As Gibson stalked after him, Speier raced to the dugout. It might have ended there, but a few weeks later Speier was at the All-Star Game, and he saw both Torre and Brock and told them that sometimes he talked a little too much, and to let Gibby know that he was a fan and held no animosity. Except for Speier's semi-apology, McCarver thought, Gibson might have let it go—Speier was an infielder, not that important a hitter, and enough time had passed since the incident to be forgotten. But in backing down from what he had said, Speier had made a mistake. The next time Speier came to bat, McCarver was sure, Gibby was going to throw at him, and in fact he did.

It was a job to him, and teammates were not to violate his professional code. You were not to wish Gibson luck on the day of a big game. He did not like that, he did not like to talk to anyone before he pitched anyway, and besides, what was happening, as far as he was concerned, was not about luck. This was his work. Once a young reporter interviewed him in the dugout and asked him if he were a money pitcher. "That's the stupidest goddamn question I've ever been asked," he said. "Why the hell else would I do this? To get my name in the paper? Of course, I'm a money pitcher." Another time a radio reporter suggested to him after he had won a game on a hot muggy afternoon that he had seemed to get stronger as the game went along. "That's about as goddamn dumb as you can get," he said. "How can you get stronger after you've thrown a hundred pitches in this heat? You might be getting better, but you're not getting stronger. I'm dead in the eighth inning. I'm going then on what I've got inside of me."

He took very good care of his body. He did not smoke, and he hated those who did; he did not want any smokers around him. The night before a game he was always in his motel room early. He might have half a bottle of wine with dinner, but he got plenty of rest. He was tense and wired on game days, and he rarely ate a full meal before a game, although before night games he would eat a little bit. More than most men he needed to control his environment, in part, friends suspected, because he wanted nothing that would strip away his hard-won place in the world. Because of that need for control, he hated coming out of a game for a relief pitcher. It was not just a matter of pride to finish what he himself had started, it was a matter of control: he did not trust others to do for him what he felt he could do better for himself. Over one stunning *ten*-year period, starting in 1963, he completed at least twenty starts every season—except one in which he broke his leg—a figure virtually unheard of in contemporary baseball.

Later, after he had achieved his position as a preeminent power pitcher, and as the reputation of his fastball preceded him, he did not have to throw the fastball so much. He could get by often on the slider and the threat of a fastball. He did not like his own curve, and went to it reluctantly. Sometimes, after a game he had won, Jack Buck, the announcer, would ask if he had gotten a particular batter with a curveball, and Gibson would say, "I don't throw any curves." "But the ball seemed to break down," Buck would insist. "That was a slider," Gibson would say. Sometimes he would go through an entire game without throwing a curve, and sometimes, when he finally did throw one, he would get hammered. He would come into the locker room afterward shaking his head and muttering, "I'll never throw another goddamn curveball in my life."

His performances had an artistic quality to them. It was his game, he was in charge, and he wanted no delays; he would set the pace and others would make their adjustments. Jack Buck once put a stopwatch on him—he threw every eight seconds. Once during a Saturday *Game of the Week* when he was pitching, he worked so briskly, coming from the dugout to the mound quickly and from there going immediately into his windup, that NBC could not get in its requisite number of commercials. In the press box an NBC producer went over to a Cardinal press officer named James Toomey and asked if Toomey could please slow Gibson down so that they could get in their commercials. "Here's the phone," Toomey said. "You make the call." No call was made. Gibson wanted no interruptions. He wanted no waste. He hated to throw over to first if there was a runner on. That was a waste. Rather, he intended to concentrate on the batter. If he had a hitter down 0-2 he did not want to waste a pitch, as baseball tradition dictated. Instead, he wanted to go for the kill right then and there and finish him off, and he and Johnny Keane argued back and forth for years over the principle of the wasted pitch.

He wanted the ball back from McCarver as quickly as the catcher could deliver it, and he was in his motion rocking back and forth even as McCarver flashed the sign. His veteran teammate Roger Craig, a man who had seen it all, from the World Series to last-place finishes, thought there was a certain genius to Gibson's authority when he was on the mound, and the speed with which he pitched was a critical part of it. It intimidated the hitter, who could never get set and never had time to guess what was coming; it pleased the umpire, who wanted to get out of there as quickly as possible and therefore probably gave him the benefit of the doubt on certain pitches; it pleased the infielders, who liked quick workers; and it kept Gibson's own arm warm between pitches.

Rarely did he turn that competitive fire on his teammates. He took defeat hard, but he assumed that they had done their best. Occasionally there were flashes of temper. In the 1965 season, which was to be a tough one for the entire team, he had been pitching with runners on first and second against Pittsburgh, and McCarver called for the fastball. Thereupon Roberto Clemente hit a twenty-bouncer to the right side to score the winning run. Gibson later turned to McCarver and said, "You've got more than one finger out there." McCarver, just as angry, retorted, "Well, goddamn it, you've got a head on your shoulders, you can shake me off—you can call for more than the fastball." They were both furious, each frustrated at the season, but the anger finally passed. On another occasion, Gibson won a 1–0 game and in the locker room McCarver told him what a hell of a game he had pitched. Gibson absolutely exploded. "Hell of a game my ass—why don't you guys score some fucking runs!" Gibson was not a man who lightly apologized, so a couple of very cool days passed between them, but then, a few days later, they were talking and there was a sort of apology or as close to an apology as Bob Gibson ever came: "You know, the other day . . . when we were talking . . . that was a hard game . . ." That was a sore point with him always—how few runs the Cardinals scored. With a runner on third and fewer than two out, McCarver, as he was ordered by the manager, would go out to the mound to talk to Gibson about what they were going to do if a ball was hit to him. "There's a man on third," McCarver would say. "Yeah, I know, I put him there," Gibson would say. "Now, Bob, you're supposed to go to first," McCarver would begin, and Gibson would answer, "The hell you say—I'm coming home with it—you guys don't score enough runs to give up a run."

If McCarver came out to the mound to talk to him, it was only because Johnny Keane had ordered him to go out. "He's pitching too quickly," Keane would say, ordering McCarver to slow Gibson down. "He doesn't want me to go out there," McCarver would protest. "I'm running this goddamn club, not Gibson," Keane would say, and McCarver would trudge out. He would still be five or six yards away from the mound when Gibson would wave him off: "What the hell are you doing out here? Get the hell back behind the plate where you belong. The only thing you know about pitching is that you can't hit it." Even on that memorable day four years later, when he was on the verge of setting a World Series strikeout record in the first game against the Tigers and McCarver came out to the mound, Gibson waved him away. "Give me the ball," Gibson had kept shouting at McCarver.

Sometimes Gibson seemed to forget how imposing he was. He knew he was threatening on the mound—that was deliberate—but he had little sense that for many people he was unapproachable and distant off the mound. He hated small talk. He did not like to go through a pretense of social interplay each spring: How's your family, Bob? Did you drive down? Did you have a good winter? Where are you staying? He did not like to waste time. He did not want people to seem to know him when they did not. Once rather late in his career, Bob Broeg, the sports editor of the *Post-Dispatch*, who greatly admired Gibson, said to him, "You know, Gibby, in all the years we've been together and I've been writing about you, you've never said a kind word to me." Gibson was stunned: he was quite fond of Broeg and had no idea that he placed a man he liked and trusted at such a distance.

He was a man who lifted an entire team. His own standards were so high that the other players did not like to let him down, and they played harder when he pitched. In time this became true on the other days as well. Years later, Steve Carlton, a pitcher who apprenticed on the Cardinals when Gibson was in his prime, would talk about how much he had learned from Gibson, which became critical to his making the Hall of Fame: the ability to focus on a game, the ability to be tough, and, perhaps even more important, the ability to create a mystique of toughness.

23

There had been rumors for more than a year that the Yankees were for sale. Dan Topping, one of the two owners, and the more active of the two because he lived in New York, wanted out, mostly for reasons of health; Del Webb, the Arizona builder, one of the men who opened the door to the Sunbelt for millions of Americans, did not have the time to be a full-time owner. During the period that Topping wanted out, the Yankees had gone about cutting back in order to make their books look better. In the previous two years there had been much talk that the Yankees were no longer the powerful organization they had once been, that their farm system was no longer particularly rich, and that, in fact, only the two sucker trades with weak franchises—first for Bob Turley and Don Larsen, and then for Roger Maris—had kept them going. Men like Bill Veeck were saying that the best young ballplayers coming into baseball were not Yankees and the best organizational skills were no longer those of the Yankee managements. The Yankee cupboard, despite the impressive arrival of Mel Stottlemyre in mid-season, was essentially empty. On August 13, the news leaked out: Topping and Webb had sold the Yankees to CBS. It was a two-part sale: in stage one CBS bought 80 percent for $11.2 million, with an option to buy the remaining 20 percent. That the Yankees were to be merged with CBS at once amused some people (there were jokes that Yogi Berra, the Yankee manager, and Walter Cronkite, the CBS anchorman, might now switch jobs) and terrified others, since CBS was so big and so rich (the price it paid for the Yankees represented only 1.9 percent of its 1963 revenues). With a limitless capacity to invest money made elsewhere, with the ability to broadcast games over a network, some critics feared, the Yankees might be made even richer and more powerful by the sale. A number of owners were upset and tried to bring the Justice Department in to block the sale for antitrust reasons. "The blackest day in baseball since the Black Sox scandal," said Roy Hofheinz, the owner of the Houston Colts. On the surface the sale seemed to make sense—the people at CBS allegedly knew a lot about sports; baseball and television were already linked in a way that seemed to enhance both; and sports was becoming a bigger part of the entertainment dollar all the time. If anything, the sale seemed like a bargain for CBS. In television and radio money alone, the Yankees were already making nearly $2 million a year in broadcast fees, $600,000 for their share of the network game of the week, and $1.2 million for the local television and radio rights.

Nothing better demonstrated the changing economics of sports in general and baseball in particular than the sale of the Yankees, for it reflected both the rising value of a team and the increasing importance of television in sports. It was an important benchmark in the rising commercialism of sports. In the nineteen years since Topping, Webb, and Larry MacPhail had bought the team from the Ruppert estate for $2.8 million, the value of the major league team, the ball park, and its principal farm operations had gone up sevenfold. Nor was this an isolated phenomenon. Throughout sports the impact of television was becoming clearer and clearer. The huge salary soon to be paid to Joe Namath reflected the fact that an experienced network, NBC, which scheduled the fledgling American Football League, needed instant stars in order to be competitive.

Already throughout sports there were signs of the increasing importance and the increasing power of television money. In Houston, Judge Hofheinz was finishing his Astrodome and it would open for the 1965 season; it was a structure that would revolutionize sports in general, making it possible to play any sport in any city in the country, despite the vagaries of local weather. No longer would the rain of Seattle, the cold of Toronto, the sweltering heat and humidity of Houston preclude the acquisition of a sports team. The cost of the new dome was estimated to be some $31 million, including the land. Throughout the country, all kinds of cities now hoped to lure baseball franchises from places where they had not flourished, and in an attempt to hold on to their teams, a number of older baseball cities were already building new ball parks. St Louis, Philadelphia, and Pittsburgh had them on the drawing board, at an average of $25 million a ball park. The last thing an owner needed to do anymore was pay for the construction of a new ball park—the cities themselves would willingly take care of that; Atlanta, eager to be seen as a major league city, and well along in negotiations designed to lure the Braves of Milwaukee to the South, had promised the owners a new ball park, with construction to be finished in time for the 1965 season. Local officials in Milwaukee tried desperately to fight back and to hold on to the team that only a few years previously they had stolen from Boston. They offered the Braves ownership all the revenue from concessions, which came to an additional $125,000 a year, and a larger radio-television package, which came to $525,000 a year for three years, an increase of $125,000 a year. The ownership, however, was excited about the prospect of getting out of a market—for that was the new word for a region in the television age—where it was merely one of three teams sharing the same audience in the greater Chicago-Milwaukee area, in order to gain a huge virgin market all to itself. Early estimates were that the Atlanta radio-television money would come to $1.1 million.

By mid-August it was a three-way American League pennant race. Baltimore was on the rise, and would win eleven more games this season than it had in 1963. It had a good young pitching staff with Wally Bunker, Steve Barber, Dave McNally, plus the veteran Robin Roberts, and it had three great players in the daily lineup: Boog Powell, twenty-three that summer and threatening for the American League home-run leadership; Brooks Robinson, just coming into his prime at twenty-seven; and Luis Aparicio, perhaps the best shortstop in the league. The Orioles were about to replace the Yankees as the best and most consistent team in the American League. Chicago was not as well balanced, but it probably had the best pitching in the league, with Gary Peters, Juan Pizarro, and Joel Horlen, and with Hoyt Wilhelm in the bullpen. More and more, the Yankees seemed patched together and carried by memories. On August 17, in third place, and two and a half games behind Baltimore, they went to Chicago for a four-game series. The day before, Mantle had jammed his knee trying to get back to first to beat a pickoff play. He was in terrible pain, with water on his knee, and he thought he would miss most of the Chicago series. In fact, he missed it all. Sportswriters covering the team, who now kept statistics of this sort, noted that it was the seventh time that year that he had been kept out because of injuries. The Chicago series was a disaster. In the first game Ralph Terry pitched well, but New York lost when Hector Lopez misplayed a ball. In the second game they lost, 4–3, when Berra stayed too long with Al Downing. Downing threw a two-hitter through the seventh inning, but then, in the eighth, he tired. Berra was wary of going to his bullpen, and Floyd Robinson hit a three-run homer off Downing to win the game. In the third game Jim Bouton pitched well but fielded poorly, and the Yankees lost, 4–2, with all the Chicago runs unearned. The next day, behind Johnny Buzhardt, Chicago shut them out, 5–0. They were four and a half games back and sinking, it seemed. "Color them black for mourning," Joe Trimble wrote in the *Daily News*. It was, he added, quite certain that there would be no pennant for New York this year.

One thing happened during that period that seriously affected the pennant race: Boog Powell, the young power hitter of the Orioles, who already had thirty-one home runs that season, hurt his wrist. At first it appeared that he had fractured it and would be out for the season. Instead, it turned out to be a minor injury, but he missed two weeks. The Orioles played fourteen games when he was out and split them. At the very least, the injury slowed down what appeared to be a serious Baltimore stretch drive. Some of the Oriole—and Yankee—players thought that if he had not been injured, Baltimore would have won the pennant.

The Yankees did not know about Powell's injury as they boarded their bus in Chicago to go to the airport. It was a brutally hot day, and they had just lost four games to a contender during a pennant drive. It was a very un-Yankeelike thing to do, especially to a team they had assumed they could beat easily in the past. The air-conditioning on the bus was not working well, and the bus got caught in Chicago rush-hour traffic. It barely moved for two hours. Tempers were short. Phil Linz, the utility infielder who was playing regularly because Tony Kubek was hurt, was playing a harmonica he had just bought, trying to learn "Mary Had a Little Lamb." Linz was angry and frustrated. He had started the first three games at shortstop and hit well, he thought, going 3 for 10, including two triples; none of the losses were in any way his fault. Then he had been benched in the fourth game, and the implication was that their failure was his failure. His music seemed to have offended the ears of Berra, as well it might have, since Linz played harmonica very badly. Berra told him to stop playing. Linz, who did not hear Berra, asked what he had said. Mantle, ever the provocateur, apparently then said, "He said play it louder." So Linz played louder. Meanwhile, Frank Crosetti, the longtime coach and, in his own mind, keeper of the Yankee flame (Linz thought Crosetti was clearly fanning the flames in this case), said, in his very distinctive squeaky voice, "That's the worst thing I've ever seen!" With that Berra got angry—his control over the club was at stake. He started coming back toward Linz, and suddenly he was looming over him. "You'd think you'd just won the goddamn pennant instead of losing four straight," he said. "Why don't you stick that goddamn harmonica up your ass." Linz, scared now, for an angry Berra was a rare sight, flipped the harmonica toward Berra, who angrily swiped at it, sending it flying toward Pepitone, whom it hit on the leg. "Corpsman! Oh, my knee, get me a corpsman!" Pepitone shouted.

The next day it was all over the newspapers, driving all other news, Linz remembered, including what was happening in Mississippi and Vietnam, off the front pages. Berra called Linz in, and Linz apologized to him. Yogi was very nice about it. "I've got to fine you, Phil, you know," he said. "That's okay, Yogi," Linz said, "I deserve it." "How about two hundred dollars?" Yogi said. "That's fine," Linz said. Two days later he got a call from a harmonica company asking him to endorse their product and offering him five thousand dollars. It was the kind of thing that happened on all ball clubs when they struggled, Linz thought, and he was sure he was being scapegoated in the media. He felt that he had played hard, and that he was playing well. As for Crosetti, it was hardly the worst thing that had ever happened on the Yankees; take, for instance, the famed incident, already recounted, in which Ryne Duren, quite drunk, squashed Ralph Houk's cigar in Houk's face during a pennant-clinching celebration. Crosetti, most assuredly, was not pleased that Linz had made money because of the incident. From then on when Linz would go to the outfield to take fly balls before a game, if Crosetti was hitting fungos, he would never hit one to Linz. He would hit to the right of him and to the left of him, but never to him.

What bothered Linz, besides the fact that he had been singled out in the press as the villain and ostensibly as the reason for the Yankee losing streak, was the way Crosetti had come down on him. There was, he thought, a double standard in everything that had happened. Crosetti was afraid to criticize the stars of the team, but he was tough on the backup players. Nor did Linz feel, as he considered the incident, that he was even one of the people who was testing Yogi. That was being done, ironically, by Mantle and Ford, Yogi's old pals and teammates. They liked Yogi, but, by instinct, they liked to push things to their limits, because there was more fun that way. That was relatively easy with Yogi, for he was not a disciplinarian. He would announce the bus was leaving at five P.M. and Ford would be a little late, perhaps deliberately so, and the bus would not leave. When Ford would amble onto the bus at ten minutes after five, Berra would not say a word. Then Whitey would deftly stick it to him, not cruelly but just as part of the constant testing in which players and managers struggled for control of turf. "Hey, Yog," Ford would ask, "what time is it?" It was not that Mantle and Ford were trying to undermine Yogi Berra that season—far from it. They were professionals and old friends. But at the same time, they went along with the idea that Yogi was a bit of a cartoon figure, and they never used their immense influence with the team to protect him and his authority.

The fact that Tony Kubek had missed most of the Chicago series at shortstop underlined a glaring vulnerability and an important change in the Yankees—a decline in the depth of the team, particularly among the middle infielders. The popular perception was that the Yankees were carried by power hitters. Their opponents thought differently: yes, they had power, and they had good pitching, but the core of their success over the years had been their balance, their depth, and, above all, the strength of their middle-infield play. The most valuable player on the team in the early part of the dynasty was not necessarily DiMaggio—"the Big Dago," as he was known by his teammates in those days—but, as DiMaggio himself had said, Phil Rizzuto, or "the Little Dago," as he had been known. According to the team culture, the infielders had to be very good fielders, with good range, and they had to be consistent. They did not have to hit. Hitting on their part was always considered a bonus. When Jerry Coleman went to spring training in 1949, he was dubious about his chances of making the main ball club because he had hit only .251 in Newark, but to the men running the club that hardly mattered; from the moment they saw Coleman play, they loved him. He was acrobatic at second, and a marvelous fielder with considerable range: how much he hit hardly mattered to them. Rizzuto, who was to be paired with him at short, understood immediately Coleman's value and how it added to the team; because Coleman had exceptional range, it enhanced Rizzuto's range and allowed him to play even deeper in the hole between short and third. Again and again in his rookie year, Rizzuto would tell the anxious Coleman not to worry about his hitting, that all he had to do was make the plays in the field.

That was the Yankee trademark: two exceptional middle infielders, and usually a backup player or two who could play any infield position and play it well. The veteran middle infielders helped train the younger ones, even if the younger players they trained were likely to be their successors. Therefore, when Bobby Richardson was about to come to the major leagues, and it was Coleman's job he would most likely take, Coleman spent long hours with him in spring training, teaching him how to make the pivot on the double play without being crunched. No one had ever been a more dedicated teacher than Coleman, Richardson later reflected: he dissected Richardson's flaws and got him to make the basic movements of a second baseman by instinct. "Come on, Bobby," Coleman was always saying, "let's do a little more today." Even Billy Martin—who shared second base for a time with Coleman, and who, with less natural talent, had been determined to maximize his ability and stay with the Yankees—worked with Richardson. Martin teased Richardson when he first showed up in camp, a pretender to Martin's job at second: "Hey, kid—I was sure you'd be in the Army by now—I already wrote your draft board telling them to take you." But Martin was helpful too, and in 1957, when he was traded, one of the most bitter days of his life, he behaved very well with Richardson. "Okay, Bobby, it's all yours now," he said.

Richardson and Kubek had played together for Ralph Houk in the minors at Denver, and had come up to the majors at roughly the same time. As he was reaching the higher echelons of the minors, Richardson was bothered by the number of middle infielders ahead of him—Martin, Gil McDougald, Andy Carey, Coleman, and Jerry Lumpe—all of whom seemed older and more experienced. In 1959, after the Yankees sent Jerry Lumpe to Kansas City, where he clearly would be able to play regularly, Richardson, by then twenty-four and feeling old and extremely frustrated with his lack of playing time and with Casey Stengel's tendency to play him and then pinch-hit for him in the early innings, went to George Weiss and asked to be traded as well. "No," said Weiss, "we're not going to trade you—we're not going to trade any more of our younger players. You're going to play regularly now." That had been the trademark of those old Yankee teams, so much depth that they could afford the luxury of breaking in their players slowly, not putting too much pressure on them at first, and confident always that there was another grace-ful-fielding shortstop and second baseman coming up through the minors. In 1961, when Ralph Houk became manager, Richardson and Kubek became the core of the infield. Kubek had been a favorite of Stengel's from the start. Stengel had known his father in the minor leagues, and Kubek's versatility appealed to Stengel. "I can play that kid anywhere," Stengel said, and he in fact did just that. Stengel came more slowly to his appreciation of Richardson, of whom he said at first, "He doesn't drink, he doesn't smoke, he doesn't chew and he doesn't cuss, and he still can't hit .250." Rich-ardson was a quiet player, and Stengel would say of his play at sec-ond base (in contrast with that of Martin, who was nothing if not volatile and verbal), "He doesn't talk much out there—I don't know if he's asleep or not."

When Houk took over as manager in 1961, he wanted to stabilize the team and believed he could do it by putting Kubek at shortstop every day and Richardson at second, and not shifting them around. He went to Richardson as soon as Stengel was forced out and told him, "The second-base job is yours. You'll play every day. I don't care if you hit .250 or .270. You're going to stay there." With that Kubek and Richardson became ever more confident, and one of the great strengths of the Yankee team in those years was its infield play. They were a very good double-play combination, quite possibly the best in the league. They always seemed to make the plays, and they were surprisingly good hitters. Mantle just edged Richardson out for American League MVP in 1962, and Mantle himself often said that if the game were on the line and the Yankees needed a hit, the player he would want up was Richardson. In fact, both Kubek and Richardson played better than their statistics showed. The recogni-tion of their excellence came slowly, in part because Kubek never looked like a great shortstop. He was not graceful, like Belanger or Aparicio, and he did not seem to have very good range. But he re-peatedly made the kind of plays that players with greater range did not. He played shortstop, it seemed, not as if it were his natural posi-tion, but through sheer willpower and determination. The key to his play, his teammates thought, was that he played with an inner toughness that he transmitted to other players on the team and seemed to carry him to a higher level in big games. He wanted to win, he expected to win, and he would not let anyone else loaf or slip beneath a standard of excellence; he was the one player on the team who would stand up to Mantle if he thought Mantle was losing focus or letting his hitting failures affect his play in the field.

Kubek liked and responded to challenges. Early on, he had heard people say that he would never be a big-league shortstop, and with that he set out to be the best shortstop in the league. He was persistent in all things, a strong union man in the Players Association when it was not a popular role and certainly did not help a player's career with management. He had his own strong sense of right and wrong and did not covet popularity. He did not like to be categorized, and if reporters wrote that he was one of the milk shake kids, hanging out with Richardson rather than with the carousers on the team, then he would hang out with Mantle and Ford for a few days, just to show them. That grittiness had always been there. Richardson remembered when they were both in the minor leagues, still at Denver, and Kubek was barely twenty. There was an argument at second base and Eddie Stanky, then the opposing team's manager, came out and seemed to bully not only the umpire but the Denver players. Kubek simply drew a line in the dirt and told Stanky, "Cross that line, I'll knock you on your ass." Those were not words that minor-league kids said to tough guys like Stanky, but it was a warning both heard and heeded. In Denver a pitcher named Frank Barnes threw at him and Kubek immediately laid down a bunt so that he could nail Barnes at first. He responded to every challenge and his intensity was palpable. Once in Detroit, after the Yankees had taken a big lead on a couple of home runs, Joe Sparma of the Tigers threw at Kubek and hit him. Kubek was furious; as soon as he could, he broke for second and took out the second baseman with a hard, rolling block. No one in the league, unless it was Roger Maris, a former football player, came in to second with as hard a block as Kubek. Then, on the next pitch, he broke for third and took out the third baseman with another hard body block. And then, on a grounder, he came home and rammed the catcher on another hard play. Then he went to the Detroit dugout, stopped right on the top step, pointed at Chuck Dressen, the Detroit manager, whom he knew had ordered the knockdown, and uttered some well-chosen words. He had been out, but the run had not mattered; what had mattered was sending a message to Dressen and Sparma.

The heart and soul of this team in the late fifties and early sixties, thought Steve Hamilton, the relief pitcher, were Kubek and Richardson. Kubek with his singular toughness, which he passed on as if by osmosis to the other players, might well be the most important player on the team, Hamilton thought, the glue that kept this aging team together. They had come up playing for winners in the farm system, and they had known nothing but winning in their early years in the majors. For the Yankee relief pitchers there was something reassuring about coming into the game, throwing your warm-up pitches, and hearing Kubek and Richardson teasing in the background. "Gee, Bobby," Kubek would say when Hamilton came in, "how's he going to get anyone out with that junk? I mean, he doesn't have *anything* today." "Yeah," Richardson would say, "I wonder how much stuff Mikkelsen has when he comes in. Let's hope he has more."

In 1964, Kubek was experiencing constant back problems. He had been badly injured playing touch football while in the army in 1962, had suffered cracked vertebrae, and his recovery had never been complete. He was only twenty-seven that season, but he could not swing properly and ended up playing in only 106 games. He hit some fifty points below his normal average, and it was, for him, a frustrating season. Within a year doctors warned him that he would have to retire or risk permanent damage to his spinal column; his career was cut down just at its height, and years later his memories of that particular season were so unpleasant that he could not bring himself to talk about them. In the past, the Yankees had been so deep that the loss of a player like Kubek would not have seemed that important. They always had an exceptional backup. Perhaps they lost twenty or thirty points in a batting average, but if the play in the field did not drop, then they did not worry about the loss of a few hits. But now it was different. Kubek was not only an exceptionally hard player to replace because of his overall value to the team, but the depth no longer existed. They were not rich in minor-league infielders, and when Richardson and Kubek both retired, they were replaced by a number of players, all of them undistinguished. In 1964, Kubek's injuries meant that Phil Linz had to play more and more shortstop that season, and that he had almost as many at bats as Kubek. Linz was a good baseball player in the eyes of his team-mates, a bit flaky but a tough kid in his own right. But he himself was the first to point out he was not Kubek, and the infield felt less solid to the pitchers with Kubek out for long stretches during this season.

24

Afterward, Lou Brock thought it was the best base he ever stole. Certainly the most important. It came just as the Cardinals were beginning to make a run at the Phillies, and after the game was over his teammates thought that if he had not pulled it off, the Phillies might have wrapped up the pennant then and there. It came on September 9, with the Cardinals playing eleven innings against the Phillies in Philadelphia. The Cards had been playing well for the last two and a half weeks; they had won 12 of their last 15, were 31-13 since July 24, and had cut five games off the Philly lead of eleven games. Curt Simmons started the game, pitched poorly, and was driven out in the fourth inning. "They can't even beat me on a bad night," he said later. The Cardinals hit Jim Bunning relatively hard and he left in the sixth inning. In the top of the ninth the Cardinals came to bat trailing 5–3. Charlie James opened the ninth with a single and Curt Flood forced him at second. Brock, at bat with one out, singled, and when Flood went to third and Cookie Rojas fumbled the ball in center field, Brock broke for second. Suddenly it appeared that the Phillies had Brock hung up between first and second. But Brock simply turned on his full speed and amazed everyone as he raced back to first past Danny Cater, the Philly first baseman. That, however, did not make him more cautious. With the count 0-2 on Bill White, Brock broke for second. It was one of forty-three bases he stole that year, but it was particularly daring because of the circumstances; if he had been out, then whatever chance the Cardinals had of tying the game up would have slipped away. Brock beat the throw from Clay Dalrymple, then Bill White hit a one-hopper to second, a perfect double-play ball; but instead of it being a double play with Flood scoring and no one left on the bases, Flood scored, Brock went to third, and White was out at first. Ken Boyer's single tied the score, and the Cardinals broke the game open in the eleventh with 5 runs. Without Brock's steal, the game would have ended in defeat for the Cards, and since the Phillies won the second game the next day, they might have ended up with an eight-game lead. "They win the game, maybe they break the whole thing open," Ken Boyer said later. "I think they may be peeking back at us now."

On September 3, with the Yankees still floundering, Roy Hamey, the former general manager, visited the team in Los Angeles, where the Yankees were in the process of losing two out of three to the Angels. "Does it look hopeless?" a reporter asked Hamey. "Well, hope is about all that is left," he answered. "This team needs a six game winning streak, but the way they're hitting, it wouldn't seem very likely they can do it. And if they get a streak going, those other guys [Baltimore and Chicago] would have to lose a few." Hamey thought that they were still a good team, but he compared them to Arnold Palmer, the great golfer, who had suddenly gone cold after being the best golfer in the country for years, and who now was coming in second in many tournaments. "I don't say they're finished. It could go down to the last week, even the last day. But they've got to start winning."

That August, Pedro Ramos, a pitcher with an exceptional fastball, was beginning to think for the first time that his professional baseball career might be coming to an end. Ramos and Birdie Tebbetts, the Cleveland manager, were most decidedly not getting along, and far more than language difficulties separated them. Ramos believed he had been promised by Tebbetts that he would be a starting pitcher, an assignment he greatly preferred, rather than working out of the bullpen. But by mid-season he was spending most of his time coming out of the bullpen. Ramos asked why, only to become convinced that Tebbetts neither appreciated the question nor was forthcoming in his answer. Tebbetts wore the number 1 on his uniform, and he turned his back, pointed to his uniform number, and said, "I'm number one here and whether you like it or not, you'll do what I say, and you'll pitch when I tell you and the way I tell you to." Ramos, then in his tenth big-league season, thought the Indians were going with younger pitchers who were not as good as he was. "But you told me I was a starting pitcher and that's what I am," he said. Tebbetts answered, "Don't you tell me what you are and what I said—I'm the manager, I know what I said, and I decide what you are."

Playing for Cleveland under Birdie Tebbetts was not where Ramos wanted to end up while he still was in his prime, for this was a team mired in sixth place. So Ramos asked to be traded. "We'd be glad to get rid of you, but no one wants you," Tebbetts told him. "What about letting me buy out my own contract and then letting me make my own deal if that's true?" asked the shrewd Ramos. "We can't do that," said Tebbetts. He did not say why they could not do that, but the idea had smacked of independence, and perhaps other players might want to purchase their contracts, too. So Ramos sat there that summer, a player of considerable ability whose misfortune it had been to play with poor second-division clubs most of his career. Worse, it seemed he would do it now as an older relief pitcher for second-division clubs. That would, of course, affect his salary negatively. Instead, he had always wanted to play for the Yankees, a team that had been his favorite when he was a boy growing up in rural Cuba. Whenever the Washington Senators, the team for whom he had labored for most of his career, played the Yankees, Ramos would sidle over to Casey Stengel and suggest that he make a deal for him. "I would pitch very good for you," he would say. "I would be a very good Yankee." Stengel always replied that he was interested, that the Yankees wanted him, but that the Washington ownership would not trade him—something others doubted, since Washington was famous for its willingness to trade or sell almost anything not nailed down. Then, in early September, Pete Ramos was called in by Gabe Paul, the general manager, and Tebbetts. "You've been traded," Tebbetts said. "I hope it's not to Kansas City," Ramos said, suddenly sensing that that might be Tebbetts's revenge, to trade him to a team even further down in the standings (the Kansas City Athletics were in tenth place at the time, some thirty games out). "Yeah, you have to go to Kansas City," Tebbetts said. There was a pause. "You're going to join the Yankees there." "I'll be on the first plane," Ramos said. Then, as he was leaving, he turned back to Tebbetts. "I thought you said no one wanted me."

Even in rural Cuba, for a little boy who helped carry the tobacco leaves on a plantation near Pinar del Río, the legend of the Yankees was powerful. Regular-season baseball games were not broadcast throughout Cuba, but World Series games were, and the Yankees always seemed to be in the World Series. The broadcaster was named Buck Canel, a very famous man in Cuba, and because of the way Canel pronounced "Yogi Berra," rolling the syllables out, it sounded like a Spanish name. So Ramos chose Berra as his favorite player, hoping that he was Spanish. That was as close to a big-league role model as a Cuban boy was going to get in the late forties. When Ramos finally signed with the Senators, the team with the strongest connection to Hispanic ballplayers in those days, he was very excited about visiting Yankee Stadium, which he had envisioned in his childhood fantasies. When he first got to the Stadium, he put his baseball uniform on and then toured the entire ball park, examining everything there, much as another man might have walked around a museum. This was the place he had always heard about as a boy, he thought, every bit as majestic as he had hoped. He loved playing against the Yankees, because they had so many great players, and his favorite player was now Mickey Mantle, who had hit one of his longest home runs off Ramos. That home run had come perilously close to going out of Yankee Stadium—leaving both Mantle and Ramos disappointed; Mantle because it was his life's ambition to hit one out, and Ramos because, in addition to being an intense competitor, he was a joyous man and realized he had just lost a moment of derivative immortality: that of having his name linked forever to Mantle's as co-authors of the longest home run in baseball history.

Liberated from Cleveland, Ramos raced for the airport and joined the Yankees in Kansas City on September 5. They were four games out and playing poorly at the time. But he was thrilled by the idea of being with his favorite team, of being in the midst of a pennant race, and, in addition, of pitching with the best infield in the American League playing behind him. He admired, as did many pitchers on opposing teams, the Yankees' infield play and their ability to pull off the pitcher's best friend, the double play. He got an example of that immediately. In his first game as a Yankee he came in to relieve Roland Sheldon in the last game of the Kansas City series. Sheldon pitched well through eight innings, had a 3–0 lead, and then walked the first batter in the ninth, Wayne Causey. Berra signaled for Ramos. The first batter was Rocky Colavito, who hit what looked like a tailor-made double-play ball to third. But the ball took a bad bounce and went off Clete Boyer's shoulder for a base hit. Then Jim Gentile singled past the mound, and Causey scored. Bill Bryan, a left-handed batter, was sent up to bat against the right-handed Ramos. Suddenly, after all those years of playing in games in which he was carried by personal ambition and pride, Pete Ramos was pitching under pressure, where a pennant could depend on his every pitch. Bryan hit a sharp ball to the right side, and for a moment Ramos thought that he had failed and that it was a base hit, but Pepitone made a nice pickup, went down to Kubek for the lead runner, and then took the relay for the double play. Then Ramos got Ed Charles to pop up for the third out.

It was Ramos's first save as a Yankee, and the first of many similar plays he would see in the weeks to come. He would throw the ball, and there would be a sharp grounder. For the moment he would feel that he had blown the game, then Kubek or Richardson would race over to make the play, and make it look easy. Afterward he would ask Kubek how he had done it, and Kubek would say that he and Richardson played the hitters in certain ways and it always seemed to work out. Good athletes, Ramos thought, and smart ones too. These were plays that had never been made for him in Washington or Cleveland, and he thought that in order to appreciate the Yankee infield play, every Yankee pitcher should be sentenced to five or six years playing for second-division clubs before he got to New York. If other members of the team thought the Yankees were wearing down and were not as disciplined as in the past, Ramos did not agree. What struck him was the professionalism of the Yankees, the belief that everything should be done right. Once when he was in the bullpen, Whitey Ford came out to talk to him, and Ford said that it was a great shame that Ramos had spent so many years with so many weak teams instead of getting to the Yankees much earlier. "Pete, if you'd been here from the start instead of the Senators," Ford said, "you could take five defeats a year, and move them over to the win column." They began to figure out his record that way. For the first nine years of his career, his record, they figured out, would have been 140-87. "Pete, you might have had a better record than me," Ford laughed.

Ramos had always had a good fastball, and when he broke in with the Senators when he was twenty, he had not even known how good it was. He played in a final preseason exhibition game against the Cincinnati Reds, and, of course, he had no idea who the Reds were, since he neither spoke nor read English. He knew they were in the National League and had red on their uniforms. The Reds crushed the Senators with their hitting that day. Late in the game Ramos was able to tell from Chuck Dressen's hand signals that Dressen wanted him in the game. So he pitched to two men, struck them out on six pitches, and got a third man to pop up. Two of the batters seemed unusually large to him. When he finished, a huge cheer went up from the crowd. Dressen, using his other players as interpreters, asked Ramos if he knew what the cheer was for. Ramos said he had no idea. "It's for you," Dressen said. Why? Ramos asked, puzzled. "Because you struck out Wally Post, Ted Kluszewski and got Gus Bell to pop up." That did not impress Ramos, so Dressen asked if his young pitcher knew who they were. No, he said. Well, said the manager, they all hit around thirty or forty home runs a year. "So the fans are happy with you," Dressen said.

His was not a great repertoire of pitches. He had a wicked fastball, a dinky curve (in his own words), and what became his famous Cuban palm ball, though everyone who hit against him said it was a spitter, which he always denied, albeit with a knowing smile. He knew exactly what he had to do every day as a relief pitcher for the Yankees. It was to get the batters to hit the ball on the ground, so he came in low all the time. In addition, he was determined not to walk anyone. The hitters were going to have to earn their hits off him. It was his happiest time in professional baseball: he could still throw hard—Ellie Howard told him he was probably throwing in the low nineties—and he was putting the ball exactly where he wanted it. Whitey Ford, who seemed to know more about pitching than any-one he had ever met, would take Ramos to the bullpen and teach him how to throw the Whitey Ford mud ball. The Yankees needed to play at home to use the mud ball, because the groundskeepers would wet down a spot near the catcher's position. When Whitey was pitching, Ellie Howard would give the ball a quick hard scratch at the mud. If the dirt was on the top, the ball would break down; if it was on the bottom, the ball would break up.

Ramos was greatly impressed by his teammates. He had never seen such a sense of purpose before. They were very relaxed as the pressure built during the stretch; no one seemed nervous, and no one was playing tight. They all seemed to put the idea of team ahead of individual accomplishment. In one game, his fourth appearance as a Yankee, he came in to relieve Whitey Ford, who had gone the first four innings with a 4–1 lead, but jammed his heel running out a base hit. Ramos gave up two hits and one run over the next five in-nings, and after the game he went over to Ford and asked why he had not gone one more inning in order to get credit for the win, which would have made his record 15-6 at the time—a lovely ac-complishment in a season marked by injury and pain for Ford. "Pete, one more win for me isn't very important—it doesn't really mean anything. But one more win for the Yankees in a pennant race means a hell of a lot right now, and it's not worth taking a chance." That win had brought them into second place, only one game out.

The Yankees were on the move now and Ramos was a key part of it. It was the best month of his professional career. He seemed to be pitching every day, with the game on the line on every pitch. Again and again Berra went to him. Finally Berra told him he needed a rest

and not to come to the ball park, because if he came Yogi might not
be able to resist the temptation to go to him. But Ramos came to the
ball park, and Yogi inevitably used him. Roy Hamey had made his
statement about the need for a winning streak on September 3, and
the next day the Yankees went on a 5-game winning streak. Then
they hit another bump in the road and lost 2 out of 3, with a five-
hitter by Al Downing against the Tigers, their only victory. On September 12, Stottlemyre, who was absolutely brilliant down the
stretch, beat Minnesota, 4–3, on a five-hitter, and it was the first
game of another winning streak. Over the combined winning
streaks, the young rookie had 5 starts and won all 5, including 3
complete games and another game in which he pitched into the
ninth. On September 26 he pitched against the Senators in Washington in what would be the Yankees' eleventh straight victory if
they won. He was awesome, and they won, 7–0. Stottlemyre gave up
two hits, got fifteen outs on groundballs, and had five hits himself.
When the second streak was over, the Yankees had won 19 out of
their last 22, and were in first place by four games. Pete Ramos had
appeared in 8 games, won 1, saved 5 (he would save 2 more before
the season was over); he had worked 20⅓ innings and given up only
eight hits and two runs. He struck out sixteen men and did not walk
a single batter. His earned run average was 1.59. As the National
League race was becoming tighter and tighter, the Yankees suddenly seemed to be putting a lock on the American League. Their
two competitors, the Orioles and the White Sox, were younger
teams and they simply flattened out: Baltimore, which actually had a
season edge over the Yankees that year, went 11-11 during the Yankee hot streak, and the White Sox went 10-9.

Most of the Yankee hitters went on batting streaks of their own.
Ellie Howard went 27 for 86 during the streak, and Bobby Richardson went 39 for 90. But if there was a key player, both offensively
and defensively, in that stretch for the Yankees, it was Roger Maris,
even though it had not been a good season for him. His nagging
injuries had allowed him to play, but not at his top level. And then,
in September, when the Yankees seemed on the verge of falling out
of contention, with both Mantle and Tom Tresh frequently injured,

Roger Maris, who had not been that dangerous a hitter for two years, caught fire and played some of the best baseball of his life. He carried the team as he might have in an earlier time if Mantle had not been a teammate. Maris hit the ball with authority. These were rocketlike line drives, hit so hard that they seemed to have topspin on them and they exploded up when they bounced toward the waiting fielders. He went 16 for 42 during that critical winning streak, and drove in critical runs in game after game—24 runs in his last 41 games. In addition, Berra, finally accepting the inevitability of Mantle's physical decline, gave Tresh a shot in center field, and then he finally decided on playing Maris there. Maris, fast and strong, a far better center fielder than Tresh, played the best center field that the Yankees had seen since Mantle was young.

25

At first it seemed a small thing. On Sunday, September 29, Tony Kubek had a frustrating day at the plate, one of many in a season of such constant health problems that he was rarely able to play up to the level of his own expectations. His batting average was down some forty points. After this game he apparently slapped his hand against a door that had appeared to him to be made of wood. It was not. It was metal, and he badly hurt his wrist, which began to swell up. Kubek did not play on Tuesday, and then he did not play again on Wednesday. Berra told reporters that he was sure that Kubek would be back in a few days, and that it was a good idea to rest him at this point of the season. But Kubek did not play again for the rest of the season and did not play in the World Series.

That September, after leading the National League for almost the entire season, often by as many as nine or ten games, the Philadelphia Phillies began to die. As the team started to make mistakes and became mired in a prolonged losing streak, the clubhouse became quieter and quieter; as the defeats mounted, they began to have ever greater psychological impact.

For Jim Bunning, the ace pitcher of the Phillies, it was the end of a storybook season. Bunning had been a star pitcher in Detroit for nine years, one of the best pitchers in the American League. Then, in 1963, he ran afoul of Chuck Dressen, who had been installed as the Tiger manager for the last part of what was a losing Detroit season. Bunning was underwhelmed by Dressen, almost as much, it seemed, as Dressen was underwhelmed by Bunning, thirty-one years old then, and in the midst of a rare losing season. Dressen seemed to think Bunning's career was over, and in September he gave several of Bunning's starts away to other pitchers, most notably to a young right-hander named Denny McLain. That enraged Bunning, who thought of himself as a good September pitcher, and afterward he felt he might have turned his 12-13 record into a winning one had he gotten all his starts. It was not just a matter of ego, but a matter of finances as well; for in those days, when players had so little leverage in contract negotiations, a losing season weakened Bunning's ability to argue for more money. Bunning regarded Dressen as a self-important man who thought that the manager was more important than the players. His favorite line to his players was that if they could hold the opposition for the first seven innings, he, Chuck Dressen, would think of some way to win the game in the last two. Was there a dumber attitude on the part of a manager in the game of baseball? Bunning wondered. At the end of 1963, Bunning asked for a trade, and the Tiger management granted his wish, sending him to Philadelphia, where he quickly became the ace of the staff. From the start, Bunning loved playing in the National League, where, as a low-ball pitcher, he found that the league's umpires regularly gave him the call on low strikes as American League umpires had not. He also thought that the Philadelphia team was very good, much better than anyone realized. Even before the season started, he thought it had a good shot at the pennant.

In the American League there was a certain deadness to the competition because the Yankees cast such a shadow that the other teams spent most of their time fighting to see who would come in second. The National League was so even that just as one injury to a key player could throw a team out of contention, so the pickup of an additional key player could turn a team into a contender. That seemed to have happened in his case with the Phillies, for his arrival not only added one very dependable starting pitcher to the Philly staff—overnight he became their stopper—but it helped the talented young left-hander, Chris Short, a pitcher of considerable skills who seemed to be uneasy with the responsibility of being the ace of the staff. Now Short thrived with the pressure on him reduced. Short had never won more than eleven games before Bunning joined the team, but in the next three years, with Bunning as the lead pitcher of the staff, Short won fifty-five games.

If the Dodgers had two of the best pitchers in Koufax and Drysdale, the Phillies, Bunning thought, might well have had the deepest starting pitching in either league with himself, Short, Art Mahaffey, Dennis Bennett, and Ray Culp. In addition, it was a team with the best middle infielders Bunning had ever played with. There were four fine infielders: two shortstops, Bobby Wine and Ruben Amaro; and two second baseman, Tony Taylor and Cookie Rojas. That gave Gene Mauch, the manager, a rare degree of flexibility and made the pitching seem even better than it was. In some ways the Phillies reminded Bunning of the New York Yankee teams that he had played against, whose secret strength had always been their superior infield play. The Philly hitting was better than people thought too: by mid-September it was obvious that Johnny Callison was having a career year and might well be the league's Most Valuable Player if the Phillies won the pennant; Richie Allen, a brilliant rookie, was quite likely to be the Rookie of the Year (which, in fact, he was). Then, in early August, the Phillies made another important pickup, trading with the Mets for Frank Thomas, the big Met first baseman. Thomas was a streaky hitter who had never played with a contending team before, and he had gone on a tear for the Phillies, hitting .294 with 7 home runs and driving in 26 runs in only 39 games. The acquisition of Thomas seemed to give the Phillies a lock.

For Bunning it seemed, if not a perfect season, something very close. On Father's Day he pitched a perfect game against the New York Mets. It was a sweltering day and he had had to change his sweatshirt three times. He ignored the superstition that a pitcher was not supposed to mention the possibility of a no-hitter or a perfect game, telling his teammates as they entered the eighth inning that there were only six more outs to go, so they should dive at anything hit. In early September Bunning's record was 16-4, he had won 9 of his last 10 decisions, and he seemed, if anything, to be getting stronger. The year of the Blue Snow, Jim Bunning called a season like this, which meant that it was a season when everything went right.

It was the general belief that Gene Mauch, then only thirty-eight years old and in his fifth year as a manager, had done a masterful job with the Phillies. No one had ever doubted Mauch's intelligence; if anything, some people thought that his problem might be that he thought too much, saw too much, and expected too much of his players. No one certainly had ever shown more skill as a bench manager—he always seemed to be about two moves ahead of everyone else. Whether his temperament was ideal for so long a season was another thing. He seemed to approach the game on a wartime footing, thought the writer Larry Merchant, as if every play in every game were taking place in the seventh game of the World Series. He had learned his trade from the mind and mouth of Leo Durocher and was a bench jockey of almost violent behavior, deliberately trying to provoke players from other teams, always trying to get them to think about him rather than the job they were supposed to be doing. Not all his players thought that his tactic was completely successful. It might break the concentration of a few players, but it was just as likely to enrage others and provoke them to play harder against the Phillies. Some of his players thought him too passionate, too wired, unable to let go, and there was always the danger that when his team got in trouble he would increase the tension among his players. If things went wrong, he could not let go of the emotion he felt. Once when Tim McCarver had beaten the Phillies with a late-inning hit, Mauch got on the team bus in a rage and sat there, repeating over and over again, perhaps ten times, McCarver was later told, *"Tim Fucking McCarver Beat You! Tim Fucking McCarver."* He was not necessarily a manager who could adjust his own temperament to the growing tightness of his team as it suddenly became burdened by a losing streak in a pennant race.

Then, on September 8, in a game against the Dodgers, Frank Thomas injured his hand. Thirty years later, Bunning, by then a congressman, could still see every detail of the play: Thomas was on second when a ground ball was hit to the left of Maury Wills, the Dodger shortstop. Thomas went out from the bag as if to decoy Wills and block his view, which was not necessarily a smart move for a player not known for his baserunning ability. He held there and then, in a fraction of a second, he realized he had stayed too long, and as Wills began to make his play to second, Thomas was suddenly vulnerable and he had to dive back to the bag. As he landed he reached for the base and broke his right thumb. Though he tried to come back before the end of the season, his effectiveness as a player was ended.

With that, other things started to go wrong. Ray Culp, who had problems with his elbow, gained his last victory on July 22 and made his last start on August 15. Now, as the team entered the home stretch, Dennis Bennett came up with a sore arm. In the same game against the Dodgers in which Thomas had been hurt, Art Mahaffey lasted only two thirds of an inning, and then four days later in a game on the West Coast against the Giants, Mahaffey again lasted only two innings. Though there did not seem to be anything wrong with his arm, Mauch lost confidence in him and did not start him for another nine days, and even then, only with obvious reluctance. Suddenly, the Philly pitching staff, which had looked so deep, was spread very thin. On September 13, Bunning beat the Giants for his seventeenth victory against only four defeats. Short and Bennett followed with victories against Houston. There was a question of who would pitch the third and final game in Houston against the Colts. Down the stretch Mauch wanted Bunning to pitch in every series the Phillies played, but that meant pitching against Houston on two days' rest: it would allow him to be ready for the final game of the series against L.A. Bunning agreed to try; he had pitched well against Houston, still an expansion club, which won only sixty-six games that season, and he had already beaten the Colts four times that year. Why not try for five? He and Mauch were trying to steal a start. But Bunning lasted only four and a third innings, Rusty Staub hit a home run off him, the Phillies lost, and Bunning went to 17-5. It was the first of six times that Mauch used both Bunning and Short with only two days of rest during the remainder of the season, and the two star pitchers ended up losing all six games.

On September 20, Bunning pitched against the Dodgers in Los Angeles and beat them on a five-hitter, 3–2. When the game was over the Phillies were 90-60 with twelve games to play and with a six-and-a-half-game lead over the rest of the league. Cincinnati was in second, and by then a half-game behind them was St. Louis. Even in that game against the Dodgers, Bunning remembered, the Phils had been shaky and had almost blown the game; there had been an easy play at first in the ninth inning when Vic Power, whom they had gotten to replace Frank Thomas, and who was normally a great fielder, seemed unable to pick up a ball and make the proper throw to Bunning. The Dodgers had scored two unearned runs in the ninth, but Bunning had struck out John Roseboro to end the game. With that the Phillies came home for a seven-game home stand, absolutely sure they could clinch the pennant. A reporter from *Sports Illustrated* was spending time with Bunning, whose record was now 18–5, and soon a photographer arrived to shoot the pitcher in color; it was said that the cover of the magazine for the week the World Series started would feature Jim Bunning on it. The next night, in the first game of the home stand, Art Mahaffey took the ball for the first time in nine days and pitched against John Tsitouris of the Reds. Mahaffey was pitching well in the sixth in what was a scoreless tie. With one out in the sixth, Chico Ruiz singled to right. Vada Pinson lined a ball off Mahaffey's glove, and the ball went past Tony Taylor toward right center field for a hit, but when Pinson tried to stretch the hit, Johnny Callison in right made a perfect throw and nailed him. Ruiz was on third with two out, and Frank Robinson, one of the most dangerous hitters, was up. On the mound Mahaffey took a big windup and fired. Robinson swung and missed. On third, Ruiz had seen Mahaffey's windup and noticed that he was not checking the runner. As Mahaffey went into the windup for his next pitch, Ruiz broke for home. It was an unthinkable play, trying to steal home with the team's big hitter up. Surprised and startled, Mahaffey threw wildly and the ball arrived high and outside; Clay Dalrymple, the catcher, jumped to spear the ball, but it rolled to the screen. Ruiz was safe. The Reds won, 1–0. The Philly lead was now five and a half games. After the game, Gene Mauch was furious— angry that he had lost, and almost as much because he had been beaten by a play that went against all the logic of baseball. *"Chico Fucking Ruiz* beats us on a bonehead play of the year. *Chico Fucking Ruiz steals home with Frank Robinson up! Can you believe it!"* he said later, still in disbelief, then adding, when he talked to reporters, that if Ruiz had gotten thrown out, he would have been on his way back to the minor leagues, which is where he belonged anyway.

The next day, still offended, still angry, Mauch rode Robinson, Ruiz, and the rest of the Reds hard from the bench. Robinson responded with a two-run homer. Chris Short pitched that game, was hit hard, and lasted only four and two thirds innings. When it was over the Philly lead was down to four and a half. That day the Phillies started accepting applications for World Series tickets, and they ended up with some ninety thousand requests. The next day Dennis Bennett, whose arm hurt badly, lasted six innings and the Phillies lost to the Reds, 6–4. Vada Pinson hit a home run and had four runs batted in, and Chico Ruiz, tired of all Mauch's screaming at him, retaliated by hitting a home run himself. The incredible shrinking Philly lead was now three and a half.

Jim Bunning came back on three days' rest against Milwaukee, a tough team for any pitcher, with its great hitters; he went six innings and lost, 5–3. Joe Torre drove in three runs with two triples. ("As slow as he runs, he really had to drive those balls," Bunning reminisced later.) In fact, both balls were misplayed by Philadelphia outfielders. The first of the two bounced over the head of rookie center fielder Adolfo Phillips, and one run scored; the second, in the eighth, went to the wall when Callison tried for a shoestring catch and missed, and two runs scored. That made it four losses in a row, and when Short pitched on two days' rest and they lost to the Braves, it was a five-game losing streak and the lead was one and a half. Mahaffey pitched the next night and lost to make it six in a row, and a half-game lead. With no one rested for the Sunday game, Jim Bunning went to Mauch and volunteered. "I'll take the ball," he said. He went out and pitched on two days' rest against Milwaukee and was hammered in a 14–8 defeat, the seventh in a row. Bunning lasted three innings, gave up ten hits and seven earned runs, and when the game was over Lee May had five hits, and Torre and Felipe Alou had three each. The streaking Cincinnati Reds were in first place with a record of 91-66, the Phillies were in second, one game out, with a record of 90-67, and the Cardinals were in third, 89-67, one and a half games out. The Phillies had played their entire seven-game home stand without a victory.

Rarely was any manager more second-guessed than Gene Mauch in those final two weeks of the 1964 season. In six different games he had gone with either Bunning or Short on two days' rest and the Phillies had lost all six games. The question was the obvious one: with a lead that big, why not concede a game or two, then come back with a rested pitcher and end the streak. Thirty years later, Jim Bunning could sit in his office in the Rayburn Building and remember each one of the final games of that season—who had pitched, what the situation was in each game, what the Philly lead was at the end of each day, and who had pitched in the other National League games as the pennant race continued to tighten. To understand what had happened, he said, you had to be there at the time, to be caught up in the excitement and emotions of that pennant race. In addition, you had to have the mind-set of a high-level athlete, which meant, in situations like this, a belief that he could prevail by sheer will. Athletes, Bunning said, always think they are invincible. "Hindsight dictates that we should have been rested and then pitched. That's obvious to everyone now," he said. "But the emotions of the moment dictated that we try for it, that we go out there and pitch on two days of rest. To say no, to refuse the ball and say that you could not pitch on short rest, was to go against every impulse superior athletes have." On that critical seventh game of the losing streak, Bunning had believed that he was the stopper of the team, that he could end the losing streak, and, moreover, that it was his personal responsibility to his team to end it. He did not feel tired when he went to the mound in those games. He felt rested, and confident, although based on the way the opposing hitters greeted him, he was obviously pitching with a good deal more fatigue than he realized.

A losing streak is contagious. Players who have played with confidence begin to lose it. Doubts begin to arise where there have been no doubts. Players run the bases poorly and throw to the wrong bases. Easy plays are missed. In the 14–8 loss to Milwaukee, Bunning watched Ruben Amaro, a shortstop who fielded beautifully, come under an easy pop-up behind short. Amaro had not dropped a pop fly all year, but now, perhaps because he heard the approach of the left fielder, he dropped the ball. Uncharacteristically, Gene Mauch became quieter and quieter as the losing streak went on.

On Monday, September 28, the Phillies went into St. Louis for a three-game series. Suddenly the schedule, if anything, seemed to favor the Cardinals. The Cards got three shots at home against a stumbling Philadelphia team, and then they closed out the season with three games against the Mets, while the Reds finished up with Philadelphia. Obscured by the run that the Reds made against the Phillies was the fact that the Cards were a hot team too. Their lead-off hitters had been getting on, and both White, who had knocked in sixty-four runs since the All-Star break, and Boyer had been hitting consistently in the clutch. Their three best pitchers were all in a groove. The Cards had started their desperate last-minute pennant run on September 22, when they went to New York to play two games against the Mets, and from there to Pittsburgh to play five against the Pirates. Bob Skinner, the old Pirate outfielder who had been traded that season to the Cards, and Dick Groat decided they needed to sweep the Mets, and then take four out of five against the Pirates: it was a tall order because Pittsburgh was a tough team. They ended up splitting with the Mets, losing to Galen Cisco, 2–1, in a game that Roger Craig pitched beautifully. "Okay, Dick, the only thing we have to do is sweep the Pirates in five," Skinner then said. They went on to do just that, helped by the fact that Bob Friend, one of the Pirates' best pitchers, missed a turn because of a sore throat, a decision that enraged the Phillies.

When the three-game Philly-Cardinal series started in St. Louis, the Cardinal players, as befit a team doing everything right, were confident and exuberant. Don Hoak, the former Pirate third baseman, was a good friend and former teammate of Groat's and now an advance scout for the Phillies. "That was a disgrace in Pittsburgh," Hoak told Groat. "They just handed you five games." "Hoaky, I bet you told them that," Groat said, "but I bet you forgot to mention the most important thing about those five games—that we didn't make a single mistake in all five of them." Hoak admitted a little sheepishly that, in fact, he had not mentioned it. "Don, did you mention Barney?" Groat asked. (In the final game at Pittsburgh, Barney Schultz had come in to relieve Roger Craig, who had pitched a shutout over seven innings. He had faced Roberto Clemente, the league's leading hitter with two men on and two out, and struck him out.) Hoak just smiled.

Rarely had baseball been so much fun for the Cards. When you woke up in the morning, thought Barney Schultz, you could not wait to get to the ball park. They should have been exhausted, but the winning streak and the apparent collapse of the Phillies was a booster shot, allowing them to play through their fatigue and despite an assortment of nagging injuries. These were injuries that in other seasons might have kept them out of games, but now they paid little attention to their physical problems. Ken Boyer was so banged up by the end of the season that the Cardinals had to hide the extent of his shoulder injury from the press when the World Series began. Curt Flood's legs were banged up and extremely sore. Both played all 162 regular-season games. Bill White had been bothered by a bad shoulder for the first half of the season yet he ended up playing in 160 games, and Dick Groat played in 161 games. Tim McCarver's legs were absolutely black and blue, and there were bumps on them the size of golf balls, Groat thought, and yet he kept playing and caught 143 games with increasingly mangled hands. Brock was with the Cardinals for 103 games and played in 103 of them; his body, befitting that of a base stealer, ached all over, particularly in his shoulder, where he had been hit by a Sandy Koufax fastball. This incident was celebrated by the ever-joyous Don Drysdale, who yelled his approval from the dugout—"All right! All right!" Drysdale later told Brock, "It's a good thing that Sandy kissed you, because I was going to kiss you the next time." "Yeah, and I was thinking of going after you when you yelled out," Brock said. "Why

didn't you?" asked Drysdale. "Because you're six-five," Brock answered.

For the Cardinals the heat of the pennant race had come so
quickly that there was no time to play under pressure. They raced
right through it. There was a strong sense of camaraderie and a
wonderful balance of personalities, the players decided, looking
back years later. Bob Uecker, who was one of the last people Devine
had picked up, was turning out to be not only a valuable player—a
good catcher with a good arm—but also a valuable addition to the
team, and he helped keep his teammates loose. Years later, Uecker
was to make a considerable living as a baseball comedian, both lec-
turing and appearing in commercials that mocked his baseball abilities. But in those days, he was performing for his own pleasure and
the pleasure of his teammates. He was someone who thought baseball should be fun; Uecker later figured that his clowning around as
a minor-league player had delayed his entry into the big leagues for
several years, because Chuck Dressen, the manager of the Braves at
the time, hated Uecker's humor. "We don't need a clown like you in
baseball," Dressen would shout at him. When a photographer had
arrived early in the season to take the Cardinal team photograph,
Uecker and Gibson had been seated next to each other, and right
before the photographer snapped the photo, Uecker whispered to
Gibson that they should smile and hold hands. Gibson had been delighted to cooperate. No one noticed what they were doing at the
time. When the photo had been produced and processed, there were
two men, one white, one black, seated in the front row with goofy
smiles on their faces, holding hands. Much to the irritation of Cardinal management, which threatened to fine Uecker, the photo had
to be retaken.

In addition, Uecker invented the game of Ugly and was the team's
best player, which was not hard since he owned and kept possession
of all fifty-two cards. Uecker had friends in the Philadelphia police
force, and whenever a particularly grim-looking man or woman was
wanted for some heinous crime, the cops saved the mug shot for
Uecker, who placed it in the Ugly deck. When he finally had fifty-
two photos, he invented the game of Ugly, which was not unlike

Hearts: there were four players, and whoever put down the ugliest of the four photos gathered up the other three. There was one photo that every player coveted, for it was the key to winning the game. It was of a woman wanted for multiple murders, and it was far and away the grimmest and ugliest picture in the deck. When Uecker played, he tended to keep it out of the pack and up his sleeve so that he could always trump at the last moment. (When Uecker had been with the Braves, he once showed the photo to Dixie Walker, then the Braves' batting coach, a man who, other than his attempt to protest Jackie Robinson's entry into the big leagues, was generally known for his courtesy and politeness. "Dixie, that's my mother. What do you think of her?" Uecker said to Walker. Walker held the photo for a long time and finally said, "She's rather attractive, isn't she?")

Uecker pitched batting practice every day, and in time he created the Uecker League, of which he was the commissioner, umpire, and scorekeeper. There were two teams of five pitchers each in the Uecker League. There was a draft among the pitchers, and they chose sides, and when the pitchers took batting practice at home (they did not get batting practice on the road), Uecker would stand on the mound and decide whether a player had gotten a hit. All ground balls and pop-ups were outs. If there were runners on base, he decided how far they advanced on a play. The pitchers themselves did the scoring and kept their batting averages. On occasion there were trades from one team to another. Once Ron Taylor, one of the bullpen pitchers, batted out of turn. A protest was immediately lodged. Uecker demanded to see the scorecard, but before he could look at it, Taylor ate it. It was said that Gibson, a very good hitter, hit more than twenty home runs and batted over .500 in the Uecker League.

As the Phillies prepared for their three games in St. Louis, Gene Mauch tried to fire up his players. "They're stealing the money right out of your pockets," he told his players. "If it was me and someone tried to steal my money there'd be a hell of a fight." Jim Bunning looked over at his friend Gus Triandos in disbelief. *Start a fight?* he had thought. *We don't need to start a fight. I need to pitch a complete game.* When the Philly players arrived on the field, the Cardinal players sensed that they were dispirited. Their pepper games were listless, and their eyes, Dick Groat thought, had a hollow look, like that of men who were in shock. Bill White thought they looked beaten already. Later, Gene Mauch would talk of how when he had called in relief pitchers during that terrible streak, he saw the fear in their eyes when they reached the mound and he gave them the ball.

In the first of the three games against the Phillies in St. Louis, Chris Short went against Bob Gibson. Short, who had beaten the Cardinals three times earlier in the season, was pitching with three days' rest. The Cardinal hitters thought he pitched well but lacked the hard, exploding fastball he had shown earlier in the season, and he tired in the middle innings. The Cardinals came up with 5 runs, and Gibson was not about to lose on this day. He gave up only 5 hits, then tired slightly in the ninth inning, giving up a single to the first batter who faced him and then walking Tony Taylor. With no one out and a 5–1 lead, Johnny Keane went to Barney Schultz immediately. It was his fourth straight relief appearance, and his twenty-seventh appearance since he had been brought up on August 1. Schultz liked to amble down to the bullpen during the sixth inning of each game in the stretch run, and once he started down in the fifth inning. Roger Craig stopped him immediately. "Hey, Barney," he said, "you can't go down there yet—it's still an inning early for you." He had become something of a talisman for them. Schultz threw a knuckleball to Clay Dalrymple and he hit into a double play, and then John Herrnstein popped the ball up. It was the Cardinals' sixth straight win, and the Phillies' eighth straight loss. At the end of the day the Reds were in first place, 91-66, the Cards in second, 90-67, one game back, and the Phillies in third, 90-68, one and a half games out.

The Phillies, if not out of gas, were out of arms. In the second game Dennis Bennett took the mound, and Jim Bunning thought Bennett's tendinitis was so bad he could barely reach the plate. Curt Simmons, who knew the personnel of the Phillies well and was a friend of some of the players, watched Bennett warming up and agreed with Bunning: Bennett had a dead arm—it was crazy to use him. Mauch, he thought, ought to start Bobby Shantz and try to patch through with his bullpen for one game, but starting Bennett was like giving a game away. Bennett predictably did not have very much, and the Cardinals scored three runs in the first two innings. Bennett left after an inning and a third, the first of six Philly pitchers to appear. Ray Sadecki pitched for the Cardinals, going for his twentieth. Before the game he had looked over and thought the Philly bench resembled a bunch of ghosts. Even their bench jockeying seemed second-rate. "You're not going to get your twentieth, Sadecki," someone yelled, and others were yelling at him that he was going to choke. Choke, he thought, that was a strange choice of words from this team. He was given a handsome early lead, and he seemed to coast through the game for his twentieth win. In the seventh inning, with two men on, two out, and Richie Allen up, Keane called for Schultz. Schultz got Allen on a pop-up, and then walked one man and retired the other six men he faced. It was his fifth straight appearance, all of them big games, during this sudden highly pressurized pennant race. With Simmons scheduled to start the next night, Sadecki went over to him and handed him the ball. "Here it is, Curt," he said. "Just keep Barney around." In Cincinnati, the Pirates behind Bob Friend ended the Reds' nine-game winning streak by pitching a shutout. Only 10,800 people showed up to see the game despite the intensity of the pennant race and the Reds' winning streak. The Cardinals and the Reds were now tied for first place at the end of the day, 91-67 each, with the Phillies still a game and a half out, with four games left.

For the final game of the series it was Bunning again pitching on two days' rest against Curt Simmons. The Cardinal players were immensely confident. Not only were they playing well, but Tim McCarver, a good low-ball hitter and a lefty, had hit Bunning with authority in the past. In the second inning, after Groat had singled, McCarver hit his ninth home run of the season for a 2–0 lead, and in the third, eight Cardinals reached base—four on hits, two on errors, and two on walks as the Phillies continued to unravel. The final score was 8–5. The Cardinals thought Bunning did not seem either sharp or fast. By contrast, Curt Simmons had pitched no-hit ball for

six and two thirds innings. The Cardinals' pitching had been spectacular since mid-season: Gibson had been 8-1, Sadecki 6-1, and
Simmons 6-0, for a total of 20-2.

The Phillies seemed finished. It was their tenth loss in a row. "We
were the best team in the league for a hundred and fifty games,"
Gene Mauch said later. They now faced the Reds for their final two
games of the season, while the Cardinals took on the Mets. In New
York the editors of *Sports Illustrated* decided to pull the cover of Jim
Bunning and go with one of Dick Butkus, the great college linebacker.

That night the Cardinal players went out to the pool at the Bel
Air East, where many of the unmarried players were staying, and
listened to the broadcast of the Reds-Pirates game from Cincinnati.
It was a classic game, two power pitchers at their best, scoreless after
nine and scoreless in extra innings; Jim Maloney pitched for the
Reds, Bob Veale for the Pirates, Maloney striking out thirteen in
eleven innings and Veale striking out sixteen over thirteen innings.
They were throwing itty-bitty baseballs, McCarver thought, and it
was as if the ball itself were getting smaller as the game went on. In
the top of the sixteenth Donn Clendenon doubled and moved to
third on Bill Mazeroski's sacrifice bunt. The batter was Jerry May, a
young catcher brought up at the end of the season. Clendenon
broke for the plate, May laid down a lovely bunt, and the Pirates had
a run. In the bottom of the sixteenth Alvin McBean put down the
Reds in order, and at the end of Wednesday's schedule, for the first
time, the Cardinals had first place to themselves. But on Thursday
the Reds beat the Pirates to cut the Cardinal lead to half a game.

It should have been easy for the Cardinals. All they had to do was
beat the Mets and the pennant was theirs. They were so hot as a
team, McCarver thought, that the only danger was an off day. Friday was a bizarre night. The Cardinals, ready to close in on the pennant, sent Gibson against Al Jackson, the talented Met left-hander,
and Gibson pitched beautifully but Jackson was better, and the Mets
won, 1–0. The game in Cincinnati was one of the weirdest of the
season. The Phillies, still sleepwalking, were behind, 3–0, in the seventh. In the bottom of the seventh, with one out and a man on sec-

ond, Chris Short hit Leo Cardenas of the Reds with a pitch. Cardenas wanted to fight, and his teammates had to stop him. Somehow, the scuffle seemed to wake up the Phillies. With one out in the eighth, a bloop hit by Frank Thomas landed near second. The Reds thought that Cardenas should have had it, but that his mind was still on the confrontation with Short. Jim O'Toole, the Cincinnati pitcher, seemed furious with Cardenas and lost his cool, walking one man and then giving up another hit. Suddenly the Phillies broke through for four runs and won the game. After the game, in the Reds' locker room, O'Toole, still furious, went after Cardenas and threw him to the ground. At that point Cardenas grabbed an ice pick and started after O'Toole, but others pulled them apart.

On Saturday the Reds and the Phillies had the day off and the Cardinals played the Mets in a day game, with Ray Sadecki pitching. Sadecki was flat. The Mets got four runs off him in the first and hammered the Cardinals, 15–5. It seemed a cruel joke to some of the Cardinal players to come this far, to play so well down the stretch, fashioning an eight-game winning streak against the league's best teams, and then lose the first two games to the Mets. If it was hard on the Cardinal players, it was equally hard on the National League schedule makers. If the Reds lost to the Phillies, and the Cards lost to the Mets on the final day, the major leagues for the first time in history would have a three-way tie. A complicated three-way mini-series was created to deal with the prospect. In Cincinnati the Phillies, behind Jim Bunning, pitching with plenty of rest, defeated the Reds, 10–0. In St. Louis, Curt Simmons started. He was not as sharp in this game as he had been against the Phillies, and in the fifth inning, when the Mets took a 3–2 lead, Johnny Keane called for Bob Gibson to come out of the bullpen. The Cards scored three in the bottom of the fifth and three more in the sixth. In the eighth they added three more. Their lead was 11–4, but in the ninth Gibson walked two. There was one out with two on when Keane went to Barney Schultz. A passed ball and a single gave the Mets a run and made the score 11–5. Then Ed Kranepool popped to McCarver. The Cardinals had won the pennant on the last day of the season.

· · ·

On October 3 the Yankees clinched the pennant at home against Cleveland. Al Downing started, and was relieved by Pete Mikkelsen, who became the winning pitcher. Ramos came in for Mikkelsen in the ninth and got the save, his seventh down the stretch as a Yankee. When the game was over, Ramos stood on the mound and turned to his former manager, Birdie Tebbetts, standing in the Indian dugout, the man who earlier that season had said that no one wanted him. Ramos planted his left hand in the crook of his right arm and then made a gesture as old as the ages to Tebbetts.

Pete Ramos was not eligible for the World Series—he had come over to the Yankees after the September 1 deadline. There had been some talk with the Phillies of allowing a player from each club to be added to the rosters, because the Phillies were short of pitching too, but when the Phillies collapsed, Ramos's chances died as well. The Cardinals had no intention of doing anything that would allow him a shot at eligibility. It was a black day, Ramos thought when he found out he could not pitch. The Yankees invited him to come with the team to St. Louis, but he had no taste for it. When they played in New York he went out to the park early to pitch batting practice, and then went to his room at the Concourse Plaza Hotel to watch the games by himself in his room.

26

There was, of course, some apprehension among the Cardinals about playing the mighty Yankees. The Yankees had been to the World Series every season since time began, it seemed, and they knew about big games. They knew how to intimidate their opponents, and somehow in a World Series, no matter where the game was played, they always managed to seem like the home team. As they came on the field for the first game, they did not trickle out of the dugout as other teams did, but came out as a team; because they were big men, they came out big. They seemed to boost themselves as they came over the last step of the dugout in order to look even bigger. On the field, watching, Lou Brock could not figure out if it was intentional, but it struck him then that they knew how to play the game of intimidation and how to look imposing. Curt Flood was standing with Brock, and he was thinking the same thing Brock was. "Hey, Lou, when they come down, they still have to play baseball," Flood said.

In fact, the Cardinals could still hardly believe they were in the World Series. Winning the pennant had come as a quick high for the Cardinals, and an equally quick downer for the Phillies. The only person who appeared to show any stress at the end was Barney Schultz. He had held up well during the last few weeks, pitching brilliantly every day, it seemed, with the game on the line on every pitch. When the Cardinals won the pennant, though, he felt the tension for the first time. Just before the World Series started he had been driving to the ball park with his old pal from the minor leagues Joe Morgan, who later went on to manage the Red Sox. Suddenly Schultz pulled over to the side of the road. "What's the matter, Barney?" Morgan asked. "I'm having trouble seeing," Schultz said. He tried to drive one more time and then pulled over again. "You better drive, Joe," he said. Schultz immediately went to see Dr. Middleman, the team doctor, who told him to wear sunglasses when he got to the field. "What you're suffering from, Barney, is stress," Middleman said. "That's all. For weeks the game has been hanging on every pitch you've thrown in every game you've pitched, and now you're showing the reaction. It's nothing very new. I've had it as a doctor—after an operation. You'll be fine. Get some dark glasses, and a good night's sleep, and try and relax. You don't even know the pressure you've been under." Schultz took his advice, began to relax, and gradually his vision came back.

On the day of the first game, Bob Uecker was shagging balls out in left field with some of the other scrubs. In order to mark the festivities, three Dixieland bands were stationed there, and at one point they took a break and put down their instruments. Uecker wandered over and picked up a tuba. For a moment he thought of trying to play it, because that might amuse the other players, but just then someone hit a slow, lazy fly out to left. Instinctively, because he was born to be a comic, Uecker circled under the ball with the waiting tuba. He tried for the catch in the mouth of the tuba, but missed. The next one he caught. Then he missed one. The players began to laugh and the crowd began to cheer. He missed two more flies and then caught one. Some of the balls dented the tuba, and the owner was not amused, sending the Cardinals and Uecker a bill for $250. His teammates, though, were delighted. It was the World Series against the mighty Yankees and the Cardinals were very relaxed.

Because Gibson had pitched so much at the end of the season, there had been no chance to rest him, so they opened with Ray Sadecki, who, true to his own projections, had been a twenty-game winner. He was pitching against Whitey Ford, who, despite injuries and declining physical ability, had nonetheless managed a record of 17-6 with an ERA of 2.13.

In the first inning there was a critical play. With one out, Brock singled. Then Groat singled to right, and Brock kept going, without hesitation, to third. It was something he had thought about before the game—testing Mantle—and he had decided he was going to do it every time. After all, he had challenged the great Roberto Clemente in the National League, and Clemente was a great defensive player at the height of his power, not an aging one playing in the wrong position, watching his skills atrophy and undermined by bad legs. Mantle, playing right, had not even bothered to make a throw. The Cardinal book on the Yankees said that they could run on Mantle, and now they started to do it, almost from the moment the game began. It was an early sign not just of his own physical decline and the fact that he was now a defensive liability, but that the Cardinals were the younger, faster, more aggressive team. Brock had come in to score when Boyer flied to Mantle.

Ray Sadecki was not sharp that day. He had pitched well at the end of the season, but in the next-to-last game against the Mets, the 15–5 defeat, he had been bombed, lasting one inning. The World Series was hard for him, he thought, because you had to go on scouting reports and that was not the way he liked to pitch; rather, he liked to rely on his personal feel for the hitters. Nor were the Yankees an easy team for him. He liked to come in with a high fastball, and the Yankees murdered high fastballs, and in the second inning Elston Howard singled, and then Tresh, a good high-fastball hitter, hit a tremendous drive into the left-center-field bleachers. The Yankees got another run on two more singles and might have gotten yet another one except that Lou Brock threw out Whitey Ford trying to score from second. The Yankees had three runs and they had gotten them on five hits. The Cardinals got one back in the bottom of the second when Mike Shannon singled and moved to second on Dal Maxvill's tapper back to Ford. Sadecki singled Shannon in. It was 3–2. In the New York fifth, the Yankees grouped three hits for one more run, making it 4–2. That was normally a nice lead to hand to Whitey Ford midway through a World Series game.

For Tim McCarver, all of twenty-two, the excitement was extraordinary. It was not just the myth of the Yankees that the Cardinals were battling that day, it was also the myth of Whitey Ford, the greatest big-game pitcher of baseball for more than a decade. He had been pitching in World Series games since Tim McCarver was nine years old, and he was the player to whom you gave the ball on critical days and who always rose to the occasion. Anyone else might have been excited and nervous on this day, McCarver thought, with the crowd at Busch Stadium and the giant press corps, not to mention the even bigger invisible crowd of 40 million at home watching on television, but Whitey Ford was as cool as could be. There was no fanfare to him, except perhaps a certain barely detectable cockiness in his stride. There he was—the pitcher with the most World Series starts, the most World Series innings pitched, the most World Series wins; he walked out to the mound like a man going out to grab a bus to take him to work in the morning.

As the game developed, though, it was clear to McCarver that Ford did not have much that day, that he was probably pitching in considerable pain. Ford had always triumphed on the basis of intelligence, placement, and a wicked curve, but on this day his curve was flat. On another day in another park with a smaller crowd and less scrutiny, Ellie Howard might have been able to cut the ball for him and then he might have been able to have given the ball some movement. But this was neither the time nor the place for that. There was a good chance they could beat him that day, McCarver decided.

It was Mike Shannon who helped get Ford in the sixth. Bing Devine had brought Shannon up in mid-season to make the Cardinals' outfield complete, and he had done just that. Shannon was big and strong, a good defensive right fielder with a wicked arm and genuine power. In half a season he had hit 9 home runs and knocked in 43 runs. His nickname was "Moon" or "Moon Man" because of his eccentricities. Someone once asked McCarver why Shannon was nicknamed Moon Man, and all McCarver had said was, "Just think

about it." Ted Simmons, who was to be McCarver's eventual replacement, remembered being with Shannon in the locker room
after a game when Shannon turned to him and said, "Teddy, I've
got something to tell you." "What is it?" Simmons asked. "Insur-
ance," Shannon answered. It was, Simmons recalled, like the scene
in *The Graduate* when someone said "Plastics" to Dustin Hoffman,
and Simmons then decided that the nickname fit.

In the bottom of the sixth Boyer singled and took second on a
passed ball. Then Bill White, trying to do too much and overswing-
ing, struck out. That brought up Shannon. He was new to the majors and new to Whitey Ford, but he thought Ford was off that day.
Shannon thought Ford had been trying to throw sliders inside and
missing. Indeed, Ford threw Shannon what looked like a slider, and
hung it, and Shannon drilled it. It was one of the hardest balls he hit
in his career, a ball with a Mantle-like orbit that went over the 358
sign and hit the B in the BUDWEISER sign. The estimates were that the
ball went some five hundred feet in the air. "The longest ball I've
ever seen him hit," Johnny Keane said afterward. There was a huge
photo on the front page of the local paper that night with a dotted
line showing the trajectory of Shannon's home run as it hit the sign,
and years later, when he was a restaurateur in St. Louis, Shannon
asked Ford to sign the picture. "You son of a bitch, you want to get
me twice, first when you hit it," Ford said, "and now when I'm supposed to sign it." The home run tied the score, and then McCarver
doubled and Al Downing replaced Ford. Ford was through for the
day, through for the Series, and in terrible pain. His left arm was
dead, and he was to undergo two operations before he got complete
feeling back in it again. The Yankees did not announce that; instead,
hoping to make the Cardinals think that their bullpen was deeper
than it was, they announced that he was bothered by a bad heel and
might still pitch again. When a reporter asked Ford himself whether
he might pitch later in the Series, he said, "There's nothing wrong
with me that a big ball park can't cure." In truth, his arm hurt so
much that he could barely cut his food.

Downing was not a natural relief pitcher. Carl Warwick, a pinch
hitter, singled, the first of his three successful pinch hits in the se-

ries, and that scored McCarver. Curt Flood drove a ball, carried by the wind, to the base of the left-field wall, and Tom Tresh finally lost it in the glare. ("I lost it in the sun. . . . When it came down I couldn't catch it, you can't catch what you can't see," he said afterward.) The ball came down three feet from his glove and went for a triple. Julian Javier, running for Warwick, scored, and that essentially was the game. The Cardinals had drawn first blood, 9–5, and had shown that they might be a tougher team in a short series due to their vastly superior speed.

27

The second game, on October 8, pitted Bob Gibson against Mel Stottlemyre. Each was the ace of the staff, and normally it was the matchup that would have taken place in the first game, but Gibson had not been ready to pitch then. He had pitched eight innings in the 1–0 loss to the Mets on October 2, and then had gone four hard innings in relief as the winning pitcher in the final game of the season on October 4, to clinch the pennant. The great question was whether he was sufficiently rested even now. In the first inning Gibson struck out Bobby Richardson, Maris, and then Mantle. If he was not entirely rested, and Tim McCarver, his catcher, did not think he was, then he was hiding it very well. Not very often did all three batters in the lead part of the Yankee batting order strike out in the first inning. In the second Gibson struck out both Ellie Howard and Tom Tresh. That made five strikeouts in two innings.

Later, in seasons that followed, as he watched Gibson intimidate opposing hitters, Tom Tresh thought the Yankees had been relatively lucky in this Series in the sense that they were new to Gibson. They were battling only his skills, no small thing in itself, instead of having to battle both that and his reputation, as teams would have to in the future. For after this World Series he would not be just Bob Gibson, he would be the great Bob Gibson, and his myth would loom bigger, and because of that, in the minds of the hitters, his fastball would be faster, the slider would break sharper and wider, and the word about how he shaved hitters with a fastball would be more ominous. The myth would work to his advantage in the future, Tresh thought, and lucky for them that the myth was still in the making.

Mel Stottlemyre looked very cool out on the mound. Young players, Tim McCarver thought, consciously or unconsciously, tended to take on the mannerisms of the best players on their teams. At the beginning of the Series the Cardinal players had watched Tom Tresh go out to his position in left field, and they had detected a slight limp. "Does he have a bad knee?" someone asked. "No," replied Ken Boyer. "He runs like that because that's the way Mantle runs." Now, as he watched Stottlemyre, McCarver decided that in some ways Stottlemyre had picked up the mannerisms of Whitey Ford. Nothing seemed to shake him. He did not look like someone who had been pitching in Richmond only a few weeks earlier; if anything, he looked like he had been dealing with pressure as long as Whitey Ford had.

Stottlemyre himself was amazed but not distracted by all the attention caused by the World Series. It seemed as if there were more reporters there than there were people back in Mabton, Washington, where he had grown up. He was surprised that there were so many people in one place whose sole purpose, it seemed, was to ask him questions, the answers to which did not seem to interest him very much, and so he doubted they would interest the strangers either. The other thing he noticed about the World Series was the noise. A low buzz seemed to be everywhere, beginning the moment he left his hotel room and got into an elevator; the closer you got to the ball park, the louder it got.

Stottlemyre had heard that Bob Gibson was a power pitcher with a great fastball, and he watched him in those early innings with true admiration. This was a highly skilled professional at work, a man of rare determination; he had a great fastball, a great slider, but most of all, thought Stottlemyre, a great presence on the mound. But Stottlemyre was careful not to be drawn outside himself. He was not overmatched in pitching against Gibson, he reminded himself. He had to be careful not to change his style and try to become a power pitcher. There was a tendency in a big game when you went against a power pitcher like Gibson to go outside your game and try to match him. That was a mistake, Stottlemyre knew. He was pleased with his stuff on that day, his ball was breaking sharply and his placement was excellent. Still, he thought, if you were inventing a pitcher for one great game like this, you would probably invent Bob Gibson.

Yet, if there were an advantage, Stottlemyre thought, it might well be his, because a power pitcher tended to wear down in the late innings, whereas a sinker-ball pitcher, like himself, might go all day. Ellie Howard had been very good with him that day, telling him not to compete with Gibson but to stay within himself, and above all not to overreach. So he fed the left-handers sliders on the outside of the plate, and the right-handers got the sinker ball.

The Yankees were supposed to be special because they always won, and Bob Gibson, new to pitching against them, at once saw that they were no better than the great players of the National League. Yet at the same time he wondered how much truth still existed to their myth. They still had the aura. They still wore the pinstripes, and their reputation made it sound like they could walk on water. It was part of his job, he believed, to bring them down to size.

The one player he was apprehensive about in their lineup was Mantle, because he had heard so much about him. Mantle was always being compared to Willie Mays, Frank Robinson, and Hank Aaron, so Gibson knew he had to be a very good hitter. He liked the idea of being pitted against the best. Tim McCarver thought that Gibson was good that day, but not prime Gibson. He was still a little tired. His fastball, McCarver thought, was good, but it did not have the explosion of Gibson at his best. The Yankees, he thought, might still see that before the Series was over.

Mantle had to bat lefty against him. The great Yankee slugger limped slightly when he came up to the plate, and then, when he swung, Gibson could see him cringe in pain, anguish obvious on his face. Gibson could see as well that Mantle could not shift his weight properly when he swung. The scouting book on him was to come inside and keep the ball away on the outside, but Gibson thought that was wrong. Gibson did not like to come inside to hitters in general, and he saw that Mantle had trouble shifting his weight. The great reputation, Gibson thought, at least when Mantle was batting left-handed, had little to do with the figure standing in front of him, who was clearly coming to the end of his career and was playing despite terrible pain. Gibson struck him out swinging in the first, got him on a called third strike in the fourth, and walked him in the sixth. In the seventh Mantle hit a hard grounder to second, where Maxvill blocked the ball and threw him out.

The Cardinals scored first in the third when Shannon singled and Maxvill hit a ground single past third, sending Shannon to second. Gibson sacrificed, advancing the runners to second and third, and when Flood grounded softly to Linz at short, Shannon scored. The Yankees tied it in the fourth. Howard doubled, and when Brock tried a shoestring catch on Pepitone, the ball got by him. Howard stopped at third. Tresh was given an intentional pass. Clete Boyer flied to Flood in center, and Howard scored. In the sixth Mantle walked, then Pepitone was allegedly hit by a pitch, a call the Cardinals bitterly disputed (and still dispute), and which the Yankees privately thought was a bad one. Mantle scored on a single by Tresh. That made it 2–1.

In the seventh the Yankees started to break it open. Phil Linz singled to left and went to third on a wild pitch. Bobby Richardson singled to center and Linz scored. The Yankees scored another run on two more hits. In the eighth the Cardinals picked up a run. Gibson came out of the game for a pinch hitter in the eighth, with the Cards trailing, 4–2, and in the top of the ninth the Yankees picked up four more runs, most memorably when Mantle hit a wicked double off reliever Gordon Richardson. Mantle came back to the dugout absolutely furious with himself. "I'd like to give them back the double—I should have hit a home run off him," he said. The Yankees won the second game, 8–3; Gibson had struck out nine men, but Stottlemyre had gotten sixteen men out on ground balls. The teams were going to New York tied, 1–1.

28

In the third game Jim Bouton pitched against Curt Simmons in Yankee Stadium, and it was probably the best played and best pitched game of the Series. Bouton thought it would be a low-scoring game. He knew that Whitey Ford had not been ready to pitch the first game, that he had been having too much trouble with his arm. Bouton, who had been pitching well in the second part of the season, felt that he or Stottlemyre should probably have started the first game. But he had also understood why Yogi went with Ford. You go with the past and with tradition, he thought, particularly when your tradition was as rich as the Yankees'. Late in the regular season, when there was a pennant race, with huge crowds in the stands, Bouton had begun to prepare himself for this occasion. He would fantasize that those were World Series games. He would tell himself that he had to deliver under pressure. Bouton had pitched in a World Series for the first time in the third game of the 1963 World Series with the Dodgers. His team was down, 2–0, in games, and he was going against the great Don Drysdale. "Hey, Jim, you nervous?" Ralph Terry, his friend, had asked. Bouton was in fact so nervous that he could barely breathe. "Well, Jim," Terry had said, "just remember that whether you win or lose, there are six hundred million Chinese out there who don't give a shit what happens one way or another."

The Cardinals were a good team for him to pitch against. He was a righty and the only three left-handed bats were White, Brock, and McCarver. White, the one true power-hitting lefty, was the hitter he feared the most. The scouting reports said that he could get Bill White out on a change, and somehow Bouton knew that White knew about the scouting report and was standing at the bat just waiting for the change. It was as if there were a voice of a friendly baseball angel coming into Bouton's ear and telling him, "Don't throw him a change, don't throw him a change. Come into him with fastballs." So Bouton threw White nothing but fastballs. He guessed right. Late in the game, sure that White had been looking for the change and gotten nothing but fastballs, Bouton went to the change, and he guessed right again. White had readied himself for a fastball and missed the change by a foot. Later, after the game, White told reporters that he had spent the entire game looking for a change, "and then as soon as I stopped looking he threw me one." Two of White's outs were balls hit to Tom Tresh in left, there was a groundout to Richardson at second, and then White got on base when he hit a slow bouncer to Boyer at third.

Curt Simmons had waited a long time to pitch in a World Series. He had been one of the Whiz Kids pitching for the Phillies in 1950 when he was only twenty-one, his third full season in the majors. The Phillies had won the pennant, but he had been called into the service because of the Korean War. At the time it had seemed like a missed opportunity, but he was sure there would be other chances, sooner rather than later; it had not occurred to him that he would have to wait fourteen years for his next chance, and that instead of being a kid of twenty-one he would be a senior player of thirty-five—no longer a power pitcher, but a skilled pitcher with a provocative motion who knew how to use hitters' strengths against them. He felt very good that day. He had great stuff, good location, and a very good breaking ball. Watching him, Bouton was impressed. Simmons kept coming inside to the left-handed hitters, going against all the rules in the book, but he was just smart enough to keep them off balance, and the Yankee hitters could not do that much with him. Simmons, for his part, could not tell that much about the young New York pitcher, Bouton. He seemed to throw surprisingly hard and his hat came off on almost every pitch, but the Cardinal hitters said that they were not that impressed. They kept coming back to the bench saying that they could get him, that he did not have that much, and yet they did not get him; later they would agree that Bouton had thrown hard and well, harder than they realized, even though he was not striking out that many batters.

The Yankees scored first, when in the second inning Elston Howard singled to center and then, with two outs and the count 0-2 on Clete Boyer, Simmons tried to waste a pitch, but got it too close to the strike zone and Boyer doubled down the left-field line. In the fifth the Cardinals tied the score. McCarver opened the inning with a single to right, and went to second when the ball went through Mantle for an error. Shannon lined to Mantle and McCarver did not advance. Then Dal Maxvill grounded out to Richardson and McCarver moved to third. When Curt Simmons lined a ball off Clete Boyer's glove, McCarver scored. That made it 1–1. It stayed that way through eight innings. The Yankees had four hits off Simmons, and the Cardinals had six off Bouton. It was a beautiful, tight baseball game. In the top of the ninth the Cardinals threatened to get to Bouton. McCarver reached first when Linz fumbled his ground ball. Shannon sacrificed him to second. Carl Warwick came up for Maxvill, and Bouton walked him. There were two on and one out. Then Bob Skinner came to bat for Simmons. Skinner liked the idea of batting against Bouton, because he was so aggressive a pitcher; he got a fastball, just as he expected, and he hammered it deep to right center field, where Maris finally hauled it in. Simmons, from the bench, watched it and thought to himself that in St. Louis it was a three-run homer on top of the roof, but in Yankee Stadium it was just a long out. It was a cold day and Simmons, his day's work done, decided to head back to the locker room to take a shower.

Barney Schultz was to pitch the ninth, and the Cardinal players were pleased because Schultz had become their invincible man that season. Somehow, when Barney came in, the game was a lock. The Yankee leadoff hitter was Mickey Mantle, and because Barney was a right-hander, Mantle would have to bat from his left, or weaker, side. Watching Mantle at the plate, Bouton had a sudden sense that the Cardinals were making a mistake, that they should not bring in a right-handed knuckleball pitcher against him. Mantle golfed the ball when he swung from the left side, swinging up, compared to his swing from the right side, which was more of a tomahawk. That golf swing could be lethal against a knuckleball pitcher because of the way the ball dropped down.

Mantle, it turned out, was thinking much the same thing. The Yankee scouts had told the hitters two things about Barney Schultz. The first was that he needed to get the first pitch over the plate because it was important for a knuckleball pitcher not to fall behind in the count. If he got the first pitch in, he could then afford to throw two more knucklers. The second thing was that for the same reason, Schultz threw the first pitch a little harder, and it did not move quite as much. It was, the scouts said, the best pitch to swing on against him. On the mound Barney Schultz was pleased with himself. The warm-up pitches he threw were very good, the ball seemed to flutter and dodge, and he was sure he had his best stuff on that day. Mantle was waiting by the plate while Schultz was warming up and Ellie Howard was in the on-deck circle. Mantle walked over to Howard. "Elston," Mantle said, "you might as well go on back to the clubhouse because I'm going to hit the first pitch out of here for a home run." It was, he later noted, the kind of boast that he had made many times, though he did not always make good on it. Schultz wound up and threw. He knew immediately it was not a good pitch: it did not dance or flutter, and it did not move away from Mantle as it should have. Instead, it glided in with precious little speed and precious little movement. Behind the plate, Tim McCarver watched the ball float toward him, ever so slowly, ever so ominously. A number of things flashed through McCarver's mind in that instant, none of them good: he could see Barney Schultz very clearly, he could see the Cardinal infielders, and he could almost feel the awesome physical surge in Mantle. For a split second McCarver wanted to stop the scenario, to reach out and interfere with Mantle's bat, but then the ball floated in, and Mantle absolutely crushed it, a tape-measure job well into the third tier in right field—his sixteenth World Series home run, which put him ahead of Babe Ruth and gave him one of his greatest thrills in baseball. Out in right field Mike Shannon went to the fence, pretending he might have a play, as if he were decoying Mantle and making him think the ball was catchable. Curt Simmons was on his way from the dugout to the locker room when he heard a tremendous roar. Simmons was an old pro, skilled at measuring crowd noise. For a moment he stopped and thought that Mantle must have hit a double, then the roar kept growing and growing, and he thought to himself, *Oh, shit, he hit a home run.* After the game, reporters crowded around Simmons's locker, and he handled them with considerable grace. "Tough day at the mill," he told them. Then he paused. "That's baseball."

After the game Whitey Ford told Mantle he had the ball, the one that had broken Ruth's record. Did Mantle want to buy it from him? Mantle said he did. How much? Ford asked. Mantle started flashing numbers with his fingers. "Will you give me one thousand bucks?" Ford asked. "Sure," said Mantle. So Ford sold him the ball, which he claimed he picked up after it bounced back on the field. All the newspaper photographers took pictures of Mantle with the ball. A few minutes later a man named John Mazzarella, his clothing torn and his leg cut, showed up with the *real* ball, wanting to *give* it to Mantle. Ford had to admit his hoax. That broke up the clubhouse. Everyone was in a great mood. The Yankees had won, 2–1, and were up in games, 2–1.

29

The fourth game was the crucial game of the 1964 World Series. With Whitey Ford finished for the season, the Yankees decided to go with Al Downing, who threw harder than anyone on the team, while the Cardinals came back with Ray Sadecki, who had been hit hard in the first game. Johnny Keane was not very confident about Sadecki, however, and just before the game Keane went over to Roger Craig, the veteran starter-reliever. "As soon as Sadecki gets out there I want you to start warming up," he said. "If you're that unsure of him," Craig said to Keane, "why don't you start me instead?"

Sadecki did not last the first inning. Phil Linz led off and doubled into the right-field corner. Then, on an attempted steal, McCarver made a great throw to third, and Linz backed off and headed back to second. The Cardinals had him hung up between second and third, but Ken Boyer slipped and threw wildly into center field and Linz ended up safely on third. With the infield partially in, Richardson doubled into the left-field corner, scoring Linz. It was a ball, Sadecki thought later, that Boyer could have gotten if he had been playing at normal depth. Instead of there being two out and no one on, one run was in and Richardson was on second. Roger Maris hit a bloop single to right and Richardson stopped at third. Mantle singled to right and Richardson scored, but when Mantle foolishly tried to stretch the single, Shannon, who had a great arm, threw him out. Maris went to third on the throw. Sadecki was finished for the day. A ten-pitch inning, a ten-pitch game, he thought to himself with disgust. The Yankees had not hit bullets off him, but he had not done the job, and the walk from the mound to the dugout was a very long one. Roger Craig, already warm in the bullpen, was called in. Ellie Howard greeted him with a single to center and the Yankees had their third run.

Three runs behind in the first inning or not, there was something magical about playing in the World Series as far as Roger Craig was concerned. As Bing Devine was putting this team together over the previous winter, one of the keys, he decided, was his acquisition of Craig from the Mets. Devine thought that a pitcher like Craig, who could work either as a spot starter or a middle relief pitcher, was what he needed; if going to a contending team from a last-place team gave Craig the proper emotional boost, and if his arm was right, he might be a determining factor—if not the winning pitcher—in some ten or fifteen games. Getting him might not seem as important in statistical terms as trading for a twenty-game winner, but in the hot days of August, important games could be either won or lost in the middle innings, when everyone was dulled by the torpor. Games slipped away then because pitchers were tired, the bullpen was overused, and the level of concentration of the team dropped. With the addition of the right pitcher, leads could be preserved, games saved, Devine thought. For Craig, going to the Cardinals had the quality of going to baseball nirvana after baseball purgatory. He had had the dubious distinction of leading the National League in games lost for the last two years, twenty-two and twenty-four respectively, and there had been one stretch in that second Met season when he had lost eighteen games in a row, in part because on seven occasions that season when he pitched, the Mets had been shut out.

Craig, in those two dreadful seasons, had tried to hold on to his sense of humor. At one dinner after the 1962 season he went to a baseball banquet along with Don Drysdale. Drysdale had won twenty-five games that year, and had gotten a huge ovation from the audience. When it was Craig's turn to be introduced, he asked Drysdale how many games he had won. "Twenty-five," said the Dodger star. "And how many did your team win?" Craig continued. "One hundred and three," Drysdale answered. "Well, Don, I guess I'm more valuable to the Mets than you are to the Dodgers because I won ten games this year and the Mets only won forty and that's a larger percentage of the team's victories than you had," he said.

Craig had always regarded his professional life as a kind of continuation of boyhood, as if he were the rare grown-up who had been allowed to go off every day and play instead of taking a real job with real hours. But in 1962 and 1963, when he pitched for the Mets, baseball had been like a job. The hours were not particularly long, two to five P.M. or eight to eleven P.M., but it was work nonetheless, and the pleasure was marginal. Still, he had pitched twenty-seven complete games in the two seasons, and seven teams had made strong offers for him at the end of the 1963 season. When he heard that it was the Cardinals who had traded for him, he was elated: "I'm going from a tenth-place team to a pennant contender overnight," he told friends. In the New York newspapers Ralph Kiner, the broadcaster, was quoted as saying that Craig could mean the pennant for the Cards. "He's a great competitor and he gives the Cards a great middle relief pitcher or a starter. He pitches hard every time he's out there."

With the Cards, Craig had loved the excitement of the pennant race, had pitched a critical shutout during those important days in September, and now was about to pitch in a World Series game. When the call came from Johnny Keane, he did not open the bullpen gate or step over the bullpen fence, his friend Bob Skinner later told him—he hurdled over the fence in his excitement. His curveball was very good that day and his control seemed almost perfect. Ellie Howard hit a good pitch, but somehow Craig felt confident. Craig got the next two men out. He was behind, 3–0, in the first inning, but somehow three runs did not seem like too much. In the second inning, the bottom of the Yankee order came up. Craig struck all three men out: Boyer, Downing, and Linz. At that point Tim McCarver thought the Yankees were going to have a hard time the rest of the way. Craig had a lot of movement and he threw at a great many different speeds. In Yankee Stadium in early October the shadows would soon fall, and that would make it even harder to hit Craig. The one moment when Craig's control weakened was in the bottom of the third, when with two out he walked both Mantle and Howard. That brought up Tresh. At second base Groat began to lull Mantle into complacency. "Mickey," he said, "that was a hell of a home run yesterday off Barney. I mean, you really hit that one." Mantle modestly thanked him. "Did you see what that spacey god-damn Shannon did?" Groat continued. No, Mantle said, he had not. "He tried to decoy you—as if there was going to be a play on it." Groat did a small imitation of Shannon pretending to make a play at the wall. "Crazy son of a bitch," Groat said. "We call him Moon Man." Roger Craig glanced over and saw the two of them and no-ticed that Mantle was not paying much attention. Roger Craig, Groat knew, had a great move to second. They had a play, Groat and Craig did—the daylight play, they called it. If Groat got inside the runner at second and there was daylight between them, they would try the pickoff. There was no signal for it. They just did it. When Craig whirled, he did not have to throw and it was not a balk. To Mantle, still leading off, Groat did a great imitation for Mantle of spacey Mike Shannon trying to decoy him at the right-field fence. He also slipped inside Mantle. Mantle began to laugh. Craig turned and threw and they picked Mantle off. Mantle headed back to the dugout, past Craig. "You son of a bitch," he said. "You show me up in front of forty million people."

If the Yankees had squandered two chances at more runs with bad baserunning, then they still had a 3–0 lead, and the Cardinals could do nothing with Al Downing. Through five innings, they had only one hit, a bloop single to center by Curt Flood in the third. Some-times Downing had good stuff but little mastery of it; on this day he had good stuff and good control. Through the first five innings he had walked only one batter. The Cardinal sixth changed things. Carl Warwick led off as a pinch hitter for Craig and grounded a hard single to left, his third pinch hit in the Series. Then Flood singled to right. Warwick held at second. That brought up Brock, who was retired on a fly ball. With one out, Groat came up and hit the ball on the ground to Richardson at second. It was a perfect double-play ball, particularly because Groat was slow. Linz moved toward second to take the throw, but the ball stuck for a moment in Richardson's glove and he couldn't dig it out quickly. By the time he got it to Linz, the shortstop was almost past the bag, partially turned toward first and vulnerable to Flood, who went into him hard. Linz couldn't hold on to the ball, and instead of the inning being over, the bases were loaded with one out. The fault on the play, Richardson thought, was his, but in addition it was a reflection of his inexperience in working with Linz. He and Kubek knew each other better, and if Kubek had been there he might have made the adjustment and they would have at least gotten the man at second. Now Ken Boyer, the Cardinal cleanup hitter, was up. He was 1-for-13 so far in the Series.

Downing's first pitch was a slider just outside for a ball. Ellie Howard called for a fastball, but Downing shook him off. Howard gave the signal, a little flutter of the hand, and called for a change: the pitch that Downing wanted. Out at shortstop Phil Linz saw the signal for the change and thought it wrong. It was already hazy out there with poor visibility because of the shadows. Downing, he thought, was a power pitcher and he had the advantage, with poor visibility and a right-handed batter facing Death Valley in Yankee Stadium. A change, he thought, subtracted from his edge. *Make them hit your best stuff, fastball, or a hard curve*, he thought. For a moment he thought of calling time but he did not, and Downing went to the change. Later it was a pitch that was often second-guessed; Downing thought it was the right pitch. He thought Boyer would be waiting on his fastball and he wanted to throw the Cardinal third baseman's timing off. He also wanted to go down and away, and he had two pitches that went there, his fastball and his change. The change had been a very good pitch for him that year, and he had given up very few hits on it. If he threw the change properly, he was sure, he would break Boyer's rhythm and get either a pop-up or a double play.

He threw Boyer a bad pitch. Usually his change sank on the hitter, but this one did not. The ball came in letter-high, not far enough out, and with very little movement on it, and Boyer jumped on it. Years later Downing could see it all very clearly. It was a poor pitch, but, nevertheless, he thought, still a good bit of hitting by a real professional. Because it was a change Boyer was well out in front of the ball, but he still managed to adjust in mid-swing, hold his weight back, and control his bat properly. The only questions from the moment he hit it were whether he was too far out in front and whether the ball would hook foul, but there was a ten-mile-an-hour wind blowing in from left field toward right, and it helped keep the ball fair as it went past the foul pole. That was it. The Cardinals, with one pitch, had gone from being behind, 3–0, to leading, 4–3.

Craig was through for the day, one of his best in professional baseball. He had given up two hits and struck out eight men in four and two thirds innings. Ron Taylor came in to pitch the last four innings and he gave the Yankees nothing. Taylor threw hard and had a running fastball. He walked one man, and other than that he retired everyone else. The game had started out as a laugher—the first five Yankees who had come to bat had gotten hits; from then on Craig and Taylor combined to throw a two-hitter for the remaining eight and two thirds innings. Instead of being a blowout for a 3–1 Yankee lead in games, they were now tied, 2–2.

30

In the fifth game the Yankees saw the real Bob Gibson. On this day
McCarver thought, he had everything working for him. The advantage of pitching in the shadows of the Stadium and against a background of the center-field bleachers made it all the more difficult for
the hitters to pick up his ball. He was ahead of the hitters almost all
day, and by the end of the game he had walked only two men and
had struck out thirteen. This was the Gibson whom the National
League hitters were already becoming accustomed to, and whom
American League hitters would learn to respect in this and two subsequent World Series: a big-game pitcher, his face an angry, cold
mask, a great athlete setting a fast tempo and never letting the hitters get set. Koufax had struck out fifteen Yankees in one of his victories in the previous World Series; Gibson on this day was every bit
as imposing. Though they were playing in Yankee Stadium, thought
Phil Linz, it was as if the Yankees were the interlopers, and this was
Gibson's territory. The Yankees would come to bat, barely have
time to dig in, and the pitch would be on its way; then, just as they
started to think about the next pitch, he was already in his windup.
How could McCarver be flashing signs that quickly? Linz wondered. Before you were ready there were already two strikes on you.
It was the most personal confrontation Linz had ever seen in baseball—as if, for the moment, there were just the two of them battling
it out together, pitcher and hitter, and all the other players had mo-
mentarily vanished from the game.

Watching the Yankees struggle that day against Gibson, Al Downing thought his team was being betrayed by the arrogance of its own scouting reports. Those reports, he and a few others on the team decided, reflected the Yankee smugness. In no way had they made clear how good this Cardinal team was, how tough it was, how hard it ran the bases. If anything, they had condescended to the Cardinal players. Lou Brock, they had said, was not that good an outfielder (of course he wasn't, thought Downing; who would be in that cow-pasture outfield in Sportsman's Park?). There was little mention of Curt Flood's exceptional ability as a center fielder, but it was clear now, as they watched him, that he was a great defensive player, and might at that moment be the best center fielder in major-league baseball, as Willie Mays was moving into his mid-thirties.

The most egregious omission was the failure to describe the sheer power, ability, and fury of Bob Gibson. When the Yankee scouts had given their briefing on the Cardinals, the report on Gibson was that he nibbled at the plate. *Bob Gibson nibbling at the plate?* The Yankee players did not know the National League that well, but they had heard something about Gibson. When the scout had said that, Downing looked at Jim Bouton, and they had both grinned. Bob Gibson was many things, but he was not a nibbler. The scouts never mentioned how important it was to score off Gibson early because he became tougher as the game went on. Al Downing liked playing for the Yankees, he liked his teammates, but as a young black man, he was aware of the prejudice against blacks that had existed in the organization. It was as if there were two Yankee organizations, he sometimes thought—the old one that had resisted change, and the new one, just beginning to recognize a new era, and the scouting report had been done by people who were part of the old era, an arrogant, smug organization that believed the Yankees were always the best. It rarely deigned to give credit to other players and other organizations, and was particularly loath to give credit to black players and to acknowledge that they were changing the nature of the game. The men who delivered that scouting report, he thought, were the same kind of men who had not signed talented young black players starting ten years ago. If there was a problem, he thought, it was that the Yankees were not entirely prepared for a team as tough as St. Louis. Now, facing the Cardinal speed, the Yankees were not responding well. Their fielding was sloppy, and their baserunning was unusually poor.

Mel Stottlemyre was pitching against Gibson again. He was probably not quite as sharp as he had been in the second game, and he was getting the ball up just a little more. With most pitchers the index of their sharpness on a given day might be strikeouts, but with Stottlemyre it was ground balls. In the second game he struck out only four, but he got sixteen hitters to go out on ground balls; on this day in seven innings he struck out six, but got only seven hitters on ground balls.

The Cardinals scored first in the fifth inning. Dal Maxvill struck out, but Gibson singled to left, a short looping fly that Tresh got to but couldn't handle. Gibson would have had a double had he not slipped and fallen as he went around first. Then Curt Flood hit a sharp grounder to Richardson, a perfect double-play ball, but Richardson booted it and both runners were safe. Lou Brock singled to right, scoring Gibson, with Flood going to third. Bill White grounded to Richardson for what looked like another double play. Richardson made the play to Linz for the first out on Brock, but Linz, feeling the pressure of so fast a base runner as Brock, hurried his throw to first and threw into the dirt. Though Pepitone dug it out, the first-base umpire, Al Smith, called White safe, a bad call, most reporters thought, and a play that allowed Flood to score.

That made it 2–0, and that was the way it stayed into the ninth. Hector Lopez batted for Stottlemyre in the seventh and struck out, and Pete Mikkelsen came in to pitch the eighth and the ninth for the Yankees. The Cardinals did not touch him, and that meant the Yankees came up trailing 2–0 in the bottom of the ninth. Mantle led off and hit a bouncer to Groat at short. Groat, thinking of the Mantle of old, charged the ball instead of waiting for the big hop. He bobbled the ball, putting Mantle on first. Gibson struck out Ellie Howard for the first out. Then a play that was probably, along with Boyer's home run, the most important play of the Series, took place.

Pepitone was up with one out. Tom Tresh was on deck. Gibson

threw his only change of the game, and Pepitone, who had a very quick bat, jumped on it and hit a shot toward the mound. Gibson had a very complete follow-through, and the ball hit him on the rear, as he completed his follow-through, right where he would keep a wallet if he were in street clothes. The ball did not just hit Gibson and drop down; instead, it bounced sharply off him toward the third base line. Watching the play, Tresh was thrilled. A sure hit, he thought. The Yankees appeared to have a rally going, and from the way that Pepitone had hit the ball, Gibson might be tiring. But then, while he watched, Gibson made one of the greatest plays Tresh had ever seen in baseball and certainly the greatest fielding play by a pitcher. Gibson was on the ball like a giant cat, turning as he finished his motion, running full speed to the third base line, and then picking it up even as his momentum carried him away from the line and away from first base. He had no time to stop and set himself, and he was forced to throw part sidearm, part underhand, but it was an underhand, sidearm fastball. Hard and on a line, it beat Pepitone, though the Yankees protested the call. McCarver, behind the plate, also thought it the most exceptional play he had ever seen by an infielder, let alone a pitcher. It was amazing, he thought, because it was all instinct; there was no way Gibson could have anticipated the move the way a great third baseman can sometimes anticipate a line shot. It was a great, great moment, Tresh thought, a superb athlete in the center of the arena, making an unbelievable play on pure ability and instinct.

The importance of the play soon became clear when Tresh hit Gibson's first pitch, a fastball into the right center-field bleachers to tie the score. It was only the fifth hit for the Yankees off Gibson. "A fastball down the middle," Gibson said later of the ball that Tresh hit, "and that's what happens to fastballs down the middle." At first Tresh thought the ball was going to stay in play, so he ran hard, hoping for a triple; then, as he neared second base, he realized it was out and started his home-run trot, yet he still seemed to be running hard. Without Gibson's play on Pepitone, the Yankees might have won the game then and there.

In the tenth Mikkelsen was still pitching for the Yankees. Bill

White walked to open the inning. Ken Boyer beat out a bunt to the right side of the mound, and White stopped at second. When Groat missed a bunt attempt, White was trapped between second and third; for a moment it appeared that the Yankees had him hung up, and he headed back to second. Ellie Howard threw to Linz at second, and suddenly White raced for third and was safe when the throw from Linz was late. White ended up being credited with a stolen base. Boyer held first. Then Groat reached base on an infield grounder as Boyer was forced out at second and White held third. With one out, that brought up McCarver, a left-handed hitter. McCarver had a hot bat in the Series. He was 7-for-16 so far, and he was seeing the ball exceptionally well. He was also a notoriously good low-ball hitter, which made him a tough opponent for Mikkelsen. Out in the bullpen Steve Hamilton, the tall, slim left-hander, was warming up. Hamilton had a reputation of being death on lefties, so some of the Yankees thought that Berra would bring Hamilton in, if only to pitch to McCarver. McCarver himself thought he would see a different pitcher, either Hamilton or Hal Reniff, but certainly not a low-ball right-hander like Mikkelsen. But Berra, who loved sinker-ball pitchers, decided to go with Mikkelsen. Mikkelsen quickly got behind in the count. On the 3-1 pitch Mikkelsen came in with what seemed like a fastball, just a little up. It was the pitch McCarver had wanted, and he ripped it, but it was foul by about four feet. McCarver was furious with himself: to be in this situation, to get the pitch you wanted, and then to blow it. He was sure he would not see anything that good again, but then Mikkelsen came in with a sinker that did not sink, and McCarver nailed it. Catchers don't catch sinkers that don't sink, he later thought. As he raced toward first, he watched Mantle's back and saw the number 7, which he tracked as Mantle headed back toward the fence. McCarver was delighted, because he knew the ball was hit deep enough to get White in from third, and not even the Mantle of old was going to spear the ball and make the right throw, not with his body momentum carrying him away from the plate. Then, as he saw Mantle continue to race toward the fence, it struck him that the ball might fall in and they could keep a rally going. As he rounded first, he saw Mantle

slow down, and he realized that it was a home run. It was a marvelous moment for him. For two years he had been struggling to meet
his own standards, to be a real professional, and it had not been easy,
a kid catcher with a veteran pitching staff. He badly wanted that
acceptance of his teammates, and it had been a hard learning process. Now, as he crossed the plate, Groat, the old pro, was bantering
with him, and Bill White, the judge, had a huge smile on his face, as
if to say, "Well, son, you really did it for us today, you're all right."
Gibson, who rarely said much in victory, was looking at him with
a very warm smile, and McCarver remembered thinking that this
was an unusually happy Gibson. It was his own coming of age,
McCarver later decided.

The Cardinals had won it in the tenth, 5–2. Later, after the game,
when the Yankees were going to the airport to catch the plane back
to St. Louis, Ralph Houk asked Steve Hamilton if he had been ready
to pitch in the tenth inning, and Hamilton said he had been. "Was
there anything wrong with your arm, Steve?" Houk asked. Hamilton said no, there was not, and he could sense that Houk was furious
over Yogi's decision to leave Mikkelsen in, and that Yogi might soon
be gone as the Yankee manager.

31

The sixth game was in some ways a repeat of the third, with Jim Bouton again pitching against Curt Simmons. For the first seven innings it was a tight, well-pitched game. For the Yankees it provided a last World Series hurrah for the home-run tandem of Maris and Mantle, when they and Joe Pepitone flashed a demonstration of that vaunted Yankee power. Simmons did not feel he pitched that well; he preferred the cold, in which he had worked earlier at the Stadium, and he had sensed that his breaking ball was not sharp on this day. As for Bouton, he was delighted to be getting his second shot in this Series. Far more than most baseball players, he was an adrenaline player, and he liked pitching under this kind of pressure. He had pitched exceptionally well in the third game of the 1963 World Series, which he had lost to Don Drysdale, 1–0, a game in which both teams got a total of only seven hits; he had given up one run and six hits in the third game of this Series, and his combined World Series earned run average for his three starts after this day was 1.48.

Bouton was puzzled by the behavior of the Yankee ownership on the morning of the sixth game. The players had been told to pack their suitcases and check out of the St. Louis hotel before they left for the ball park. If they lost, they would leave for New York right after the game; if they won, they would return to the hotel and check back in. Management clearly did not want to be charged for an extra day in St. Louis if they were going to lose the game and the Series. That stunned Bouton: in the past the Yankees had always been both arrogant and parsimonious, but this was the first time he could ever remember their parsimoniousness outweighing their arrogance. It was, he thought, the work of people with a loser's mentality. But Bouton felt good on this day; he loved being the center of attention and being given the ball in a game this big.

The Cardinals scored in the first inning. Curt Flood opened the game with a single to left, then went to third on Lou Brock's single to center. Flood scored when Bill White hit into a double play. The Yankees tied it in the fifth; Tom Tresh, who had hit the Cardinal pitching hard all week, lined a ground-rule double down the left-field line, moved to third when Clete Boyer grounded out, and scored when Bouton himself singled to left-center. In the sixth the Yankees nailed Simmons. Richardson, the team's leading hitter in the Series, popped up. Up came Maris, who had been a notoriously poor hitter in this and previous World Series games. Simmons hung a curve to Maris and Maris jumped on it, hitting it up on the roof in right, the ball landing just fair. Then Mantle came up and Simmons threw him a fastball; Mantle batting righty, hit it on a line to the roof in right field. This gave the Yankees a 3–1 lead. Then, in the eighth, with Simmons out of the game and first Barney Schultz, then Gordon Richardson, on the mound for the Cardinals, the Yankees scored five more times, including four runs on a Joe Pepitone grand-slam home run. The final score was 8–3, and the Yankees had to check back into their St. Louis hotel.

In the seventh game Bob Gibson took the ball. There was a time, only recently past, when that would have surprised people, a black pitcher getting the call in a decisive seventh game of the World Series, for it had long been part of the myth of white America that blacks were not mentally as tough as whites and therefore could not be counted on in the clutch: it was the performances of such athletes as Gibson that destroyed that particularly scabrous fiction. In a way Gibson's very presence on the mound in so big a game showed how much baseball had changed in its ethnic makeup in so short a time.

Only fifteen years earlier, in the final regular-season American League game that would decide the pennant, neither team had a black player on its roster, and when the Yankees took the field, four of the nine players, DiMaggio, Rizzuto, Berra, and Raschi, were Italian-American. Now four of the nine Cardinal starters were black, and if Julian Javier had not been injured, the total would have been five black or Hispanic players. The only black starter for the Yankees was Ellie Howard. Now Gibson, starting the seventh game of the World Series for the Cardinals, was a long, long way from the moment seven years earlier, when he had been pitching for Columbus in the Sally League, a brief unhappy stint lasting only eight games, and someone had yelled out at him, "Alligator bait! Gibson, you're nothing but alligator bait!" *Alligator bait*, he thought, *what the hell is that?* for he had no idea at all what it meant. Later he was told it was an old Deep South expression, and it recalled the good old days when the good old boys went into the swamps in search of alligators and tied a rope around a black man, or so they claimed, and threw him in the water as bait.

In the seventh game Bob Gibson was battling his own fatigue as well as the New York Yankees. He was determined not to give in to it. Most pitchers as tired as Gibson was on this day, with only two days' rest, slowed down their rhythm so that they could rest between pitches. Not Gibson. If anything he sped up his pace so the Yankees would not know that he was tired. He did not want to show even the slightest hint of weakness, and so he set a blistering pace. Gibby was struggling, Tim McCarver, who was catching him, thought. He was sure that Gibson was more tired than he had been when he pitched against the Mets in the final game of the season. Then, McCarver had been able to see the fatigue in his face, but on this day he could see it even more clearly in Gibson's pitches. Against the Mets his breaking ball had been a little flat, but now, in his third World Series start in a week, it was not only his breaking ball that was flat, it was his fastball as well. It did not explode in the strike zone the way a Gibson fastball normally did.

And yet even with all that, he had the Yankees off balance. Gibson was still a very fast, very smart pitcher, and even more, a great competitor. The Yankees might be a great fastball-hitting team, but that did not mean that hitting Bob Gibson was going to be easy. When the Cardinals played against Koufax or Maloney or Bob Veale, Gibson used to tease his teammates: "Okay, all you fastball hitters, there he is, now just go out there and have a field day." It was like telling a kid who liked ice cream to eat a gallon of it at one sitting, McCarver thought. Gibson was going to do that on this day; he was going to make the Yankees earn every hit.

In baseball, thought McCarver, players admired the ability of a pitcher who could reach back and find something extra. More than anyone he had ever played with, Bob Gibson could do that. He might be exhausted, but he seemed to understand even on the worst days that he would be finished in two and half hours. That allowed him to force his body to do things it did not want to do. It was a triumph of the spirit over body; since he refused to be defeated, he was not defeated. He would walk off the mound after one of those games, his arm aching, and he would sit in the locker room icing his arm, saying that he was going to quit, that it was not worth it, that the pain was too great. The constant use of his slider had literally bent his arm out of shape. When Gibson and McCarver went to the tailor together, the tailor would tell Gibson to drop both his arms straight down so that he could measure their length; the left arm dropped normally, but the right arm remained bent just slightly. "Let your arm hang straight, Bob," the tailor would say, and Gibson would say, "It *is* hanging straight." That was as good as he could do. The slider had done it to him. He always knew the price he was paying for the success he sought.

Normally, the day after he pitched his arm was all right, and then on the second day, it ached terribly, and on the third day the ache began to go away. It was not the rest of his body that was tired, only his arm. In those days he, like other pitchers, took Darvon to kill the pain. Gibson thought he had rather good stuff early in the game, and he struck out three batters in the first two innings, including Mickey Mantle.

The Yankees went with Mel Stottlemyre, who had gone, in a few brief weeks, from ingenue to rookie sensation to ace of the staff.

Yogi Berra and the coaches came to him and asked if he could pitch on two days' rest. The other possibilities were Ralph Terry, whom they had not used much late in the season and who had not had a good year, and Al Downing, about whom they clearly were uncertain. So Stottlemyre said yes, and he felt reasonably good when he went to the mound. He thought he was pitching fairly well, although his slider had less bite on it and his ball had less movement than usual. But the Cardinals were hitting the ball on the ground.

But in the fourth inning the Yankees self-destructed. They had fielded poorly throughout the Series, and though when it was over they were charged with nine errors to the Cardinals' four, in reality their fielding had been far worse than that. There had been numerous bad throws and bonehead plays, which were not counted as errors but which cost them dearly, just as their poor baserunning had cost them on offense. Ken Boyer started the home fourth with a single to center. Dick Groat walked on four pitches. Then Tim McCarver hit a bouncer to Pepitone that looked like a double-play ball. Pepitone made a good pickup and threw to Linz at second for the force on Groat. Stottlemyre covered first for the return throw, but the throw from Linz, which should have beaten McCarver easily, was wide of first and rolled to the stands. Backing up the play, Bobby Richardson picked up the ball and threw home, but Boyer scored for the first run of the game. Mike Shannon's single sent McCarver to third. So far in the Series, the Cardinals had been relatively cautious in their baserunning, but they decided in this game that they would challenge Howard and the Yankees, and they tried the double steal. Shannon broke for second, and behind the plate Ellie Howard double-pumped; then Howard bit and threw to second, but his throw was high and to the right, and Shannon slid in safely. When Howard threw, McCarver raced for home, and he scored when Richardson's throw was in the dirt and went through Howard. Dal Maxvill singled to right, and Mantle got to the ball quickly. A good throw from Mantle might have caught Shannon, but Mantle threw wide and Howard dove for Shannon and missed. The Cardinals had three runs on only one Yankee error, but four bad Yankee throws. The once-great Yankees, wrote Dick Young, "had looked more like the Mets than the Mets. Linz made a bad play. Howard made a bad play. Richardson made a bad play. Mantle made a bad throw and up went three ragged runs for St. Louis and the Yankees were never in the ball game again."

Worse, Stottlemyre jammed his shoulder diving for the ball from Linz, and it quickly stiffened on him. The Yankees sent up a pinch hitter for him in the fifth, and then sent Al Downing to the mound in the bottom of the fifth. Brock greeted Downing with a four-hundred-foot drive to the pavilion roof in right-center. Then Bill White singled to center and Boyer doubled to right, sending White to third. That was it for Downing, and Roland Sheldon came in to pitch. Groat grounded to Richardson, who had to throw to first and had no chance to get White, who scored. Boyer went to third. That made it 5–0. Then McCarver hit a soft fly to right and Boyer beat Mantle's throw, which skidded through Howard again. That made it 6–0.

In the top of the sixth the Yankees began to struggle back. Richardson beat out a slow roller to Ken Boyer at third. Maris hit a ground single to right, with Richardson stopping at second. All during the Series Gibson had pitched Mantle outside, going against the book. McCarver had thought the scouting reports were right, but Gibson was Gibson—he did not like coming inside on power hitters; he believed the outside of the plate belonged to him, and he was not a man easily argued out of anything. So far his strategy had worked. Mantle had been 1-10 against him in the Series. But now Gibson was really beginning to tire and he came outside, and Mantle hit the ball into the left center field bleachers to make the score 6–3. It was Mantle's third home run of the Series and his record eighteenth in World Series competition.

But even then the Yankees could not hold the Cardinals. Ken Boyer hit a solo home run off Steve Hamilton in the home seventh. By the seventh inning Gibson knew he was tiring, but Johnny Keane left him in, in part because he had a four-run lead, in part out of respect for Gibson as a competitor, and in part because of his anxiety about his own bullpen. Gibson hated to come out for a relief pitcher in any circumstance, and he most certainly did not want to come out of this game. But by the seventh inning he was finding it harder and harder to put the ball where he wanted. He had to put more effort into getting extra break on the ball, and as he did that, he lost location. There was a danger at a moment like this, he well knew, of slipping, of pushing rather than firing the ball, of losing both location and speed, and then of beginning to fall behind the hitters. The other danger, he thought, was that it was easy to become lazy without knowing it, to give in to your body and stop reaching back. So he spent those last three innings talking to himself on the mound, trying to keep himself alert: *Let's go asshole, don't quit now. . . . This is where you've always wanted to be, the seventh game of the World Series with you pitching for everything against the New York Yankees . . . this is not the time to get lazy and get soft.* Out on the mound his throat was dry because every time he threw, he grunted from the effort.

In the seventh the Yankees hit the ball relatively hard on him. With two out Richardson singled to center, and Maris hit a line shot to right field, but directly at Mike Shannon for the third out. The eighth was easier. Mantle flied to center. Ellie Howard struck out, which was a relief for it showed Gibson still had some pop on the ball. Then Pepitone popped up to Maxvill. The Cardinals did not score in the bottom of the eighth. Now it was time for the top half of the ninth. Rarely had Bob Gibson wanted anything so badly as to finish this game. When it was time to go out on the mound for the ninth, Johnny Keane, *who knew he was tired and knew he was wearing down*, came over to Gibson and told him he was going to stay with him, and reminded him that he had a four-run lead. "Bob, I'm going with you in the ninth. Just throw it over the plate," he said. "Don't be cute. Don't go for the corners. Just get it over. They're not going to hit four home runs off you." What Gibson had always wanted was the confidence of his manager, and on this day he had it more than any pitcher could ever ask for. He did not want to betray that trust in the ninth.

He struck out Tom Tresh, the first batter. Then Clete Boyer came up and hit a home run into the left-field bleachers. *That's one home run*, Gibson thought to himself. Johnny Blanchard batted for Pete Mikkelsen and struck out. Two outs now, both strikeouts.

Then Phil Linz came up, and he hit the ball into the left-field bleachers, making it 7–5. *That's two home runs*, Gibson thought. *Maybe Keane is wrong.* Up came Bobby Richardson, who already had thirteen hits in the Series. Out in the bullpen, Ray Sadecki was warming up. Aware that he had not pitched well in the Series, and that Johnny Keane was down on him, he wondered whether Keane would go to him if Richardson got on. Until then Keane said he never thought of lifting Gibson. But if Richardson had gotten on, he would have gone to Sadecki. Keane went out to the mound to talk with his pitcher for a moment. McCarver did not go all the way out because he knew Gibson hated it when the catcher came out, and besides, there was nothing to say. The count was 1-1. Richardson liked the ball high and out over the plate, and Gibson made a very good pitch to him, a fastball that moved in on him at the last instant. Richardson popped it up, and Dal Maxvill gathered it in a second.

Afterward Gibson realized for the first time how hard he had fought against his fatigue and how much his arm hurt. It would hurt on and off for an entire month, but it was a month in which he did not have to pitch. He had struck out nine men, which gave him a total of thirty-one for the Series, a Series record, which he would soon break. He was voted the Most Valuable Player in the World Series, just ahead of McCarver. After the game, when reporters crowded around Johnny Keane, they asked the manager why he had left Gibson in during the ninth when he was so obviously tiring. Keane answered with one of the nicest things a manager ever said about a baseball player: "I had a commitment to his heart."

Epilogue

Yogi Berra thought he had done a good job managing the Yankees. He had brought them from behind to win the pennant, and though he had lost his ace pitcher in the first game of the World Series, he believed he had done a good job of patching an aging team together. He had not panicked when the team was doing poorly. Baseball men compared what he had done in New York to what Gene Mauch had done in Philadelphia and concluded that Berra's lighter touch and willingness to let the players find their own way was the superior job—particularly for a team that had suffered so many injuries. He had no idea that Houk believed he had lost control of the team in mid-season and had decided much earlier to replace him. In fact, Houk had been aware that Johnny Keane was about to be fired by Gussie Busch and Houk had covertly offered Keane Berra's job. Flying back from St. Louis with Bobby Richardson and his wife, Betsy, Berra asked them, as he had asked others, whether when he met with management in the next few days he should ask for a two-year contract. "Why not," said Betsy Richardson, teasing him and teasing her husband. "If it hadn't been for Bobby, you'd have won the Series." He was therefore stunned when he was told he was out. Later on the day that Berra got the bad news, Jerry Coleman ran into him outside the Yankee offices. "Hey, Yog," said Coleman, "did you get the two-year contract?" "They fired me," said Berra, his face ashen.

Meanwhile, in St. Louis the Cardinals called a press conference in

which Gussie Busch intended to announce that he had rehired
Johnny Keane. Everyone was ready to start the conference, but
Keane was a little late to it. When he finally arrived, he handed
Busch a letter. Busch took no notice of it, and was eager to get on
with the press conference when an aide read the letter. He pushed it
over to Busch and insisted the owner read it before he started the
press conference. In it Johnny Keane announced his resignation.
When reporters asked about Keane's future plans, he said he was
going to do some fishing. The truth was he was going to fly to New
York to take the Yankee job.

It would be the wrong team for him. He was a manager who was
better with younger players than older ones, and this was a team of
aging stars whose best years were behind them. They were accustomed to going their own way and setting their own hours, and they
soon came to regard Keane as a martinet—a man with too many
rules and too little flexibility. They longed for the return of Berra.

The Yankee decline was about to accelerate. Ralph Terry was
gone, traded to Cleveland as part of the Ramos deal. Al Downing
occasionally pitched well for the Yankees but never achieved the
greatness some had predicted; he was traded at the end of the 1969
season. Bouton's arm went bad; he had thrown too hard for too
long, and in 1965 he was 4-15, often pitching in great pain, and
nearly two full runs were added on to his earned run average. He
was effectively finished as a big-league power pitcher at twenty-six.
Of the younger Yankee pitchers only Mel Stottlemyre lived up to
his potential. Arriving in New York in time to help save the pennant
and pitch the Yankees into the World Series, he had assumed that
there would be annual pennant races and World Series games;
though he became one of the best pitchers in Yankee history, with a
career earned run average of 2.97, he never pitched in another
championship game.

Under Keane the Yankees had a losing record, 77-85, and fell to
sixth place, and when they started the 1966 season they won only
four of their first twenty games. Johnny Keane was fired and replaced by Ralph Houk. The Yankee players were thrilled by the return of Houk and were sure that Houk would bring back the old

Yankee magic. But the magic was gone and Houk's team finished in tenth place. CBS, it turned out, had bought a logo and not a great deal more. Less than a year after being fired in New York, Keane died at the age of fifty-five of a heart attack in Houston, Texas. His former players thought the decision to go to New York had been a tragic one and that managing that particular team had taken a terrible toll on him.

Ernie Banks and Lou Brock were already good friends when Brock had been traded to St. Louis, so Banks had told the younger player, "Don't worry, Lou, you'll still be able to get into the Series—I'll send a ticket down to you in St. Louis." When the Cardinals won the Series, Brock sent his pal the box that his World Series ring came in, without, of course, the ring. Banks called him up immediately. "You son of a bitch," he said over the phone.

Bob Howsam, who replaced Bing Devine, later went on to become a very good baseball man in Cincinnati, but he had arrived in St. Louis as an alien on a team that was not his own; he did not do it modestly, in the eyes of the players, since he had never played or managed in the big leagues. The players, who were fond of Bing Devine, and who regarded this as rightfully Devine's team, were prepared to resent him, and they quickly found reason to justify their resentments. It was not merely that when the team began to win, Howsam took, they thought, an undue amount of credit, but there were also the memos. Howsam liked memos, and there were a good many of them, which seemed like nit-picking to veteran players: about the length of hair, for Howsam seemed to believe that short hair led to victory; about the need to wear a cap during batting practice; about how low the stirrups on the socks were supposed to be. There was also a memo at the end of the season to Curt Simmons suggesting that Simmons work on his pickoff move to first during the off-season. Since at the time Curt Simmons was thirty-five and had been in the major leagues with two teams for seventeen years, winning more than 160 games in that time, there were a number of jokes about sending *Howsam* a memo regarding how long his hair should be and how high his socks were to be worn. He was soon replaced by Stan Musial.

Bing Devine was voted baseball executive of the year, which pleased him and almost everyone who had worked for him. In a rare moment of candor a few years later, Gussie Busch admitted that firing him had been a mistake. Devine left St. Louis to go to work in the front office for the Mets. There, much as he had once had to share power with Rickey, he had to work alongside George Weiss, exiled there after having been squeezed out by the Yankees. To Devine, Weiss was very much like Rickey, a once-great figure unable to adjust to new circumstances. Shorn of the great Yankee machinery, and shorn of Kansas City as a virtual farm club, Weiss seemed largely paralyzed by his new job. He still disliked paying a great deal of money for players, and he was very much against the Mets going into a one-shot pool for a young pitcher named Tom Seaver because he thought it too costly. Others in the front office, impressed with Seaver's talent, pressured him and he finally relented—largely, Devine believed, because Weiss thought the odds of the Mets actually winning the rights to Seaver were so slim. In one case, though, his thriftiness actually helped the Mets. They were just about to cut loose a young minor-league player named Jerry Koosman, who had so far disappointed them. The decision had been made to release him, but then someone noticed that Koosman owed the club five hundred dollars. "If there's one thing George can't stand it's to release a player who owes the club money," one of his subordinates said, so they kept Koosman on until the accounts could be settled; in the meantime Koosman began to turn his career around.

Lou Brock was uniformly admired by his teammates for what he had done and how hard he had played in 1964. If there was ever a player who set out to be the best ever, his teammates thought, it was Brock. Nor was it so much his great physical ability that made him special. He was one of the most cerebral players of his generation. He studied the game and, in particular, he studied pitchers—not as Ted Williams had studied them, for tip-offs on what they might throw, but instead for the telltale signs that would help him steal bases. Brock had heard that Maury Wills, at the time the standard against whom all base stealers were measured, kept a little black book filled with the idiosyncracies of the league's pitchers. "Hey, Maury, got that little book?" he once asked the Dodger veteran, but it turned out that Wills was in no hurry to share his secrets with a younger player from a rival team. So, starting late in the 1964 season, Brock got an eight-millimeter camera and began to film the various pitchers in the league as they were on the mound, as they got set, as they threw home, and as they threw to first. "My home movies," he called them. One day he was filming Don Drysdale, as tough a pitcher as existed in the league. "What the hell you doing with that camera, Brock?" "Just taking home movies," said Brock. "I don't want to be in your goddamn movies, Brock," Drysdale said, and threw at him the next time he was up.

The films were helpful, and Brock began to pick up on little movements, twitches almost, that might have escaped the naked eye. All pitchers had some kind of twitch, he decided, and so he began to improve as a base stealer, stealing sixty-three in 1965, and then leading the league in eight of the next nine years. Because of his increasing knowledge and improving technique, he realized that he could steal more than one hundred bases in a season, and in 1974 he did just that. *If Wills had his black book*, Brock thought, *I've got my camera—I'm a man of modern technology*.

Brock was different from Maury Wills in other ways too. Maury was always talking about how base stealing beat you up. He was always talking about the need to take a big lead off first. If you did not have to dive back, he liked to say, you had not taken a big enough lead. For a time Lou Brock did the same, but after a while he decided to change his style. What convinced him was a game against the Giants in which he had to dive back to first three times, and each time Willie McCovey beat him so hard with the tag that he could barely move. First basemen, he observed, were big, powerful men, while second basemen were slighter, often smaller than Brock himself. He decided that in order to preserve his own body, he was going to take smaller leads and go into second very hard. If anyone was going to do any beating up, he was, not the McCoveys of the world. In time Lou Brock broke Ty Cobb's record, once considered unreachable, of 892 stolen bases; his own career mark was 938.

At the meeting of the owners in August, spurred by the rising cost of bonus players, there had been a good deal of talk about going to some sort of draft system for young players, not unlike that used by professional football and basketball. What encouraged the talk more than anything else was the competition for an outfielder named Rick Reichardt, who played for the University of Wisconsin. Reichardt was big and strong, and some said he would be the next Mantle. With ever richer owners and greater pressure than ever for instant success, the bidding for Reichardt soared above the previous ceilings. That summer Reichardt signed with the Angels for what was said to be a record bonus of $250,000. He was not the next Mantle, though no one knew that at the time. Reichardt's impact on the owners was greater than his impact on the American League's pitchers: he proved to be a good, not great, player who, in his better years, hit about 15 home runs, knocked in 60 runs, and batted around .260. But his bonus terrified the owners, for it was as close as they had yet come to a free-market situation. A bonus like that, some owners realized (looking at the CBS and Anheuser-Busch millions), might be only the beginning. Later that same year, Charley Finley, the owner of the Kansas City Athletics, revealed that he had paid out $634,000 in bonuses that year to sign some eighty players. The National League teams adopted the idea of a draft enthusiastically, whereas at the American League meeting, only three teams voted in favor of it. Those franchises that had traditionally been successful and had powerful scouting systems were wary of such radical change. But gradually the tide shifted in favor of some sort of draft. At the meeting of all the major league teams held in Houston in early December 1964, the draft was passed with little opposition. Hearing of it, Tom Greenwade, the great Yankee scout, told his son Bunch, "They've just taken the bat out of my hand."

. . .

Given his intelligence and sense of humor, it was not surprising that Bob Gibson soon became the dominating force in the Cardinal locker room. He remained a great mimic and put-on artist, aided now by his success and seniority. At one point there was a young player on the team named Hal Gilson. For a time it appeared that Bob Gibson's phone calls and messages were being routed to Hal Gilson, which did not please Gibson. "Gilson, I'm warning you," he said. "You've got to stop taking my messages or I'll have to trade you," and it was part of Cardinal locker-room lore that shortly thereafter, Hal Gilson was traded to Houston.

One of Gibson's favorite stunts was to list the entire roster on the blackboard in the clubhouse at the end of the year, and then go down the list, deciding who was going to be traded during the off-season. He spared no one, save himself and Lou Brock, and later, when he became a great Cardinal hitter, Joe Torre. Everyone else was ticketed out, including Red Schoendienst, who had replaced Johnny Keane as the manager. One year Bing Devine, back from the Mets for his second tour as general manager, walked in when Gibson was going through his routine, and Devine was amused until Gibson looked up and said, "It's okay to laugh, Bing, but you're gone too."

With the retirement of Sandy Koufax, Gibson became the premier pitcher in baseball. Remarkably, there was, in the 1967 and 1968 seasons, a huge improvement in his control. To the amazement of his teammates and his peers, he reached an ever higher level of excellence, and finally attained that rarefied place inhabited in recent years only by Sandy Koufax. Gibson was the dominating pitcher in the 1967 World Series, after a season in which he had missed a third of his starts with a broken leg. Then he continued to improve and was virtually unbeatable in the 1968 season. In 1968, in what was a dazzling season, he had won 22, lost only 9, he had struck out a league-leading 268 batters in 304⅔ innings, he had walked only 62, he had an ERA of 1.12, he had pitched 13 shutouts, and he had completed 28 of the 34 games he started. It was, for a pitcher who only a few years earlier had contended with serious control problems, a demonstration of the rarest kind of pitching, which combined uncommon power with pinpoint control. Rarely has a single player been so overwhelming in World Series play as Gibson was in the World Series in both 1967 and 1968.

The first game of the 1968 World Series was his masterpiece. Gibson was going against Denny McLain of the Tigers, the first thirty-game winner in the major leagues in thirty-three years. McLain, who flew his own plane and played the organ in nightclubs around the Midwest when he wasn't pitching, caught the attention of the media that season in his quest for thirty; to say that he had gotten more publicity and more endorsements than Gibson was an understatement, just as Carl Yastrzemski had gotten more endorsements than Gibson after the 1967 Series. Koufax, one of the network broadcasters that day, mentioned to his audience that he thought the difference in commercials and publicity that the two players had received might just fire up Gibson. He was right. Again and again the television cameras cut to close-ups of Gibson's face displaying The Look, cold and unsparing, as Gibson struck out one Detroit hitter after another. The Detroit team was considered a good fastball-hitting team, but it barely mattered that day. In the ninth, Gibson, holding a comfortable 4–0 lead, struck out Al Kaline for his fifteenth strikeout of the game, tying the record set by Koufax in 1963. On the scoreboard the statistician flashed the news that Gibson had just tied the record of fifteen for World Series play set five years earlier by Sandy Koufax. Tim McCarver walked partway out to the mound to call his attention to it, hoping Gibson would soak in some of the glory of the moment. "Give me the ball," Gibson yelled at him. McCarver tried to point to the scoreboard. "Give me the ball!" he repeated. Again McCarver tried to tell him what he had done and why the crowd was cheering, and finally Gibson understood. In a softer tone he said, "All right, now give me the ball." Then he struck out Norm Cash for the third time that day. That broke Koufax's record. "Who follows Cash?" he asked McCarver. "What difference does it make?" McCarver said. It was Willie Horton, a fearsome hitter in his own right. With two strikes on him, Horton backed away from a slider that looked like it was going to hit him but then broke wickedly back over the plate, for the seventeenth strikeout of the game. McCarver thought the ball must have broken eighteen inches. "To this day I believe Willie Horton thinks the ball hit him," McCarver later said.

Gibson was almost as impressive in the fourth game, striking out ten batters to give St. Louis a 3‑1 lead in games. If anything, Tim McCarver later reflected, Gibson's capacity to rise to such heights in World Series games might have made the Cardinals overconfident by the middle of that Series. Confident that they would have Gibby in the seventh game, and that he was unbeatable in big-game situations, the Cardinals might have let up in Games five and six, McCarver thought. In the seventh he was again overwhelming, but Mickey Lolich pitched very well for the Tigers, and when Curt Flood misplayed a ball in center field, the Tigers went on to win the game and the Series.

Harry Walker remained fond of Bill White, and when Bill White was made president of the National League, Harry Walker was delighted. One day in 1990 Harry Walker, by then living in Leeds, Alabama, called up White and said that he would like to visit him at his home in Pennsylvania. White said that Harry Walker ought to know that he was divorced now and that the woman he was living with was not black. Walker laughed and said, "Bill, that stuff doesn't bother me anymore—I'm way past that." So he came up to visit with White, and his visit became something of an annual trip. White was touched by how much one man had changed over the years.

The Cardinals slipped badly in 1965, going from first place to seventh, winning 80 games while losing 81. Curt Simmons seemed to age overnight, and his record went to 9-15; Ray Sadecki had a dreadful season, winning 6, losing 15, and seeing his ERA balloon up to 5.21. There were signs that Bill White and Ken Boyer might be slipping: their respective run productions were down; Boyer was thirty-four, and Bill White was about to be thirty-two. So the Cardinals began to move for youth. Ken Boyer went to the Mets for Al Jackson, the fine left-hander, and Charley Smith; Bill White, Dick

Groat, and Bob Uecker were traded to the Phils for Art Mahaffey, Alex Johnson, and Pat Corrales; and Ray Sadecki was traded to San Francisco for Orlando Cepeda. The 1966 team improved its win-loss record to 83-79 and moved up to sixth place.

Then, in 1967, the team came together. Viewed by his employers in San Francisco as a morose, somewhat alien malingerer, Orlando Cepeda blossomed on this racially harmonious team, and at critical moments he seemed to carry the whole team with his bat. Roger Maris came over from the Yankees to play for two more years, de-lighted to be liberated from the declining Yankees and out of the city he had come to hate, to play now, instead, in a city where he felt at ease, and where expectations of what he could do were far less grandiose. Still bothered by a bad wrist, he was no longer a power hitter, but he was an excellent all-around player, and he gave the Cardinals what was probably the best outfield in the league. Mike Shannon, who became his close friend, went to third base, and Dal Maxvill became one of the best shortstops in the league. In addition, Steve Carlton, Nelson Briles, and Ray Washburn were finally sur-facing as dependable starting pitchers, with Carlton showing signs of potential greatness. The 1967 team, led on the field and off by Gibson and Cepeda, won the National League pennant by ten games. Gibson, in particular, loved playing with Cepeda, who drove in 111 runs in 1967. When Gibson was pitching and it was time for the bus to leave the hotel for the park, Red Schoendienst would look at his watch and give the word to the driver to go. But Gibson would check out who was there and who was not there, and if Cepeda was not aboard, he would stop the bus. "No way we go until Cepeda is on board," he would say. No one contradicted Bob Gibson on the day he pitched, and so the bus would wait.

In 1968, what was essentially the same team won by almost the same margin. The Cardinal players were uncommonly proud to be part of those teams, for they won not by dint of pure talent or pure power—San Francisco was far richer in terms of pure talent. Rather, they won through intelligence, playing hard and aggressively, and because they had a sense of purpose that cut across racial lines in a way that was still extremely unusual in the world of sports.

That special cohesiveness came to an end after the 1968 World Series. There was a glimmer of what was to come, a *Sports Illustrated* cover near the end of the season about them as the most expensive team in baseball, and revealing the salaries of each of the starting nine players and their manager. Although the total was only $607,000—less than what a utility player would get some twenty-five years later—it seemed a fortune at the time, and it changed the way the team was perceived by sportswriters, by some fans, and, in the end, by their owner. (The salaries hardly seem that grand now: Maris—$75,000, McCarver—$60,000, Gibson—$85,000, Shannon—$40,000, Brock—$70,000, Cepeda—$80,000, Flood—$72,500, Javier—$45,000, Maxvill—$37,500, and Schoendienst, the manager—$42,000). Bob Burnes, the sports columnist for the *St. Louis Globe Democrat*, a man not known by the players for working the locker room hard or for his personal knowledge of the players, wrote a column after their bitter final-game World Series defeat in which he theorized that the Cardinals had lost because they had thought more about their clothes than about winning. That column struck many of the players as perhaps the stupidest thing ever written about them, and thirty years later they still seethed about it.

In the off-season after the 1968 season, Gussie Busch, deeply offended by the rising salary demands of his players, and by the growing pressure for a strong union and by a brief strike, made the first of several mistakes that helped destroy his own team. What may have set him off as much as anything else was the rejection by Curt Flood of an offer for $77,500. Flood told Busch that if he wanted to sign a player who was the best center fielder in baseball and a .300 hitter as well, it would cost him $90,000, "which is not seventy-seven five, and is not eighty-nine thousand, nine hundred and ninety-nine." Flood got his contract, but to Busch, who remembered how he had helped Flood out earlier when he had financial troubles, this was one more sign of the player as ingrate. In late March 1969, Busch called a special meeting of the team; he walked into the Cardinal locker room during spring training, and, accompanied by aides from The Brewery and by the press, whose members were there at his specific invitation, he dressed down his players. It was a memorable, humiliating experience for the team, an odd, rambling, somewhat incoherent speech in which the principal theme was that the players were cheating their fans. The owner himself seemed to think that the Cardinals were a nonprofit organization, a kind of athletic charity he sponsored out of civic pride. He outlined all that The Brewery had done for the players and for baseball, how much it had invested in the facilities in St. Louis. The person who was taking the risk each season, he said, was the owner, not the players. "You don't put two million people into a stadium by wishful thinking," he said. "It takes hundreds of people, working every day to make it possible for eighteen men to play a game of baseball that lasts for about two hours." Busch reminded the players of the investment made in the new ball park by civic-minded businessmen. Why, he himself was seventy years old, and the last thing in the world he needed, he said, was a new ball park. So much was being done for the players, he said, and they did not seem to appreciate it.

The fans, he said, were beginning to turn away from the sport. "If you don't already know it, I can tell you right now—from the letters, phone calls, and conversations we've had recently—that fans are no longer as sure as they were before about their high regard for the game and the players." He then complained to them about their outside business activities. The players, he said, had lost touch. "Too many fans are saying our players are getting fat . . . that they now only think of money . . . and less of the game itself. . . . Fans are telling us now that if we intend to raise prices to pay for the high salaries and so on and on, they will stop coming to the games, they will not watch and will not listen. They say they can do other things with their time and their money." He ended with a peroration about the fans: "I urge you to watch your attitudes. I plead with you not to kill the enthusiasm of the fans and the kids for whom you have become such idols. They are the ones who make you popular. They are the ones who make your salary and your pension possible." Then he urged them to go out and show the world that they were still champions. Then, just to make sure that the message got through, the Cardinals traded Cepeda, whom the other players thought the heart of the team, to Atlanta for Joe Torre, who was a good player but who did not arrive in St. Louis under optimum circumstances. The 1969 team was clearly a better team than the Mets, who went on to win the division, but it was an embittered team that played well below its potential.

The whole new thrust of baseball—a more aggressive union, higher salaries, and, soon, greater player freedom—was alien to Gussie Busch, who saw the Cardinals as *his* success, not the success of his players. He was a businessman and he had made a fatal mistake—he had turned the salary dispute with his players into a personal matter. He had allowed his very considerable ego to get between him and what was good for the ball club. That meant he was sure to be the loser. In February 1972 he gave orders to trade Steve Carlton, then on the threshold of being one of the greatest left-handers in baseball history, because of a ten-thousand-dollar difference in salary negotiations; a few weeks later he got rid of Jerry Reuss, a promising young left-handed pitcher, because Reuss had refused to shave off his mustache and because he too had held out.

But perhaps the most important trade the Cardinals made or tried to make was one after the 1969 season, when they tried to package McCarver, Curt Flood, and several other players to the Phillies for, among others, Richie Allen. At that moment Flood was thirty-one, the best center fielder in baseball, and a career .293 hitter. He had asked for $100,000. Busch, already angered by the previous set of negotiations, had had enough. As happens in these matters, Curt Flood found out that he was no longer working for the St. Louis Cardinals when a local reporter called to find out what he thought about the trade.

Curt Flood was the quiet man. Bob Gibson, his friend and longtime road roommate, remembered a certain delicacy about him, a sensibility and an aesthetic that could easily have been ground down by the system—not just of baseball, but of race in America in those years. Baseball was a tough place: other men like him, talented enough to play baseball, had not been strong enough and had unraveled under the pressure of the life around them. What saved Curt Flood, Gibson believed, was a rare inner toughness. It allowed him to survive and triumph in the racist world of minor-league baseball, in which he had never let local prejudice and cruelty define him. He went on to play for more than a decade in the majors. At first his inner toughness was something that perhaps only his teammates and some of the opposing players saw, although the Philadelphia Phillies, the St. Louis ownership, and indeed the rest of organized baseball would eventually learn how determined and willful he could be.

"If I had been a foot-shuffling porter, they might at least have given me a pocket watch," he wrote of finding out he was being traded to the Phillies. At the time Flood, just thirty-two, son of poor people who worked myriad menial jobs to support their six children, did the unthinkable: he refused to report. It was what many an established player, unexpectedly traded, had thought of doing. In retrospect, though, it was not surprising that the first baseball player to draw the line on the reserve clause was black. Blacks felt far more alienated from the norms of society than did whites, and in the case of athletes, they were far more sensitive to being thought of as chattel.

White athletes, often privileged and pampered since they were teenagers, were rarely skeptical about those who had treated them, on the surface, at least, so lovingly; they tended to accept society and the game at face value. Flood himself wrote of Stan Musial, a man he greatly admired, that Musial often said loving things about the game and the Cardinal organization, "not because he felt it was politic to do so, but because he believed every word he spoke." The black players emerging in the sports world in this new era were different. In basketball, a professional sport steadily gaining in national acceptance, the leadership for a model professional athlete's union had already come from a generation of exceptionally thoughtful black athletes. Almost all had been to college and many were graduates of the nation's best schools, whereas most baseball players tended to be country boys, their political viewpoints fixed when they were teenagers, and thus they were far more malleable to the owners.

Unlike Gibson, Brock, and White, Curt Flood had never been to college, but like them he was intelligent, and driven. He was a serious painter who had something of an ancillary career doing portrait work. He listened carefully, not just to what people said but to what they did not say. He was articulate about any number of things that grated on black players in those days—the great differences in endorsements, the wariness of some white reporters to interview black athletes and to treat them with respect in newspaper articles. In the past, ballplayers who got into fights on the field and who were scrappy and verbal were considered tough; Curt Flood brought a whole new definition of toughness to the game. There had been certain tipoffs in the past as to what kind of man he was, a willingness to play in exceptional pain, and a willingness to stand in against Don Drysdale—who, along with Gibson, was one of the two most terrifying pitchers in baseball, a man who loved to throw at hitters, and who said of Curt Flood that he was the toughest out for him in baseball.

Flood was the first to challenge what to him was a demonstrably unfair labor law, one that bestowed all rights on the owners at the expense of the players. "I want to go out like a man instead of a bottle cap," Flood told Marvin Miller, who became the head of the baseball players' union.

When Flood mounted his lonely challenge to baseball's reserve clause, Miller was cautious at first, and played the devil's advocate to see if he would have the staying power for so hard a struggle. Miller was aware from his own experiences of the pressure that would be brought to bear on Flood by the owners and by the commissioner. Miller went down the list of things that could happen, and found that Flood remained determined to make his challenge. He was, thought Miller, a flinty young man. It did not surprise Miller that the first challenge had come from a black player on the Cardinals. The Cardinals struck him as being different from other teams in the way they had managed to deal with the issue of race: the black players whom he had first met on the Cardinals struck him as men of exceptional character—good baseball players, but by no means only baseball players.

Flood's friends, such as Tim McCarver, with whom he had played and with whom he was being traded, tried to impress on him the serious consequences of what he was doing. "You'll never get another job in baseball," McCarver told his friend. "I know that," Flood answered. Miller asked Flood to come before a meeting of all the players' representatives, and after a long tough session in which they asked him hard questions—such as what he would do if the owners offered him a lot of money to drop the case—he said he would go forward. "I can't be bought," he said. Tom Haller of the Dodgers asked how much of what drove him was race. After all, Haller pointed out, it was a time of black militance. Flood thought it a fair question and answered that yes, what black players went through was often worse and more difficult than what white players did, but what he was doing was for *all* baseball players. It was time, he said, to draw the line. No other profession in the country left talented men so little control over their own destiny and deprived them of true market value.

So Curt Flood did not play for Philadelphia. Instead he sat out the season and went ahead with a lawsuit that went all the way to the Supreme Court, where he finally lost a close decision (the more conservative Nixon appointees tended to vote against him), but in so doing he began the process that would soon bring baseball players free agency, and thereby change the face and structure of baseball negotiations.

Tony Kubek and Bobby Richardson were close friends as well as roommates, and they remained friends after their professional careers were over. Kubek went on to become an announcer for NBC on the *Game of the Week*, and then for the Yankees, where he distinguished himself by his independence and willingness to make calls that angered the Yankee owner, George Steinbrenner. Richardson, a seriously religious Christian fundamentalist, became the baseball coach at the University of South Carolina and later at the Reverend Jerry Falwell's Liberty University. At one point he decided to run for Congress, as a conservative Republican. He asked several of his former Yankee colleagues to help campaign for him, and Mickey Mantle showed up, enjoying himself immensely, going around repeating over the loudspeaker that this was Mickey Mantle and that he would not vote for Bobby Richardson for dog catcher. Joe Di-

Maggio also showed up. But when Richardson asked his closest friend on the team, Kubek, to help out, Kubek called back and said that he had checked out with the Democratic party, and that the man Richardson was running against was not a bad man, and that it was hard for Kubek to back Richardson since he was a liberal Democrat. Well, that's Tony, Richardson thought, stubborn as ever.

Marty Appel, who had lionized Mantle as a boy growing up in suburban New York, eventually went to work for the Yankees, and one of his most important early jobs was going over Mantle's mail with him. Appel loved doing it because it always gave him some prime time with the player he had so admired, and when Appel decided on a career, he became a baseball executive and in time worked doing the production of Yankee baseball; he went on to write several books about baseball as well. As he grew older he watched Mantle age and he came to feel a growing affection for him. One of the saddest days in Appel's professional career came when, after the star had lingered on too long in his career, the team statistician had come in to Appel's office and said that it was his melancholy responsibility to report that either on that day or on the following day Mantle's lifetime batting average was going to fall beneath .300. That meant, Appel thought, that he was going to fall off the list of the immortals, the lifetime .300 hitters—which he did, ending up with a career .298 average. If it was not a happy day for Appel, it was not a happy day for Mantle either, and he often told friends that he wished he had retired in 1964, the last great season. He hated the fact that when he looked at the baseball encyclopedias, he always saw the figure .298.

Mickey Mantle's final years in baseball were hard ones. His body had worn down and his talents were eroded, and he was playing, in his final four years, for weak teams. Opposing pitchers had a luxury they had never enjoyed in the past—that of pitching around him. He saw few good pitches and he never hit .300 again. Mantle stayed on after the 1964 season in part because management pleaded with him to and he felt a strong personal loyalty to the Yankee organization, and in part because he was extremely well paid for playing and had nothing much else to do. In the years after baseball, particularly as he lived into his sixties, he was extremely hard on himself. Rather than accepting his magnificent career for what it was, he became haunted by the fact that he had not been better, that he had not taken better care of his body and stayed in shape during the off season, that instead of being the best ever, or one of the very best ever, he had in his own mind slipped below the level of the greatest players of his era, such as Willie Mays and Hank Aaron. In contrast to him, they had taken good care of their bodies and as such had prolonged their careers, as he had not. At night he had terrible recurring anxiety dreams. In one of them he would arrive at the ball park late only to find that the game had started without him, and he would have to find some way of getting through the wire fence so that he could play with his teammates. In another he got to the team bus just in time and got to the game and came up to bat. He would hit the ball hard, but then he would seem immobilized at the plate and he would be thrown out at first by a good throw from the outfield.

His drinking, which had been heavy when he was a player—it was a world, he later said, where everyone was always pushing a drink at you, a couple of beers in the clubhouse after the game, and then some drinks before dinner, and then some more drinks after dinner—became worse after his retirement. He missed his teammates, and he missed the game, for this was the only world he felt comfortable in, and he felt ill prepared to deal with the more complicated social situations of his life after baseball. He remained shy and reserved, and most of the work he found in his post-baseball life was promotional, and he was thrown again and again into situations where he was with strangers, and where he felt ill at ease.

In 1985, when his teammate Roger Maris died of cancer at the age of fifty-one, Mantle took it particularly hard, in no small part because Maris, to his mind, had been so much better a family man than Mantle had. It was as if he felt that if one of them had had to die young, it should have been himself, not Maris. At some point he became a full-fledged alcoholic. His behavior, late in the evening, became darker and darker. His friends—and he had many of them, for there was a part of him that remained warm, generous, and genuine—were bothered by his drinking and what seemed to be increasingly self-destructive behavior. He was funny and often exuberant earlier in the day, but as he drank he had the ability to turn ugly. Increasingly he was unable to recall his behavior the next day.

That he had a serious drinking problem was hardly a secret and strangers were warned that they ought to try and get to him relatively early in the day. In 1994, at the age of sixty-two, warned by his doctors that his liver was deteriorating at an alarming rate and that he might not live much longer, Mantle checked himself into the Betty Ford clinic in California, and when he came out he had stopped drinking. His friends felt a vast sense of relief. When he went before a national television audience, his face was obviously worn down by those years of hard living, but he was candid and unsparing about how self-destructive he had been, and how embarrassed by his own behavior he was. There was a certain poignancy to the scene, for the interviewer was Bob Costas, the talented young NBC broadcaster, who, growing up in Long Island, had been the prototypical Mantle fan, a walking encyclopedia of Mantle trivia. As an adult he still carried Mantle's bubble-gum card with him as a talisman. On the occasion of Costas's wedding day eleven years earlier, Mantle had left a message on his phone service wishing him a happy life. He had been a hero in his youth because of his limitless athletic gifts: now, as a man in his sixties, going before the nation to explain his weaknesses with such remarkable candor, he was performing what his former teammate Steve Hamilton thought was the most courageous act of his life.

Many of the St. Louis players went on to unusually successful lives after baseball. Both Lou Brock and Bob Gibson went to the Hall of Fame. Gibson, as imposing in his years after baseball as he was during his career, did some coaching for his friend Joe Torre in Atlanta and later with the Mets, though there was a sense that he was too driven and too fierce to deal with many of the modern ballplayers, young men who seemed to arrive in his care with handsome guaranteed contracts, and whose backgrounds and attitudes toward life were so different from his own. For a time he ran a restaurant in his hometown of Omaha. Some of his friends thought he would be an excellent broadcaster, but his demeanor and his reputation for bluntness made many professional baseball people nervous. Brock became an entrepreneurial business figure, and had a sports business and a restaurant in St. Louis. Tim McCarver, with his love of both the language and the game, became one of the game's best announcers, though he felt a growing distance between himself and many of the younger players, a difference that was highly publicized in a celebrated moment when during a play-off game he made critical comments about Deion Sanders, a talented if immature and egocentric young man who played both professional football and baseball. Sanders responded by dousing McCarver with a bucket of ice water during his team's victory celebration. Bill White went into an extremely successful career in broadcasting and eventually became president of the National League, where he came to be regarded as a man of exceptional judiciousness and fairness. Curt Flood, whose place in American life transcended baseball because of his historic early challenge to the reserve clause, had a difficult time for a number of years after his career ended, struggling with a drinking problem, but eventually he steadied himself, did some announcing on the West Coast, and emerged as a proud, dignified figure who turned down the Players Association when it talked to him about making some kind of belated compensation for what he had gone through in his legal challenge. Mike Shannon, his career cut short by an unusual illness, became an announcer and restaurateur in St. Louis, his hometown. Julian Javier named his son after his beloved teammate Stan Musial, and in time Stan Javier became a major-league player. Dal Maxvill, a young player catapulted into the starting lineup during the Series because of injuries to Javier, stayed in professional baseball and eventually became general manager of the Cardinals. Ken Boyer was traded to the Mets, which was traumatic for his family back in Alba, since his parents believed that he would be with the Cardinals all his life. He played for several more years, and ended up managing the Cardinals for three years, before dying at the age of fifty-one of cancer. Curt Simmons ran a golf course in Philadelphia with his longtime teammate and friend Robin Roberts.

Ray Sadecki coached in the minor-league system for the Chicago Cubs. Roger Craig stayed in baseball for much of his life, first as a coach and then as a manager for the San Diego Padres and the San Francisco Giants. Barney Schultz's lifetime of loving baseball was capped by that one marvelous season in St. Louis. He remained in baseball much of his life as a coach, and then retired to the town just outside Philadelphia where he had grown up. At the time of publication of this book Bing Devine was doing some scouting for the Philadelphia Phillies. Ironically, of all those Cardinals, Bob Uecker, who had been thought of as perhaps the most marginal player on the team, became the best known by dint of a series of beer commercials highlighting the limits of his playing ability and his role in a television sitcom, and at reunions of the team he had to stay at a separate hotel, away from the other members, in order to avoid the crush of fans.

Whitey Ford retired like his close friend Mickey Mantle and went to the Hall of Fame shortly afterward. They remained close friends and still ran a baseball fantasy camp, designed to allow middle-aged men to think for a moment that they were younger and playing in their own league of dreams. Of the other Yankees, Clete Boyer was soon traded to Atlanta, and he finished up his career playing baseball in Japan, where he managed to distinguish himself in the eyes of the Japanese by making an effort to learn the language and customs. He eventually returned to the Yankees as a coach and still coaches for his old team. Jake Gibbs, who never quite reached the heights that Yankees scouts had hoped for, also became a coach for the Yankees. Gibbs spent the second half of his professional career as the baseball coach at Ole Miss, where he had starred in both baseball and football. Elston Howard was traded late in his career to the Red Sox, but came back as a coach, and had he not died young of a stroke, he might have ended up as one of baseball's early black managers. Joe Pepitone was traded in time to Houston and then to Chicago, and eventually ended up playing for a good deal of money in Japan. There, his tendency to say he could not play because of injuries but his ability to turn up on the floor of a disco did not amuse the Japanese baseball world, and his career there was abbreviated. Bob Whiting pointed out in his wonderful book on Americans who played baseball in Japan, *The Chrysanthemum and the Bat*, all American players who were believed to be dogging it came to be known by the Japanese as "Pepitones." He had some unfortunate run-ins with the law upon his return to America, and eventually became a hitting instructor for the Yankees. Ralph Terry, just as he suspected, was the player to be named later in the Ramos deal, went to the Indians, and made a brief return to New York (with the Mets) in 1965; he went from baseball to a second career playing on the senior golf circuit. Phil Linz ran a restaurant in New York for a time and then moved to suburban New York, where he was in the life-insurance business. Mel Stottlemyre, spent much of his second career as a pitching coach for the crosstown Mets. At the writing of this book, he was the pitching coach for the Houston Astros. Always politically irreverent, Jim Bouton wrote a book, *Ball Four*, which was a major best-seller and was an early iconoclastic view of life among the Yankees. He was completing a novel about baseball at the writing of this book. Tom Tresh's career was cut short by injuries and he went back to coach at Central Michigan. Hector Lopez did some major-league scouting and then retired to a small town outside Tampa. Steve Hamilton coached at his own alma mater, Morehead State, and eventually became its athletic director; and Pete Mikkelsen bought some land in the state of Washington and became a grape farmer. Pete Ramos coached junior-college ball in Miami and did some scouting for the California Angels. Being fired by the Yankees did not end Yogi Berra's career. He managed for the Mets, and took them to the 1973 World Series, where they lost in the seventh game; he came back to manage for a second time with the Yankees in the mid-eighties. When he was abruptly fired by George Steinbrenner, he decided as a point of honor not to return to the Stadium for old-timers' games. He remained something of phenomenon in baseball and on Madison Avenue, and as this book was written, some forty-eight years after he first broke in with the Yankees, he could be seen regularly in a major commercial pronouncing one of his most famous Yogiisms, saying that it wasn't over until it was over.

Tom Greenwade died a week short of his eighty-second birthday in 1986. He remained the great Yankee scout of his generation. His last great discovery, Bobby Murcer, hailed as Mantle's successor, proved to be a good but not great ballplayer, as some of the front office had earlier claimed. It was Murcer's misfortune that he arrived during the team's prolonged decline. The decision of the major leagues to go to a formal draft not unlike basketball and football profoundly changed Greenwade's freedom in signing players. Buck O'Neil finally retired after scouting for many years for the Cubs. He remained in Kansas City, where he had made his home when he played and managed for the Monarchs and where he now runs the Negro League Baseball Hall of Fame. Interviewing him was one of the singular pleasures that came with writing this book.

Interviewees

Interviewees: Maury Allen, Marty Appel, Ernie Banks, Bill Bergesch, Jim Bouton, Clete Boyer, Bob Boyle, Lou Brock, Bob Broeg, Ernie Broglio, Jim Brosnan, Bill Bruton, Jack Buck, Jim Bunning, Shirley Clurman, Jerry Coleman, Pat Conmy, Bob Costas, Roger Craig, Al Downing, Bing Devine, John Gregory Dunne, Mike Eisenbath, David Fine, Roy Firestone, Al Fleishman, Jake Gibbs, Buddy Gilbert, Bob Gibson (who was exceptionally gracious even though he was working on his own memoirs at the time), Bunch Greenwade, Florence (Mrs. Tom) Greenwade, Angie Greenwade McCroskey, Dick Groat, Steve Hamilton, Solly Hemus, Tommy Henrich, Jerome Holtzman, Arlene (Mrs. Elston) Howard, Big Julie Isaacson, Gene Johnson, Leonard Koppett, Bruce Kornblatt, Phil Linz, Hector Lopez, Tim McCarver, Larry Merchant, Tom Metcalf, Pete Mikkelsen, Marvin Miller, Doug Minnis, Stan Musial, Billy Muffett, Buck O'Neil, Pedro Ramos, Bobby Richardson, Arthur Richman, Neal Russo, Ray Sadecki, Johnny Sain, Barney Schultz, Tom Seaver, Mike Shannon, Charlie Silvera, Curt Simmons, Ted Simmons, Bob Skinner, Mel Stottlemyre, Andy Strasberg, Ralph Terry, James Toomey, Joe Torre, Tom Tresh, Bob Uecker, Tom Weinberg, Harry (The Hat) Walker, Billy White. I tried to connect with as many players as possible. Some I missed out on because we could not coordinate schedules or because I was in their region when they were not. Only two important players were unwilling to talk: Tony Kubek, because, in his own words, it was the least happy season of his career—he was out with an injury for the World Series and had been slowed by injuries much of the season; and Curt Flood, who was told by his lawyers that talking with me might jeopardize a chance to make the story of his life into a movie. Mickey Mantle agreed to sit for an interview, but by the time I was ready to visit with him, he was in the Betty Ford clinic, and my deadline had passed. I want to acknowledge in addition, even though I have already listed him as an interviewee, the help of Maury Allen, who covered the Yankees for the *New York Post* and was an original journalistic Chipmunk; since he was with the team that year and I was not, his judgment was invaluable, and he proved helpful on this book, as on a previous one, far beyond the call of duty. That is true also of Bob Broeg and Jack Buck in St. Louis, both of whom were exceptionally generous and thoughtful in dealing with me.

Bibliography

Aaron, Hank, with Lonnie Wheeler. *I Had a Hammer*. New York: Harper-Collins, 1992.

Allen, Maury. *Roger Maris: A Man for All Seasons*. New York: Donald I. Fine, 1986.

———. *Jackie Robinson: A Life Remembered*. New York: Franklin Watts, 1987.

Anderson, Dave. *Pennant Races: Baseball at Its Best*. New York: Doubleday, 1994.

———, Murray Chass, Robert Creamer, and Harold Rosenthal. *The Yankees: The Four Fabulous Eras of Baseball's Most Famous Team*. New York: Random House, 1981.

Angell, Roger. *Once More Around the Park: A Baseball Reader*. New York: Ballantine Books, 1991.

Ashe, Arthur R., Jr. *A Hard Road to Glory: A History of the African-American Athlete, 1619–1918*. New York: Warner Books, 1988.

———. *A Hard Road to Glory: A History of the African-American Athlete 1919–1945*. New York: Warner Books, 1988.

———. *A Hard Road to Glory: A History of the African-American Athlete Since 1946*. New York: Warner Books, 1988.

Barber, Lylah. *Lylah: A Memoir—A North Florida Childhood and the Years as Wife of Baseball's Hall of Fame Broadcaster*. Chapel Hill, N.C.: Algonquin, 1985.

Bouton, Jim. *Ball Four Plus Ball Five*. New York: Stein and Day, 1981.

———. *Ball Four: Twentieth Anniversary Edition*. New York: Collier Books, 1990.

Brock, Lou and Franz Schulze. *Stealing Is My Game*. New Jersey: Prentice-Hall, Inc., 1976.

Brosnan, Jim. *The Long Season*. New York: Harper & Brothers, 1960.

Cairns, Bob. *Pen Men*. New York: St. Martin's Press, 1992.

Caray, Harry, with Bob Verdi. *Holy Cow*. New York: Villard Books, 1989.

Cohen, Stanley. *A Magic Summer: The '69 Mets*. California: Harcourt Brace Jovanovich, 1989.

Craft, David, and Tom Owens. *Redbirds Revisted*. Chicago: Bonus Books, 1990.

Creamer, Robert W. *Stengel: His Life and Times*. New York: Fireside Books, 1989.

Dickson, Paul. *Baseball's Greatest Quotations*. New York: Harper Perennial, 1992.

Durocher, Leo, with Ed Linn. *Nice Guys Finish Last*. New York: Simon & Schuster, 1975.

Etkin, Jack. *Innings Ago: Recollections by Kansas City Ballplayers of Their Days in the Game*. Missouri: Normandy Square Publications, 1987.

Fedo, Michael. *One Shining Season*. New York: Pharos Books, 1991.

Firestone, Roy, with Scott Ostler. *Up Close*. New York: Hyperion, 1993.

Flood, Curt, with Richard Carter. *The Way It Is*. New York: Trident Press, 1970.

Ford, Whitey, with Phil Pepe. *Slick: My Life in and Around Baseball*. New York: William Morrow & Co., 1987.

———, Mickey Mantle, and Joseph Durso. *Whitey and Mickey: An Autobiography of the Yankee Years*. New York: Viking Press, 1977.

Forker, Dom. *Sweet Seasons: Recollections of the 1955–64 New York Yankees*. Texas: Taylor Publishing Co., 1990.

———. *The Men of Autumn: An Oral History of the 1949–53 World Champion New York Yankees*. New York: Signet, 1990.

Gallen, David, ed. *The Baseball Chronicles*. New York: Carroll & Graf, 1991.

Gibson, Bob, with Phil Pepe. *From Ghetto to Glory: The Story of Bob Gibson*. New Jersey: Prentice-Hall, 1968.

Gibson, Charline, and Michael Rich, with notes from the mound by Bob Gibson. *A Wife's Guide to Baseball*. New York: Viking Press, 1970.

Golenbock, Peter. *Dynasty: The New York Yankees 1949–1964*. New York: Berkley Books, 1985.

Halberstam, David. *Summer of '49*. New York: William Morrow & Co., 1989.

Henrich, Tommy, with Bill Gilbert. *Five O'Clock Lightning: Ruth, Gehrig, DiMaggio, Mantle and the Glory Years of the New York Yankees*. New York: Carol Publishing Group, 1992.

Hernon, Peter, and Terry Ganey. *Under the Influence: The Unauthorized Story of the Anheuser-Busch Dynasty.* New York: Avon Books, 1991.

Holway, John B. *Blackball Stars: Negro League Pioneers.* New York: Carroll & Graf Publishers, 1992.

————. *Black Diamonds: Life in the Negro Leagues from the Men Who Lived It.* New York: Stadium Books, 1991.

————. *Josh and Satch: The Life and Times of Josh Gibson and Satchel Paige.* New York: Carroll & Graf Publishers, 1991.

————. *Voices from the Great Black Baseball Leagues.* New York: Da Capo Press, 1992.

Houk, Ralph, and Robert W. Creamer. *Season of Glory: The Amazing Saga of the 1961 New York Yankees.* New York: G. P. Putnam's Sons, 1988.

Kahn, Roger. *The Era: 1947–1957, When the Yankees, the Giants and the Dodgers Ruled the World.* New York: Ticknor & Fields, 1993.

Koppett, Leonard. *The Man in the Dugout.* New York: Crown Publishers, 1993.

Kubek, Tony, and Terry Pluto. *Sixty-One: The Team, The Record, The Men.* New York: Macmillan Publishing Co., 1987.

Kuklick, Bruce. *To Every Thing a Season: Shibe Park and Urban Philadelphia, 1909–1976.* New Jersey: Princeton University Press, 1991.

Lowenfish, Lee. *The Imperfect Diamond: A History of Baseball's Labor Wars* New York: Da Capo Press, 1991.

Mangano, Joseph J. *Living Legacy: How 1964 Changed America.* Maryland: University Press of America, 1994.

Mann, Jack. *The Decline and Fall of the New York Yankees.* New York: Simon & Schuster, 1967.

Mantle, Mickey, with Herb Gluck. *The Mick.* New York: Jove Books, 1986.

———— and Phil Pepe. *My Favorite Summer, 1956.* New York: Doubleday, 1991.

————. *The Quality of Courage.* New York: Doubleday, 1964.

Maris, Roger, and Jim Ogle. *Roger Maris at Bat.* Des Moines: Meredith Press, 1962.

McCarver, Tim, with Ray Robinson. *Oh, Baby I Love It!.* New York: Dell Books, 1987.

Mead, William B. *Two Spectacular Seasons.* New York: Macmillan Publishing Co., 1990.

Miller, Marvin. *A Whole Different Ball Game: The Sport and Business of Baseball.* New York: Birch Lane Press, 1991.

Mulvoy, Mark, ed. *Baseball: Four Decades of Sports Illustrated's finest Writing on America's Favorite Pastime.* Alabama: Oxmoor House, 1993.

Nathan, David H., ed. *Baseball Quotations.* New York: Ballantine Books, 1991.

Peary, Danny, ed. *Cult Baseball Players.* New York: Simon & Schuster, 1990.

————. *We Played the Game: 65 Players Remember Baseball's Greatest Era, 1947–1964.* New York: Hyperion, 1994.

Pepitone, Joe, with Berry Stainback. *Joe, You Coulda Made Us Proud.* Illinois: Playboy Press, 1975.

Peterson, Robert. *Only the Ball Was White: A History of Legendary Black Players and All-Black Professional Teams.* New York: McGraw-Hill, 1970.

Rains, Rob. *The St. Louis Cardinals.* New York: St. Martin's Press, 1992.

Robinson, Jackie, as told to Alfred Duckett. *I Never Had It Made.* New York: G. P. Putnam's Sons, 1972.

Rogosin, Donn. *Invisible Men: Life in Baseball's Negro Leagues.* New York: Atheneum, 1983.

Shecter, Leonard. *The Jocks.* Indianapolis: Bobbs-Merrill Co., 1969.

Smith, Curt. *Voices of the Game: The Acclaimed Chronicle of Baseball Radio and Television Broadcasting—from 1921 to the Present.* New York: Fireside, 1992.

Thorn, John, ed. *The Armchair Book of Baseball.* New York: Collier Books, 1985.

Tygiel, Jules. *Baseball's Great Experiment: Jackie Robinson and His Legacy.* New York: Oxford University Press, 1983.

Uecker, Bob, and Mickey Herskowitz. *Catcher in the Wry.* New York: Jove Books, 1983.

Acknowledgments

I would like to acknowledge the help of Philip Roome, who did much of the travel arrangements for me; my editor, Doug Stumpf; Leslie Chang, Jacqueline Deval, Kathy Schneider, Amy Edelman, Leta Evanthes, Richard Aquan, Russ Lake, copy editor Randee Marullo, book designers Lilly Langotsky and Jo Ann Metsch, and jacket designer Bradford Foltz, all at Villard Books; Kate Lardner for her assistance; Carolyn Parqueth, who did transcriptions of tapes; Nick Scharlatt in New York, who assembled photocopies of old Yankee games; and Mike Eisenbath in St. Louis, who did the same with old Cardinal games; Arthur Richman of the Yankees and Marty Hendin of the Cardinals; Phyllis Merhige of the American League and Katy Feeney of the National League; Jay Horwitz of the Mets; Chris Brush of Upper Deck; and Arthur Schack of the Players Association, all of whom were extremely helpful. I am also grateful to Wendy Selig-Prieb and Mary Burns of the Milwaukee Brewers; John Lowe of the *Detroit Free Press;* Rob Fleder and Dave Minget of *Sports Illustrated;* Thomas Craig of the National Baseball Library and Archive at the Baseball Hall of Fame; in St. Louis, Bob and Randy Costas, Richmond Bry, Lee Liberman, Barbara and Tom Eagleton, and Joe Ostremeier; and David Black, Bruce Blockley, Ken Starr, Robert Schaffer, Marty Garbus, Bob Solomon, and Bruce Plotkin.

About the Author

DAVID HALBERSTAM was the author of numerous other books, including his highly praised trilogy on power in America, *The Best and the Brightest, The Powers That Be,* and *The Reckoning*. His book *Summer of '49* was a number one *New York Times* hardcover bestseller. He won every major journalistic award, including the Pulitzer Prize.